T0355775

'*Boy Jesus* considers all the ancient texts and archaeological data connected with Jesus' birth and early years and comes up with some surprising conclusions. Most strikingly, it challenges the usual scepticism surrounding the Gospel infancy narratives, arguing that they do indeed contain "family memories" associated with Jesus' earliest years. This is Joan Taylor at her best, offering an original, imaginative, clearly written and deeply thoughtful analysis of a range of exceptionally powerful texts. Her deep erudition and balanced judgement are everywhere on display.'
Helen K. Bond FRSE, Professor of Christian Origins, University of Edinburgh

'*Boy Jesus* is perhaps the most thorough, accessible and compelling contextual treatment of Jesus' life to date. Everything from his tribal identity to his family and trade are given close examination. This book will be prized by anyone studying the historical Jesus or the Gospels, scholar or pastor alike.'
Gary M. Burge, Adjunct Professor of New Testament, Calvin Theological Seminary, Grand Rapids, Michigan

'A thought-provoking and innovative investigation of a subject usually supposed beyond the reach of historians.'
Ken Dark, Visiting Professor of Archaeology and History, King's College London

'Enlightening and engaging, this is a must-read for everyone interested in the historical Jesus and the birth of Christianity.'
Nick Holmes, author of *The Roman Revolution: Crisis and Christianity in Ancient Rome*

'Original, engaging and smart, Taylor's volume brilliantly challenges conventional readings of the nativity stories and so of Jesus' upbringing.'
Amy-Jill Levine, Professor of New Testament and Jewish Studies Emerita, Vanderbilt University, Nashville, Tennessee

'Beautifully written and richly illustrated, *Boy Jesus* weaves recent archaeological discoveries with insightful textual analyses to construct the crucial background for understanding the world and memories behind the Jesus of the Gospels. A must-read for anyone interested in the historical Jesus and Christian origins.'

Jonathan L. Reed, Professor of Philosophy and Religion, University of La Verne, California

Joan Taylor is Professor Emerita of Christian Origins and Second Temple Judaism, King's College London, and Honorary Professor in Biblical and Early Christian Studies, Australian Catholic University, Melbourne. Her recent books include *The Essenes, the Scrolls and the Dead Sea* (Oxford University Press, 2012), *What Did Jesus Look Like?* (Bloomsbury T&T Clark, 2018) and (with Helen Bond) *Women Remembered: Jesus' female disciples* (Hodder & Stoughton, 2022).

BOY JESUS

Growing up Judaean in turbulent times

Joan Taylor

First published in Great Britain in 2025

SPCK
SPCK Group
Studio 101
The Record Hall
16–16A Baldwin's Gardens
London EC1N 7RJ
www.spckpublishing.co.uk

British Library Cataloguing-in-Publication Data
A catalogue record for this book is available from the British Library

ISBN 978–0–281–08498–2
eBook ISBN 978–0–281–08499–9

1 3 5 7 9 10 8 6 4 2

Typeset by Fakenham Prepress Solutions, Fakenham, Norfolk NR21 8NL
First printed in Great Britain by Clays Ltd

eBook by Fakenham Prepress Solutions, Fakenham, Norfolk NR21 8NL

Produced on paper from sustainable sources

For my family

The word of the Lord came to me saying:
'Before I formed you in the womb I knew you,
and before you were born I sanctified you.
I appointed you as a prophet to the nations.'
So I said, 'Oh no, Lord God,
look, I don't know how to speak,
because I'm just a boy!'
But the Lord said to me,
'Don't say, "I'm just a boy,"
because to everyone I send you, you will go,
and everything that I tell you to speak, you will say.
Don't be afraid of them,
because I am with you, to keep you safe,
says the Lord.'
(Jer. 1:4–8)

Contents

List of illustrations   x

Acknowledgements   xiii

Timeline   xiv

1 Identity: Jew, Judahite, Judaean   1

2 Heritage: seed of David   25

3 Location: Bethlehem   49

4 Born Jesus: the Gospel of Matthew   71

5 Born Jesus: Luke and beyond   116

6 Refugee: into Egypt   144

7 Return: a time of hope   161

8 Growing up Galilean   185

9 Growing up Jesus   207

10 Boy Jesus in the Temple   236

Conclusions   244

List of abbreviations   246

Notes   254

Further reading   332

Index   335

Illustrations

Plates

1 The ancient Lower Aqueduct running through Bethlehem in a French plan from Baedeker's guide 1912 (Public domain)

2 A view of Bethlehem to the north with Herodion on the horizon, 1867 (Photograph by Henry Phillips. Courtesy of the Palestine Exploration Fund, London)

3 View from Bethlehem to Herodion (© Joan Taylor)

4 View from Herodion hill to Bethlehem (© Joan Taylor)

5 The Holy Spirit imagined as a feminine divine manifestation. Wall painting from the third-century synagogue of Dura Europos, Syria (National Museum of Damascus. Public domain)

6 Artefacts from Judaean refugees in the Christmas Cave east of Bethlehem (© John Allegro. Reproduced with permission from the Allegro estate)

7 Coin of Herod showing *pilos* cap and *tau-rho* abbreviation (Wikimedia Commons, Staatliche Museen zu Berlin. Creative Commons Public Domain Mark 1.0)

8 Coins of Herod showing X in diadem (Wikimedia Commons from Glyphmark. Creative Commons Attribution-Share Alike 4.0 International License)

9 The Temple and Antonia Fortress – model in the Israel Museum, Jerusalem (© Joan Taylor)

10 View over upper Sepphoris south-west towards Nazareth (© Joan Taylor)

11 Panoramic view of Nazareth and its vicinity, 1866 (Photograph by Henry Phillips. Courtesy of the Palestine Exploration Fund)

12 Entrance to triple silo (hiding place) in first-century house, Mary of Nazareth International Centre, Nazareth (© Joan Taylor)

13 Remains in area outside the Church of the Annunciation, Nazareth (© Joan Taylor)

14 Holy Caves of Nazareth, Greek Orthodox property, Nazareth (© Joan Taylor)

15 Woodworker in the Tower of Babel mosaic panel, Huqoq synagogue (c.400 CE), Israel (Photograph by Jim Haberman; courtesy of Jodi Magness)

16 Courtyard of the Mosque of al-Azhar, built in 970–2, Cairo, Egypt (Albumen print by Felix Bonfils, late 1800s. © Victoria and Albert Museum, London)

Figures

All figures are drawn by the author unless otherwise indicated.

1.1 Judaea around the time of Jesus' birth (c.6 BCE) 3

2.1 Ossuary inscription: shel be David, 'of [the] house of David' (IAA Inventory number 1971-410. Drawing by Joan Taylor) 31

3.1 The region south of Jerusalem, with ancient roads and Lower Aqueduct 51

3.2 Bethlehem in the late first century BCE, as presently known. The word 'caves' appears where the Basilica of the Nativity would later stand 55

3.3 Caves under the Basilica of the Nativity, Bethlehem 57

6.1 Map of region from Syria to Egypt, 6 BCE 145

6.2 Roman Egypt 154

8.1 The western part of Galilee, 6 CE, with ancient roads 189

8.2 Survey of Western Palestine map 1880. Detail of Sepphoris, Nazareth and Japhia (Courtesy of the Palestine Exploration Fund, London) 190

9.1 Areas of Nazareth where archaeological remains have been found 209

9.2 Remaining walls of lower level of first-century house, Mary of Nazareth International Centre, Nazareth 211

9.3 Triple silo (hiding place) in first-century house, Mary of Nazareth International Centre, Nazareth 213

Tables

1.1 The twelve sons of Jacob/Israel with their mothers   16

2.1 Two genealogies: Jesus' Davidic lineage according to
Matthew and Luke   40

5.1 Lukan answers to questions raised by Matthew's Gospel   122

10.1 The story of the boy Jesus in the Temple as told in Luke's
Gospel and the *Paidika*   238

Acknowledgements

This book has developed over quite some time and there are many people who have helped in one way or another. I would like to thank especially my family for all their support as I have explored the evidence and moved forward with writing, and for accompanying me on trips investigating sites. I thank especially Helen Bond and Ken Dark for their important comments on this book, and Ken particularly for many hours of conversation on Nazareth and the resources he generously shared. I also thank others who have sent me comments and materials, especially Leila Sansour, Mina Monier, Shimon Gibson, James Crossley, Robert Myles, Jodi Magness, and Wayne Te Kaawa, and also my student Katie Worner, who wrote about the family of Jesus in her master's dissertation in 2019. I thank Guy Stiebel for his expert tour of Herodion. I am grateful also for the valuable comments received in the Historical Jesus section at the Studiorum Novi Testamenti Societas meeting in Melbourne in July 2024, chaired by Sarah Rollens. I thank King's College London for research support. Many thanks to Philip Law of SPCK for his guidance and patience, also production editor Rima Devereaux and copy-editor Mollie Barker. I am grateful to Ildi Clarke for the index.

Timeline

BCE

18th–14th century   Hebrews, Canaanites, Amorites and other ethnic groups in land of Canaan under Egyptian hegemony

Before 13th century   Egyptian enslavement of Hebrews; prophet Moses leads Hebrews/Israel out of Egypt; return to Canaan

By 12th century   Judah and other tribes of Israel resettle alongside Canaanites and Amorites in tribal territories

1200–1025   Period of the judges; extensive warfare; Philistines settle coast and further inland

1010–970   King David rules over united kingdom of twelve tribes of Israel; extensive warfare

970–931   King Solomon rules (First Jerusalem Temple)

c.931–721   Northern kingdom of Israel (till vanquished by the Assyrians)

c.931–586   Southern kingdom of Judah (and Benjamin), ruled by Davidic descendants

586   Jerusalem destroyed, including Temple; Judahite exile in Babylon

538   Return of exiles from Babylon to Judah

520   Jerusalem Temple rebuilt (Second Temple)

333   Alexander the Great defeats Persians, conquers Judaea

323–c.200   Hellenistic Egyptian Ptolemies rule Syria Palestina

c.200–167   Hellenistic Syrian Seleucids rule Syria Palestina

167   Profanation of the Temple by Antiochus IV Epiphanes

166   Judas Maccabeus revolts in Judaea

164   Rededication of the Temple (Hanukkah)

152	Judas's brother Jonathan becomes governor and high priest: Hasmonean royal dynasty begins
134–104	John Hyrcanus expands Judaean rule to Idumaea and Samaria
104–103	Aristobulus I expands Judaean rule to Galilee
103–76	Alexander Jannaeus expands Judaean rule east of Dead Sea
67–63	Hyrcanus II rules, but rival brother Aristobulus II takes power
63	Roman general Pompey defeats Aristobulus II; Hyrcanus II reinstalled as high priest but with Antipater as Roman client governor
47	Julius Caesar appoints Hyrcanus II high priest and ethnarch; Antipater's son Herod governor of Galilee
44	Assassination of Julius Caesar
43	Second triumvirate: Roman Empire ruled by alliance of Octavian, Mark Antony and Lepidus
40	Antigonus Mattathias, son of Aristobulus II, invades with help from Parthians, usurps rule, exiles Hyrcanus II to Parthia; Herod flees and massacres Judaean fighters near Bethlehem; appointed king of Judaeans in Rome
37	Roman army of Mark Antony defeats Antigonus in Jerusalem; Herod the Great begins reign as Roman client king of the Judaeans
35	Herod kills the high priest Aristobulus III
27	Octavian is given titles Augustus 'illustrious one', and *imperator*, 'emperor'
10	Herod enters and loots the Tomb of David in Jerusalem
c.7	Herod executes his sons Alexander and Aristobulus
c.6	Jesus born (Matthew's chronology)
4	Herod executes his son Antipater; rebellion in Temple; Herod executes rebel teachers Judas and Matthias and their students; Herod dies
4–2	Archelaus takes charge, massacres 3,000 people

in Temple; revolts of Judas son of Hezekiah, Simon, Athronges and others; Roman legate Varus quashes rebellion; mass executions: the War of Varus. Archelaus appointed Roman client ethnarch of Judaea; Herod Antipas Roman client tetrarch of Galilee and Peraea; Herod Philip Roman client tetrarch of Ituraea and other areas; Herod's sister Salome granted cities; period of continued social turbulence

CE	
6	Archelaus deposed; census of Judaea; revolt fomented by Judas the Galilean (from Gamala)
6–66	Judaea a Roman province administered by prefects and then procurators, who appoint high priests as national rulers, for government, religion and judiciary; intermittent protest movements involving popular prophets and militant leaders
c.30	Jesus crucified
62	James, Jesus' brother, executed
66	First Revolt in whole of Judaea begins; Judaean independence from Rome declared
68	Vespasian's forces crush revolt in Galilee and elsewhere
70	After long siege, Roman forces under Titus take Jerusalem, destroy Temple
70–132	Judaea administered by Roman legates in Syria; partial rule of Agrippa II (till c.100)
c.115	Revolt in Jewish Diaspora communities and in Judaea, quashed by Roman general Quietus: the Kitos War
132–6	Second or Bar Kochba Revolt; partial Judaean independence, culminating in Roman forces' eviction of Judaeans from Judaea; Roman province of Syria Palestina established; end of Judaean nationhood

1

Identity: Jew, Judahite, Judaean

In a story told in the Gospel of John, recorded sometime towards the end of the first century CE, Jesus meets a woman by a spring. He is not supposed to talk to her, because she has one identity and he has another, and there has been a rupture between people with these identities.

Implicitly, the story is set in a region the Graeco-Roman world under-stood as Syria Palestina.[1] The Gospel-writer knows that there were two groups who claimed to be 'Israel' and that they were deeply hostile to each other: the Judaeans (living in 'Judaea') and the Samaritans (living in 'Samaria'). Around the year 50 CE, Samaritans murdered a Judaean pilgrim at Gema (modern Jenin), and Judaeans responded by torching Samaritan villages in the territory of Akraba (modern Aqraba) and killing the villagers.[2] This kind of violent incident appears to have been known to the author: Jesus is portrayed as being on the way from Jerusalem to Galilee in the north, and it is said, in Greek, that 'he *had to pass* (*edei . . . dierchesthai*) through Samaria', as if compelled when there was danger:

> He [Jesus] left Judaea and went off again to Galilee, and he had to pass through Samaria. He came then to a city of Samaria called Sychar, near the plot of land that Jacob gave to his son Joseph, and the Spring of Jacob was there. Jesus was exhausted from the journey, so he sat down at the Spring. It was about the sixth hour. A woman of Samaria came to draw water, and Jesus said to her: 'Give me something to drink?' . . . But the Samaritan woman said to him, 'How come you, a Judaean (*Ioudaios*), ask me for a drink?' That is because Judaeans do not associate with Samaritans.
> (John 4:3–9)

We see here a story of a named man and an unnamed woman, and there are gendered roles: a man does not pull up his own water from a spring

1

pool; the woman must be doing this, using an appropriate vessel. For Jesus, as a man, it is acceptable to ask for water to be given to him by a woman, but for a *Ioudaios*, a Judaean, to talk to a Samaritan is something else.

The unnamed Samaritan woman immediately recognises Jesus as a *Ioudaios*. Was this to do with his appearance? They would both have looked similarly Middle Eastern, with medium-brown skin and black hair, and both Samaritan and Judaean men were supposed to wear a tallith, a distinctive mantle with blue tassels at the corners.[3] But was there something about Jesus that didn't look Samaritan? Or was it to do with his accent when he asked for her help to draw water for him? Whatever it was, it is a clear indicator that Jesus was remembered as having a recognisable identity.[4]

The story goes on to explore Jesus' identity as meaning something more than what appeared on the surface, and it also refers to religious issues that Judaeans and Samaritans fought over, such as where God should be worshipped: should it be in Jerusalem (on Mount Moriah) or in Samaria (on Mount Gerizim; see John 4:20–1)? The Spring of Jacob is itself a kind of metaphor for two peoples claiming a common descent. Jacob's name was also 'Israel': the water they both drink should unite them. So the term *Ioudaios* here is something more than regional. Indeed, Jesus asserts: '*You* worship what you don't know; *we* worship what we know, because salvation is from the Judaeans' (4:22). Jesus here, emphatically using 'we' (*hēmeis*), identifies himself firmly as a Judaean.

Later on in the Gospel, the title placed on Jesus' cross by the Roman governor Pontius Pilate reads 'King of the *Ioudaioi* (Judaeans)' in three languages (John 19:19–22; cf. Mark 15:26; Matt. 27:37; Luke 23:38). The Gospel also asserts that 'he came to his own, and his own people did not accept him' (John 1:11). The writer thus has a negative assessment of *Ioudaioi*,[5] and wishes to stress the deeper identity of Jesus as Son of God, the pre-existent divine *Logos* or Word (John 1:1–18). But here, by the Spring of Jacob, we have Jesus shown as one would meet him, as a *Ioudaios*.

This memory of Jesus' identity is found in another story of him with an unnamed woman, this time in the Gospel of Mark (7:24–30), written around the year 70 CE. It is one of the most awkward recollections of the early church, given how Jesus responds to someone he perceives as different. In this story, Jesus has travelled north-west from the boundaries of Galilee, apparently to visit villages where Judaeans lived in the territory of Tyre and Sidon (see Fig. 1.1), in Syria Phoenicia. He enters a house, and a Hellenic woman (*Hellēnis*, Greek-cultured), a 'Syro-Phoenician', arrives. Her little daughter is 'possessed by an unclean spirit' and she falls at his feet, begging him – as an expert exorcist – to

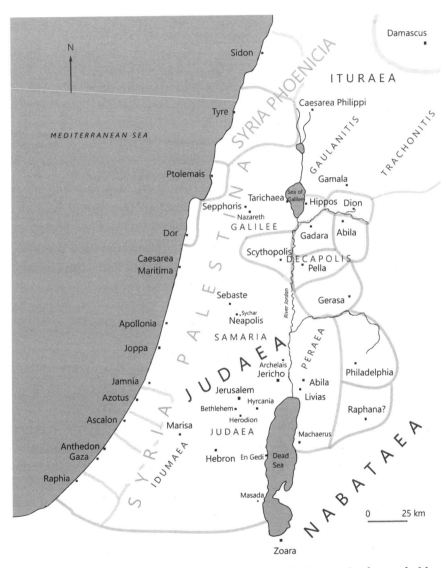

Figure 1.1 Judaea around the time of Jesus' birth (*c.*6 BCE) when ruled by the Roman client king Herod

(Drawing by Joan Taylor)

cast the demon out. Jesus responds: 'Let the children be fed first, for it's not right to take the children's food and throw it to the dogs.' The picture Jesus paints is of hungry children sitting at a table eating, needing this food, and someone brutally taking away their food and throwing it to the dogs before they have finished. Jesus is presenting himself as a carer. The healing he provides (symbolised as food) would be squandered if offered to Syro-Phoenicians. The woman replies, 'Yes indeed, master, but even the dogs under the table eat the children's crumbs.' She cannily enters the picture Jesus paints, accepting being a dog, yet imagines the dogs as household pets under the table, gulping morsels of the 'food' of healing.[6] Jesus is impressed, and so asserts that the demon has left her daughter. She goes home, finds her daughter in bed, and the demon is gone.[7]

When the authors of the later Gospels of Matthew and Luke encountered this passage in their retellings of Mark, they dealt with Jesus' attitude to the woman in two very different ways. In Matthew, Israel's history is invoked.[8] However, in Luke, the whole problematic passage is simply omitted. It's no wonder why. The Lukan church had made its home in the 'Hellenic' (Greek-cultured) world among those who would readily identify with the Syro-Phoenician woman. Her humble acceptance of secondary marginality was not one guaranteed to win hearts and minds. However, Jesus' response in Mark is the earliest version of the story, and it creates an initial statement of 'us' and 'you' that speaks to his own identity.

Jesus, as remembered, could therefore see Samaritans as 'other' than himself as a Judaean, while accepting them as having a common heritage within Israel, but look upon Hellenic Syro-Phoenicians as outsiders from Israel who were marginal to his mission. Our identity is composed not only of what we are but also of what we are not, and here in these stories we see what Jesus was not. They present a Jesus looking beyond the boundary of who he is.

Today, there is a vast literature on identity and how it is forged in childhood and adolescence. Studies of ego identity began in earnest with the work of the Freudian psychoanalyst Erik Erikson and psychologist James Marcia in the 1960s,[9] and there is a plethora of approaches and theories attaching to it. Here, in this historical study, we can simply note that identity is about selfhood developed through social interaction. It governs how we relate to others and the world. It can include gender, ethnicity, culture, heritage, family, tribe, race, socio-economic class, occupation, politics, nationality, place, religion, physicality, sex, sexuality, parenthood, relationship status, age, ability/skill, and other elements besides. Importantly, one's identity can be linked to trauma (among survivors of crime, abuse, wars, health crises or disasters, for example).[10] When we think about Jesus as a child, we might focus on many aspects of identity, and we will do so in this book. But we will begin with these Gospel passages because they ground Jesus in a certain time and place, and are striking examples of Jesus' having a recognisable identity. He was a *Ioudaios*.

In most translations of the New Testament this Greek word *Ioudaios* is found as 'Jew'. Our term 'Jew', in English, is actually just a contraction ('Ju') of the equivalent Latin term *Iudaeus*. The word *Ioudaios* is itself a rendering of Hebrew *Yehudi*, or Aramaic *Yehuda'i*. But to be defined as a *Ioudaios* was to belong to a complex category,[11] and there is no one word in English that would suffice to capture all dimensions. We may translate *Ioudaios* as 'Jew' in terms of an ethnoreligious identity; as 'Judahite' in terms of tribal heritage as a descendant of Jacob's son Judah; or as 'Judaean' in terms of regionality, associated with someone who lived in a country named 'Judaea'. All these dimensions represent different facets of identity. We need to probe, then, the different dimensions of *how* Jesus was a *Ioudaios*.

Jesus the Jew

To be a Jew in antiquity was to be part of an ethnoreligious group. One belonged to a people (Greek *patria*) or 'nation' (*ethnos*)[12] that was connected with the *patris* (homeland) of Judaea, and whose members had particular distinctive beliefs and customs concerning their *thrēskeia*, or 'worship system' or 'religion'.[13] *Ioudaismos*, Judaism, is specifically defined as a kind of *thrēskeia* in Acts 26:5.[14] One adhered to the beliefs and praxis of Judaism, with central foci on the interpretation of Scripture and the cult of the Jerusalem Temple. Jews from far and wide came to Jerusalem for key festivals, particularly the Passover, where they met, networked, studied and debated in the Temple's vast precincts. This activity connected Jerusalem to many other lands, as we see in the story

5

of Acts 2:5 when, fired by the Spirit, the disciples communicate with 'Jews living in Jerusalem [who] were people from every nation under heaven'.

If we look at Jesus' identity within this rubric, it is helpful to start with our earliest evidence: the letters of the apostle Paul, composed c.48–60 CE.[15] Paul was not himself part of Jesus' group in Galilee or Jerusalem; indeed, he tried to stamp out the Jesus movement by arresting and punishing Jesus' disciples, but after his conversion on the road to Damascus – thanks to an astonishing vision[16] – he became one of its foremost missionaries. Paul did not therefore know Jesus personally, but he visited Jerusalem and talked to Jesus' closest disciples there, including members of Jesus' family. While there, we can assume he picked things up, and so Paul incidentally mentions matters about Jesus as a man, presuming that everyone knew much the same things. This makes what he says very important. Despite this, almost all scholars of the historical Jesus skip over Paul's evidence quite lightly,[17] and it is quite easy to see why. Reading the New Testament in order, with the Gospels first, by the time we get to Paul we already know, as he says, that Jesus was crucified (1 Cor. 1:17 – 2:5; Gal. 3:1; 6:14; Phil. 2:8) by the 'rulers of this age' (1 Cor. 2:8) and that he was buried in a tomb (1 Cor. 15:4; Rom. 6:4). We know he had disciples and apostles (1 Cor. 15:5–7), including a group designated as 'the Twelve' (1 Cor. 15:5), one of whom was called 'Cephas', which is Aramaic for 'Rock' (in Greek *Petros* = Peter; Gal. 2:7–8), and another of whom was called John (Gal. 2:9). We know very well that he was a teacher who taught his disciples (1 Cor. 7:10–11) and that he had a last supper on the night he was arrested at which he asked them to remember him (1 Cor. 11:23–5).

But Paul also provides some historical details that we do not immediately know from the Gospels, for example that Jesus' *brother* James was so important that he witnessed one of Jesus' resurrection appearances and led the church in Jerusalem (1 Cor. 15:7; Gal. 1:19; 2:9, 12), or that Jesus' siblings as a whole were a leadership group (1 Cor. 9:5; 15:7), or that Jesus' male apostles travelled around with female companions, called 'sister-wives', as did the 'brothers of the Lord' (1 Cor. 9:5).[18] This kind of incidental historical information in our earliest source should make us reflect on the fact that our Gospel authors do not aim to tell us everything about Jesus, but only the things that matter to the writers. Paul's incidental information is vital because it is the well-known ground on which he builds his points;

it has to be firm for the points to stand. For this reason it is likely to be true. At the time when Paul was writing, many of Jesus' disciples were around, Jesus' brother James was still alive, and his other siblings probably were too.

Paul's writing is important for defining Jesus as a Jew, because when he says in his letter to the Galatian church that Jesus was 'born of a woman, born under the Law' (Gal. 4:4), he tells his non-Jewish readers that Jesus' identity was distinctively different from theirs. Here Paul defines Jews as normatively being 'under Law'. By 'Law', he means the core part of Jewish Scripture: Torah, known in Greek as the 'Pentateuch', the five books believed to have been written by the prophet Moses.

In this letter, Paul clarifies what it means to follow Christ for non-Jews in a context outside Judaea: he argues that even though Jesus was a Jew this did not mean all his followers should be, because they could be considered equally righteous by God as non-Jews.[19] If Paul knew the story of the Syro-Phoenician woman, he would likely have wanted to adjust it to ensure that in the picture painted by Jesus she is included as a hungry child being fed at the table, not as a little dog underneath it. In fact, Paul preferred quite a different picture. Just a few lines earlier, Paul created an image of the Law being like a guardian over a place where Israel was looked after (Gal. 3:23–5). It was customary to have unmarried virgins kept safe and guarded inside the house.[20] Jesus himself was like this, like all Jews: guarded and protected by being 'under' the Law.

Paul therefore mentions Jesus as a born Jew, a *Ioudaios*, but someone not to emulate exactly in all respects. A Syro-Phoenician, or a Galatian, or a Roman, could be accounted just as worthy and righteous as a Jew without having to be one. Clearly, his readers were saying: 'Paul, we just want to be like Jesus.' But Paul said Jesus' identity did not need to be replicated.

Paul then gives us some idea about Jesus. We see here how Jesus' identity is a combination of physical descent (born of a woman) and religious affiliation (under the guardianship of the Mosaic law). Being born of a Jewish woman is a critical thing, because the determining factor in the Jewish identity of a newborn is the mother.[21] This would have been noted by Paul's readers, because some Jews were not born of a Jewish mother but rather adopted into 'Judaism' (*Ioudaismos*) by conversion; indeed, some of his readers had gone through conversion themselves, a matter he considered plain 'stupid' (Gal. 3:1).

7

By focusing on the body's physicality, we see here a biological dimension to the term *Ioudaios*,[22] but the fact that people could convert to Judaism and be counted as Jews meant the category of being a member of a *patria*, in Greek, was not entirely about biology. As a convert you were adopted into what we might call an ethnicity, or 'people' (in Latin a *gens*; Pliny, *Nat. Hist.* 13:4:46). But Paul could also separate out the ethnic[23] and the religious elements of the category *Ioudaios*, which only serves to demonstrate the complexity of the term. For example, in debate with those who wanted non-Jews (Gentiles) in Galatia to follow Jewish customs and law, including circumcision of males, Paul scorns the supposed hypocrisy of Jesus' disciple Peter and states: 'We are Jews by nature, and not Gentile sinners' (Gal. 2:15). Peter and Paul are both Jews 'by nature', that is, physically, by descent. That marks them as different from non-Jews by descent, who – simply on these grounds – can be defined as 'sinners'. But paradoxically, in the same breath, Paul could claim that 'through the law I died to the law that I might live to God' (Gal. 2:19). By this he means that the Mosaic law actually predicted Christ, if interpreted correctly, and for him Christ's death – regarded as inaugurating a new covenant between humanity and God – released him from needing to follow that law. Paul could note that '[his] former manner of life' in Judaism (*Ioudaismos*) was one in which he was earnest for 'the traditions of [his] ancestors' (Gal. 1:13–14), but he now rejected that. Paul rejected the necessity of the practice of the law, even though 'by nature' (in terms of physical descent) he was still a Jew. The ethnic element was therefore detached in some way from the religious.

The category of 'law' itself is confusing. In Paul's context within the Jewish Diaspora of the Roman East, which was largely Hellenic (Greek) in culture, Jews followed Jewish law as part of their identity within a given city, in a wider environment in which each city had its own law.[24] For example, in Alexandria, in Egypt, legal matters concerning the Jewish community (*politeuma*) were governed within the city by a Jewish magistrate (alabarch) and a council of elders (*gerousia*).[25] Alexandria was a paramount Diaspora centre, though there were others, from Rome to Babylon. Jews here, as elsewhere, had their own legal operations.

As a Jew in the Diaspora, you could choose to step out of a Jewish legal framework of the law (*nomos*) and become 'un-lawed' (*anomos*) as an apostate, thereby detaching the 'religious' element from your ethnicity 'by nature'. It is this that Paul cheekily plays with. For Paul, Gentiles were 'unlawed' (and therefore 'sinners', Gal. 2:15); so, in his first letter to the Corinthian church, Paul also calls himself 'unlawed', like a Gentile, but one who could move back and forth on this very issue of following law depending on context. So he says:

> I became to the *Ioudaioi* like a *Ioudaios*, in order to win *Ioudaioi*; to those under law (*nomos*) as under law, not being myself under law, in order to win those under law; to those unlawed (*anomos*) as one unlawed, not being God's unlawed but Christ's in-lawed (*ennomos*), in order to win the unlawed.
> (1 Cor. 9:20–1)

In Greek, Paul's language is as repetitive, rhyming and rhythmic as a rap. He clearly loves the repetition of the word *nomos*, 'law', in various forms. But in saying he was *anomos*, 'unlawed', Paul was not claiming to be 'un-Scriptured'. At the point where he proclaims himself as 'unlawed', he has just quoted 'law' (Deut. 25:4) as indicating the deeper meaning that workers should be allowed to eat, that is, earn their keep (1 Cor. 9:9–12). For Paul, Jewish Scripture, read in this symbolic/allegorical way, led to truth, but it did not lead Gentiles to the practice of the law, because that would mean a literal reading and, as he said, 'the letter kills, but the Spirit gives life' (2 Cor. 3:6). The Spirit guides you to the correct interpretation of the law, which can undo the literal meaning, and point to Christ.

Therefore, when Paul referred to Jesus as being born 'under the Law' (Gal. 4:4), he defined him as a Jew, categorically. Unlike himself, Paul never indicated that Jesus was anything but a 'lawed' Jew. Not once in his surviving letters did Paul appeal to Jesus as an example of someone who broke the Jewish law in order to justify what Paul himself did; for example, while not following a *kosher* diet, Paul did not quote Jesus as having declared all foods to be 'clean'.[26] Jesus was born and remained under that law which Paul defined as 'material' (cf. Gal. 3.3; 4:24–31). Paul knew that *he* was the anomaly, not Jesus. For Paul, the possibility of living in an 'unlawed' way, as a Jew, was only available by means of the death and resurrection of Jesus, not the life of Jesus.[27]

That Jesus was a Jew might seem extremely obvious today,[28] but this was not so obvious in the past.[29] It was recognised that Jesus kept Jewish

9

festivals, and that he saw the Sabbath as given by God, though he was concerned about what was and was not binding in terms of Sabbath laws (as in his saying: 'The Sabbath was made for humanity, not humanity for the Sabbath, so the son of humanity is lord also of the Sabbath', Mark 2:27–8). It was recognised that he claimed that not one 'jot and tittle' of the Jewish law would pass away until all was accomplished (see Matt. 5:17–20), but there was more emphasis placed on the points that Jesus argued for in his stance against what was seen as Jewish legalism. Jesus' refusal to accept the interpretations and practice of the legal school known as the 'Pharisees', and his criticism of the 'scribes and Pharisees' as hypocritical and unkind (e.g. in Matt. 23), were read as indicating that Jesus spurned Jewish law itself. In other words, internal *debates within* Judaism were read by Christian scholars as *debates with* Judaism. Judaism was deemed rigid, while Jesus emphasised compassion and forgiveness. As T. W. Manson stated in 1935:

> The difference between the ethic of Jesus and that of Judaism is . . . simply this, that with Jesus the fact that the good heart is fundamental is accepted and carried to its logical conclusion while in Judaism the whole apparatus of Law and Tradition is still maintained beside the moral principle which renders it obsolete.[30]

This crushing dismissal of the Judaism of Jesus' time as involving a law and tradition that should be obsolete next to the moral principle of the good heart is shocking for us to read now. In Judaism in antiquity, as now, a good heart is a core part of the law and tradition. It is the basis of it all, not a moral principle in opposition to it: 'I desire compassion, and not sacrifice; the knowledge of God, rather than burnt offerings', says the prophet Hosea (Hos. 6:6).[31]

The idea of Jesus not really being *that* Jewish was challenged most successfully by Geza Vermes, who in 1973 published a book simply entitled *Jesus the Jew*. Here he inserted 'the Jesus of the Gospels into the geographical and historical realities and into the charismatic religious framework of first-century Judaism', where 'Jesus the Galilean *hasid* or holy man begins to take on substance'.[32] For Vermes, Jesus was a holy man, a type of charismatic wonder-worker similar to figures mentioned in rabbinic texts: men named Hanina ben Dosa and Honi the Circle

Drawer, for example. Additionally, Vermes sought to understand key terms used of Jesus, such as 'son of God' and 'son of man', by reference to idiomatic Jewish Palestinian Aramaic, the language that Jesus spoke. The historical Jesus became a man understandable only by contextualising him in his religious culture.[33]

Vermes was an illustrious Jewish scholar. He was eminently suited to be the one to champion the cause of a Jewish Jesus. Four years earlier, the Israeli scholar David Flusser had published in English his book *Jesus*, with its cover image of the name *Yeshua* – 'Jesus' in Aramaic – advertising the Jewishness of Jesus.[34] But it was Vermes' work that had a major global impact, seizing the imagination of an international audience in the year of Norman Jewison's film version of the rock opera *Jesus Christ Superstar*,[35] when the time was ripe for a thorough re-examination of who Jesus was. His book was a scholarly best-seller and set the path for everyone to follow.

A new (Christian) perspective on Judaism came with the publication of E. P. Sanders' *Paul and Palestinian Judaism* (1977) and with Sanders' corresponding work *Judaism: Practice and belief, 63 BCE to 66 CE* (1992) in which he set out a Judaism in which Jesus clearly belonged.[36] Sanders' 'common Judaism' was Temple-focused, Scripture-esteeming and bonded by behaviours rather than belief. James Dunn, in his *Partings of the Ways* (1991), famously defined 'Four Pillars' of Judaism: monotheism (asserting the One God), election of Israel as Servant, a covenant agreement focused on Torah, and a land focused on Temple. Jews were an *ethnos*, maintaining certain practices that separated them from non-Jews: circumcision of boys, for example. These behaviours maintained identity as boundary-markers. In searching to answer the question 'Who is a Jew?' Dunn also noted that the religious dimensions of this term are inherent in cases where people are defined as apostates: one cannot normally be an apostate from an entirely ethnic category.[37] So we are left with the normative multivalency, a composite ethnoreligious category, even though the ethnic and religious dimension can be separated out. More exactly, you could lose your religion but not your ethnicity.

In John J. Collins' exploration of the type of Judaism in Jesus' time – Second Temple Judaism[38] – he concluded that 'there was no simple normative definition which determined Jewish identity in the Hellenistic Diaspora' and notes only some 'persistent tendencies', including what could be construed as 'covenantal nomism' (law based on a covenantal agreement between God and Israel), but also ethnic pride 'with little regard for religious laws or for anything that could be called nomism'. Collins noted there was also a moral system and code of conduct, namely loyalty to the Jewish community, the common thread coming from the reliance on the 'Jewish tradition'. This tradition, in the way Collins framed it, is Scripture.[39] In the description by the Jewish historian Josephus of the conversion of the influential queen of Adiabene, Helena, and her son Izates in c.30 CE, just around the time of Jesus' death (c.30 CE), instruction in Scripture was an essential part of the conversion process,[40] but Izates gained two opinions from Jewish teachers on whether circumcision was absolutely necessary or not.

What is clear now is that Second Temple Judaism was very variegated. The more we have learned about it in the past sixty years, the more the possibilities of what a Jew could be, and believe, have expanded. The charismatic, revelatory, mystical side of Judaism has been recognised in the literature of the Dead Sea Scrolls and also in other ancient texts that were previously unknown or ignored, such as 'Enochic' or apocalyptic literature, in which otherworldly visions play a powerful role. Jewish writers of the Graeco-Roman world, such as Philo and Josephus, have been much more widely studied. The diversity and richness of early rabbinic literature has been better appreciated. The word 'legalistic' has been sent packing.

This has led some to talk not about 'Second Temple Judaism' but about 'Second Temple Judaisms'.[41] There were differences between expressions of Judaism in the Jewish Diaspora and in Judaea, but also within Jewish groups of the land: fractures of class, regionality and legal interpretation, differences between those who interpreted Scripture literally and those who read it allegorically for hidden meanings. Ways of reading were as important as the issue of which scriptures were being read, in which versions.

More expansively still, though, Judaism was more than an ethnicity–religion blend: it was also a philosophy. Both *thrēskeia* in Greek and *religio* in Latin, though translated as 'religion', actually mean doing the right thing towards the divine (Cicero, *On the Nature of the Gods* 2:28) in cultic and household rituals, but ethics, metaphysics and lifestyle choices were in the realms of *philosophia*, philosophy.[42] Judaism blended cultic worship and philosophy together: there was indeed the Temple in Jerusalem where sacrifices and other rituals were enacted, but there was also an ethical lifestyle of obedience to a particular moral philosophy enshrined in the law of Moses, and there were metaphysical ideas about the nature of the universe. For Philo, Moses was the prime philosopher,[43] so synagogues were schools of this philosophy.[44] Thus, Paul's ejection of Moses' law still retained the philosophy, now reinterpreted.

Jesus, as a Jewish child, would have become embedded not only in the cultic praxis of honouring God at the Temple in Jerusalem but also in all the moral and metaphysical (cosmological) aspects of the *philosophia* of Judaism, absorbing all this as a template for how the world was and how one should behave within it.

This *philosophia* had long been influenced by currents of thinking from further east, from the region of present-day Iran and Iraq. In Jesus' day this was the seat of the Parthian Empire. The Parthians were successors to the hugely powerful Persians (*Parthava* means 'Persia' in the old Persian language) whose conquests stretching to Greece in the fifth century BCE had fired Alexander the Great's determination to retaliate, to counter-conquer and to destroy their great cities. The Parthians had fought off Alexander's colonisers in the third century BCE, and now their empire encompassed all of the fertile crescent between the Euphrates and Tigris rivers and much more besides, right up to the edges of Cappadocia and northern Syria. The Parthians were Zoroastrian, following the prophet Zoroaster (also known as Zarathustra), who probably lived sometime in the sixth century BCE and composed (as is thought) sacred writings: the Yasnas and the Gathas.[45] Like the Jews, they had Scripture.

Zoroastrianism asserted a mythological reality underpinning all of human existence that involved a cosmic battle between good and evil, between one great good God and an evil entity, with a world inhabited by dangerous *daevas* responsible for harm, including illness, who were countered by mighty Beneficent Immortals (angels). Human life choices led to final judgement (life or death). Cultic worship was conducted by white-clad priests, who sent praises and prayers to the one good God in fire temples where the Divine was understood as all Light and Truth. The priests were also philosophical experts in both the nature of the universe and human morality. It has long been understood that the period of

Persian rule in Judaea, from the sixth to the fourth century BCE, allowed Zoroastrian ideas to affect Jewish concepts.[46] While in Jewish Scripture illness, and various calamities, could be attributed to God (as we see famously explicated in the book of Job), now these were attributed to demons. A similar belief system permeated the eastern Hellenistic world, as we see with the Syro-Phoenician woman. As an adult, especially in his exorcistic work, we see Jesus accepting that human life was deeply afflicted by demons: there is a cosmic battle between God and Satan.[47] He grew up in a world steeped in such concepts.

Nevertheless, unlike in Zoroastrianism, in Judaism ethnic heritage counted for much, and so did place. There was one central cult site – in Jerusalem. Zoroastrians, like Jews, had twelve months in a year, but in Judaism time was also organised into weeks: regular cycles of seven days, the seventh of which was a holy day of rest, the Sabbath. Dotted throughout the months were the festivals, hinging on memory, agriculture and collective assembly in Jerusalem, and embedded in all were patterns of how things should be done: in terms of food, the body, clothing, taxes, charity, purity, and so on. All these things should be done for the sake of righteousness, since God's purpose for Israel among all peoples was to be an ethical light to the nations (Isa. 49:6).[48] Here we can see Jesus' perspective: children 'fed at the table' should be rewarded for that. He was sitting at the same table.

Contemporary scholarship, following Vermes, understands Jesus as a Jew religiously, arguing that he needs to be understood 'within not outside Judaism', as Halvor Moxnes puts it.[49] Indeed, in the dynamic, feisty and creative milieu of Second Temple Judaism, Jesus makes perfect sense as a Jew of his age. There is not a scholar today, of any persuasion, who would dispute the importance of recognising that Jesus was a Jew, understandable in his Jewish context. Jesus might be seen as a kind of apocalyptic prophet, as suggested by Paula Fredriksen, Bart Ehrman and Dale Allison;[50] or a Galilean sage championing the peasant class, as John Dominic Crossan presents him;[51] or a wisdom teacher of an egalitarian ethos as Elisabeth Schüssler Fiorenza indicates,[52] or even a radical zealot as portrayed by Reza Aslan;[53] but he is a Jew.[54] The question is: what kind of Jew was Jesus?

If we think of Jesus as a child, growing up as a Jew, we can see him gaining an identity from a distinct *story* told in Scripture, one that involves a relationship to the Divine and to others. We can see him following the laws and festivals of Judaism, the Sabbaths and the seders. We can see him as part of a vibrant philosophical world where there were debates and different groups following different interpretations. We can see him being educated in these matters as a Jewish boy. In all these things, he would have learned the boundaries between 'us' and 'them'.

Jesus the Judahite

Being a *Ioudaios* could also mean something quite particular. Paul is not only specific about Jesus being a *Ioudaios* by nature; he is also specific that he was 'born from the seed of David, according to flesh (*kata sarka*)' (Rom. 1:3). The 'seed of David' is a way of saying that he was a physical descendant of the great King David, who lived around a thousand years earlier but whose royal line had continued to rule in the land of Judah until the sixth century BCE. David in turn was a descendant of the patriarch Judah, son of Jacob (also known as Israel). Paul states in his letter to the Roman church, written *c.*56 CE, that Jesus was physically (*kata sarka*, 'according to flesh') descended from the 'ancestors' of Israel (Rom. 9:5). In this he again points to the importance of Jesus' ancestral identity. In the letter to the Hebrews, this is spelled out precisely: 'It is clear that our Lord arose from Judah' (Heb. 7:14). Jesus was *tribally* a 'Judahite': he was a descendant of the great ancestor Judah. In this way, he is understood as being part of a *patria* in a more particular sense.[55]

The idea of Jesus belonging to a tribe has not made much sense to most European and North American scholars, but in many indigenous cultures a tribal or nation identity remains an important part of your sense of self. To trace your lineage back to a founding ancestor provides you with a place within a group and a shared history with others. The story of Jewish Scripture is in fact largely the story of Judah, as a tribe, from its development within the broader tribes of Israel (e.g. Gen. 35:22; 42:13, 32; 49:28; Exod. 24:4) to the establishment of the renewed nation in the Persian period (sixth to fourth centuries BCE), following the invasion and destruction of Judah by the Babylonians in 586 BCE (see Timeline).[56] This story would have been told to Jesus. With this renewal, from 538 BCE onwards, the Judahites claimed to be the legitimate survivors of the multiple cataclysms that had wrecked a twelve-tribe model within Israel. All this informs the response Jesus gives to the Samaritan woman in the Gospel of John.

Given how fundamental this story would have been to any Jewish child, it is worthwhile remembering the concept of the 'whole' of the twelve tribes of Israel. In the narrative of Genesis, Abraham was known as the ancestor of many peoples of the region, but through Isaac his line became the 'Hebrews'.[57] As Genesis records it, Jacob – renamed 'Israel' after wrestling with an angel at the shrine of Bethel (Gen. 32:22–31) – married two wives, Leah and Rachel. He had twelve sons with these women and also with the slaves Bilhah and Zilpah. The sons of Jacob/ Israel are, then, the patriarchs of the twelve tribes, as shown in Table 1.1 with the names of their respective mothers.

Table 1.1 The twelve sons of Jacob/Israel with their mothers

Mother	Son
Leah	Reuben, Simeon, Levi, Judah, Issachar, Zebulun
Rachel	Joseph, Benjamin
Bilhah	Dan, Naphtali
Zilpah	Gad, Asher

The twelve-tribe model was not actually this simple, because the tribe of Joseph was actually split between two sons – Ephraim and Manasseh – and the tribe of Benjamin became linked in with Judah,[58] but the story of the twelve tribes underlies Scripture: from the book of Deuteronomy through to 2 Kings, and the retelling in 1–2 Chronicles. In Ezra and Nehemiah it is the physical return to the land of Judah, and what it means to be Judahite, that directs the narrative.

As a counterpoint to being Judahite, in Jesus' time there was a community known as the Samaritans, who saw themselves as Israelites,[59] the true descendants of Ephraim and Manasseh (sons of Joseph). These tribes had been subject to deportation (by the Assyrians in the eighth century BCE), but they also remained in the land as a 'remnant of Israel' (2 Chr. 34:9). Archaeological excavations of their holy cult site on Mount Gerizim have uncovered the Samaritan temple there, dating from the fifth century BCE.[60] The Samaritans followed the Mosaic law, claiming they were authentically Israel. The survival of Ephraim alongside Judah is acknowledged in the writings of the Judahite prophet Ezekiel (37:15–16) in the sixth century BCE, but otherwise within Judahite traditions the Samaritans did not have legitimacy: only the Judahites were the true representatives of Israel, and the Samaritans could even be represented as foreigners.[61] This too informs the interactions, as portrayed, between Jesus and the Samaritan woman.

The fact that Jesus grew up in Galilee, as we will explore, does not take away his tribal affiliation as Judahite, even though there has been in scholarship some determined effort to sever him from this.[62] This makes Jesus somewhat different from Paul, who (though a Jew) defined himself as being from the tribe of Benjamin (Phil. 3:5; and see Rom. 11:1).[63]

As a Judahite, belonging to a tribe with a sense of physical descent from a common ancestor, Jesus may well have had a particular 'look'. In some cultures, we can determine race or tribe on the basis of an individual's appearance, but people in the modern West are often desensitised to such subtleties. In terms of Jesus' physical appearance, studies of skeletal remains in post-exilic Judah/Judaea have indicated that this population group had affinities with the appearance of Babylonian Jews. Their appearance was somewhat different from the pre-exilic tribes.

In John 4:3–43, Jesus and his disciples were plainly en route, travelling back to Galilee from the Judahite cultic centre of Jerusalem, through the conquered lands of the tribes of Ephraim and Manasseh (Samaria). That in itself would have provided a clue to the Samaritan woman.

As a Judahite, Jesus would have learned of his ancestral heritage inscribed in Scripture, and it is likely he would have received a broader knowledge passed on orally through stories. The stories of these ancestors were part of a family heritage that was connected to places and tombs. The patriarchs themselves lay together in death and in Scripture. In the *Testament of Judah*, initially composed in the first century BCE, Judah himself is said to be buried in Hebron 'with his ancestors' (*Test. Jud.* 26:4), meaning his tomb was remembered as being in the ancient Cave of Machpelah (Ramat el-Khalil), where there were also the burial places of Sarah and Abraham, Rebecca and Isaac, and Leah and Jacob/Israel (Gen. 23:1–20; 25:5–8; 35:28–9; 49:30; 50:1–14). It was a vital centre of reverence at the time of Jesus, evidenced today by the fine renovations and expansions of the late first century BCE.[64]

To be a Judahite was to consider yourself a survivor, in terms of your identity, first from an ancestral persecution in Egypt as one of the Hebrew tribes of Israel oppressed there in ancient times (so Exodus; Deut. 1 – 11), and then again from having a heritage among those who survived after the Babylonian captivity (so Ezra–Nehemiah). As with any survivor, there was a deep cognisance of those who did not survive: the remaining tribes, in this case. We see in the writings of the prophet Ezekiel a vision of restoration: in a valley a great mass of dry bones come together to form whole skeletons, revivified by the Spirit, and then they become bodies with muscles, organs and flesh, reconstituting Israel (Ezek. 37:15–28). In his adult life, Jesus would in fact use a fresh model of the twelve tribes: the 'Twelve' he appoints as his envoys in Galilee would, so he claimed, 'sit on twelve thrones to judge the twelve tribes of Israel' (Matt. 19:28//Luke 22:28–30). Perhaps this indicates a kind of nostalgia for a past whole (of Israel) that might still exist in a way known only to God.[65] At the very least, though, it suggests that the idea of the twelve tribes remained live and meaningful in the environment Jesus knew, and that it was meaningful to him also.

Jesus the Judaean

The final dimension of being a *Ioudaios* in terms of Jesus' identity concerns land and nationhood. Being a Judahite in terms of ancestral heritage was also about connection to place, in this case the land of traditional Judah, *Ioudaia* in Greek, or Judaea as it was known in Latin: this was his country (*chōra*) with many sites (hills, valleys, rivers) associated with the past. A *patria*, as an ethnic group, belongs to a *patris*, a homeland, a place of the ancestors, where their tombs lie.[66] While much has been made in scholarship of Jesus as a Galilean,[67] the idea of Jesus as a Judaean in terms of regionality has not been so prevalent. But Jesus was remembered as totally a Judaean: he was born in the town of Bethlehem of Judaea (see Chapter 3), where his family came from and where his ancestors were.

In stating this, we should not think of a 'country' in modern nation-state terms. Judaea was where *Ioudaioi* lived, where there was Judaean governance from Jerusalem, and where Jewish law was the law of the land. Law, in the Hellenistic East, was connected to cities and their village-filled territories rather than to nation-states as we have them. Thus, in some ways 'Judaea' was a nation that encompassed the territory governed by the central Judaean *metropolis* (mother-city) of Jerusalem, which then ruled over other cities and their territories, as well as the Jewish communities of the Diaspora.[68] Judaea was by no means a backwater to the Romans: it was extremely important strategically. This was because adjacent Nabataea ('Arabia'), ruled by the hugely powerful king Aretas IV Philopatris (9 BCE – 40 CE), was the principal buffer to the Parthian Empire: Rome's foe.

Judaea was 'the country of Judaeans' (*hē Ioudaiōn . . . chōra*), as the Jewish historian Josephus would put it (*War* 3:58).[69] It lay within Syria, on the eastern Mediterranean, largely inland from the coast. Syria included Syria Phoenicia in the north, and Syria Palestina in the south, and the latter was subdivided into both Judaea and a cluster of Syro-Palestinian cities. South-west was Egypt. Arabia lay to the south-east and east.

The history of the land would have been part of the knowledge handed down to Jesus. Part of this history was in Scripture, but part was beyond it, and it is important to reflect on this knowledge. Traditional Judah, as a Judahite tribal area, had for centuries been a relatively small region, centred on the holy city of Jerusalem and stretching south to Hebron. This was still the case following the restoration of Judah after the exile in Babylon, in 538 BCE, when the Judahite tribal territory existed as a peaceful western province of the Persian Empire.

However, the whole area of Syria (including Syria Palestina) was taken by the armies of Alexander the Great in 333 BCE and held tightly by one or the other of his successors, either the Ptolemies ruling from Alexandria in Egypt (through to 200 BCE) or the Seleucids ruling from Antioch (to 164 BCE). In this phase, hellenisation – Greek cultural imperialism – spread to Judaea. In archaeological, epigraphic and literary sources, Hellenic influence is clearly apparent in architecture, dress, civic structure, theatres, and weights and measures, with inscriptions indicating that Greek was spoken in many cities. At this time, Judaea bordered the Edomite region of Idumaea in the south-west, and the Idumaean capital Marisa had clearly 'gone Greek', with its population identifying with illustrious Sidon, further north, as evidenced from their tomb art and Greek writing.[70]

In 164 BCE, Judaea gained independence from the Seleucids and established a hierocracy of priest-kings: the Hasmonean dynasty. Their rise came in the wake of a battle for independence to safeguard the Judaean cult from having to equate the God of Israel with the Greek god Zeus after the Seleucid king Antiochus IV Epiphanes proclaimed himself a manifestation of said god, demanded pig sacrifices in the Jerusalem Temple, banned circumcision and put Judaean protesters to death (see 1 and 2 Maccabees). Given such horrors, hellenisation was subsequently somewhat checked by the Hasmoneans in order to preserve Judaea's identity.

The Hasmonean phase of Judaean independence went along with a significant expansion of geographical boundaries, which pushed back the threat of foreign dominion. The idea was that Judaean governance should embrace all the land promised to the tribes of Israel (so Josh. 13 – 19). It was the people's 'ancestral heritage' (1 Macc. 15:33–5). Soon, Judaea spanned the traditional extent of the area inhabited by the twelve tribes of Israel, stretching from Mount Libanus in the north to the Negev Desert in the south, and the remaining populations were required to be subject to Judaean law (i.e. to either convert or leave).[71] Under Jonathan (152–142 BCE), Engeddi by the Dead Sea was included, as was a cluster of towns to the north and west (including Gophna and Lydda). Under his son Simon (142–134 BCE), Gezer and Joppa, a port on the coast, were added. With John Hyrcanus (134–104 BCE), swathes of Idumaea in the south and Samaria in the north came under Judaean governance. John Hyrcanus destroyed the Samaritan temple (so Josephus, *Ant.* 11:322–34, *c*.111–110 BCE)[72] as part of the Judaean expansion. Galilee was included under his son Aristobulus I (104–103 BCE). Under Alexander Jannaeus, Judaean rule was expanded over areas east of the Jordan Valley and Dead Sea (*c*.103–76 BCE).[73] This complicates our terminology, because there was still traditional Judaea, regarded as the old tribal territory of Judah, but now also a greater Judaea carved into Syro-Palestinian/Phoenician areas.

While Jews already resided in many places as part of long-standing patterns of Diaspora,[74] the old Judaeans (Judahites) soon moved into the new territories: to Galilee, Gaulanitis, Peraea, Idumaea. In this environment, converted and ancestral Judaeans could marry one another, and ultimately, through the system of male lineage, the converts would become absorbed into Judahite ancestral patterns. But the difference between a recent convert and someone with a long Judahite lineage was surely felt.

However, Hasmonean expansion did not always stick, and independence was short-lived. In the year 63 BCE, under the Roman general Pompey, the Romans took the opportunity of a civil war between the Hasmonean high-priestly royal rulers Hyrcanus II and Aristobulus II, the sons of Alexander Jannaeus, to sack Jerusalem, after which Judaea paid tribute to Rome. Rome installed its own chosen procurator, an Idumaean named Antipater, as the administrative ruler over the area, alongside the Hasmonean high priest Hyrcanus II, who continued as the nation's leader to rule over the law courts, Temple and matters of government but was effectively robbed of military authority. Further civil war ultimately led to the end of the Hasmonean dynasty. Rome favoured Antipater's son Herod and eventually, in 40 BCE, appointed him as client 'King of the Judaeans'. Seeing the Hasmoneans as a threat, Herod had the young high priest Aristobulus III drowned in his swimming pool in Jericho (Josephus, *War* 2:206; *Ant.* 15:53–5).

It was in the last years of Herod's reign (c.6–4 BCE) that Jesus was born. He grew up in a land that had stabilised and somewhat shrunk down after the maximal extent of conquests of the past. Judaea comprised five key regions: Galilee, Samaria, Peraea, Idumaea and traditional Judaea, though Jews lived in other surrounding cities and territories besides.[75] Galilee, a rich and populous agricultural area, was divided into an upper and lower part, with its administrative centre in Sepphoris (Josephus, *War* 3:35–9).[76] Samaria was a hilly region which lay between Galilee and traditional Judaea (Josephus, *War* 3:48–50), inhabited by Samaritans and Syro-Palestinians. In practical terms, despite the Hasmonean conquering of this territory and the destruction of the Samaritan temple, the two Hellenic cities of Sebaste and Neapolis seem to have functioned independently. Samaritans held on to a separate identity, harbouring much resentment against Judaeans.

Jerusalem was in the north of traditional Judaea, but now it was located towards the south of the whole land, even if conceptualised as the centre of the earth (*Jub.* 8:19). There was then Idumaea, in the south, named after the Edomites, who had moved westwards into this region (that was once part of southern Judah) with the encroachment of Nabataeans into their land east of the Dead Sea. Tracing their ancestry to Ishmael, son of

Abraham's female slave Hagar, they were an Arab people, but with the expansion of Judaea they had converted. 'Idumaea' was configured as a single city with a territory (Josephus, *War* 3:55), though its principal cities were actually Adora (see 1 Macc. 13:20) and Marisa (*Ant.* 13:257).

On the east, within Judaea, there was Peraea (Josephus, *War* 3:44–7), meaning 'Beyond', a term with a decidedly Judaean perspective since it was 'beyond' the River Jordan when viewed from a location on the west of it, in Judaea. A rather dry and rugged region, apart from land east of the Jordan Valley, it lay south of the Decapolis, through to the eastern edges of the Dead Sea and down to the River Arnon, bordering Nabataea. There was also Gaulanitis, an arid zone which stretched northeast to border wild Trachonitis. It included Jewish villages, but it does not seem to have been counted within Judaea.

After the era of the Hasmoneans, many Syro-Palestinian cities retained or restored their independence and were not part of Judaea proper. The core group of these in the east were named the Decapolis ('Ten-Cities'), a list that the Roman writer Pliny presents as 'adjoining Judaea on the side of Syria': Damascus, Philadelphia (modern-day Amman), Raphana, Gerasa, Pella, Scythopolis (Nysa), Gadara, Hippos, Dion, Pella and Kanatha (*Nat. Hist.* 5:4:16 [74]). Some of the coastal cities were independent Syro-Palestinian cities too, but under Syrian administration: Gaza, Ascalon, Dora and Ptolemais. Jamnia and Azotus were governed as imperial estates.

As a Judaean then, geographically, when history told of frequent occasions when your neighbours overran your homeland, you would feel a sense of being surrounded by threatening foreigners.[77] Given the loop of Syro-Palestinian and Syro-Phoenician cities all around, and their Nabataean neighbours, Judaeans would also have known of many temples and shrines for different deities and heroes. The ancient Greek deities had been syncretised with the Roman ones (Zeus = Jupiter, Ares = Mars, Aphrodite = Venus, and so on) and then blended with local divinities (for example, Atargatis = Aphrodite, Hadad = Zeus). Dionysus, the god of wine, was strongly associated with Scythopolis: its alternative name, Nysa, had been the name of his wet-nurse. Additionally, the Roman imperial cult joined all devotions into a system of loyalty to the Roman emperor and his family. The emperors functioned as quasi-deities themselves under the benign gaze of the goddess Roma, and – thanks to Herod – the Roman imperial cult temples were dotted around what was ostensibly (though only just) the country of the Judaeans itself: in Sebaste (Samaria), Caesarea Philippi (Omrit) and Caesarea Maritima.[78] This meant that the 'others' were never very far away. In such an environment, Judaeans would have experienced a sense of 'us' and 'them' being in close proximity. When Jesus responds to the Syro-Phoenician woman by talking about throwing the children's food to the 'dogs' (Mark 7:24–30), he is using a known slur against the 'others': the group to which she belonged would have been expected to honour the dying-and-rising god Melkart-Heracles, not the God of Israel.[79]

Jesus was 'under the Law', as Paul says (Gal. 4:4), but – unlike in the Diaspora where Paul lived – in the country of the Judaeans this was largely the law of the land of Judaea.[80] Law was administered in local courts under the authority of the high priest in Jerusalem, who was advised by a select council (the Sanhedrin, from Greek *sunedrion*). Council selection was not by a democratic process. In Judaea, there were leading priestly families, and alliances of wealthy houses, that made up a ruling class (the 'chief priests' of the Gospels).[81]

Jesus then dwelt in a country, a nation, with a particular character and history. It had a narrative of struggle, but Judaea was also colonial, in that places beyond traditional Judaea (Judah) had become subject to Judaean laws and government, even though this was configured as a reclamation of ancestral heritage.

As with any land, there were cultural aspects. Language was part of Judaean regional identity. Scripture was written in Hebrew, the ancient language of Israel, but since the Persian conquest of the sixth century BCE the common language of the region had shifted to Aramaic. Hebrew nevertheless remained as a spoken language around Jerusalem, and literacy in Hebrew was strongly maintained by the scribal elite there: it is thus no wonder that the majority of the Dead Sea Scrolls were written in Hebrew. This maintenance of Hebrew was partly linked with a desire to maintain national identity over against various linguistic, cultural and religious threats.[82] If from Bethlehem, a town close to Jerusalem, Jesus' family may well then have spoken Hebrew, even if, as a Galilean adult, Jesus spoke Aramaic.[83] Both Hebrew and Aramaic were spoken within a wider context of prevalent Greek, the common language of the eastern Mediterranean world, spoken in the hellenised Syro-Palestinian cities of the Decapolis and from Rapha to Ptolemais. Oral multilinguality, to various degrees, was probably common.

Regionality was reflected in speech accents.[84] In Samaritan Aramaic you dropped 'aitches', effectively, and other guttural sounds, as in the English regional accents of London and Essex (where you say ''at' for 'hat').[85] Whatever the case, in the story of John 4:3–9, as we saw, it is assumed that the Samaritan woman could easily identify Jesus as a *Ioudaios*.

Culture within a country also encompasses customary ways of dressing[86] and distinctive food. We know today how much different dishes can vary according to region. There were undoubtedly distinctive songs, and a musical tradition, along with art and architecture. In all these aspects, we need to see Jesus growing up within a particular *place*, in which Judaism was woven into daily life but was not all of daily life.

So we have begun thinking of Jesus as a boy with an exploration of Jesus' identity as a *Ioudaios* and have unpacked the various dimensions of the term. Jesus was a Jew in terms of an ethnic and religious category, which involved philosophy. He was descended from the patriarch Judah and thus tribally a Judahite. He was a Judaean, a resident of the country of the Judaeans. These three dimensions of identity are all found within one Greek, Latin or Hebrew/Aramaic word, but they can be pulled apart. Jesus' connection with land, country, nation, heritage, ancestry, culture, philosophy and religion were all tied up together in being a *Ioudaios*. He could not have been more of a *Ioudaios*, in fact. He was a *Ioudaios* in every dimension: a Jew, a Judahite and a Judaean.

Thinking about his identity as a *Ioudaios* has also allowed us to explore Jesus' context in terms of land, history and culture. These things are vital to understand as we seek to reflect on Jesus as a child. Judaea was far from a peaceful place, and – as we have seen – there is one further aspect of Jesus' identity, mentioned by Paul, that was very specific. He was a descendant of the royal line of David.

2

Heritage: seed of David

One's identity can come from many sources, and ancestral heritage is one of them. Who we are can be locked into who our forebears were, and what they did. In pre-modern societies, what your forebears did often determined what your job would be, as an artisan, midwife, farmer or fisher. To be born into a noble family came with expectations of living up to a certain standard of achievement, or wealth, along with certain privileges. The ancient world was one where good birth mattered a great deal, and hierarchies of birth were widely acknowledged. Illustrious ancestry was closely preserved in family archives and memory, and by social acknowledgement.

The Greek term for being 'noble' was *eugenēs*, literally 'well born', and for Jews of Jesus' world such as Josephus and Philo this carried with it social expectations about how you would behave, namely with virtue, generosity (with one's wealth), courage and intellectual superiority, and by looking well presented (Philo, *Jos.* 106). It was expected that you showed 'nobleness' of character, sticking to certain principles (see Josephus, *Ant.* 12:255) and exhibiting refined sensibility (Philo, *Contempl.* 69). For Philo, Moses himself as an infant seemed 'well born (*eugenēs*) and refined (*asteios*)' (*Mos.* 1:18). In Acts 17:11, the author commends the Jews of Beroea, a city of Greece, for being 'more well born (*eugenesteroi*) than those of Thessalonika in that they received the teaching (of Paul) with total readiness of mind (*prothumia*), and searched the Scriptures every day to see if things were so'. To be 'well born' carried the associations of the term 'well bred' in English (Aristotle, *Pol.* 5:1/1301b:1–4; *Hist. Anim.* 1:1/488b:18–20). Being 'well born' made someone fit to rule.

In the letters of Paul, Jesus was remembered as a descendant of King David: he was 'from the seed of David' (Rom. 1:3), from the royal line. This is one of our most securely and widely attested pieces of information about Jesus. In another letter attributed to Paul (2 Timothy), the author states also that Jesus was 'from the seed of David' (2 Tim. 2:8). This memory appears in the book of Revelation: Jesus is the 'Lion from the tribe of Judah, the root from David' (Rev. 5:5; cf. Isa. 11:1, 10), and is 'the root and family of David' (Rev. 22:16). In the Gospels, it is repeatedly stated that Jesus was the son of David, thirteen times in Matthew.[1] This assertion forms an important part of the nativity stories of Matthew (1 – 2) and Luke (1 – 2). Jesus is the son of David, as was Joseph his father (Matt. 1:1, 20). In Luke's Gospel, Joseph is one 'from the house of David' (Luke 1:27), 'from the house and the family of David' (Luke 2:4).[2] Jesus will inherit the throne of 'his father David' (Luke 1:32). He is 'in the house of David' (Luke 1:69). In Acts, Peter proclaims that God made a promise to David that one 'from the fruit of his loins' would sit on the throne (Acts 2:29–30); Jesus is the seed of David (Acts 2:23–4; and see 2:32–7).[3] This truly is physical descent and not simply legal, as a result of Joseph somehow adopting Jesus: such legal adoption likely was not practised by Jews in the first century.[4]

In other Christian literature from the early second century, Jesus' physical descent from David through the male line ('seed') was also much remembered. For Ignatius of Antioch, Jesus was 'seed of David' (*Ephes.* 18:2; 20:2; *Trall.* 9). In the *Didache*, an early church manual, the eucharistic blessing over the cup (of wine) was as follows: 'We give thanks to you, our Father, for the holy vine of your servant/child (*pais*) David which you have made known to us through your servant/child Jesus.' With the eucharistic wine identified as Jesus' blood,[5] David has produced the 'holy vine' whose blood has flowed into Jesus (*Did.* 9:2).[6]

Given the importance of *eugenia*, and the earliness of these attestations, it is quite hard to dismiss them all. Strangely, however, while some scholars of the historical Jesus have accepted that Jesus was of Davidic lineage,[7] many have suggested that Jesus' Davidic descent is highly questionable. Geza Vermes, whose work was so important for stressing the Jewishness of Jesus, noted that *c*.200 CE Davidic descent was claimed by the leader of the later rabbinic academy Judah ha-Nasi (via the sage Hillel), and by the Babylonian exilarch,[8] and he considered such claims doubtful, including that of Jesus. Jens Schröter cites Jesus' Davidic descent as part of a list of 'mythical' elements:

the traditions about Jesus' birth and childhood are shaped by legendary motifs which express the conviction of his divine origin, his Davidic descent and the fulfilment of the Scriptures of Israel by Mary's conception and Jesus' birth. Consequently, [genuine] memories of Jesus did not begin with his childhood and youth, but only with his public ministry.[9]

Reza Aslan is more equivocal about whether Jesus was actually descended from David:

Whether it was true is impossible to say. Many people claimed lineage to the great Israelite king (who lived a thousand years before Jesus of Nazareth), and frankly none of them could either prove such a lineage or disprove it.[10]

This is an interesting observation, because it takes us into what was claimed, or rather 'remembered', in terms of identity, rather than simply focusing on what is verifiably true. That helps us here, because if Jesus' family *believed* they were descended from the Davidic kings, it doesn't matter whether Jesus was or was not; it was still an important identity-marker for the family and for Jesus himself.

This also takes us to the fundamental approach we will adopt here, which is concerned with memory.[11] For understanding Jesus as a child, we can look to a range of literature which tells us about how Jesus' defining identity was remembered during the decades after he lived. Memories, as transmitted, are not necessarily perfectly accurately retold or written down, and elements can be forgotten, shaped and moved. Nevertheless, in any process of memory transmission, there are constraints on individual invention when there is an existing community holding memories of the past, especially when those with living memories can still tell their stories. Thus, when we have many attestations of Jesus being a descendant of David in our earliest records, from different places, it is overly sceptical for historians to dismiss them all as innovations designed to bolster Jesus' messianic status. These memories existed and were transmitted among the earliest Christian groups because they were held to be both meaningful and true.

Remembering David and his royal line

So who was David? What was remembered of David is found in Scripture, in a story strongly connected to land. The book of Joshua presents a situation in which the land of Canaan, once conquered by the Israelite armies, is divided between the 'twelve tribes' of Israel, with the Canaanites largely killed, absorbed or evicted. The tribe of Judah was allocated a large block of the land in the south (Josh. 13 – 19), as we have seen. The book of Judges presents a confederation of tribes, led by tribal chiefs (judges), with the Canaanites, Moabites and Amorites of the land remaining a threat. There is no king (Judg. 17:6; 21:25). This period is usually thought to correlate with a historical time period of 1200–1025 BCE (see Timeline).

The books of 1 and 2 Samuel tell of a radical change in terms of the leadership of the confederation. Saul, from the tribe of Benjamin, is chosen and anointed as king by the prophet Samuel at a time of increasing warfare with neighbouring groups, notably the Philistines, who occupied the western regions. This narrative is thought to correlate with a time period of c.1025–1010 BCE.

Then, we meet David. David is essentially a nobody, not well born in any way. He is the son of a certain Jesse, a Judahite (more specifically an Ephrathite – a regional designation) from Bethlehem, but he is just a boy shepherd minding flocks. David exemplifies how a nobody can become the greatest hero of the day. Chosen by God for greater things, and incredibly good-looking, he famously slays the Philistine Goliath with a slingshot. David becomes Saul's son-in-law, marrying his daughter Michal. But not all goes well. Saul feels threatened, and suspects he is in revolt against him. There is a tense cat-and-mouse struggle between Saul and David in which Saul's son Jonathan loves David far more than he loves his father.

After his sons are killed in a battle with the Philistines on Mount Gilboa, Saul dies by his own hand, and David is chosen by his men as the new king of Judah (2 Sam. 2:4). In due course, David gains all the territory of the Israelite tribes in the north and the south (c.1010–970 BCE), ruling his kingdom from Jerusalem, in Judah, and it is said that under his son Solomon (c.970–931 BCE) the first Temple was constructed and dedicated there (1 Kgs 6 – 8). David is so acclaimed that the prophet Nathan says to him: 'Your house and your kingdom will be made sure for ever before me; your throne will be established for ever' (2 Sam. 7:16).

David was remembered for his great successes in battle, for being astute, and also for his personal story, which was not always one of moral excellence: beginning an adulterous relationship with a beautiful married woman, Bathsheba, he ensured that her Hittite husband Uriah was conveniently killed in battle so that he could marry her, after he got her pregnant. He was also remembered for lyre-playing and composing prophetic songs, which were in due course collected together within the book of Psalms; seventy-three psalms are attributed to him.[12] In the eyes of his subjects, God had chosen him and favoured him. In the words of the prophet Samuel, speaking to David as if directly from God:

> When your days are complete and you lie down with your ancestors,
> I will raise up your seed after you, who will come forth from inside
> your body, and I will establish his kingdom. He shall build a house
> for my name, and I will establish the throne of his kingdom for ever.
> I will be a father to him and he will be a son to me.
> (2 Sam. 7:12–14a)

A Davidic king was thus accounted as 'son' of God (and see Ps. 2:7).

After the reign of David's son Solomon, c.931 BCE, the united tribal kingdom fractured, and the northern kingdom, designated 'Israel', split from the southern kingdom, Judah. According to 1–2 Kings and 1–2 Chronicles, the Davidic dynasty continued to rule in Judah, though not in the northern kingdom of Israel, through a time period that can at times be correlated with Assyrian records stretching from the tenth through to the sixth century BCE (see Timeline).[13] These biblical books are then likely based on some historical records of the dynasty.

But things went wrong. The nineteenth king of this line, Jehoiachin (598–597 BCE), also known as Jeconiah (Jer. 27:20), ran headlong into the critique of the prophet Jeremiah, who predicted that no descendant of his would ever sit on the throne (Jer. 21 – 22). Indeed, Jehoiachin was dethroned and taken captive by the invading army of Nebuchadnezzar, who took him and his children to Babylon. In terms of the historicity of this event, it has been stunningly confirmed by ration tablets, found in excavations in Babylon, which outline what rations were due to him and his family.[14] This is not the only archaeological evidence of David's line. King Jehoshaphat (2 Kgs 3:5–27) is mentioned in an inscribed black basalt stela, found in 1868 in Dibhan, known as the Mesha Stela (and dated to c.840 BCE). Now on display in the Louvre, it also records 'the house of David' as being the royal rulers of Judah.[15] An inscription found in Tel Dan in northern Israel in 1993, dated to the later ninth century BCE, commemorates the Aramaean king Hazael's defeat of Joram and Ahaziah of 'the house of David' in 841 BCE (2 Kgs 8:28–9).[16]

The last (Davidic) king of Judah was Jehoiachin's uncle Mattaniah, renamed Zedekiah (596–586 BCE), who was installed by Nebuchadnezzar II in 597 BCE as a client king for the short-lived Neo-Babylonian Empire. Zedekiah led the country into a disastrous revolt in c.586 BCE, which ended up in a horrific siege and the destruction of Jerusalem, including the Temple, and the wholesale deportation of Judah's ruling class, and many others besides. Zedekiah's sons were killed in front of him, after which his eyes were put out, and he too was sent off captive to Babylon (2 Kgs 24 – 25). At the conclusion of 2 Kings, we are presented with an ignominious end to a dazzling dynasty that represented both the heights and depths of greatness and folly, as told by those who chronicled the nation's history.

The Davidic line was not remembered as evaporating at this point, however. When the new Persian ruler, Cyrus, allowed the exiled Judahite captives in Babylon to return to Judah, now a Persian province named Yehud, a grandson of Jehoiachin, Zerubbabel, was appointed as governor of Jerusalem (Zech. 4:1–9; Ezra 3:1–2, 8). The idea that the Davidic dynasty should rule was thus still alive and well. Zerubbabel was important in rebuilding the Temple, and his children's names were also recorded (1 Chr. 3:19–20). This takes the memory of the Davidic line to the end of the sixth century BCE.

But given that this is still 500 years before Jesus, the question has been whether calling someone 'seed of David' really means that Jesus was physically connected with this dynasty. Was Jesus brought up with the idea that he was of Davidic lineage, or was calling him 'seed of David' a symbolic attribution of his kingship? While we have ancestry.com and other ways of working out our lineage, how plausible is it that families in ancient Judah/Judaea kept their ancestry up to date, especially without good written records?

Actually, people did remember descent, because a first-century ossuary has been discovered with a tiny Aramaic inscription on the right side's upper rim reading: *shel be David*, 'of [the] house of David,' or 'of David's house' (see Fig. 2.1). This inscription misses the final letter *tau* of the word *beth* ('house of'), which accurately reflects pronunciation in that the letter would not be vocalised.

Figure 2.1 Ossuary inscription: *shel be David*, 'of [the] house of David'
(IAA Inventory number: 1971-410. Drawing by Joan Taylor)

Located in a Jewish tomb of the Second Temple period excavated in present-day Givat ha-Mivtar, near Mount Scopus, Jerusalem, it is a finely decorated limestone box with two rosettes and a zigzag frame. This inscription clearly shows that people remembered that someone was a descendant of David.[17] On the decorated side there is written 'Shalom Hillel', which is striking given that the great sage Hillel was reputed to be a descendant of David (see above), but this ossuary contained bones of someone aged about 25 years. Perhaps, though, this man was from the Hillel family.

This was not an inscription for the public, but for the family, who here wanted to record identity. The relationship between this particular son of David and the others buried in the tomb is unknown. Was he a man who married into the family, or were all of the other entombed people also descended from David? Despite these unknowns, the inscription shows that this memory was not merely symbolic: it was about identity.

The son of David as God's Anointed

Being part of the lineage of David provided not only the identity of being a well-born person but also a destiny, since there was the promise of future leadership.[18] People believed there would be a king from the descendants of David who would save Israel from oppression. The Davidic king-Messiah was not the only type of messianic figure who could be expected,[19] but this figure is found repeatedly attested.

The promise was in Scripture. There was the aforementioned prophecy of Nathan: 'Your house and your kingdom will be made sure for ever before me; your throne will be established for ever' (2 Sam. 7:16). Amos predicts that God would build up 'the booth of David that is fallen' in Israel (Amos 9:11). Isaiah 9:6–7 looks to a coming righteous king on the 'throne of David'. Imagining a growth like a new shoot springing from an old stump of a tree, Isaiah predicts there would be 'a sprout (*khoter*) from the stump of Jesse, and a branch (*netser*) from his roots shall bear fruit' (Isa. 11:1); the Spirit of God would rest on him to enable him to judge and rule in righteousness. Micah (5:1–3) proclaims that a ruler would come from Bethlehem (like David), in the land of Judah, to shepherd Israel. In Jeremiah, 'Righteous Branch for David' (*leDavid tsemakh tsaddiq*) is a title for a king from the royal house of Judah (Jer. 23:5; 33:15).[20]

In the exilic writings of Ezekiel (34:23–4; 37:24–8), from the sixth century BCE, there is a prediction of the arrival of a 'shepherd, [God's] servant David', a future prince who will re-establish Israel in the land.[21] Israel would be reconstituted. Ezekiel sees in his vision of a valley of dry bones that are brought together into skeletons, enfleshed, and revivified by the Spirit, that the tribes of Ephraim (Samaritans) and Judah are joined under the rule of David again. Elsewhere, this expected king was called God's Anointed,[22] in Hebrew *Mashiakh*, transliterated into Greek as *Messias* (hence: Messiah) or translated into Greek as *Christos* (Christ). Since a king was anointed as part of the coronation ceremony in ancient Israel, a king was also an 'anointed' (e.g. 1 Sam. 10:1; 16:2–13; 1 Kgs 1:39).[23]

Several psalms were interpreted as pointing to the arrival of the Anointed. For example, in Psalm 89:3–4 God states:

I have made a covenant with my chosen one.
I have sworn to David, my servant.
I will establish your seed for ever,
and build up your throne through all generations.

This Davidic king who would rule Judah, and Israel as a whole, was a powerful source of hope after the exile. In the *Psalms of Solomon*, a first-century BCE collection of poems that did not get included in scriptural canons, there are two psalms (17 and 18) which imagine the return of a king named the Son of David (see esp. *Pss Sol.* 17:21–4, using Pss 17:22 and 2:9)[24] and 'the Lord's Anointed' (*Pss Sol.* 18:7). Such terminology is found in other literature from around this time (*1 Enoch* 48:10; 52:4; *4 Ezra*

7:28; 12:32). In the Dead Sea Scrolls, a priestly 'Anointed' was also at times expected,[25] but clearly the 'Branch of David' is a title of an expected king who would save Israel (e.g. 4Q174 frag. 1:1:11–13; 4Q252 5:3–4).[26] In the Qumran scroll known as 4Q174 (*4QFlorilegium*) 10–13 we read:

> 'I will establish the throne of his kingdom [for ever. I will be] his father and he shall be my son' [2 Sam. 7:12–14]. He is the Branch of David (*tsemakh David*) who will arise with the Interpreter of the Law [to rule] in Zion [at the end] of time. As it is written, 'I will raise up the tent of David that is fallen' [Amos 9:11], that is to say, the fallen tent of David is he who shall arise to save Israel.

For those who wrote the Scrolls, the Anointed (Messiah) was expected to do remarkable things: not only to restore Israel as a royal ruler but also to heal (4Q521, drawing on Isa. 61:1 and Ps. 146:8).[27] The descendants of David are important: 'For to him (David) and to his descendants has been given the covenant of royalty over his people for all everlasting generations' (4Q252 5:4). Given all this expectation, it would be odd if descendants of the house of David simply forgot where they came from. The line of David was of crucial importance for the hopes of Israel.

Jesus as son of David

In Mark's Gospel, Jesus is directly addressed as 'son of David', as if his identity is well known. This is in the story of the healing of a blind beggar named Bartimaeus (Mark 10:46–52). Bartimaeus is sitting by the roadside when Jesus is leaving Jericho with his disciples and a 'great crowd'. He calls out, 'Jesus, son of David, have mercy on me!' It is said that 'many' wanted him to be quiet and tried to get him to stop shouting, but he shouted all the louder. At this point Jesus stops, says to his disciples 'Call him', and asks him what he wants. Bartimaeus asks to have his sight restored. Jesus does this, miraculously, and Bartimaeus then 'followed Jesus on the road' to Jerusalem. The question is: why did anyone want him to be quiet?

Soon after, in Mark, when Jesus comes to Jerusalem, people also engage in shouting about David. They say, '"Hosanna, blessed is the one coming in the name of the Lord", blessed is the coming kingdom of our father David!' (Mark 11:9–10).[28] The first part of this acclamation is a quote from Psalm 118:25–6. The second part seems to be an interpretation: the coming one is supposed to bring in a restoration of the kingdom of David; that is, he is the Davidic Messiah. The term 'father' was a term of respect.[29] Jesus is said to have entered Jerusalem sitting on a donkey colt, rather than walking as he had done previously, and this would have recalled the messianic prophecy of Zechariah 9:9: 'Look, your king is coming to you, humble and mounted on a donkey: on a colt, on the foal of a donkey.'

In both cases, it seems people are actually shouting about Jesus with different hopes. Bartimaeus wanted healing, and the people of Jerusalem wanted 'the kingdom of our father David'. In the second case, it is not mentioned that anyone, least of all Jesus, wants the people to be quiet, but, nevertheless, allowing them to say these things openly looks like a dangerous step, since in the end the Jerusalem authorities plan to arrest Jesus and have him put to death (Mark 14:1).

These two stories of the healing in Jericho and the arrival in Jerusalem were retold in the Gospels of Matthew and Luke. Matthew even tells the healing story twice (9:27–31; 20:29–34), and in both cases there are two blind men shouting 'Have mercy on us, son of David'. In the second story it is the crowd who want the men to be quiet, and Jesus himself calls the men over. Both follow him. This double duplication of both the blind men and the story itself serves to emphasise the proclamation of Jesus as son of David, and answers the question Matthew places on the lips of the crowd in 12:23: 'Could this be the Son of David?' At this point, it is clear that there is an identification of Jesus not just as a descendant of David, but as the expected (messianic) Son of David.

In Luke (18:35–43), the healing story is situated as Jesus is nearing the city of Jericho rather than leaving it. He is with a crowd, and 'those . . . in front' tell the unnamed blind man to be quiet. The blind man follows Jesus, and it is made clear how important his witness was: 'and all the people, when they saw it, gave praise to God'.

In terms of the entry-to-Jerusalem story, Matthew (21:1–9), like Mark, has the proclamation 'Son of David' (understood as a title) flow right on to the 'messianic' arrival of Jesus in the holy city, and this Gospel even quotes Zechariah 9:9 in full.[30] Luke (19:28–40), however, interrupts this sequence with the story of Zacchaeus in Jericho, and Jesus' parable of the ten pounds, told 'because he was near Jerusalem, and they supposed the kingdom of God was going to appear immediately' (Luke 19:11). In Luke, when Jesus arrives on the donkey it is Jesus' disciples who do the shouting, not additional crowds, and they testify concerning 'all the miracles they had seen'. The term 'Son of David' is not mentioned; instead the disciples cry, 'Blessed is the king who comes in the name of the Lord', so that the 'coming one' of Psalm 118 is explicitly defined.[31] In this case it is some of the Pharisees from the crowd who say, 'Teacher, rebuke your disciples [for saying this]', and Jesus retorts, 'I tell you, if these are silent the stones will cry out', here quoting Habakkuk 2:11. Jesus appears quite content to be proclaimed as the expected Davidic king.

In John, the story of Bartimaeus in Jericho is not included, but Jesus' arrival in Jerusalem is (John 12:12–19). A chunk of Zechariah 9:9 is provided to explain the significance of the donkey. Like Luke, John drops the reference to the Son of David, but refers to the 'King of Israel', as an equivalent term. There is an interesting note that Jesus' disciples did not understand this initially but when Jesus was glorified they then remembered that this had been written of him and done to him. Because of such a statement, scholars are able to dismiss the references to Jesus being called 'Son of David' or 'King of Israel' as a retroactive fit when the disciples of Jesus had a sudden new 'memory' involving useful biblical references.[32] But it is likely indicative of later reflection about meaning, given that Jesus was crucified (hence 'glorified' in Johannine terms, John 12:23–50).

Why would Mark have had the disciples hush this up? Being proclaimed a Son of David very loudly in public carried with it a sense of powerful expectation, given the prophecies. To hail someone as 'Son of David' was a revolutionary statement, proclaiming Jesus to be the expected royal leader who would overthrow the existing rulers. Jesus' arrival in Jerusalem, as told in the Gospels, indicates both his ancestral identity and the intense anticipation he attracted.

In Mark, then, the issue is what people expected of Jesus. The story of Bartimaeus follows immediately after Jesus has told his disciples that he will be killed in Jerusalem, and was sent to serve, not be served (Mark 10:32–45). If the 'Son of Humanity'[33] came not to be served but to serve, and give his life as a ransom for many, being proclaimed 'Son of David' as he was leaving Jericho (Mark 10:45–6), en route to Jerusalem, asks readers to reflect on what this expectation entailed.[34]

For Mark, the concept of the glorified Son of Humanity (from Dan. 7:13) as Messiah was in many ways more important than the concept of the Son of David with its physical lineage and hopes for a restored Israel in the land. This emphasis follows that of *1 Enoch*, a composite first-century BCE work that was Scripture to the people who authored the Dead Sea Scrolls but which became marginalised later, surviving in the canon of the Ethiopian church. In a section known as the Parables of Enoch (*1 Enoch* 37 – 71), there is a powerful heavenly figure, the Son of Humanity, who is the Lord's Anointed (*1 Enoch* 46:1–4; 48:2–7; 69:26–9) but not, apparently, a descendant of David.[35] Scholars have debated about the date of the Parables, since no fragment from this section has been found in the Qumran caves, but there is a growing consensus that these traditions predate Jesus.[36] It is one of several texts of the time which indicate a different kind of Messiah concept from that of a king of the Davidic royal line.

However, as Max Botner has well argued, in Mark the two concepts of the Son of Humanity and Son of David should not be seen as antithetical. Mark's Gospel has a structure in which numerous incidents draw on references to the Davidic messianic concept (e.g. Ps. 2 in Mark 1:11; 9:7; 12:6; 14:61).[37] It was thought that David had received the divine Spirit and thus prophesied (1 Sam. 16:14–23; Josephus, *Ant.* 6:166) and indeed exorcised. In 1 Samuel 16:23, after all, David drives away the evil spirit in Saul by his Spirit-filled lyre-playing. In an anonymous work of the first century known as the *Liber antiquitatum biblicarum* (*Biblical Antiquities*), royal rule and exorcistic power go together (*LAB* 60). Mark's descriptions of Jesus' actions as a prophetic exorcist-healer are meant to confirm how very Davidic he was. In Mark, Jesus is *of course* the Son of David, but he is really much more: the Son of God.[38]

Mark describes the very moment that Jesus is accounted Son by God, after Jesus has undergone the 'immersion of repentance for the remission of sins' (1:4) by John the Baptist in the River Jordan. At this point, immediately upon coming up out of the water, Jesus 'saw the heavens rent apart and the Spirit like a dove descending into him, and a voice came from the heavens: "You are my son, the beloved one. In you I am well pleased"' (1:10–11). This Voice blends scriptural elements: Psalm 2:7, understood as a Davidic psalm (Acts 4:24–6) about the 'reign of the Lord's Anointed' ('You are my son'), and Isaiah 42:1, which speaks about God's servant in whom God has placed his Spirit and with whom God is pleased (Isa. 11:2). Jesus' messiahship thus incorporates much more than a simple descent from David, but, as Botner states, Mark 'simply took the point for granted'.[39]

Therefore, in Mark 12:35–7, there is the following teaching of Jesus, given after his arrival in Jerusalem when he taught in the Temple:

> How can the scribes say that the Christ is 'son of David'? David himself, in the Holy Spirit, stated: 'The Lord said to my Lord, "Sit at my right hand, until I put your enemies under your feet."' David calls him 'Lord', so how is he also his son?

Here Jesus engages with Psalm 110:1, which was understood to have been composed by David. This statement follows on from Jesus being hailed as the Son of David in Jericho and during his entry into Jerusalem. It looks as if Jesus has been wrestling with the interpretation himself and is going to explain much more about what being the Christ (Messiah) is all about, picking up on what he has said about the need for the Son of Humanity to suffer and be raised (Mark 8:31–3; 9:30–2; 10:45), but he leaves everyone with a question, and his explanation is not recorded.[40]

As Richard France has noted in his commentary on this text, it simply cannot be that this teaching of Jesus is recorded in order to correct Bartimaeus and the Jerusalem crowd, so as to present Jesus as *not* being a descendant of David after all, because – as we have seen – Jesus' descent from David was widely remembered by the early church[41] and taken for granted by Mark. However, the title Son of David 'might be felt to encourage too nationalistic and political an understanding of Jesus' mission', and France noted how in Matthew's developed version of Jesus' statement there is an additional question: 'Whose son is he?', and thus: 'there can be little doubt that Matthew and his readers would have supplied the answer "the Son of God"'.[42] Matthew steps in then to make it clearer to readers what is expected as an answer, as implied in Mark. While in terms of his heritage Jesus is indeed the Son of David, Jesus is actually 'Lord' to David because of his more important identity as Son of God and future glorification as the Danielic Son of Humanity.[43]

In the Gospel of John, the question about Jesus being Son of David appears in another way. In response to Andrew saying, 'We've found the Messiah!' (John 1:41), and Philip saying, 'We've found the one Moses in the

Law and the Prophets wrote about' (1:45), Nathaniel scoffs: 'Can anything good come from Nazareth?' (1:46). Jesus' provenance from Nazareth means he could not be the Messiah since, as we learn later in the Gospel, 'the Christ comes from the seed of David, and from Bethlehem, the village where David was' (John 7:42; cf. v. 52, drawing on Mic. 5:1–3).[44] Since nothing in Scripture suggests the Messiah should come from Nazareth, what good can come from there? But the whole Gospel is constructed on a pattern of knowledge versus ignorance, and thus this may be Johannine irony.[45] We will return to the question of Bethlehem in due course, but in terms of John's readers, familiar with Luke (and likely with Matthew),[46] they would have known that Jesus fulfilled the criteria of messiahship perfectly.

In short, Jesus was remembered by early Christians as being a descendant of David, but this identity was qualified in terms of the character of his own messiahship. Given the way Jesus is shown as questioning what the idea of the Son of David might mean, we are asked to think about the kind of expectations he grew up with, within a Davidic family.

Genealogies as identity statements: a focus on Matthew

There are two genealogies for Jesus in our Gospels, one in Matthew (1:1–17) and one in Luke (3:23–38), both tracing him to David. In the earliest Gospel, Mark, there is no Davidic genealogy or ancestry, but the opening of the Gospel may well recall it. Helen Bond has noted that the first sentence of Mark (1:1), 'The beginning of the good news of Anointed Jesus, Son of God,'[47] recalls the opening of Proverbs: 'The proverbs of Solomon, son of David, king of Israel' (Prov. 1:1).[48]

One reason for scepticism among scholars about Jesus' lineage is that Matthew and Luke give two different Davidic pathways, though both of these trace Jesus' physical descent through Joseph as Jesus' biological father.[49] In Matthew, Joseph is the son of Jacob, son of Matthan, son of Eleazar, while in the Gospel of Luke Joseph is the son of Heli, the son of Matthat son of Levi. How can Joseph have been both the son of Jacob and the son of Heli?

However, the Christian writer Julius Africanus, in the early third century, stated that the anomaly in genealogies was a result of levirate marriage, whereby a man was required to father a child for a deceased sonless brother by having sex with his widow (Deut. 25:5–10).[50] In this case, then, Joseph's father Jacob was actually the maternal brother (same mother, named Estha, different fathers) of his 'proper' father Heli. Heli was a man who actually died childless, while Jacob was his biological father, thus sending the genealogies off in different directions.

Notably, in terms of the line, Matthew (1:1–17) starts from Abraham and goes forward through time, and Luke (3:23–38) starts from Joseph and goes backwards, all the way to the first man, Adam. Matthew also has Jesus descended from Solomon, while Luke has Jesus descended from another son of David, Nathan. In both cases the line is entirely patrilineal. This was vital, because royal descent was traced only through the male line (Sir. 45:25).[51] In Matthew this royal descent is emphasised by mention of 'David *the king*' (1:6). Matthew starts with an announcement that it is the record of 'Jesus Christ son of David, son of Abraham', with the identity of David placed first.

For ease of reference, this Davidic lineage of Jesus as it appears in the genealogies is shown side by side in Table 2.1, so that the differences and similarities can be seen clearly.

The striking agreement in all this is that Matthew and Luke both have Jesus descended from Zerubbabel.[52] However, in Matthew's genealogy (1:1–17) there is a curious neatness about how things are arranged. There are three sets of names in total, running from Abraham to David, from David to Jeconiah, and from Jeconiah to Joseph, and each set has fourteen names. This is stressed as if it is a vital factor hinging on David: 'So all the generations from Abraham to David are fourteen generations. From David to the exile to Babylon there are fourteen generations, and from the taking away to Babylon to the Christ there are fourteen generations' (Matt. 1:17).[53] This emphasis on the number 14 probably points to a symbolic, numerological meaning. In Hebrew, each letter is also a number. The Hebrew letters that spell David (DVD), when added up, make 14, since *dalet* (D) = 4, and *waw* (V) = 6. As such, this underscores the Davidic lineage of Jesus,[54] and also suggests a Hebrew or Aramaic original text.

The pattern of fourteen was so important that in fact some kings of Judah, attested in Scripture, were skipped over,[55] and the skipping continues through the lineage from Zerubbabel. Therefore, while Matthew has only nine generations between Zerubbabel and Joseph, Luke has eighteen (a far more likely number given the span of the

Table 2.1 Two genealogies: Jesus' Davidic lineage according to Matthew and Luke

Matthew	Luke
David the king	David
Solomon, 'by she of Uriah'	Nathan
Rehoboam	Mattatha
Abijah	Menna
Asaph (= Asa)	Melea
Jehoshaphat	Jonam
Joram (= Jehoram)	Joseph
–	Judah
–	Simeon
–	Levi
Uzziah	Matthat
Jotham	Jorim
Ahaz	Eliezer
Hezekiah	Joshua
Manasseh	Er
Amos (= Amon)	Elmadam
Josiah	Cosam
–	Addi
Jeconiah (= Jehoiachin)	Melchi
–	Neri
Shealtiel	Shealtiel
Zerubbabel	Zerubbabel
–	Rhesa
–	Joanan
–	Joda
–	Josech
–	Semein
–	Mattathias
–	Maath
–	Naggai
–	Esli
Abiud	Nahum

Table 2.1 (*continued*)

Matthew	Luke
Eliakim	Amos
Azor	Mattathias
Zadok	Joseph
Achim	Jannai
Eliud	Melchi
Eleazar	Levi
Matthan	Matthat
Jacob	Heli
Joseph	Joseph
Jesus	Jesus

centuries). This demonstrates that for Matthew the genealogy was more than a simple factual record; it was something to be understood in terms of its meaning for Jesus' identity and for his birth and naming.

While Luke also affirms the Davidic ancestry of Jesus (1:27, 69; 2:4, 11), the genealogy goes off in a completely different direction, tracing an unknown line from Nathan, the son of David (2 Sam. 5:14; 1 Chr. 3:5; 14:4), and an otherwise unattested son Mattatha. There are far fewer kings; it is a list of names of largely unknown people. The number of generations fits with the number there should be between Zerubbabel and Joseph. But actually, this genealogy is also shaped. As Richard Bauckham has explored, there are seventy names after the name of Enoch. In the revelation to Enoch (*1 Enoch* 10:12) there are seventy generations until the day of judgement; therefore Jesus (counted from Enoch) is in the final generation.[56]

As noted, like many others Vermes was sceptical about the veracity of the genealogies and stated that the 'secondary, and consequently historically insignificant, nature of these genealogies is no longer denied by responsible New Testament scholars'.[57] Rather, while 'the possibility of genealogical knowledge in the first century AD cannot be a priori excluded', Vermes concluded:

because of the intense dogmatic, apologetical and polemical tendencies of the relevant New Testament documents it would be useless to try to ascertain whether the family of Jesus actually claimed affiliation to the tribe of Judah and the royal clan of David.[58]

He suggested that both Matthew and Luke used different records they found of random Davidic ancestries and attached them to Jesus.[59]

But claims to identity could not have come from nowhere. Accuracy was clearly important to people regarding a good, noble birth. Recording some form of genealogy is part of historical biography (Diogenes Laertius, *Lives* 3:5) and autobiography (Josephus, *Life* 1–6). In Suetonius's biography of the Vitellius family (*Vit.* 1:1 – 2:2), their genealogy is not given in detail, but he summarises it to note that there are two versions: one which proves they are of noble lineage and another which proves the opposite.[60] According to Josephus, there were even public records of priestly descent (*Life* 6; *Apion* 1:31, 36). Matthew (1:1), in mentioning a *biblos*, a written papyrus 'roll' or 'book', points to something written down as he proclaims at the outset that here is 'the roll of the generations of Jesus, the son of David, the son of Abraham' (cf. Gen. 5:1 LXX). It is possible the author of Luke knew another genealogy and judged it to be more accurate.

After all, David was remembered as having eleven children with seven wives, so the chances of there being surviving descendants 500 years later are quite good. Why would these people have forgotten their ancestry? Even in the modern world there are countless cases of people who are aware of lineages they can trace to important ancestors. What is harder for us to remember are the names of all the ancestors one by one.

But this is a modern Western problem, because we don't go in for oral recitation and memory exercises. Among the Māori people of Aotearoa New Zealand, remembering one's *whakapapa* (ancestral lineage), with each person named, is an important part of education and essential identity. The word literally means 'grounding': *whaka* means 'to make', while *papa* means the 'earth' or 'ground'. Many people can be descended from one tribal ancestor, going back centuries in time. *Whakapapa* are not only privately preserved but also openly recited in gatherings in a *marae* (community ritual centre), and they form part of your self-introduction in a public setting, which connects you not only with ancestors but also with land. The memory of descent has long been done via oral recitation, not by means of written records. In a doctoral thesis completed at the University of Otago, Wayne Te Kaawa analysed the genealogies of Jesus in the Gospels through a Māori lens.[61] Read in this way, the genealogies themselves tell a story about identity.

At the start of the Gospel of Matthew, then, the whole work begins with a genealogy and should alert everyone that we are in an ancient Judaean mentality. For many contemporary readers, this might well be skim read because we are interested in the action of the nativity story. Yet, for the writer of this Gospel, it is absolutely fitting that Jesus should be introduced by a genealogy. The fact that Ezra the priest is introduced by a genealogy (Ezra 7:1–5) indicates that a public presentation of some sort could involve the recitation of a genealogy in ancient Judah. Likewise, the book of Chronicles begins with genealogies that last nine chapters, taking the reader from Adam to the death of King Saul and the rise of David and his line, and there are other genealogies in Chronicles also.

In other words, the genealogy of Jesus as 'son of David' at the start of Matthew is not just informational: it is a weighty statement of the importance of Jesus' descent as the basis for his identity in terms of having a noble birth that qualifies him for kingship. Jesus' kingship continues as a key theme of the nativity story: the magi ask, 'Where is the King?' (Matt. 2:2). Likewise in Luke, Jesus' Davidic descent is meaningful in the light of the number of generations until God would act in history. Both the genealogies tell a story. However, such shaping does not invalidate the central core of what they state: Jesus was descended from David.

Jesus' Davidic siblings

One of the points to remember about the identity of Jesus as a descendant of David is that Jesus' siblings were remembered as likewise Davidic. Jesus' ancestral heritage is not actually his alone but belonged to all his family.[62] Given that Jesus' brother James lived to the year 62 CE,[63] anyone could have asked him for his genealogy. Perhaps he recited it. The author of Luke[64] may well have had access to James's account of his genealogy or that of other members of Jesus' family, and the circumstances of gathering historical evidence clearly mattered to this writer (Luke 1:1–4; Acts 1:1–2).

James is in some ways a mysterious figure, because the canonical Gospels do not make much of him. But he suddenly appears as a resurrection witness in charge of the Judaean churches in the letters of Paul (Gal. 1:19; 2:9–12; 1 Cor. 15:3–7). Paul also knew other 'brothers of the Lord' in Jerusalem (1 Cor. 9:5; cf. Acts 1:14), as we saw.[65] We remember again that the letters of Paul are our earliest historical evidence for Jesus' life. That it was really James in charge is indicated when c.42 CE 'certain people came from James' (Gal. 2:12) to Paul and Peter in Antioch, and assumed authority. This is also made clear in Acts (12:17; 15:13; 21:18) and in a second-century gnostic work known as the *Gospel of Thomas* (12) where Jesus himself appoints James as his successor in leadership.[66] Nothing is said about why James should have been the one to lead the community, but his Davidic ancestry and family connection with Jesus seem intrinsic to this role.

According to Eusebius, James was described as the 'brother of the Lord' and as Joseph's son – with Joseph known also as 'the father of Christ' – and James was also called 'the Righteous' and placed as overseer (*episkopos*) of the church in Jerusalem (Eusebius, *Hist. Eccles.* 2:1:1–10; 4:22:8).[67] As told by Josephus, a hard-line high priest named Ananus ordered James and several others to be executed by stoning for breaking the law, but many in Jerusalem were incensed by this action (*Ant.* 20:200–1). An early Christian chronicler, Hegesippus, quoted by Eusebius, tells the story of James's mode of life and his execution (*Hist. Eccles.* 2:23:4–20): he was taken up to the Temple parapet by his accusers in Jerusalem and there testified to the 'door of Jesus' as indicating the 'Son of Humanity . . . sitting at the right hand of the Great Power', at which point people cried out: 'Hosanna to the son of David!'[68] Hegesippus relates that, after James was executed, 'those who were related to the Lord according to the flesh' continued to be a leadership group. The new overseer of the Jerusalem church after James was Simeon, the son of Clopas, who was the cousin of Jesus, because Clopas was the brother of Joseph (Eusebius, *Hist. Eccles.* 3:11:1–2).[69] Davidic lineage appears, then, to have been important to the earliest Jerusalem church in defining its own top position, as if it were a miniature Israel establishing the messianic kingdom. To remember Jesus' Davidic lineage was to remember the Davidic lineage of all of Jesus' family.

It is therefore not for nothing that the siblings of Jesus are specifically named in the Gospel of Mark. When Jesus comes to Nazareth, the local crowd asks: 'Isn't this the carpenter, son of Mary, and brother of James, Joset,[70] Judas and Simon? And aren't his sisters here with us?' (Mark 6:3//

44

Matt. 13:55–6, and implied also in Mark 3:35//Matt. 12:46//Luke 8:19).[71] Actually, while the brothers are named, the sisters are not (as with other notable women in Mark), but their existence is clear. Later on, their names were known to be Mary and Salome (Epiphanius, *Pan.* 78:8:1; 78:9:6; cf. *Ancoratus* 60:1, where they are Anna and Salome),[72] information which may also come from Hegesippus.[73] A Mary is also referred to as a sister of Jesus in the second-century *Gospel of Philip* (59:10–11), one of three Marys who 'always walked with the Lord', the others being Mary the mother and Mary Magdalene, his companion.[74] In the fourth-century *Apostolic Constitutions* (3:6), the sisters of Jesus are among Jesus' disciples.[75] In the Gospel of John the mother and siblings of Jesus are among Jesus' disciples in Galilee (John 2:12; 7:3). However, little is said of them, as if it is simply well known that they are associated with Jesus as an important group.

Within the New Testament, the Letter of James was held to be written by the brother of Jesus, though there is no clear indication of this in the letter itself, while the Letter of Jude is also held to have been written by Jesus' brother Jude/Judas; but here the author is identified as 'the brother of James' (Jude 1:1) rather than 'the Lord's brother'. Jude is nevertheless remembered as 'the Lord's brother according to the flesh (*kata sarka*)' (Eusebius, *Hist. Eccles.* 1:7:11; 3:20:1).[76] James was also considered to be the author of revelatory works esteemed by gnostic Christians: the *Apocryphon of James*, the *First Apocalypse of James* and the *Second Apocalypse of James*.[77]

In addition, the identities of Jesus' siblings are preserved in a popular second-century Christian work known as the *Protevangelium of James*, purportedly written by Jesus' brother James (25:1).[78] They are mentioned here as children of Joseph from his first marriage (9:6), and they travel with Mary and Joseph to Bethlehem after a call 'from Au[gu]stus the King for all who were in Bethlehem of Judaea to be registered' (17:1–2; and see 9:2; 18:1; 25:1). Mary, in this work, is given a backstory that involves being one of the seven 'undefiled virgins from the tribe of David' (10:2, 4) who is summoned to weave the Temple veil.

With Jesus' siblings being remembered in key leadership positions and being involved in his mission early on, their shared ancestral heritage would have been known and disseminated. However, to be of this line was indeed dangerous, as indicated in early Christian evidence.

The difficulties that Davidic descent could attract is evidenced by Julius Africanus. As we saw, in his *Letter to Aristides* he tried to reconcile the different genealogies of Matthew and Luke by reference to levirate marriage.[79] Along with this, he recorded that Jesus' family got into trouble with the Roman authorities for being of the Davidic line (*Let. Arist.* 21–2 = Eusebius, *Hist. Eccles.* 1:7:14; 3:12.19–20, 32). He notes: 'the relatives of Jesus according to the flesh' handed on the Davidic genealogy (*Hist. Eccles.* 1:7:11) and were 'called *desposunoi*'.[80] This term *desposunos*, a rare Greek word, can mean 'belonging to the master (*despotēs*)' in relation to things or perhaps slaves. However, the word *desposunos* is also another way of saying *despotēs*, 'master' or 'noble'.[81] In fact, it is this meaning that is understood in the translation of Julius Africanus into Syriac in the fifth century.[82] The word *desposunoi* is rendered as *marawatha*, which is an honorific term: 'sirs', 'lords' or 'nobles'.[83] This is also the sense of the term in Palestinian Jewish Aramaic.[84]

Translated in this way, Julius Africanus writes about the preservation of the family genealogy as follows:

> However, a few of the careful ones who had personal records for themselves, or had a recollection of the names or otherwise having [them] from copies, pride themselves on the memory of the noble descent having been preserved. Among these were the aforementioned people, called 'nobles' (*desposunoi*) because of the connection to the saving line (*to sōtērion genos*) . . . and so as far as they were able they recited the genealogy laid out before from the Book of Days[85] [and from memory] as far as they could.[86]

Mention of 'the saving line (*to sōtērion genos*)' recalls the language of the *Didache* (9:2): 'the holy vine of your servant/child David'. Interestingly, Africanus writes of the 'nobles' going around reciting this genealogy, as if it was indeed an important part of their identity. The 'saving line' is surely that of David, since Scripture predicted that the Messiah, who would save Israel, would be from this line.[87]

However, all did not go very well for the Davidic family of Jesus and their genealogical recitations. According to Hegesippus, the grandsons of Jesus' brother Jude[88] were arrested during the reign of Domitian (80–96 CE) for being descended from David, with the threat of death (*Hist. Eccles.* 3:19:1 – 3:20:5). They were asked about their finances and their capacity to raise an army: two matters you might expect of royal revolutionaries. They were also asked about what they thought of the Messiah and his kingdom. With amazing detail, it is recorded that they owned '39 plethra' (about 10 hectares) of land on which they paid their taxes, and farmed it by their own labour, and they had about 9,000 denarii between them, which was actually the land value. They showed their calloused hands from working the land. Their interrogator, dubbed 'Domitian Caesar' (i.e. a representative of Rome), dismissed them as posing no threat. On their release they then 'presided over every church' and lived until the reign of Trajan (Eusebius, *Hist. Eccles.* 3:32:6; cf. 20:6).[89]

They were lucky. Hegesippus had already noted that after the conquest of Jerusalem (in 70 CE), the emperor Vespasian ordered those of David's lineage to be sought out so that 'none of the royal tribe should be left among the Judaeans', which resulted in a terrible persecution (*Hist. Eccles.* 3:12). As mentioned above, Simeon, who had become the leader of the Jerusalem church after the death of James, was the cousin of Jesus, since he was the son of Joseph's brother Clopas.[90] He survived this persecution and sheltered the Jerusalem community for a time in Pella, across the Jordan. However, there was more trouble. Correlating with what we know of a further revolt, spreading from Jews in Cyrene (north Africa) *c.*115 CE,[91] it is said that in the reign of Trajan and the governorship of a certain Atticus, Simeon was killed for being a descendant of David and a Christian: a fatal combination. He was tortured and crucified (*Hist. Eccles.* 3:32:1–6).[92]

We can therefore be fairly certain on the basis of a swathe of evidence that Jesus was a descendant of David. As such, Jesus' family would surely have felt a weight of prophecy on their shoulders. Messianic concepts were diverse at this time, but one key expectation concerned the Davidic line. Jesus and his family had a heritage of royalty, and a claim. No wonder the earliest churches looked to them as leaders. Jesus himself would have been educated in all the scriptural passages identified above as being meaningful about the Davidic line. This heritage was a mark of honour, but it was also dangerous. If the evidence from Hegesippus and Africanus is sound, then being a descendant of David meant you could be subject to arrest and death if anyone caused trouble, even if you were not directly involved. This certainly explains why the Gospel-writers have people trying to hush up anyone calling out 'Son of David' to Jesus, and why anyone would write 'of the house of David' on an ossuary only in very small and inconspicuous letters. It suggests that Jesus' family might have been proud of their royal lineage on one hand, and very nervous about it on the other. Jesus would have been brought up as a boy hearing a complex narrative in which fear of the present rulers would have formed a part.

3

Location: Bethlehem

In Chapter 1 we explored Jesus' identity through the lens of the ancient Greek term *Ioudaios*, which echoes the Hebrew *Yehudi*. We thought about a dimension of this term as meaning a Judaean, in terms of referring to someone living in a particular geographical region: Judah/Judaea. This region traditionally was connected with both heritage (Judahite ancestry) and religion (Judaism), and would have had cultural aspects we cannot now access. In this chapter, we narrow the focus to one location within Judaea and explore more about what it would have meant to people who lived there. This is important because we gain a sense of identity about ourselves from where we are born and grow up. This is 'place identity', and it was first theorised by the psychologist Harold Proshansky in the 1970s and then further developed by Anssi Paasi.[1] It involves a pattern of conscious and unconscious ideas, behaviours and values as a result of being born and raised somewhere.

Jesus' birthplace is firmly named as Bethlehem in both Matthew (2:1, 5, 8, 16) and Luke (2:4, 11, 15), and this location is absolutely standard in Christian tradition.[2] There was another Bethlehem, not far from Nazareth in Galilee, recorded in Judges 12:8–10 and Joshua 19:15,[3] but the Gospels are clear that Jesus was born in 'Bethlehem *of Judaea*' (Matt. 2:1; Luke 2:4).[4] He is never thought to have been born in Nazareth, though this is often assumed by those involved in contemporary historical studies of Jesus.[5] Such scholars hold that Jesus' identity as someone from Nazareth indicates his birthplace, and that the Bethlehem tradition was made up to bolster Jesus' messianic credentials. But methodologically it is flawed to assert that anything that bolsters Jesus' messianic credentials is likely false.[6] Many people have a birthplace that is different from the place that shaped their adult identity. Furthermore, no anti-Christian writer of the first centuries (e.g. Celsus or Porphyry) doubted Jesus' birth in Bethlehem, as far as we know.

The town of Bethlehem

Bethlehem was an ancient town lying 5 miles (8 km) south of Jerusalem, built on an L-shaped hill, some 770 m above sea level. The famous Christmas carol 'O Little Town of Bethlehem' may well bring to mind a sleepy and quiet hamlet, but very little official archaeology has taken place in Bethlehem and so its extent at the time of Jesus is unknown.[7] Josephus repeatedly refers to it as a 'city' (*polis*) rather than a 'village' (*kōmē*),[8] though his terminology can be loose.

There is something material that suggests it was not a tiny settlement. In the ancient Mediterranean world, access to water was vital for a place to flourish, and the size of a settlement was often determined by how much water could be harnessed to support the population. While villages usually made do with wells and/or cisterns, cities and towns required larger water systems. Bethlehem had an aqueduct running through it. Attested *c.*150 BCE in a Jewish work called the *Letter of Aristeas* (91), the so-called Lower Aqueduct from Solomon's Pools to Jerusalem was a major feat of engineering, constructed of covered channels, and it ran directly through the hill on which Bethlehem lay. The aqueduct otherwise looped around the hilly landscape to maintain a gentle gradient (from 765 to 744 m) to allow water to flow north by means of gravity (see Fig. 3.1). To go to Bethlehem, the aqueduct needed to detour. This would have required additional labour, expertise and cost.

If Bethlehem were just a tiny village, the engineers who constructed this aqueduct might have bypassed it and gone more directly northwards to the Holy City, and indeed a century later engineers built another water system (the Upper Aqueduct) that more neatly ran to the west of Bethlehem. But for the Lower Aqueduct they went to the trouble of cutting out a long tunnel (over 200 m) running directly through the Bethlehem hill, with pools on either side for the population to draw water.[9] One of these, the Bir el-Qana ('the waterway pool'), on the south side, existed until modern times. The aqueduct construction would have allowed water to be used by the town's inhabitants for household needs, for washing, to irrigate terraced field systems and to support industry that needed water. It is reasonable to think that local Bethlehem workers were particularly involved in its construction and that the town's leaders

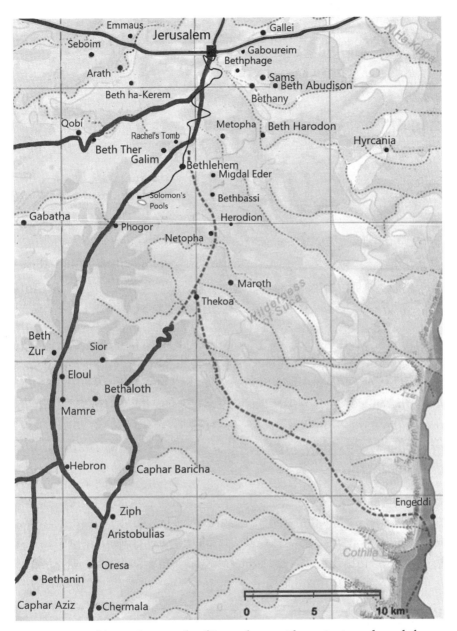

Figure 3.1 The region south of Jerusalem, with ancient roads and the course of the Lower Aqueduct. Broken lines indicate ancient roads not yet fully surveyed. Dotted lines are smaller roads

(Drawing by Joan Taylor, adapted from *Palestine in the Fourth Century: The Onomasticon by Eusebius of Caesarea*, introduced and edited by Joan E. Taylor, translated by Greville Freeman-Grenville and indexed by Rupert Chapman III (Jerusalem: Carta, 2003), plate 7, detail)

had an important role to play in maintaining this valuable watercourse serving Jerusalem. It was a magnificent structure, and so well done that it remained in use (with various repairs over the years) until the twentieth century. It is even mapped out in early tourist guidebooks for visitors to see (see Plate 1).[10] The ample water supply itself would have enabled the population to grow. Bethlehem was therefore a decent-sized town.

Bethlehem remembered

Bethlehem was famous. It was known for its association with the royal line of Judah. It was the 'city of David' (Luke 2:4, 11). Meaning 'house of bread' in Hebrew (*bet-lekhem*), Scripture recorded that Bethlehem was once called Ephrath, and the matriarch Rachel, wife of Jacob, was buried in a tomb on the roadside nearby (Gen. 35:16, 19; 48:7).[11] In a genealogy in which places were also people, as in some indigenous cultures, 'Bethlehem' is the great-great-great-great-grandson of 'Judah' (1 Chr. 2:51, 54; 4:4). Bethlehem is mentioned as a significant place: Rehoboam fortified it (2 Chr. 11:6),[12] and the Philistines had a garrison there (1 Sam. 17:14). It was also remembered as being the home of a judge of Israel named Ibzan (Judg. 12:8–10).[13] It was the home of a Levite who became a priest for Micah in Ephraim (Judg. 17:1–13),[14] and of the concubine of an unnamed Levite who was horribly raped and killed by Benjaminites (Judg. 19 – 20). It was the home of Elimelech, husband of Naomi, and of Boaz, who married the Moabite Ruth (Ruth 2:4).[15] But most importantly of all, it was the home of David, son of Jesse, great-grandson of Ruth and Boaz, king of Judah and Israel (1 Sam. 16:18; 17:12).[16] It was where the prophet Samuel went and anointed David as king (1 Sam. 16:4, 13).[17] It was where Asahel, the nephew of David, was buried in an ancestral tomb (2 Sam. 2:32).[18]

Importantly, Micah 5:2[19] reads:

And you, Bethlehem Ephrathah,
You are small among the thousands of Judah,
But from you will come forth to me a ruler,
Who will shepherd my people Israel.

As noted in the Gospel of John 7:42, some people believed then that 'the Christ comes from the seed of David, and from Bethlehem, the village (*kōmē*) where David was'.[20] This belief is found in a Jewish text attributed to a second-century sage, Eleazar (*Pirqe deRabbi Eliezer* 3). The Jerusalem Talmud (third to fifth century CE) has a story about an Arab who tells a Judaean on the day that the Temple has been destroyed that the Messiah has been born in the 'king's palace in Bethlehem of Judaea' (*j.Ber.* 2:4). So the idea of Bethlehem as a town itself bringing forth a king still mattered centuries after Jesus. While there were a variety of messianic ideas in Second Temple Judaism, and it was not absolutely necessary for a messiah to be born in Bethlehem, as rightly pointed out by Jonathan Rowlands,[21] Bethlehem appears to have been a site of hope for people who trusted that a royal 'Son of David' would restore the nation.

According to Luke 2:4, Joseph, then in Nazareth, went up to Judaea for a Roman census, 'to the city of David, which is called Bethlehem, because he was of the house and family of David'. This implies an association between Davidic descendants and the town. Did the 'house of David' still live there? There is a memory of 123 'children of Bethlehem' who returned after the Babylonian captivity in works written in the fifth century BCE (Ezra 2:21; 188 'people of Bethlehem and Netophah' in Neh. 7:26). But what was the situation in the late first century BCE?

There is one clue. In the Mishnah (*Ta'an.* 4:5), dating from the late second century CE, the 'sons of David' are designated as having a particular duty in regard to the Jerusalem Temple. This is another instance of people being recognised as having Davidic descent in the time of Jesus, as this passage concerns praxis regarding the Second Temple (520 BCE – 70 CE). The sons of David are one of the groups with a specific responsibility to supply wood to burn on the altar of burnt offering to keep it alight at all times (as required in Lev. 6:12–13). This wood offering[22] was supplied nine times a year by specific families of Judah/Judaea and Benjamin: the 'sons of David of the tribe of Judah' were supposed to bring wood on the twentieth day of the month of Tammuz. Tammuz in the Jewish calendar is the tenth month of the year, which is around midsummer. The amount of wood required would have been considerable given the needs of the Temple, and gathering it would have involved much community effort. It is not specifically stated that the 'sons of David' lived in Bethlehem, but they would have needed to be somewhere like Bethlehem, which is near Jerusalem. In Cyril of Jerusalem's *Catechetical Lectures* (12:20, *c.*348 CE), he writes that 'until recently' the area around Bethlehem was wooded. We do not have definitive proof, but it is plausible to think that at least some of the Davidic descendants still lived in their ancestral town. Their duty required people to have the skills to chop and process the wood in an appropriate way. Having this responsibility would have been an important part of clan identity.

Tombs of the house of David

As with any town, the inhabitants of Bethlehem would have told their stories about what happened recently and long before, and it is likely that they tied some of the stories into particular locations still to be seen and pointed out. The memory of the town's association with David's descendants was not only to be found in Scripture: it would also have been inscribed in the land, and especially in tombs. Since ancestry formed an essential part of Jesus' identity, as indicated in Matthew and Luke and the wider memory of his heritage as a descendant of David, we need to remember that ancestors are buried in particular plots of land, and these are loci of identity where families gather to bury and commemorate the dead. You were not just born in a particular place; you expected to also die in that place and be buried where your parents, grandparents and ancestors were buried. To this day, in many indigenous and traditional cultures, places of ancestral burial are sacred or ritually restricted. With Bethlehem being so closely associated with David's line, we would expect descendants of David to have been buried there – even if the royal tombs of the kings of Judah themselves were located in Jerusalem – and for the living to have a strong tie to their burial places in terms of their own identities.

Where were these tombs? The L-shaped double hill of Bethlehem is surrounded by deep valleys (Plates 1 and 2),[23] except to the north-west (see Fig. 3.2). Several tombs have been found in these valleys.[24] One from Iron Age II (1000–586 BCE) was discovered in 1969 in the valley just to the north of present-day Manger Square, the Wadi ed-Djem.[25] In 2013, a tomb complex on the slope of a valley about a mile (2 km) south-east of Bethlehem, halfway between Bethlehem and Herodion, was uncovered, and excavations have revealed that it too was much used in Iron Age II (1000–586 BCE).[26] The very far eastern side, where the Basilica of the

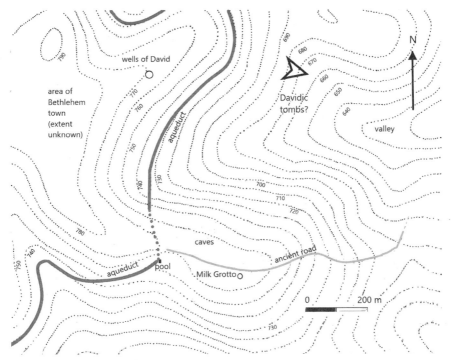

Figure 3.2 Bethlehem in the late first century BCE, as presently known. The word 'caves' appears where the Basilica of the Nativity would later stand
(Drawing by Joan Taylor)

Nativity stands, was probably not part of the town's urban settlement, and it may be that this area was used for burials, since part of an ossuary and first-century pottery were found in a recent investigation in an area of the Armenian monastery known as Jerome's Hall.[27]

Evidence for any specific tomb of the descendants of David has not yet been found in archaeological excavations, but there is intriguing evidence for such a tomb in records from the early fourth century. A list of biblical places was compiled by Eusebius, bishop of Caesarea, who presented all the information in a compendium known as the *Onomasticon* (written 313–25 CE).[28] In this work, Eusebius writes of Bethlehem: 'Of the tribe of Judah. Six miles away from Ailia (= Jerusalem) on the southern side, on the Hebron road, *where the tomb of Jesse and David is pointed out*' (*Onom.* 42:10, italics mine).

This mention of the tomb is interesting, because Eusebius compiled his list *before* the Christians took over such sites for pilgrimage development. Who pointed it out? Jerome, some eighty years later, stated that the god Tammuz-Adonis had been worshipped in a cave and a sacred wood, where Christians contrarily identified the birthplace of Jesus.[29] This suggests a Syro-Palestinian population. But might local Jews have been responsible for the identification of the royal tomb?

It is difficult to know how many Jews there were in this area at the time of Eusebius. The Judaeans of Jerusalem and its surrounding area, including Bethlehem, had been brutally evicted by the Romans after the failure of the Second Revolt in 132–6 CE.[30] This revolt, led by Simon bar Kosiba, called 'Son of a Star' (Bar Kokhba), led to catastrophe for Judaea. The main description of this is found in the surviving epitome (summary) of Cassius Dio (*Hist. Rom.* 69:12:1–14:3), who uses official Roman military records to note that fifty of the secret outposts of the rebels were destroyed, 985 towns and villages were razed to the ground, a total of 580,000 fighting men were killed in battle, and the number of people who died as a result of starvation, disease and the burning of the towns and villages was impossible to reckon: 'So, almost all of Judaea was turned into a wilderness' (*Hist. Rom.* 69:14:2). Archaeology has confirmed this report, with the discovery now of over 440 subterranean hiding settlement-complexes in 252 sites in the Judaean foothills, Hebron mountains and Bethel region, and evidence of the destruction of over 330 settlements in Judaea at this time.[31] It thus seems very likely that Bethlehem would also have been destroyed.

There was then a ban on Judaeans living in a large part of the former core homeland of Judaea,[32] and Judaeans relocated to Galilee and Idumaea. Judaea as a province was erased, and rebranded in line with its regional name of 'Palestina'. Jerusalem became the Roman *colonia* Aelia Capitolina, devoted to the worship of the Capitoline gods.[33] But there is a question about how far this eviction stretched in time as an effective ban. Eusebius writes elsewhere that 'the people who live at the place, the tradition having come down to them from their *ancestors*, bear witness to the account to those who come to Bethlehem, for the sake of an interpretation of the places' (*Dem. Evang.* 7:2:14, italics mine). Excavations at the nearby Tomb of Rachel, on the road to Bethlehem from Jerusalem, have revealed possible Jewish tombs from the third century, indicating that Jews had returned.[34] This ancient site had been venerated over many centuries by Judaeans.[35] It is not mentioned by Josephus, but it is noted by Eusebius (*Onom.* 82:11–13) as 'being shown today', four milestones from Jerusalem. Again, this may

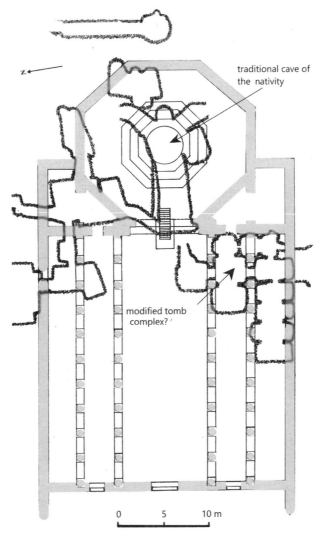

traditional cave of
the nativity

modified tomb
complex?

0   5   10 m

Figure 3.3 Caves under the Constantinian Basilica of the Nativity,
Bethlehem. The shape and size of caves in the south may indicate that
Jewish *kokhim* tombs were cut into and modified
(Drawing by Joan Taylor, adapted from Louis-Hugues Vincent, 'Bethléem, le Sanctuaire de
la Nativité d'après les fouilles récentes', *RB* 45 (1936), pp. 544–74, plate II)

suggest that local Jews lived in the area.[36] In the records of a journey of
an Irish monk named Arculf in the seventh century, written by Adomnan
(*Loc. Sanct.* 7), it is said to have a pyramidical roof, which is typical of
Second Temple period monumental tombs (see 1 Macc. 13:27–9).[37]

We need to be forensic, to work out what Eusebius' 'tomb of Jesse and David' really was. The actual Tomb of David was long known as being in the City of David, which was in Jerusalem (1 Kgs 2:10; Neh. 3:16; and see below). The City of David was the fortress of Zion, named as such after David defeated the Jebusites and captured it (2 Sam. 5:7, 9). It was a core part of Jerusalem for centuries (Neh. 3:15; 12:37), identified as the Upper City by Josephus (*War* 5:136–7; 7:61–4).

But memories can attach to different sites, and new sites can be more convenient in various ways. After Eusebius, things changed radically in Palestine and particularly in Bethlehem. A basilica was built, commissioned by the newly Christian Roman emperor Constantine. It was placed on the eastern spur of the Bethlehem hill, on a site reputed to be where Jesus was born in a cave beneath, which is actually part of a cluster of other underground caverns (see Fig. 3.3).[38]

Dedicated on 31 May 339 (Eusebius, *Vita Const.* 3:43), it became a huge draw for pilgrims from far and wide. From the fourth to the sixth centuries all kinds of other sites relevant to Christians were identified in Palestine, often on the basis of dreams and other forms of revelation rather than tradition, in the service of developing Christian pilgrimage and the idea of the 'Holy Land'.[39] Before Constantine, the few intrepid Christians who visited the area relied on old local memories, as told by Palestinian Christians who acted as their guides.[40] Therefore, it is the earliest evidence of site identification that is most crucial for history, but even in these tellings memories could shift.

In 333 CE, and still in the early days of Christian pilgrimage, an anonymous pilgrim from Bordeaux noted the presence of the new Constantinian basilica and said, 'Not far away is the tomb of Ezechihel, Asaph, Job,[41] also Jesse, David and Solomon. Their names are written in Hebrew letters on the wall as you go down into the vault itself' (*Itin.* 598).[42] This indicates that there was a tomb that you stepped down into, as was typical of Jewish tombs of Jesus' day, and the Hebrew inscription is clearly not made for any newly arrived Greek- or Latin-speaking Christian tourists. Were the names Jesse, David and Solomon ancestors?

What the Bordeaux Pilgrim states in terms of names is important because Ezechihel, Asaph and Job don't neatly map on to recognisable royal rulers in the lists of the kings of Judah (see 1 Chr. 3:10–16), and so this tends to confirm that such names really were to be found on the walls of the tomb, and were recorded by the pilgrim as well as possible. The name 'Asaph' occurs in the genealogy of Matthew 1:7–8, where Asaph is the father of Jehoshaphat. Perhaps the spelling Ezechihel could indicate Hezekiah; the pilgrim records the *domus Ezechiae* (house of Hezekiah) in Jerusalem earlier (*Itin.* 592), but the correspondence is not exact. Perhaps it indicates Asahel (2 Sam. 2:18–32), one of three nephews of David, who was buried in an ancestral tomb in Bethlehem by his brothers Abishai and Joab, as noted also by Josephus (*Ant.* 7:19). But if this tomb relates to this family, then they are sons of David's sister Zeruiah and the inscription mentioning Jesse, David and Solomon suggests the Solomonic line. In other words, the first three names of the inscription read more like a genuine list of men whose names reflect those of the Davidic house, but not exactly.

Furthermore, mention of Hebrew letters is intriguing. Letters at the time of the royal rulers of Judah in Iron Age II were written in paleo-Hebrew script, unlikely to have been read by Christians in the fourth century. If they were in Aramaic square script, read by Christian Jews, then this would date the tomb to the Second Temple period, not Iron Age II.

Christian pilgrims' descriptions of the form of the tomb also allow us to date it to the Second Temple period and even to locate it. In the late fourth century, Jerome (who lived in Bethlehem from 384 until he died, and who read Hebrew) wrote of the 'mausoleum' of David in Bethlehem (*Ep.* 46:13), though he says little about it. But around the same time the Spanish pilgrim Egeria noted: 'The well from which David wanted water is next to the mouth of a cave, and in a valley in Bethlehem are the tombs of the kings of Judah' (*Itin.*: Peter the Deacon, L1). In the sixth century, the so-called Piacenza Pilgrim wrote that the tombs were in the valley lying just to the north of Bethlehem town, about 'half a mile' away: here 'David's body lies with that of Solomon, and they have separate tombs. The basilica is called At Saint David' (Piacenza Pilgrim, *Itin.* 29). Adomnan (*Loc. Sanct.* 2:4:1–4) states that 'the [entrance to the] Tomb of David was in the middle of a church'.[43] Like the Piacenza Pilgrim, he indicates that the church (connecting to the mausoleum) was 'outside the city wall in the valley which adjoins the hill of Bethlehem on the north'. This shows that there was a church built here, to commemorate David, erected to provide access to the tomb. With such a precise localisation, archaeology could one day reveal this site, but for now it has been buried by time.

One reason for the Byzantine Christians to think the tomb was really that of David is the ambiguity of Scripture. In 1 Kings 2:10 we read, 'David slept with his ancestors and was buried in the City of David.' However, if David was buried with his *ancestors*, in the 'City of David', this might not indicate Jerusalem, because Luke 2:4 and 11 identify Bethlehem as the 'City of David'. In Acts 2:29, Peter announces that the Tomb of David 'is with us to this day', but he does not say where it is. This gave Christians scope.

However, as noted above, at the time of Jesus the Tomb of David and Solomon was very much known in Jerusalem, as we see in Josephus (*War* 1:61; *Ant*. 13:349; 7:392–4; 16:179–83).[44] Their tombs were situated close to other tombs of the Davidic kings of Judah, lying where they had been for centuries.[45] Again, a Second Temple tomb in *Bethlehem*, in which Jesse, David and Solomon were mentioned, would better indicate the burial place of descendants of David who were not themselves royal rulers. This would have been a tomb known to Jesus' family.

One of the telling things mentioned by the Piacenza Pilgrim (*Itin*. 29) in regard to the tomb is that 'the children slaughtered by Herod also have their tomb there, and they all lie buried together', so apparently children's bones could be viewed within this chamber. One of the distinctive features of later Second Temple Jewish burials, and not of Iron Age II (or the Byzantine period), is the use of ossuaries – bone boxes made of stone, which look like small coffins – for children, and perhaps this is indicated. But, more particularly, the mention of the tombs of David, Solomon and the children being separated parallels typical Second Temple burial layouts, whereby different chambers lead off a central vestibule. But where was this?

Both Adomnan and the Piacenza Pilgrim place the tomb north of the city wall. In terms of this city wall, we do not have archaeological remains, but we can be reasonably clear that in the Byzantine period (fourth to seventh centuries) it ran around the edges of the southern part of the Bethlehem hill and north of today's Peace Centre on Manger Square, where a large Byzantine public building has been found.[46] The Christian pilgrims note that the town of Bethlehem lay 5 miles (8 km) south of Jerusalem (6 miles or 9.5 km to the Bordeaux Pilgrim, *Itin*. 598) on a hill next to the main road from Jerusalem to Hebron. The extent of the town then did not reach over the northern hill but was more confined to the south in a straight line (the bottom stroke of the 'L'). Adomnan says of Bethlehem:

> It lies on a narrow ridge completely surrounded by valleys. This ridge of land measures about a mile in length from west to east, and round the very edge of the flat top of this small hill runs a low wall without towers,[47] rising above the surrounding valleys, and enclosing a longish space within which the houses of the inhabitants are distributed. (*Loc. Sanct.* 2:1:2–4)[48]

The Basilica of the Nativity stood on the eastern edge within the town. The wall then probably lay quite close on the northern flank of the hill. The pilgrims placed the royal tombs half a mile north (anywhere north-west to north-east) of their Bethlehem in a valley. The measure of half a (Roman) mile (= 0.4 miles or 0.7 km) is a pilgrim's estimate, and we may give it leeway of plus or minus some 100 m (see Fig. 3.2).

Some 600 m north of the Byzantine town, just at the top part of the 'L' on the northern hill, there are the Wells of David, *Biar Dawd*, now seen within the property of the Franciscan Catholic Action Circle on King David Street. Traditionally, these cisterns are associated with a story in 2 Samuel 23:15–17 (1 Chr. 11.1–18) where David says, 'Oh that someone would give me a drink of water from the cistern that is by the gate of Bethlehem!' (and see *j.Sanh.* 2:5; *b.BQ* 60b). A gate of the town was thus remembered as being in existence at some point in the Iron Age. In 1895, some mosaics from a Byzantine church were discovered east of the wells in this property, including one with a quotation from Psalm 117:19–20:

> Open for me the gates of justice.
> I will go in and give thanks to the Lord.
> This gate is the Lord's,
> Where the upright go in.

The mention of a gate indicates that the writers of this inscription assumed some connection between the church and a gate. That there was a proper church is important, because Christian pilgrims often assembled for prayer and song in a church near a site of memory. But this gate is too far north to have been suitable for the Byzantine town, which lay only on the southern hill. It may well, then, indicate a memory of the more ancient gate.

The Franciscan archaeologists clarified that in their property there were three openings (wells) from one ancient rock-cut underground cistern, and two openings (wells) from a second cistern in the property of the Greek Orthodox church across the road. The wells' use in the Iron Age I period (1200–1000 BCE) has been confirmed by the recovery of fragments of two collared-rim jars, distinctive of this time.[49] Furthermore, a Christian necropolis was then revealed under the church in the Franciscan property.[50] There was a painted cross and graffiti of names at the bottom of steps leading down into a vault. While the excavators thought this might indicate the very tomb of David mentioned by pilgrims, the catacombs and arcosolia niches uncovered were dated to the fourth century CE on the basis of pottery and the wall inscriptions. Further cut tombs of this time have also been found to the west of the wells.[51] It is interesting to have this Byzantine church, with a burial ground, lying hard by the wells, because this connects it with what is stated by Egeria (*Itin.*: Peter the Deacon, L1), that 'the well from which David wanted water is next to the mouth of a cave'. The mausoleum developed by the Christians is therefore quite likely formed from the 'cave' mentioned here, by the small church commemorating the wells and gate.

This is significant for locating the Davidic tomb because Adomnan states that the church providing access to the royal tomb was not on the top of the hill, where the wells are located, but in the valley, so it cannot be the wells church by the gate excavated by the Franciscans. But in Egeria's account of her pilgrimage, she mentions the royal tombs right after the wells, as if that was the next stop for her, close by. It would make sense if the Byzantine Christians built the church and their own necropolis at the top of the hill, by the ancient wells and gate, *above* where the royal tombs (as they identified them) were located, further down on the north-eastern slope.

In Figure 3.2, an arrow gives an indication of the most likely area for the location of the tomb, further down in the valley, provided here in the hope that the Davidic tomb and its associated church may yet one day be found. Until quite recently, the sides of the hill were terraced for olive and vine orchards and other agriculture (see Plate 2), as it would have been in Jesus' time, but this area is now mostly used for housing.[52]

Such a tomb, inscribed with names (as the Bordeaux Pilgrim states) can survive in memory for a very long time, as with the nearby Tomb of Rachel, or the Tomb of the Patriarchs in Hebron. But of course many tombs are also long forgotten, and one may wonder how that could be. The story of Bethlehem through time is a story of many conquests and destructions, and people needed to be pragmatic. As archaeologist Lorenzo Nigro states:

> Due to natural conformation of the local carsic limestone, caves and tunnels in the bedrock were used through centuries for tombs, shepherds' shelters, storage facilities, workshops and dwellings. It is, thus, very difficult to date back the earliest utilization of such underground devices, which were re-employed many times by the inhabitants of the town.[53]

Therefore, a site can be forgotten, and only revealed by rediscovery and archaeological excavations.

What does all this mean for Jesus as a child? Here the issue is not only place identity, and the kinds of stories that were told about places as he was growing up. Jesus' birth in Bethlehem also connected him with expectation, and the future, and indeed with a long past: with the ancestors mentioned in the genealogy we reflected on in the previous chapter. They were likely not just names but also *people* buried in rock-cut tombs in the valleys of Bethlehem. In indigenous and traditional cultures, grave sites of ancestors are an important part of the experience of belonging to people and place. Funerals bring families together, even when they have gone to live in other towns. In this, there is social identity, in which one is connected by duties and status, as sociologist Ward Goodenough explored.[54] Jewish literature and tradition today retains mourning rituals that date back to the time of Jesus.[55] Studies of identity in the archaeology of funerary remains tend to focus on the identity of the deceased,[56] but in funerary rites it is actually the identities of the *living* that are affirmed, both relationally in terms of the deceased, and socially in terms of the group that gathers.

The tombs of the Davidic house in Bethlehem, and the living descendants of David there, likely remained at the time of Jesus. They were buried elsewhere too, as we see in the ossuary inscription of someone 'of the house of David' buried in a tomb in Givat ha-Mivtar (see Fig. 2.1).[57] But Bethlehem, in terms of memory and connection, surely remained central.

Another king: the tomb of Herod

A further reason to believe that there was something special about Bethlehem in terms of both memory and expectation is found close by, in a very different tomb: the tomb of Herod, the Roman client king of the Judaeans (37–4 BCE).[58] The tomb has quite recently been discovered, embedded in the side of a hill where Herod had built a grand fortress-palace, named Herodion, with an associated village for his staff, family and friends. From Bethlehem you can look to the south and see the distinctive flat-topped triangle of Herodion, 3 miles (5 km) away (see Fig. 3.1; Plates 2 and 3). Why might Herod have chosen this location for his tomb, and not a position outside Jerusalem? Standing at this site, you look north to Bethlehem (see Plate 4). It is as if this tomb was positioned to say, 'I am watching you.'

As with all tombs, there is memory associated with it. Herod apparently built Herodion near the site of a battle victory at a time when Judaea was in the midst of a bloody civil war, which was in some ways a conflict between two superpowers by proxy. Rome and Parthia were at war here, with the Judaeans nervously favouring one or the other of two rival high-priestly rulers, each backed by one of these enemy empires. On one side was Hyrcanus II, who was appointed ethnarch[59] by the Romans, with Herod and his brother Phasael as tetrarchs,[60] and on the other was Antigonus Mattathias, son of the ousted high priest Aristobulus II, supported by the Parthians, who claimed he was the rightful priest-king ruler of Judaea.

In 40 BCE, Antigonus arrived with a mighty Parthian army. Herod fled fearfully from Jerusalem with his household, at night, and made for the fortress of Masada, necessarily via Engeddi by the Dead Sea. En route, the party was attacked by 'Judaeans' (Josephus, *Ant.* 14:359–60; *War* 1:265) at a distance of 60 stadia (*c.*9 miles or 12 km) from the city of Jerusalem.[61] If we consider the story in the light of the road system (see Fig. 3.1), the party would have just gone past Bethlehem and then been attacked. There is no indication that Herod sought help from any villagers; rather the opposite. Though Bethlehem is not mentioned here, the attackers appear to have been locals: while the Parthians in Jerusalem chased him, it is said by Josephus that Herod 'found the Judaeans more burdensome than the Parthians' (*War* 1:265) because they continually attacked him on the way. Near Bethlehem, then, just after Herod's party had gone by, there was a serious battle between Herod's militia and local Judaeans, and Herod 'slaughtered many of them' in the place he would build his palace-fortress and eventual tomb (*War* 1:265). Thus, while Josephus does not describe the 'slaughter of the innocents' of the Gospel of Matthew (2:16–18), he does describe the slaughter of the (young) men of Bethlehem and vicinity in 40 BCE.

According to Josephus, Herod survived and got away to Arabia (Nabataea, where his mother Cypros had come from), and then eventually he made his way to Rome. There, as an ally of Rome against the Parthians, he was hugely celebrated. He was declared by the Roman Senate to be the rightful 'King of the Judaeans', and left the Senate meeting grandly walking between the illustrious Mark Antony and Caesar Octavian, later Augustus (Josephus, *War* 1:284–5). He then returned to Judaea to oust Antigonus. Given the attitude of the Judaeans of the Bethlehem area, they supported Antigonus. However, in 37 BCE, bolstered by the army of Mark Antony led by the Roman governor of Syria, Sossius, Herod and his forces captured Jerusalem, and slaughtered and abused huge numbers of the city inhabitants. Antigonus was seized, and, chillingly, having been 'treated as a woman' (*hōs gunaika . . . phrousas*) and called 'Antigone' (a woman's name) by Sossius, he was then sent to Mark Antony in Syria, where he was horribly put to death. Josephus records that Antony had him beheaded with an axe (Josephus, *War* 1:345–58),[62] but the Roman historian Cassius Dio states that 'Antigonus he bound to a cross and scourged, a punishment no other king had suffered at the hands of the Romans, and so slew him' (*Hist. Rom.* 49:22).

Herod established himself as Roman client king against the hopes of those who had supported Antigonus, and demonstrated just how cruel the Romans could be with anyone who dared to challenge Rome. Herod then founded Herodion to commemorate his victory over pro-Antigonus Judaean attackers near Bethlehem.[63] He built it at the very place where he had slaughtered them, where the victims' families would see it. Herod would have gone past Bethlehem every time he went to and from his palaces in Jerusalem and Herodion with his retinue. He was breathing down the neck of Bethlehem, where the descendants of David had their own tombs and their own place.

Herodion was huge, covering over 12 hectares, and its construction involved a massive undertaking of engineering. On an existing hill, Herod built up a gigantic additional mountain of earth, with a flat top, creating a large mound rising above everywhere else. Around this there were concentric walls and a circle of four round towers, the highest being in the east, with the palace buildings sunk in the centre as if in the crater of a volcano. Excavations[64] have shown that the interior was fabulous, boasting great luxury and wealth, which spelled status and victory. A theatre was built into the north side of the hill, decorated with beautiful murals. In other words, the site of Herodion had much to do with Herod glorifying himself in his identity as rightful king of the Judaeans, and he looked down on his subjects (most closely those of Bethlehem) from there.

New archaeological excavations at the site have clarified that Herod began building this palace-fortress early on, in the 30s, not long after he defeated Antigonus. It was conveniently situated near the border between Judaea and Idumaea, on a crossroads. There was already an abandoned military post on the hill.[65] It was a very useful site for a military post, not far from Jerusalem to the south, and on the road to Idumaea. Furthermore, once built, Herod established Herodion as the capital of a new administrative district (toparchy), replacing Beth-Zur, in an area that would encompass Bethlehem.[66] Perhaps even the distinction between Herodion and Bethlehem became slightly blurred, which would explain why in the Jerusalem Talmud there is a reference to the 'king's palace in Bethlehem of Judaea' (*j.Ber.* 2:4).

The precise location of the tomb of Herod itself (*War* 1:673; *Ant.* 17:199) was for a long time unknown, despite extensive archaeological excavations at the site. However, in May 2007 the director of Herodion excavations, Ehud Netzer, announced that it had been found. Rather than being situated safely inside the hill, it was built into the outer slope of fill on the north-eastern side, on a platform beside a monumental stairway, and was clearly designed to be seen from afar: constructed from a white *meleke* limestone that catches the late rays of the sun.[67] It was Hellenistic in style and extremely tall. Built on a podium 10 m square, it rose up two storeys, with a conical roof, to an estimated total height of 25 m.

Archaeologist Jodi Magness has compared the tomb with other tombs of Hellenistic kings, showing how in its construction it heralded Herod as being one of the great rulers of the Graeco-Roman world.[68] Moreover, she notes that its location close to Bethlehem was specifically chosen by Herod as a proclamation about his claims to kingship. Indeed, even in its reconstructed form today, at perhaps a fifth of the original size, it is a shining finger pointing up from the side of the Herodion hill (see Plate 3).

Herod versus David

What did all this do to the feelings of those who dwelt in Bethlehem, who had already lost sons in 40 BCE? From their readings of Micah 5:2 and other texts, people were expecting the return of a Davidic king who would liberate and rule a united Israel, and they believed this king would come from David's city, Bethlehem. However, Herod had absolutely no credentials that would make him a legitimate king in the eyes of the Judaean population; he had instead the authority of Rome. The former high-priestly dynasty of the Hasmonean house had claimed kingship on the basis of their priestly credentials alone. Now, according to Josephus, Herod proclaimed he was king by 'the will of God' (*Ant.* 15:384, 387).[69]

Herod was the child of Jewish converts, not Judahite. Herod's father Antipater was an Idumaean Jewish convert, and his mother Cypros was a Nabataean (Arab).[70] However, there was some attempt made to suggest a more illustrious ancestry for Herod. Josephus says that according to Nicolaus of Damascus, a chronicler at Herod's court whom he used for information,[71] Antipater was actually descended from the foremost Judaeans who returned from Babylon (*Ant.* 14:9), but, Josephus adds, this was just said to 'gratify Herod'. Historian Abraham Schalit nevertheless has suggested on the basis of this that Herod even saw himself as the Messiah, with Davidic ancestry.[72] However, the issue for Herod, lacking even Judahite forebears, was simply to justify being king at all. That the claim of his Judaean descent was made to 'gratify' Herod suggests that Herod was edgy about criticism concerning his legitimacy.

Nicolaus of Damascus does seem to have presented Herod as a David-like king, as Tal Ilan has pointed out,[73] probably as a means of flattering Herod. For Josephus, though, the crown 'came to Herod the [son] of Antipater, being of an ordinary house and a common family and one subject to the kings' (*Ant.* 14:491). He was not well born. Given this kind of criticism, Herod seems to have gone on the attack. Julius Africanus, who recorded the survival of the *desposunoi*, the 'nobles' of Jesus' family, states that up to the time of Herod

> the genealogies of the Hebrews were recorded in the public archives, and those even went back to the proselytes, to Achior the Ammonite, and Ruth the Moabitess [i.e. the Davidic line], and the mixed crowd which left Egypt along with the Israelites. Herod, knowing that *the lineage of the Israelites contributed nothing to him*, and bruised by the knowledge of his ignoble birth, burned the records of their families, supposing that *he might appear to be well-born*, if no one else could reckon his line by the public register to the patriarchs or to the proselytes, and to that mixed race called *geiorai*.[74]
> (Eusebius, *Hist. Eccles.* 1:7:13, italics mine)

This indicates that there were genealogical records held in a public archive in Jerusalem of people who could trace their lineage very far back in time, and there was a fire that resulted in the loss of these, for which Herod was blamed.

The antagonism between the descendants of David (in Bethlehem) and Herod is also shown by a particular incident. We learn from Josephus that Herod targeted the Tomb of David. As noted above, Josephus states that David was buried in a tomb 'in Jerusalem' (*Ant.* 7:392–4). The Hasmonean priest-king John Hyrcanus (135–105 BCE) had already 'opened the Tomb of David, who was the wealthiest of kings' and extracted 3,000 talents of silver (*War* 1:61; *Ant.* 7:392–3; 13:249–50).[75] But this was to pay money to a besieging army and to increase the forces that would defend Judaea. As for Herod, Josephus writes of how he just wanted revenue.

According to the story Josephus relates, Herod himself went with his closest friends and his men to the Tomb of David by night, in secret, and found gold ornamentation and precious goods, which they took away. But Herod wanted more: he apparently wanted to see the graves of David and Solomon. Then something happened: a flame burst out from deep inside and two of his armed guards were injured, 'so it was said'. Therefore, in much fear, Herod 'built a propitiatory monument (*hilastērion mnēma*) of white stone at the mouth [of the tomb], at great expense' (*Ant.* 16:179–83).

The term 'propitiatory' (*hilastērion*) suggests an inscription: Herod seems to have wished to propitiate the deity for something in connection with David and his memory. Perhaps all the circumstances were not quite as Josephus's informants indicate, but nevertheless there was something for all to see: an expensive white monument at the mouth of the Tomb of David, in Jerusalem, built by Herod. At the very least, the story suggests again some awkward relationship with the 'house of David'. And it was considered extremely wrong of Herod to rob this tomb. As Josephus writes, Herod's own court historian mentioned him building the monument, but he did not record what he did in the tomb, 'since he believed the action was not proper' (*Ant.* 16:183). For those descended from David, it would have been an act of utter desecration.

As a final note on matters to do with burial, the tomb of Herod's son Archelaus, ethnarch of Judaea after the death of his father, was – according to Jerome (<u>*Lib.*</u> *Loc.* 45:1–2) – 'at the beginning of the fork from the public highway to our cells'.[76] In the fourth century, when Jerome wrote this, the monastic cells were connected to the Basilica of the Nativity. The main highway route to Bethlehem town was via the Hebron road, lying to the west (Eusebius, *Onom.* 42), but the eastern side of Bethlehem, where the church and cells were located, was more easily accessed by another public road going south from Jerusalem and connecting to Migdal Eder (see Fig. 3.1).[77] There was then a fork off this to the road leading up to the cells: the Milk Grotto road of today. If this tradition about Archelaus is true, then Herod's son and heir decided to encroach far more into David's town than even his father had done.[78] Again, this shows a special interest.

Bethlehem was not just anywhere; it had prophecy attached to it. There was hope that someone coming from the house of David would rule Israel. People who traced their descent to David's line still existed and even had a role to play in terms of Temple operations. There is no reason to suppose that they did not live in Bethlehem and still have their tombs lying outside the town, in the valleys; indeed the evidence of early Christian pilgrims suggests this. Herod built his own tomb at Herodion to tower over Bethlehem, as if to trump any tombs below. He had slaughtered his Judaean attackers, from the Bethlehem region, who supported his rival Antigonus. He is said to have burned records of noble lineage and violated the Tomb of David and Solomon in Jerusalem. Such stories, even if they are not entirely true, indicate Herod's attitude to the Davidic line.

To be born Davidic in Bethlehem, then, was to be born into a landscape of expectation and violence. Your identity as a descendant of David and a Bethlehemite would be associated with trauma.

4

Born Jesus: the Gospel of Matthew

In any family, stories are told of the past: of events, ancestors and child-hoods. In the Gospels, there are two stories about the birth of Jesus, in Matthew and Luke respectively, known to many today through countless nativity plays and other remembrances. In performances, the two stories are fused together as a composite, but we need to look at them separately in order to assess them as memories. Stories about your birth and early childhood provide a sense of identity, belonging, relationships and expec-tations. Might there then have been stories told within Jesus' family?

In historical Jesus studies, there has been little interest in the nativity stories, as the underlying assumption is that they are not at all 'historical' but rather composed by the Gospel authors to make theological points about Jesus and to underscore the themes of their work.[1] As E. P. Sanders concluded, the 'clearest cases of invention are in the birth narratives'.[2] An implicit assumption for many historians is that the Gospel authors had licence to make things up from scratch. The scriptural references have been thought to show that these stories were made up in order to create fulfilment of key passages with a messianic significance. There have been many literary studies, but in these there is a hesitancy about making claims about truth.[3] When historians have ventured into the realms of the nativity stories, they have sometimes asserted that they are cover-ups, designed to obscure a real story about Jesus' illegitimacy.[4]

This scepticism is founded on a long history in Western scholarship of being nervous regarding oral traditions. History itself as a discipline is founded on the idea of literary records, so anything in the human past in which no literary records are available is 'pre-historic'. Lands and people who did not have literary records prior to colonisation could also be considered 'pre-historic' societies. In societies where literacy has been largely the preserve of men, no one wants to credit 'old wives' tales'.

While in Gospel studies it is widely understood that there was a period of oral telling of stories prior to anything being written down, historians fight shy of speculating on what that might have entailed, and have often looked only at the actual evidence of the literary works we have, plumbing their depths to understand the author and the authorial context (*Sitz im Leben*) and defining editorial shaping before proposing what is reliable as actuality. When it comes to the nativity stories of the Gospels, each one is quite distinctive, and each one looks as if it claims to be founded on oral tradition from one or the other of Jesus' parents. It has been easy for historians to sweep this tradition aside as more fictional than factual, as the details are unverifiable, it is thought, and – if so – they could have been made up.

However, in her examination of early Jewish birth stories and social memory, Antoinette Clark Wire has looked at the birth narratives of Jesus among other similar Jewish recollections of auspicious births. She considered how stories were told in contexts that could even include singing and other practices particularly associated with women. The birth stories of prophets were modelled on actual birth stories told in families, and there could be prophecies and visions associated with auspicious births. Ultimately, Wire concludes: 'Since such a prophecy or account of a vision cannot readily be falsified, I suggest that it is best respected as a family tradition, in which accuracy in detail is not as much the point as credibility of the speaker, and of the God in whose name the prediction is spoken.'[5]

In societies such as those in the modern West where patterns of individualistic life are normative, and also for theological reasons, Jesus is imagined as quite singular, solitary and distinctive. In this way, Jesus is presented as the 'Great Man' who 'changed history by himself', as James Crossley puts it.[6] He has only one close family connection, namely with his mother Mary. The rest of his family, especially the members of his extended family (of David), even Joseph, are a vague and shadowy backdrop. Only a few scholars have ventured into exploring this subject, especially in thinking about Jesus' brother James, but their work has not been met with much interest within historical Jesus circles, even though it is sometimes popular with the wider public.[7] The important work of John Painter, who has examined carefully all the early traditions about Jesus' brother James as the influential leader of the Judaean church and successor to Jesus' own leadership,[8] may well now change this, and it leads us into the present exploration. We ask: what are the boundaries of invention?

Given that Jesus' family continued to play an important leadership role in the Judaean churches through to the first part of the second century, is it reasonable to think that they told a story – or stories – about Jesus' birth and his early years? Conversely, is it *unreasonable* to think that stories could have been written down in a Judaean and wider Syrian context without any constraints on the basis of what Jesus' family remembered and said?

In this chapter, then, we will think about what stories could have been told as part of the family tradition of Joseph, Mary and their children: Jesus, James, Joset, Judas and Simon, and their sisters, remembered as Mary and Salome.[9] The interest is not in historicity precisely, but in stories. These family stories themselves might not have been all true. The question will be whether the stories – as *stories* – are plausibly early. If so, what impact would they have had on Jesus as a boy?

This investigation involves us in issues related to how we approach our reading. It is certainly much easier to say there is nothing of historical value in the nativity accounts and to leave them be as inventions of the early church. If we are to think about how stories came to be told, and who told them, we are on uncertain ground. The Gospels were clearly written in different social environments and at different times, but the earlier they are, the more the writers would need to be aware of people who had living memories of Jesus or his family. More imaginative developments of our canonical Gospel stories, with additional elements, can certainly be seen as time goes by, on through the second century and into the sixth, in writings known as the 'Infancy Gospels' (for which see the next chapter and Chapter 10). These show steps in the process of authors having freer creativity, as we shall see. But authors' freedom to fictionalise correlates with their distance from their subjects. There are constraints on invention the closer a writing is to the time of an event, or to the people involved. In addition, to make matters more complex, later more fictionalised stories can still contain nuggets of actuality embedded in their accounts.

We are usually best helped if we turn to the earliest evidence, and so again we need to begin with Paul, writing in the 50s and early 60s of the first century. Paul states that Jesus was 'born of a woman' like any other human being (Gal. 4:4; and see Rom. 1:3; Phil. 2:7), and the 'seed of David' he refers to indicates a human father (Gal. 3:16, 19). In the first century there was a widespread Aristotelian notion that conception arose when the male seed was planted in the female 'ground' or blood in the womb, from which the child would grow (see Philo, *Quaest. Gen.* 3:47). Jesus was recognised as the 'son of Joseph' (Matt. 13:55; Luke 4:22; John 1:45; 6:42),[10] and hence Davidic, as we have seen. Therefore, the earliest nativity story told should correlate with this understanding.

Matthew: the stories

The earliest story told about Jesus' birth and early childhood is found in the Gospel of Matthew. This work is generally understood to be the product of someone writing in the area of Syria (Phoenicia/Palestine) sometime in the mid-80s CE.[11] The author is sometimes identified as a 'Jewish-Christian', meaning he was a Jew in ethnoreligious terms who maintained Jewish praxis (regarding festivals, food, Sabbath observance, and so on; see Matt. 5:17–18), but he was writing for a community in which Gentiles were included in this Jewish milieu.[12] The work is written in Greek, using Mark (written *c.*70 CE), which is largely incorporated into it, and another prior gospel, often referred to as 'Q' (from *Quelle*, meaning 'Source' in German), defined on the basis of overlaps with the Gospel of Luke, where it is also incorporated (possibly via Matthew).

This prior gospel is largely composed of sayings, including ethical teaching (e.g. Matt. 5–7) and parables. Some argue that this material was incorporated into Luke only via Matthew (the Two Gospel hypothesis), but the Q hypothesis is more accepted.[13]

Who wrote the lost gospel Q? Papias of Hierapolis (*c.*125 CE) records that there was indeed a work containing *logia* ('oracles', 'statements') originally recorded by Jesus' apostle Matthew in 'Hebrew', translated into Greek (Eusebius, *Hist. Eccles.* 3:39:16). If this prior work by Jesus' apostle Matthew was incorporated into our Matthew, it explains the continuation of author attribution in the expanded work, as Maurice Casey has argued.[14] Q itself is Syrian, in that it has strong affinities with another early Syrian work known as the *Didache*, or *Teaching of the Twelve Apostles*, and also the Letter of James: a letter attributed to Jesus' brother.[15]

Anything in Matthew not in either Mark or in Q is often attributed to a separate source scholars call 'M', though sometimes M might be parts of Q omitted by Luke (e.g. certain parables, such as that in Matt. 20:1–16). The birth and infancy narrative of Matthew in chapters 1 and 2 are not part of Q, in being different stylistically and also in content, while Q begins with John the Baptist,[16] so they are M. The origins of M are a mystery, and we do not necessarily have this source preserved perfectly. We can see that the Gospel of Matthew shapes, restructures and modifies Mark, and adds editorial elements, and therefore very likely does the same with the other source material (both Q and M).

In looking further at the birth–infancy narrative of Matthew 1 – 2, we need then to be alert to two levels: the level of the pre-Matthean source material and the level of the final edition. Within this narrative there are several sections, though they flow together to form a continuous unit that takes us from Jesus' ancestry to his arrival in Nazareth. We have already explored how the section of the genealogy of Jesus in Matthew 1:1–17 is itself a story. It tells of Jesus' Davidic descent. This story is not separate from what now follows: it continues in the begetting, birth and naming of Jesus.

At the outset, we would expect the genealogy to conclude by stating that Jesus is descended from Joseph, in order to clinch his Davidic credentials as 'seed of David'. However, in most early manuscripts of the Greek New Testament, Matthew's genealogy ends oddly with: 'and Jacob begot Joseph, the husband of Mary, to whom was born Jesus, called Christ' (Matt. 1:16). By the time our most important early manuscripts were written down, in the fourth century, it was doctrinal orthodoxy to believe that Joseph himself did *not* father Jesus physically. As Eusebius wrote: 'Christ was not the son of Joseph, but the son of Holy Spirit and Mary . . . Christ was not fathered by Joseph, and has no physical connection with him' (*Quaest. Steph.* 1:1).[17]

Such a doctrine makes it quite incredible that a different version of this verse ever appears in any manuscripts at all: a reading that really does have Joseph fathering Jesus. In the late second century, an Assyrian Christian named Tatian carefully conflated the Gospels of Matthew, Mark, Luke and John into one continuous narrative, known as the *Diatessaron*. It proved so popular that it was the definitive 'Gospel' in many Syrian churches through to the fourth century, at which point it was withdrawn by those who wanted to streamline doctrine. Their suppression of this work was so successful that a full text of the *Diatessaron* in Greek or Syriac has not even survived. The work is probably best attested in a later Arabic translation, and, in the earliest form of the manuscripts testifying to this (A), it reads: 'Jacob begot Joseph, the husband of Mary, who begot from her Jesus the Christ'. The words 'from her' are actually an addition, written just above the line.[18] If this was the second-century reading of Matthew, incorporated into the *Diatessaron*, then Joseph is clearly Jesus' biological father, as we might expect from Paul.

A similar reading is found in another early translation of Matthew into Syriac. Syriac was a form of Aramaic spoken in Syria over a wide area, including northern Palestine, written in the Estrangela script. The Greek canonical Gospels were translated into Syriac sometime in the third century.[19] There are two manuscripts testifying to this version dating from the late fourth or early fifth century. One of these, the Sinaitic Syriac, has: 'Jacob begat Joseph – to whom was betrothed Mary – who begat Jesus who is called the Christ'.[20] In a Greek manuscript from the ninth century (the Koridethi) and a family of manuscripts related to this (*f*13) the text is (ambiguously): 'and Jacob begat Joseph, to whom was betrothed the virgin Mary, [and] he begat/she bore (*egennēsen*) Jesus who was called Christ'.[21] This reading is attested similarly by seven early manuscripts in the old Latin version (second to fourth century). There are echoes too. In the sixth-century *Dialogue of Timothy and Aquila* (17:3a), there may be a conflation between the doctrinally correct text and an alternative text (here in italics): 'Jacob begat Joseph, the husband of Mary, from whom was born Jesus who is called Christ, *and Joseph begat Jesus who is called Christ*.'[22]

All these manuscripts seem to reflect in some way a reading that has Joseph as the real father of Jesus. This wide range of doctrinally *incorrect* versions is amazing, because Joseph's paternity was also a common view among 'Jewish-Christians'. These were various groups defined as heterodox by the standards of fourth-century theological orthodoxy,[23] an orthodoxy now backed by imperial authority in the form of Constantine and his heirs at a time when there was little tolerance for dissent.

The Aramaic version of Matthew

What then if the manuscripts' doctrinally incorrect version (by later standards) was a more accurate reading? At this point we need to think about who used which gospels, and narrow down our focus in terms of the 'Jewish-Christians' who saw Joseph as Jesus' real father. Late in the second century, Irenaeus had spurned the understanding of the (first-century) 'apostle' Cerinthus that Jesus was 'the son of Joseph and Mary in the same way as all other people' (*Adv. Haer.* 1:26:1). Irenaeus noted that Cerinthus and his ilk used only the Gospel of Mark, when they should really use all four to ensure theological correctness.[24] However, more commonly, Jewish Christ-followers – who could be dubbed 'Nazarenes', 'Ebionites'[25] or 'Hebrews' by Gentile Christian scholars – are said to have used the Gospel of Matthew.[26] Jerome places these 'Hebrews' or *Nazareni* in southern Syria and the Golan (Jerome, *Comm. Isa.* 8:14:19–22; 9:1–4; 29:17–21; 31:6–9),[27] including Beria (= Aleppo, *Vir. Ill.* 3) and the village of Choba, near Damascus (Eusebius, *Onom.* 172:1–3; cf. Jerome, *Lib. Loc.* 112).[28] He translated their gospel into Greek (*Comm. Matt.* 12:13)[29] and states that it is *iuxta Matthaeum*, 'equivalent to Matthew', written in 'the Chaldean or Syrian language' (namely Aramaic) in Hebrew characters,[30] as was in fact normative in Palestinian Jewish Aramaic: the language of Jesus. The Gospel could therefore be called the 'Gospel of the Nazarenes' or the 'Gospel of the Hebrews',[31] though it is actually attested as an Aramaic version of Matthew, available in the church library of Caesarea, as Jeremiah Coogan has pointed out.[32] It might be referred to variously, but it is the same work. Jerome even thought initially that it was the original Hebrew Matthew mentioned by Papias.[33] Small variants in this 'Jewish gospel' of Matthew could be noted in manuscripts.[34] But at no point does Jerome or anyone else state that this gospel was lacking the first two chapters of our usual Matthew.[35] In fact, Jerome refers to its reading in his commentary on Matthew 2:5.[36]

However, the 'Ebionites' (Christian Jews) who only used (Aramaic) Matthew held that Jesus was the son of Joseph, as noted by Irenaeus (*Adv. Haer.* 3:21:1; 5:1:3).[37] Eusebius writes of how 'Ebionites' asserted that Jesus was 'born of the intercourse of a man and Mary' (*Hist. Eccles.* 3:27:2; 5:8:10). But curiously they could also hold that Mary was a virgin when Jesus was conceived. Origen (*Against Celsus* 5:61), writing in Palestine in the third century, identified two types of 'Ebionites': one type held Jesus to be conceived of a virgin, and the other type denied this and said he was conceived like the rest of humanity.[38] However, in both cases Jesus was understood as the child of both Mary and Joseph.[39] Jerome too mentions 'Ebionites' who believed that Jesus was born of 'Mary the Virgin' (*Ep.* 112:13).

Further back in time, even Ignatius – who was bishop of Antioch in Syria in the early second century, and someone who used the Gospel of Matthew[40] – states that Jesus was 'conceived by Mary according to God's plan, both from seed of David *and* Holy Spirit' (*Ephes.* 18:2). The seed of David is understood in a bodily sense, since he was 'of the family of David according to flesh, son of God by will and power, truly born of a virgin' (*Smyrn.* 1:1).

If the male seed of David travelled down through the male line to Joseph and then Jesus, one may ask then: how did anyone read Matthew and understand that Jesus was born of Mary as a virgin and yet think he was also the seed of Joseph, as a descendant of David? We need to explore interpretation.

Joseph's story

We thus approach Matthew's narrative. As a tool for our analysis, we will think about presumed knowledge. We will think about who is identified as the key character or observer, as that makes a claim about a story's origin. We will also define what elements cohere with what we otherwise know from history. We will probe these stories to see what memories are contained in them.

The story of Jesus' birth in Matthew runs as follows (1:18–25):

[18]The birth of Jesus the Anointed[41] was like this. His mother Mary was betrothed to Joseph, but before they came together (*sunelthein*) she was found to be pregnant from (*ek*) Holy Spirit. [19]Joseph her husband, being a righteous man (*dikaios*) and not wishing to expose her publicly (*deigmatisai*), decided to send her away (*apolusai*) secretly (*lathra*). [20]Having pondered these things, look, an angel of the Lord in a dream appeared to him saying, 'Joseph, son of David,

don't be afraid to take along (*paralabein*) Mary your wife, for what is conceived in her is from (*ek*) Holy Spirit. ²¹She will bear a son and you will call his name Jesus, for he will save his people from their wrongdoings. ²²All this happened to fulfil what was spoken by the Lord through the prophet: ²³"Look, the virgin will conceive, and she will bear a son, and they will call his name Emmanuel, which is translated 'God with us.'" ²⁴When Joseph woke up from the sleep he did as the angel of the Lord had instructed, and took along (*parelaben*) his wife, ²⁵and he did not have sex (*eginōsken*) with her until she had given birth to a son, and he called his name Jesus.

This story is clearly told from Joseph's point of view; it is not told from Mary's perspective. We are not told how she felt about anything, and indeed we are not told anything either about the wider background, situation of the families, date or place. We do not at this stage know anything about Joseph; it is as if we are expected to have some prior knowledge. It is only later that we discover that he was a *tektōn*, a 'carpenter' or 'constructor', when in Matthew 13:55 Jesus is called the 'son of a *tektōn*' (see Mark 6:3). He was someone who worked with his hands to earn his living. He was not, then, one of the big landholders who gained wealth from property and agriculture. We need to imagine his house as fairly modest, not a luxury villa, and likely one with a workshop. In an era when a son gained his expertise from his father, it is likely that Joseph's father was also a *tektōn*. However, none of this is part of our introduction to Joseph. The key information given here is only that Joseph was righteous (*dikaios*) and a 'son of David' (1:20). This is the important link with the preceding genealogy that leads us to this point.

So now, as in standard exegetical practice, we need to interrogate some Greek words. Often the best way of understanding the use of particular words is to consider how they are employed by an author in a particular work, or in the general oeuvre of that author, beyond simply the dictionary definitions. The Greek word *sunelthein*, a form of the word *sunerchomai*, is a very general one simply meaning 'come together', but in marriage contracts it implies the consummation of that marriage.[42] It is only found in this one instance in Matthew, but it seems to have this technical meaning. Eusebius actually makes much of this, and thinks that it was just before the couple were going to consummate the marriage that Joseph discovered Mary was pregnant (*Quaest. Steph.* 4). Joseph alone seems to have discovered Mary's condition. This is actually quite important, because this shows that the wedding proper had occurred.

From rabbinic evidence and also the archaeological discoveries of ancient Jewish marriage documents, much can be known about what was considered normal in betrothal and marriage.[43] The betrothal (*erusin*) involved signing the agreed contract (*ketubbah*) and presenting gifts to the bride's family, which created the formal agreement between the father of the husband (or the husband)[44] and the father of the bride. It established the marital partnership, with a concomitant allowance for the couple's privacy, but the bride remained living in her father's house.[45] After the betrothal there was usually a period of waiting, which could be long if the girl was below the age of puberty, but more commonly was no more than thirty days.[46] During the time of betrothal, it was not anticipated that the couple would have penetrative sex,[47] though there was no scriptural law actually forbidding it. The second part of the marriage involved a procession from the girl's home to her husband's house (*nissuin*), completing the transfer of the dowry and authority (guardianship) from father (or other responsible male) to husband. In the procession, the girl (often aged 12–14 years) would be carried in a litter with her hair unbound (*m.Ket.* 7:1). There was a wedding feast, at which both the bride and the bridegroom put on 'crowns' (*m.Sot.* 9:14) and people sang marriage songs. Then came the consummation of the marriage in a bridal chamber, followed by cohabitation. The 'bridal chamber' – a bedroom or tent – had been decorated and prepared as a place where the couple could consummate the marriage.

But in the story of Matthew, things did not go as planned. A virgin of marriageable age (post puberty) was supposed to stay within the home until betrothal and marriage, and not appear publicly until her wedding procession.[48] The usual quite loose clothing of this era, with a band under the breast line rather than around the waist,[49] could easily cover up early pregnancy. If we read with Eusebius, in the bridal chamber Joseph discovered that there was a child in Mary's womb. However, Matthew's language is not active; rather, 'she was found to be pregnant' (1:18), literally 'she was found [as] having [a baby] in [her] belly' (*eurethē en gastri echousa*). The issue was not about virginity, which was normally established by the girl bleeding on first marital intercourse (Deut. 22:13–21; *b.Ket.*16b). This passive tense implies that before intercourse Mary was recognised as pregnant. Reading with Eusebius, Joseph would then have recognised this on their wedding night. But it is highly likely that others were involved in this determination, namely the senior women of the household. This was women's business. In one of the Dead Sea Scrolls (4Q159 2–4) there is a case where 'trustworthy [women] will examine her' if a girl is accused of not being a virgin. Likewise, in another text '[examination] by reliable [women]' will establish virginity in the case of a girl with 'a bad name about her virginity in her father's home' (4Q271 3).[50] This is the kind of inspection for virginity that is presented in such texts as the second-century Infancy Gospel, the *Protevangelium of James* (19 – 20), when the midwife Salome inspects Mary after the birth of Jesus. It was not for Joseph alone to decide either pregnancy or virginity, or for Mary alone to proclaim it.

In terms of the results of the implied examination, it appears that it was not Mary's virginity that was questioned. Joseph never doubts this. But her pregnancy was the issue. It then becomes Joseph's problem to make a decision as Mary's husband and guardian. He is presented as the only active party here because it is his moral quandary: he thinks *he* could send her off from *his* home, or else keep her. He does not suggest this as an option to her father, so Mary has already been transferred to his care. There is no negotiation with Mary's father at all.

After Joseph's recognition of Mary's pregnancy, what he wanted to avoid is represented by the term *deigmatisai* (from *deigmatizō*): 'to expose'. It is found in ancient texts and papyri as indicating an exposing to public disgrace.[51] Public shame and humiliation for Mary would have been a terrible thing for her, and in this society honour was important social credit.[52]

Joseph pondered his options. What should he do? The term *apolusai*, from *apoluō*, means 'release' or 'send away'. While it is often translated as 'divorce', this is not necessarily accurate.[53] The simple meaning of 'send away' is found in Matthew 15:32, and the meaning of 'divorce' is found in Matthew 19:3, 7–8. The key to the meaning is in the term *lathra*, 'secretly'. Given the importance of a betrothal and marriage, not only to the couple concerned but also to the families, it was not possible for a man to 'divorce' a woman 'secretly' (*lathra*) in a judicial sense.[54] The contract was between Joseph and Mary's father or other male guardian. This contract (*ketubbah*) would have been broken, and there would be issues about the bridal gifts. As John Collins notes, while 'divorce could be obtained at will by either party [husband or father of the bride], it was not to be taken lightly, for it had well-defined economic consequences'.[55] Added to these problems, the two households would have been in uproar. People would have wanted to know the reason for the divorce, the family would have been embarrassed, and Mary would have been 'exposed'.

As was noted above, at no point does the story represent Mary's feelings or how she herself reacts or explains anything to Joseph. It is as if she is completely mute. She is found to be pregnant, but she does not provide any reason for it. She does not explain, or indicate she has given consent in terms of any sexual interactions. She does not blame anyone, weep or express fear, or reveal why she thinks she is pregnant. Her emotions are utterly passed over. She does not express a preference for what Joseph should do, but it does seem to be implied that what he eventually decides is in her best interest. Her silence and inactivity only serve to emphasise how much this is about Joseph and his perspective.

There seems to be a deliberately ambiguous use of words in this story. However, it is important to consider exactly what Joseph was afraid of doing, as Philip Esler has explored.[56] He ponders, and an angel in a dream directs him not to be afraid of 'taking along' Mary. The words *paralabein* (v. 20) and *parelaben* (v. 24) are forms of the verb *paralambano*, which means 'take with/along' (Matt. 2:13–14, 20–1; 4:5, 8; 12:45; 17:1; 18:16; 24:40–1; 26:37; 27:27), though it can also mean 'take on one side' (Matt. 20:17). *Paralambano* is not found in ancient marriage contracts for 'marry',[57] but it connects with the ancient colloquial language of marriage. A husband in Greek idiom 'led' a wife (see Josephus, *Ant.* 14:300; 18:21), and thus to 'take her along' would mean to be with her properly in marriage. In this passage it reads as the opposite of 'send away', quite literally. Either Joseph takes her along, in marriage, or he sends her away, but secretly.[58] Joseph chooses not to send Mary away but to keep her with him, *despite* discovering her condition, and thereby he accepts the public disgrace this would entail for *him* as a righteous man (see Sirach 26:5). This reputation would have been tarnished if the couple had had sex before the betrothal. For a man to force himself on a non-consenting virgin (i.e. to rape her) could be understood as a form of betrothal (based on Deut. 22:25–7), but this was considered immoral (though the girl's reputation was preserved).[59] Sex during the betrothal was certainly not considered ideal.[60] Clearly, the major issue for Joseph would have been if Mary was so pregnant that her pregnancy must have happened prior to the betrothal. He could then: (1) expose her to public disgrace, and divorce her; (2) send her away secretly; or (3) live with her as his wife, come what may.

While it is common to suppose that Joseph initially thought Mary had had sex with someone else, as does Lincoln in fact,[61] in this story there is actually no indication of that at all. As we noted above, there is no question about Mary's virginity. Joseph doesn't look for a culprit or show any sign of outrage. Eusebius himself noted that had Joseph thought she was pregnant through having sex with someone else, he would have brought her to court to be publicly prosecuted (*Quaest. Steph.* 6), given that the rules against adultery covered the period of betrothal.[62] For Eusebius, this showed that Joseph always knew that the conception was miraculously enacted by the Holy Spirit. Indeed, the family would have been required to find the culprit. It would have been mayhem.

Therefore, the alternatives are given plainly in Matthew 1:19: 'being a righteous man (*dikaios*) and not wishing to expose her publicly, he decided to send her away secretly.' Joseph's sense of being a righteous man is tied up with his wish to cover everything up. He could have kept his reputation by simply announcing that Mary was pregnant by another man, and divorcing her, and therefore maintained his righteousness, while tarnishing hers. But this is not suggested. His righteousness is actually deeper: he wants to protect and look after Mary, but he is afraid of living with her as his wife, given what might be said. He decides to send her away secretly.

In Joseph's thinking, then, in sending her away, Mary would still return with a baby some time later. No one would need to know that she was already significantly pregnant at the time of marriage.

Joseph then initially makes a decision to follow option 2: send her away secretly. However, he ponders. He then receives a dream in which an angel speaks and quotes Scripture, directing him not to be afraid to follow the course of option 3. Read in this way, Joseph's final decision is to 'take her along'. The Gospel presents a story in which Jesus is born with both parents exposed to some public disapprobation, because people would have thought Mary had had sex with Joseph while in her father's house. The final obvious stages of her pregnancy would have led to tittle-tattle that would mean Joseph was perceived as less than righteous, and that would have hurt him. But no one would have thought for a moment that he would ever have married (and not divorced) a girl pregnant with someone else's child.

In all this, we need now to reflect on meaning. Matthew has begun with an emphasis in the genealogy on Jesus as son of David. How does this story fit as a clinching identity-marker? It is often thought that the whole story results from the Greek version of the prophecy of Isaiah 7:14, cited in Matthew 1:23: 'the virgin will conceive a child and will bear a son'. In this view, Matthew invented a virginal conception of Jesus as a result of this messianic prediction. However, there is no evidence that this was ever a messianic prophecy; later Jewish interpretation did not see it as such.[63] Even if it were a messianic prophecy, the wording in Hebrew does not indicate a virginal conception; the passage in Hebrew reads only that a young woman (*almah*) would conceive and bear a child, quite normally. In the Greek Septuagint there is the word 'virgin' (*parthenos*) instead of 'young woman', but really the sense was the same. As we read the Gospel text, it seems more that this vague verse about a young woman's conception has been seized upon as prefiguring Mary's pregnancy.

Whose interpretation was this? Joseph is identified not only as righteous but also as an admirable expert in the arts of prediction, using both Scripture and dreams, through which angels communicate. The art of oneiromancy, or dream-interpretation, was long understood as a method of predicting the future and understanding the present, though a dream's significance could require an interpreter.[64] The import of dreams might also be questioned: the prophet Jeremiah decries false prophets who say, 'I had a dream! I had a dream!' (Jer. 23:25). Dreams alone might reveal divine purposes, but the combination of both a dream and an interpretation of a scriptural passage became a particularly valued method of prediction. Josephus attributes expertise in predictive arts to the Essenes via the interpretation of both dreams (*War* 2:112–13; *Ant.* 17:345–8) and Scripture (*War* 2:159; *Ant.* 13:310–13).[65] He also credits the Pharisees with being able to predict the future on the basis of Scripture (*Ant.* 14:172–6; 15:3–4; 17:41–5). Josephus himself would combine a dream and a scriptural interpretation in his own prediction of Vespasian's rule as emperor (*War* 3:351–4, 400–2).[66] Both dreams and Scripture could be interpreted similarly: among the Dead Sea Scrolls, the interpretation texts (*pesharim*) illustrate the way in which Scripture was read symbolically, similarly to the way dreams were understood, in order to indicate current events, the recent past and the future.[67] Words of Scripture are 'mysteries' (*razim*) that need to be unlocked by an expert (1QpHab 2:8–9; 7:1–5).[68] Angels – divine messengers – could themselves appear in dreams and interpret what was going on (as in Dan. 7 – 12). Josephus himself believed he received angelic reassurance in a dream (*Life* 42). He knew of this happening to others, such as the high priest Jaddua (*Ant.* 11:326–7).[69]

Therefore, Joseph is presented in Matthew not just as a righteous man and son of David: he is someone who is so adept at the interpretation of both dreams and Scripture that he can understand both the present and the future. In Josephus's presentation, this ability was the preserve of the scribal elite of the legal schools and priesthood. It is a radical claim in Matthew to indicate that Joseph, as a *tektōn*, had such skills.

But why tell this story? There seems to be a hidden clue in the genealogy itself, and so we need to return to it.

The message of the mothers

It is often noted that, despite the male line being all-important in the identity of the expected Davidic king, there are women mentioned in the genealogy of Matthew (1:1–16): mothers, not just fathers: Tamar the Canaanite, Rahab of Jericho, Ruth from Moab and 'she [= the wife] of Uriah' (Bathsheba).[70] There is a formula: N (masc.) begot (*egennēsen*) a son from (*ek*) N (fem.) (Matt. 2:2:3, 5, 6). Wayne Te Kaawa points out that these women are 'people of the land' of Canaan: effectively colonised indigenous peoples.[71] This points forward to the story of the 'Canaanite' (Syro-Phoenician) woman who teaches Jesus about faith (Matt. 15:21–8), whom we have met already, and so their 'inclusion in the genealogy of Jesus makes Jesus himself indigenous to the land of his Canaanite ancestors, as well as to his Israelite conquering ancestors'.[72] While scholars have long noted that the women included in the genealogy point to Matthew's Gentile mission (so Matt. 28:19), this observation of what the genealogy is trying to do actually draws the focus more narrowly in to focus on land,[73] and in fact to the areas that were conquered by David.

However, a long-standing problem for the Gentile-inclusive characterisation of the mothers in the Matthean genealogy has been that the
'wife of Uriah', Bathsheba, is not actually a Gentile. She is married to a
Hittite, but she is the daughter of Eliam (2 Sam. 11:3, or Ammiel in 1 Chr.
3:5), who was remembered as the same man as Eliam son of Ahithopel,
a Judahite from Gilon (2 Sam. 23:34), and in later Judaism she is never
considered to be a Gentile.[74] Furthermore, the next woman mentioned is
Mary, and she too is not a Gentile.[75]

Another explanation for the women's inclusion has been that the
women were sinful, which points to scandal.[76] Jerome (*Comm. Matt.* 1:3)
claims there is in the genealogy no mention of holy women but only of
women whom Scripture reprehends, so that we should understand that
Christ has come for the sake of sinners. However, as Raymond Brown
notes, Ruth was not a sinner but a role model for loyalty.[77]

There is a further suggestion that there was something irregular
or unusual about their conceptions. Turned around slightly, this can
also be viewed as female initiative, with a focus on celebrating Mary.[78]
Raymond Brown combines this with a suggestion of scandal about
Mary's pregnancy, given that Mary was in danger of social condemnation
on account of her pregnancy before the consummation of her marriage
to Joseph.[79] But, as Craig Keener has noted, if the aim was to defend
Mary from an accusation of immorality, why include women who were
actually considered immoral: Tamar, who behaved like a prostitute, and
Bathsheba, who was an adulterer?[80] If an unusual conception was key,
why not include Sarah's (Gen. 17:15–21; 21:1–3)?

Again, we need to bring this back to the theme of defining Jesus as
the appropriate and long-awaited son of David through Joseph. The
story runs to Joseph, son of David, and his quandary about what to do
regarding Mary's surprising pregnancy (Matt. 1:18–25). It is Joseph's
story, as a man. We should, then, be thinking particularly about the
behaviour of the *men* of the Davidic line in relation to the women, but
not so much the direct correlation of the women with Mary. If we work
with this focus, the inclusion of the mothers asks us to think about their
stories holistically, as Eusebius noted long ago: the evangelist 'is inviting
us to look carefully at the story about them all' (*Quaest. Steph.* 7:2). Are
there features of the men's behaviour that repeat?

In Genesis 38 we have the story of Tamar and Judah. Tamar was initially Judah's daughter-in-law, as she married his son Er; when Er died childless, Judah married her off to his second son Onan, according to the rule of levirate marriage (Deut. 25:5–10). Onan was supposed to raise up a son for Er, but Onan 'spilled his seed on the ground' to avoid conception; he then died. Judah told Tamar to live as a widow in her father's house again until his son Shelah was old enough to marry, but in reality he viewed Tamar as a curse and resisted the levirate arrangement. After Judah's wife died, however, Tamar covered her face in the style of a prostitute (interestingly) and went off to the entrance road of Timnah, offering herself to Judah, anonymously, in order to continue Judah's line (actually following what Deut. 25:5–10 intended). As payment she received his staff, seal and cord in security for a goat. After this encounter, when she was accused of prostitution on account of becoming pregnant, she sent the staff, seal and cord to Judah as proof that he had caused the pregnancy, after which he dropped the accusation. He said, 'She is more righteous than I am, in that I did not give her my son Shelah' (Gen. 38:26). It is implied that Judah then married her, and she gave birth to twins Perez and Zerah, but he had no further relations with her (Gen. 38:24–30). In this story the indication is that there was something culpable about Judah in not following the Mosaic law (even though he was usually righteous), and visiting a prostitute on the road was hardly a case of moral excellence. It is Tamar who is actually more righteous. Judah eventually does the right thing, but does the wrong thing first. Eusebius in fact tells the story of Judah and Tamar in a similar way, exonerating Tamar and blaming Judah (*Quaest. Steph.* 7:1–2).

The story of Salmon and Rahab is not recorded in Scripture, and thus in their case the genealogy asks readers to draw knowledge from wider Jewish oral storytelling, indeed a midrashic story that has now been lost. In Scripture, Salmon is noted as the father of Boaz (Ruth 4:21; 1 Chr. 2:11). Rahab's story is told in Joshua 2: while working as a prostitute she hid two Israelite spies in Jericho, knowing that God had given the land to Israel. The Israelites spare her and her family when they take Jericho (6:25), but there is no mention of any marriage with Salmon. However, in Deuteronomy 7:1–4 it is said of the Canaanites (such as Rahab) that the Israelites should show 'no favour to them' and 'you shall not marry them; you shall not give your daughters to their sons, nor shall you take their daughters for your sons'. So, in Salmon marrying Rahab, Salmon contravenes the law of Deuteronomy, yet marries someone who is remembered as truly faithful and righteous. Rahab (spelled *Raab*) is applauded in Hebrews 11:31 for her faith, and in James 2:25 she is identified as 'righteous', which indicates a memory of Rahab in which she is far from immoral but rather held in great esteem.[81] This trajectory would continue: she was remembered by later rabbis as being so righteous that she was considered the model proselyte and was said to have married the Israelite leader Joshua.[82] They seem to know nothing of Salmon, but here we might assume that in a lost story Salmon, like Judah, does the right thing in marrying her, though it might not look like it, given that she is a Canaanite and a prostitute.

The book of Ruth belongs to the time of the judges when Israel was at war with the Canaanites and other peoples (Judg. 1:1, 3). The Moabites are derided as the children of Lot by incest with one of his daughters (Gen. 19:37–8). In Deuteronomy 23:3 there is a total ban on marriage to Moabites: no Moabite is allowed to enter the congregation of Israel through marriage, including to their tenth generation. However, in this story a man of Bethlehem, Elimelech, went with his wife Naomi and two sons to stay in the land of Moab, and the sons of Elimelech flouted this rule by marrying Moabite women, and then died, leaving the Moabite Ruth and her sister-in-law Orpah as widows. Orpah stayed in Moab, but Ruth came to live with Naomi in Bethlehem. The Bethlehemites were – as expected – scornful of her (Ruth 1:19), and the error here is that no man in the wider family of Elimelech would come forward to raise up a child to his name or to that of his son, so again there was a breakdown of levirate marriage. But Boaz, a kinsman of Elimelech, accepted that Ruth should feed herself and her mother-in-law by harvesting the edges of his grain field. Naomi, seeking Ruth's marriage to Boaz, devised a plan whereby Ruth slept at his feet by the harvested grain and basically asked him to marry her in order to 'redeem' her from widowhood; he would also be required to purchase a field that had belonged to Elimelech. Boaz first offered the opportunity for this marriage to a man who was a closer relative, but he rejected it, since to marry Ruth would have jeopardised his own inheritance (4:6), and so finally Boaz married Ruth, and they had a son, Obed, father of Jesse, father of David. Obed was considered the replacement son of Elimelech and Naomi (4:16–17).[83] Ruth had acted ingeniously to further the law of Deuteronomy 25:5–10 while the men of the family showed no initiative. Boaz stepped in as a righteous man who showed compassion and did what was right in the end. While the law stated that no one should marry a Moabite, the rule to raise up sons for the fallen male line is hereby shown as more important. Boaz did the right thing while apparently also doing the wrong thing.

In the story of 2 Samuel 11, David saw Bathsheba, the wife of the Hittite Uriah, taking a bath while he was on the roof of his palace, and – despite knowing she was married – he called for her and had sex with her. This contravened the law regarding adultery (Deut. 5:18). Bathsheba became pregnant, and David then got Uriah killed in battle by placing him in the front line, and after that Bathsheba became David's wife. In Matthew, calling her 'she of Uriah' (Matt. 1:6) has the effect of emphasising David's adultery. After Nathan the prophet reprimanded David for his actions (2 Sam. 12), the child conceived by his adulterous and coercive action died. At the end, though, David and Bathsheba became the parents of the great king Solomon, and thus, after breaking the law and repenting, David was rewarded with a fine son. He did the wrong thing, and then he did the right thing.

The genealogy, therefore, presents instances in which men who were supposed to be righteous did not do the right thing regarding progeny, and yet a God-given rightful conception was worked out anyway. Judah recognised his error, while Salmon and Boaz simply ignored the rule not to marry either a Canaanite or a Moabite. David erred terribly but then fathered Solomon with Bathsheba as his wife. The most egregious error was that of David.

In the story of Matthew, Joseph, who was righteous, is right in not wanting to publicly expose Mary, even though to divorce her was his prerogative and would seem socially correct, but he was clearly wrong for initially thinking of sending Mary away for the sake of social propriety. Then, in living with her as his wife and in doing the right thing, he would have been considered wrong by the public, in that people would have supposed he had fathered Jesus prior to the right time for the consummation of the marriage, and possibly even before the betrothal. He was a true son of David.

Conceived in iniquity?

Importantly, David's intense repentance for his error was expressed in one of the most poignant psalms: Psalm 51, with its title indicating it was written as 'a psalm of David when Nathan the prophet came to him after he had gone in to Bathsheba'. Given the title, the psalm should also be considered in our reading of the genealogy. It is noteworthy that it is also a psalm of inward cleansing (Ps. 51:7, 10), outlining what David will do for God in the future: 'I will teach transgressors your ways, and sinners will be converted to you' (Ps. 51:13). It culminates in a future hope with a strongly messianic ring: 'By your grace do good to Zion, build up the walls of Jerusalem!' (Ps. 51:18). Jesus, so named, will 'save his people from their wrongdoings' (Matt. 1:21), after all.

There is also a curious statement in David's repentant outpouring of Psalm 51 regarding his own conception: 'I was generated in iniquity; in sin my mother conceived me' (Ps. 51:5).[84] In due course this gave rise to the idea that there was something not quite right in terms of David's conception. A midrashic text that quotes this passage,[85] *Leviticus Rabbah* (14:5), goes on:

> Even if one be the most pious of the pious, it is impossible that he should have no streak of iniquity in him. David said before the Holy One, blessed be He: 'O Lord of the Universe! Did my father Jesse have the intention of bringing me into the world? Why, his intention was his own enjoyment; the proof for this is that after they had accomplished their desire, he turned his face in one direction and she turned her face in the opposite direction, and it was Thou that didst cause every single drop [of semen] to enter, and this is what David meant when he said, 'For though my father and my mother forsook me, the Lord did gather me in.'[86]

This picks up on the fact that the whole of Psalm 51 – the psalm of David composed after his adultery with Bathsheba – is strongly focused on repentance and inward purification. It brings in also Ecclesiastes 7:20: 'Truly there is no one so righteous so as to do good without ever sinning.'[87] The details of David's conception are even graphically presented, whereby the 'iniquity' was about some form of non-penetrative sex or coitus interruptus, done for pleasure rather than for purpose, so that semen was not deposited in the womb. Non-penetrative sex was specifically decried in Genesis 38:1–10 (as the 'sin' of Onan). Despite this, God put 'every drop [of semen]' into David's mother's womb.[88] In the Second Temple period, sex was understood by Jews to be justified only for procreation, so in the first-century CE Jewish text Pseudo-Phocylides it is commanded that a man should not have sex with his wife when she is pregnant (*Sent.* 186),[89] a rule we find Joseph adhering to in Matthew 1:25. This in itself implies that Joseph had high standards of behaviour for himself.

Matthew's story flows on directly from the emphatic mention at the end of the genealogy that from Abraham to David there were fourteen generations, from David to the deportation to Babylon there were fourteen generations, and from the deportation to the Anointed there were fourteen generations (Matt. 1:17), which, as we have seen, emphasises the numerical value of the name 'David' (DVD), so that Matthew is even prepared to jump over ancestors to ensure the neat fit.[90] For Matthew the key theme is that Jesus – through Joseph – is Davidic. When it comes to Jesus' birth, it forms a conclusion of the genealogy that should then also cohere with the Davidic theme. The genealogy should end with some clinching indication. As such, it is indicated that a certain moral quandary and vacillation over action would be entirely in keeping with ancestral stories.

So was Joseph assured, then, that the seed he did not plant in Mary's womb was his, as *Leviticus Rabbah* indicates regarding David's conception by Jesse? *Leviticus Rabbah* was written down in the fifth century CE,[91] and even though it purports to include ancient traditions, it is always an issue to know how far back they can be traced.[92] Many such stories (such as the one about Salmon and Rahab) did not survive at all, but by the time this one was written down it may have been different from what was circulating in the first century BCE. Nevertheless, Psalm 51:5 states what it states, purportedly from David. In the light of it, given Jesus' Davidic identity, it was appropriate for a certain 'iniquity' to be perceived in Jesus' birth. Like David, in Psalm 51:5, there was the issue of whether Jesus' conception, as a descendant of David, was considered quite right. Moreover, given the ideas lying behind the portrayal of David's conception in *Leviticus Rabbah*, Matthew's story could also be read as saying that God miraculously acted in Mary's womb with Joseph's seed, despite no penetrative sex (or any other intimate behaviour), and this only proved how much Jesus was the expected Son of David. Joseph's righteous reputation might well have been tarnished, but for a good reason.

Read this way, this is all about Joseph being affirmed as Jesus' real father.

The action of the Holy Spirit

Given that a reading of the fatherhood of Joseph is being indicated in this story in Matthew, the miraculous action of Holy Spirit is appealed to here as a means of attributing the pregnancy to Joseph despite Mary's virginity. Joseph is reassured by the angel's words. While previous male ancestors 'begot' sons from (*ek*) certain women, Mary is pregnant 'from (*ek*) Holy Spirit' (Matt. 1:18) and 'what is conceived (*gennēthen*, a passive form) is from (*ek*) Holy Spirit' (1:20). Ambiguously, the word *ek* in Greek can signify various relationships with the noun it governs, including origin (material, parentage, place, author),[93] but it can also indicate cause, instrument or the means by which something is done.[94] Mary's conception is presented as a miracle, given her virginity, but, as we know now, and as any family-planning clinic will warn us, a child can be conceived in female bodies without penetrative sex with a male.[95] Joseph is asked to trust this conception: the Holy Spirit has acted on the 'ground' of Mary's womb to create it.

What exactly, then, does the Holy Spirit do? Andrew Lincoln has noted how God can 'open' wombs or close them, as we see with Rachel, whose womb is finally opened by God (Gen. 30:1–2, 22–3), and thus in Psalm 139:13–16, a psalm of David, it is said: 'You formed my inward parts, you wove me together in my mother's womb.' That does not imply a miracle; it is simply what God does to create human life. God fashions human beings in the womb (Job 10:8–12; 31:15; Isa. 44:2, 24; 49:1–6; Jer. 1:5). There are three involved in the creation of a baby: a male, a female, and God, who does the work of growing the child. Therefore, the role of the male seed, even in a divine intervention, would simply be assumed.[96] In Scripture, God miraculously creates conceptions several times: Isaac in the womb of elderly Sarah, as mentioned (Gen. 18:10–14); Samson in the womb of Manoah (Judg. 13:2–3); Samuel in the womb of Hannah (1 Sam. 1:20). Therefore, in this story, it can be read that God has created this pregnancy miraculously (from the action of Holy Spirit), taking Joseph's seed and implanting it in Mary's womb; thus, it is 'from Holy Spirit'.[97]

In this reading, the conception of Jesus is still imagined as miraculous, but not involving divine 'seed'. Indeed, as a story told by Joseph, or his family, or early Nazarenes, it is unlikely that anyone could possibly have believed that the 'Holy Spirit' of God acted in lieu of human male seed. While there were stories of angels (understood as male) fathering human children (Gen. 6:1–4; *1 Enoch* 1 – 36),[98] the Holy Spirit is not an angel. In Judaism the Holy Spirit was understood to be a guide (Isa. 63:11–12; Ps. 2:10–12).[99] This is all consistent with the idea that God's Spirit can be equated with Wisdom (*Hokmah*; in Greek *Sophia*), a feminine dimension of God who in the book of Proverbs guides Israel and inspires prophets (Prov. 1:20–1; 2:2–4; 3:14–18; 4:7–8; 8:1–36; 9:1–12).

However, there is another dimension of Wisdom (as Holy Spirit). Wisdom was also established from the beginning of creation and acts as creative energy (Wisd. Sol. 7:22 – 8:8; Prov. 8:22–30).[100] In Psalm 104:30, addressing God, the psalmist states: 'You send out your Spirit, and they are created'. In Job 33:4 we read: 'The Spirit of God has made me, and the breath of the Almighty gives me life.' In the writings of the Jewish philosopher Philo, Wisdom is the archetypal divine daughter. She is 'the Mother and Nurse of all' (*Ebr.* 31), the Mother 'through whom the universe came to be' (*Fug.* 109).

The Spirit as creative energy, then, is essentially a feminine dimension of God for Jews of the Second Temple period. Jerome notes that in the Aramaic Matthew used by the Nazarenes there is a saying of Jesus that indicated Jesus himself thought of the Holy Spirit as his divine Mother:[101]

> But in the Gospel which is written according to the Hebrews, read by the Nazaraei, the Lord says: 'A short time ago my Mother, the Holy Spirit, took me up.' But no one ought to be scandalised by this, because the Hebrews speak of the Spirit in feminine gender, with our language (Latin) we use the masculine gender, and Greek the neuter. (*Comm. Isa.* 40:9–11)

This is also found quoted in Origen (*Comm. Joh.* 2:12:87; *Hom. Jer.* 15:4): 'Just now my Mother, the Holy Spirit, took me up by one of my hairs and carried me up to the great mountain, Tabor.'[102] In the same gospel, at Jesus' baptism by John 'the entire fount of the Holy Spirit descends upon him'. The Spirit is the divine Mother, as she speaks to him saying, 'My son, in all the prophets I was waiting for you, that you would come, and I would rest in you. For you are my rest, you are my firstborn son, who will rule forever.'[103]

Indeed, as Jerome well knew,[104] in Hebrew the term *ruakh haqqodesh*, 'Holy Spirit', is feminine, and also in Aramaic: *rukha d-qudsha*, 'spirit of holiness', or *rukha qaddishta*, 'Holy Spirit'; in Greek it is *to pneuma to hagion* (neuter) and in Latin it is *spiritus sanctus* (masculine). Anyone speaking Hebrew and Aramaic would more naturally incline to understand this dimension of God in feminine terms. Christian Jews, using Aramaic Matthew, could not have read Jesus' conception from Holy Spirit as involving divine male seed. Even in a Gentile Christian context this was not accepted: in the *Gospel of Philip*, a second/third-century gnostic work written in Syria,[105] the idea that the Holy Spirit somehow 'fathered' Jesus is directly dismissed: 'Some said, "Mary conceived by the Holy Spirit." They are in error. They do not know what they are saying. When did a woman ever conceive by a woman?' (*Gos. Phil.* 55:23–6). In this thinking, the virgin and feminine Holy Spirit could be understood to 'birth' Jesus at the time of his baptism in the River Jordan (*Gos. Phil.* 71:3–16).[106] As the Valentinian *Testimony of Truth* (39:26–30) has it: 'The Holy Spirit came down upon him as a dove [at his baptism], therefore we accept that he was born of a Virgin.'

We can see the personification of the Spirit of God in Syrian Judaism in a wall painting from the third-century synagogue in Dura Europos, now in the Damascus Museum (see Plate 5). Here, the Spirit – presented much like the Greek goddess Psyche – is shown in stop motion descending from heaven, and then bending over dead bodies to revivify them, fulfilling God's proclamation: 'I will put my Spirit in you and you will live' (Ezek. 37:14; and see 37:15–28).[107] Thus, in a reading of Matthew, in Aramaic/Syriac, the action of Holy Spirit would have been that of a creative, life-giving feminine entity.[108]

All in all, then, Matthew's story of the conception and birth of Jesus can well be read as indicating that Joseph is the actual father of Jesus, whose seed (of David) was miraculously implanted in Mary's womb *from the action of* the Holy Spirit of God. It is Joseph's story, and he is shown as being an exemplary son of David with interpretative skills involving dreams and Scripture, aided by angels. We are directed in this story only to think of him and his moral quandary, and Mary is muted. Joseph initially made the wrong choice, but – thanks to his pondering on dreams and Scripture – he made the right choice in the end, accepting that he would endure public criticism. Thus he provides a model in his own right, and Jesus' curious conception too is shown to be quite appropriate for one of Davidic descent.

Naming

This section of Matthew's Gospel ends with the naming of Jesus, as if all the auspicious conception story would provide a reason for his name. In many traditional societies, your name's meaning is significant and an important part of your identity, as has been much studied anthropologically in the field of onomastics.[109] A naming ceremony provides an opportunity to explain why a particular name is chosen. In Matthew 1:18–25 the story concludes with Joseph's naming of the baby. This naming would normally have taken place at the circumcision ceremony, on the eighth day after birth, but the circumcision of Jesus is here not mentioned.

The angel in Joseph's dream instructs him to call the baby both Immanuel, meaning 'God with us', from Isaiah 7:14, and *Iēsous*, Jesus, 'for he will save his people from their wrongdoings' (Matt. 1:21). The passage in Isaiah is a promise that God will act to overthrow oppressive rulers while Immanuel is still a young boy: 'the land of two kings will be laid waste' (7:16). It was not understood as a messianic prediction. Rather, this might well be a message of liberation from both Herod and the Roman emperor, Augustus, who were a threat to both the family and Judaea as a whole. Joseph duly does what he is told. After the child was born, 'he called his name *Iēsous*' (1:25). This suggests that Joseph was conscious of the significance of the name, and in giving this name he expected great things. Jesus would be named after the famous military leader of Israel, Joshua – in Hebrew *Yehoshua* or Aramaic *Yeshua* – who established the twelve tribes in the land: transcribed into the Greek of the Septuagint, Joshua's name was *Iēsous*, Jesus.

We know now from ossuaries found in many tombs in ancient Judaea, especially in Jerusalem, that forms of this name were common in the Second Temple period.[110] The name Joshua/Jesus was understood to mean 'safety/salvation of the Lord' (*sōtēria kuriou*) by the Greek-speaking

Philo of Alexandria (*Mut.* 121).[111] This is not correct in biblical Hebrew: *Yehoshua* probably means 'Yahweh helps'. Nevertheless, also in the Greek (LXX) version of Sirach 46:1–2 it is said that Joshua was named appropriately because 'he became great concerning the salvation/deliverance of his chosen people'. This shows an influence from Aramaic, where *Yeshua* does indeed mean 'salvation', 'redemption' or 'deliverance'.[112] Deliverance here is national, not personal. In Isaiah, God allows Israel to be defeated by enemies because of the nation's wrongdoings (e.g. Isa. 5:7–30), but hope will arise: there will be a prince of peace on the throne of David (Isa. 9:2–7). This reflects a view associated with the narrative of Deuteronomy (esp. chs 31 – 32) in which Israel's wrongdoings are followed by God's judgement and then restoration, a cycle widely accepted in Second Temple writings.[113] It was quite a provocative name to give to a child of the line of David. This name alone would have signalled to a growing boy that there were certain expectations of him acting in a way that would lead to benefits for Israel.

In Matthew 1:11–25, then, from the genealogy to the miraculous conception and birth of Jesus and his naming, this is a story of 'Anointed Jesus, Son of David', whose naming would stamp him with hope. If told as part of the stories of the family, Jesus himself would have grown up with a sense that he was expected to do great things.

The magi and the star

Once the story of the ancestry and birth of Jesus as son of David is completed, a new story unit begins (Matt. 2:1–18). It launches into something that seems different in terms of focus, but it will loop back to Joseph. His experience and implied memories remain central. It is stated: 'After Jesus was born in Bethlehem in Judaea, in the days of Herod the king, magi (*magoi*) from the East came to Jerusalem'. Given that we have had no clues to location or date hitherto, readers[114] are suddenly grounded. We are told where the location is: Bethlehem of Judaea. We have Jerusalem named too, with an implication of proximity, but there is no further introduction about where these locations are; it is as if they are familiar. This was 'in the days of Herod the king'. His days are not now. We are looking back. But readers are expected to know who 'Herod the king' is, as ruler of Judaea. The reference implies Judaean memory.[115]

It seems to be assumed that readers also know there is a terrible relationship between the descendants of David, living in Bethlehem, and Herod, who is dangerous and cannot be trusted. As we have seen, Herod the Great, the Roman client king of the Judaeans (37–4 BCE), built a fortress-palace named Herodion close to Bethlehem to commemorate a battle victory over 'Judaeans' supportive of the Parthian-backed rival king Antigonus Mattathias, who had attacked him. Building Herodion in such close proximity to Bethlehem, it was as if Herod wanted to send a signal to everyone there. His tomb trumped any tombs down in the valleys and created a massive white landmark visible for miles around.[116]

Herod had nine wives and numerous children, who were resident in his various palaces, but by 6 BCE he had killed his favourite wife Mariamme, and her mother Alexandra, and two of his sons (*War* 1:445–581; *Ant.* 16:66 – 17:61). Before his death, he would kill one more son, and a host of other people, and we will return to this presently. For now, we can note simply that in the story told by Josephus, based on the records of Herod's courtier Nicolaus, the king was fanatically alert to any sign that anyone would seize his throne. We have already seen how Josephus presents him pillaging the Tomb of David in Jerusalem, and there was a memory that he burned family records of the Davidic line.

We learn that magi arrived from 'the East' in Jerusalem, but there is no country specified. It is said that they asked where the new king was, since they had followed a star 'when it rose' and had come to honour (*proskunēsai*) him. Herod was stirred up (*etarachthē*) 'and all Jerusalem with him', and thus Herod was positioned there in the city at the time, and there is an appeal to social memory of disturbance. The authoritative 'chief priests and scribes' identified Bethlehem as the correct location for the future king, citing the all-important reference to Micah 5:2. This identification relies on knowledge that this priestly class were authoritative in scriptural interpretation.

Herod is clearly the enemy: untrustworthy and manipulative. As it is written, Herod secretly (*lathra*) called for these magi and gained information about when the star appeared; then he sent them off to Bethlehem and asked them to search for the child and report back to him, 'so that I too may come and honour (*proskunēsō*) him' (2:8). At this point, the story relies on a reader response that would assume Herod to be a terrible threat, though as yet within the text nothing has been indicated as a clue, apart from the fact that Herod was stirred up.

The story goes on to tell how the magi went on their way from Jerusalem to Bethlehem 'and the star they had seen when it rose went ahead of them until it halted over the place where the child was' (Matt. 2:9). They found the child after the star they had tracked went on before them until it came and stayed in position. On coming to the household (*oikia*), they saw Mary and the child, fell down and honoured (*prosekunēsan*) him. They gave him gold, frankincense and myrrh. They then learned of God's wishes in a dream, and they did not go back to Herod but 'returned to their country by another road' (2:12).

In this narrative unit, from a small family crisis focused on one household we suddenly pull back to a grand drama about a king in Jerusalem, visiting astronomers, a disturbed population and the Davidic line in Bethlehem. We are led to imagine the vista of the sky, a sweep of stars, and journeys over landscapes. Furthermore, despite much being made in the former unit of the naming of Jesus, in this story he is repeatedly just called 'the child' (*to paidion*). The only specific identifier comes in Matthew 2:11 when there is reference to 'the child with Mary his mother'. The story seems to have been shaped, in that it demonstrates aspects of Matthew's own way of expressing things. For example, Matthew is fond of the verb *proskuneō*, 'to honour' or 'to worship', which literally means 'kiss towards' as an act of devotion. In Matthew, quite distinctively, it is the fitting attitude towards Jesus of a leper (8:2) and the Canaanite woman (15:25) later on in the Gospel, and the appropriate attitude of the two Marys, or the disciples as a whole, on seeing the risen Jesus (28:9, 17). In total it is used thirteen times (2:2, 8, 11; 8:2; 9:18; 14:33; 15:25; 20:20; 28:9, 17). This is how the magi are said to respond to the 'child'.

An unusual star seems to be appealed to as part of social memory. The star would have been momentous in terms of meaning. The arrival of a star is particularly linked with the birth of the Anointed (King, Messiah, Christ) who would rule over Israel and vanquish all of Israel's enemies, because it was associated with the star in the ancient prophecy of the non-Jewish diviner Balaam:

A star shall come out of Jacob
And a sceptre will rise out of Israel.

It shall crush the foreheads of Moab
And break down the sons of Sheth.
(Num. 24:17b–19)

Matthew does not explicitly quote this passage, but it is probably implied, since it was very widely known as a prediction of the future king.[117] In the first century, Philo of Alexandria refers to the prophecy of Balaam concerning this future ruler in his *Life of Moses*: 'There shall come forth from you one day a man and he shall rule over many nations, and his kingdom spreading every day shall be exalted on high' (*Mos.* 1:290). The story of Balaam is given much space in Josephus's *Antiquities* (4:102–58).[118] In the second century, Rabbi Akiba apparently identified the revolutionary leader Bar Kosiba as the expected 'Star' (*j. Ta'an.* 4:68d), and he duly became known as 'Bar Kokhba', Son of the Star.

In Matthew, the astronomers who recognise the expected Messiah of the Judaeans are foreigners, but it is not clear where they came from. The word *magoi*, for the magi, was known in the West, because in the fifth century BCE Herodotus mentions them as an order of Persian priests (*Hist.* 3:61–80; 7:37), though they are not here associated with expertise in astronomy. Xenophon identifies them as an order of priests established by Cyrus (*Cyropaedia* 8:1:23). They were considered to be dream-interpreters (Cicero, *On Divination* 1:46). Given the association with Persia – and therefore Parthia – George van Kooten has well explored the implications in the light of Roman–Parthian relations,[119] though there is a fundamental problem in seeing them as Parthians in the story as we have it, given the Parthians' backing of Antigonus Mattathias. Herod, with the Roman army of Mark Antony under Sossius, had in 37 BCE crushed not only Antigonus but also the Parthians who supported him. Their chosen ruler on the throne of Judaea was replaced by Rome-backed Herod. It is quite hard to imagine that three decades later three Parthian priests would turn up in Jerusalem to state that they had worked out that another rightful king had been born in Judaea, and this king was not anyone in the house of Herod. Perhaps, though, this story is some relic of the Parthian support for Antigonus, vindicating him as the rightful king by virtue of astrology.

But were the magi, or rather the *magoi*, Parthians? Philo knows that *magoi* may be expert Persians (= Parthians) who 'silently research the faces of nature to gain knowledge of the truth through visions clearer than speech, and give and receive the revelations of divine excellency' (*Prob.* 74), but he states that there are cheap local imitations (*Spec.* 3:100), and he can even use the term *magoi* to indicate magicians generally who appear along with 'wise men', *sophoi* (*Mos.* 1:92), and sorcerer-druggists, *pharmakeutai* (*Spec.* 3:100). In Philo's *Life of Moses* (1:276) the word *magos* is used for Balaam, whose skill in *magikos*, 'magic', is trumped by an actual prophetic spirit, which possessed him and made him predict the future ruler as a star despite himself (Num. 24:17). Balaam is described here as coming from Mesopotamia (*Mos.* 1:264, 278), which for Philo indicates he was a Chaldean (*Abr.* 188): a Babylonian, expert in astrology/astronomy. Philo writes about them in a number of his works, and he associates Abraham with one who has particular knowledge of this science.[120]

Origen would see the *magoi* as descendants of Balaam (*Hom. Num.* 13:7; 15:4–5),[121] an understanding followed by other Christian scholars,[122] but the provenance of Balaam is vague, regarded as being somewhere in the East.[123] Clement, bishop of Rome at the end of the first century, in fact understood 'the East' to refer to 'Arabia and the countries round about' (*1 Clem.* 25:1). Such a notion is found in the comments of Justin Martyr in the second century:

> And that one is about to arise like a star from the family of Abraham, Moses intimated this, saying [through Balaam] that 'a star shall arise from Jacob, and a leader from Israel' [Num. 24:17], and another [passage of] Scripture says, 'Behold a man; his name is East' [Zech. 6:12 LXX].' Therefore, when a star actually rose in heaven at the time of his birth, as written in the memoirs of his apostles, the *magoi* from Arabia came to a decision from this and came and honoured (*prosekunēsan*) him.
> (*Dial.* 106:4)

Justin by this time had 'memoirs of the apostles', perhaps the four canonical Gospels, and also local knowledge since he hailed from Sebaste in Palestine. For him, it was so clear that the magi came from Arabia that he hardly mentions them without also defining their provenance; they are the '*magoi* from Arabia' (*Dial.* 77:4, 78:1 (×2), 5, 7; 88:1; 102:2, 103:3).

Justin knew that Arabia encompassed the kingdom of the Nabataeans, which had become the Roman 'Provincia Arabia' in the year 104 CE, but that earlier it had included Damascus.[124] He relates this to a prophecy of Isaiah, 'he shall take the power of Damascus and the spoils of Samaria' (Isa. 8:4), stating that the *magoi* coming to honour Jesus fulfilled this scripture because the evil demon's power in Damascus – to which the *magoi* were held in bondage – was then overcome by Christ.[125]

If the magi were Arabs this also makes sense of the comment that the magi 'returned to their country by another road' (2:12), after Bethlehem, as if more than one particular road led to it. Nabataea bordered on Judaea on the east, while Parthia hugged the River Euphrates, hundreds of miles away. This statement also suggests very local knowledge. While many towns and villages were situated so that someone arriving from elsewhere would have to backtrack to get home, people travelling from Arabia could go towards Jerusalem from the east, and then south to Bethlehem, but return from Bethlehem without going back to Jerusalem: they would go south past Herodion, then on to Thekoa and Engeddi, then travel around the southern Dead Sea to Nabataea, or take a vessel over the water (the route Herod took when fleeing from Antigonus and the Parthians, and see Fig. 3:1).

Also, it is clear now that Arabians (Nabataeans) included astral interests in their religion, particularly evidenced in the temple excavated at Khirbet Tannur, where the goddess Allat (meaning 'Goddess') is surrounded by a distinctive zodiac, and the zodiac has a prominent position also in the temple of Khirbet ed-Dharih.[126] The hellenised Nabataeans would have been *au fait* with the permutations of Hellenistic astronomy/astrology and had close ties with Hellenistic Egypt where there was a sophisticated study of the stars based at the temples of Serapis.[127] Strabo refers to the Nabataeans worshipping the sun, with altars on the roofs of their temples, where they burn frankincense (*Geogr.* 16:4:26).

Indeed, the gifts of frankincense and myrrh given to Jesus are typical of Arabia, not of Parthia. The first-century BCE historian Diodorus Siculus states:

> While there are many Arabian tribes who use the desert as pasture, the Nabataeans far surpass the others in wealth although they are not much more than ten thousand in number; for not a few of them

are accustomed to bring down to the sea frankincense and myrrh and the most valuable kinds of spices, which they procure from those who convey them from what is called Arabia Eudaemon. (*Bibl. Hist.* 94:4–6)

Diodorus then describes how Athenaeus, the general of the Macedonian king Demetrius Poliorcetes, took Petra (in 312 BCE) and seized these precious items (*Bibl. Hist.* 95:2–3): 'and of the frankincense and myrrh he gathered together the larger part, and about five hundred talents of silver.' Thus precious metals, frankincense and myrrh are defined as particularly Arabian. The bringing of gifts was common practice in the honouring of royalty. In his second visit to Babylon, Alexander the Great apparently received aromatic gifts from Chaldean priests (known to be astronomers) who had predicted that a great king would come (Diodorus Siculus, *Bibl. Hist.* 17:112).[128] And Herod was likely to accept a Nabataean delegation. Herod's mother Cypros was Nabataean, and, though he had a fraught relationship with the Nabataeans and had fought them in significant battles,[129] they were an ally of Rome, unlike the Parthians.

While the star in Matthew functions as a geographical pointer to the birth of a king in Judaea, and a clinching indication that Jesus is the Anointed, scholars have long wondered if there was some memory of an actual astronomical event. If there was, then it is very likely that stories of various kinds were told about it. All ancient societies in the region were involved in understanding the stars in various ways for navigation, calendars, science, cult and predictions. The Judaean people too were speculating a great deal about the meaning of astrological phenomena.[130] Josephus notes that many *sophoi* (wise ones) were thinking about signs in the heavens (*War* 6:312–13). The importance of the stars in Judaism is shown in the breastplate worn by the high priest, which had twelve precious stones that related both to the twelve tribes of Israel and to the twelve signs of the zodiac. The zodiac is a common image on synagogue floors of the fourth to sixth centuries.[131] The Dead Sea Scrolls contain numerous astrological texts, which indicates an interest in the science of prediction.[132] As such, it is quite remarkable that in this story it is *foreign* astrologers who are said to work out the birth of a king in Judaea.

There are other records of a star, but they are not exactly as in Matthew. The memory of a star connected with Jesus' birth is recorded in Ignatius of Antioch's *Letter to the Ephesians* where he writes:

How then was [Christ] revealed to the aeons: a star shone in heaven brighter than all the stars and its light was ineffable, and its novelty caused astonishment. All the other stars together with the sun and moon became a chorus for the star and it outshone them all with its light and there was perplexity about where this novelty so unlike them came from, so all magic was destroyed and every bond vanished.
(*Ephes.* 19:2–3)

The second-century *Protevangelium of James*, which we will consider later on, similarly states that 'an indescribably great star shone among these stars and dimmed them, so that they no longer shone' (*Prot. Jas* 17:21). Likewise, an early gnostic Christian named Theodotus, a disciple of the gnostic teacher Valentinus, apparently stated:

Therefore the Lord came down, bringing those on earth the peace that is from heaven . . . a strange and new star arose, doing away with the old astral decree, shining with a new unearthly light, which revolved on a new path of salvation, as the Lord himself, a guide for all people, came to transfer from Fate to his providence those who believed in Christ.[133]
(Clement of Alexandria, *Exc. Theod.* 74)

These attestations are about a very bright new star, rather than one 'in the east' that rested over Bethlehem (Matt. 2:2, 9–10), suggesting that there were other stories about a momentous star in circulation.

One of the problems in defining the star, and any memory of it if it existed, is that the date when all this was supposed to occur is debated. This would be even more complicated if the star was actually an echo from an earlier time, namely the Parthian endorsement of the kingship of Antigonus. If associated with Jesus' birth, the star might have appeared some two years before the *magoi* arrived, given that Herod wanted to kill all boys under the age of 2 after they left (Matt. 2:16), but Matthew gives no precise timeframe for anything. The *magoi* are said to arrive sometime before Herod died, but when was this? The date of his death is usually arrived at by means of Josephus's comment that his son Philip ruled for thirty-seven years and died in the twentieth year of the emperor Tiberius (October 32 – October 33 CE), so, working backwards, Herod would have died in 4 BCE (*Ant.* 17:79–81). Josephus says that Herod died just after a lunar eclipse and prior to Passover (*Ant.* 17:167). There was apparently a partial lunar eclipse on 13 March 4 BCE, but there were total eclipses in 5 BCE and 1 BCE, determined on the basis of comparing different astronomical records. The usual chronology, and the one followed here, favours 4 BCE.

In Matthew, it seems that only the *magoi* really knew about the star and could follow it. Herod had to ask them when they had spotted it (2:7), so it required a very high level of expertise and discernment. It was, then, not so very bright. That it was moving and stopping would probably indicate a planet, and the strange behaviour of the planet Jupiter is most suggestive, because Jupiter was associated with kingship. So, if we look to planetary events around this time, there was a close conjunction of Jupiter and Saturn on 29 May 7 BCE, and a close conjunction of Venus and Jupiter on 12 August 3 BCE. Among the many to work on the problem, astronomer David Hughes has explored how the conjunction of Jupiter and Saturn occurred three times in a row – a triple conjunction – in 7 BCE. This would not have made a very bright star, because the planets would not have been so close to veritably overlap, but it would have led to a particular interpretation: Jupiter, when associated with Saturn, represented royal change.[134]

On the other hand, given that there was a method of star interpretation which concerned the rise and fall of rulers, and the astrological horoscope charts associated with them,[135] we need to be alert to how this might have correlated with astronomical features. Michael Molnar has proposed that the *magoi* determined a natal horoscope of a ruler born in Judaea. The star was an occultation of Jupiter by the moon when Jupiter was in the east (the heliacal rising of Jupiter), which explains why the *magoi* saw a star in the east and went west. He thinks that this is indicated on a coin from the city of Antioch in Syria first issued by the Roman legate Quirinius in 6 CE. This coin shows the Ram (Aries) looking backwards with a star above.[136] Molnar defines the occultation as occurring much earlier than the date of the coin's issue, precisely on 17 April 6 BCE, when the sun, moon and Saturn were all in Aries.[137] He notes that the Egyptian astronomer Ptolemy (*Tetrabiblos* 2:3) associated Aries with Judaea.

However, Stephen Heilen notes that Ptolemy also associated Aries with Britain, Gaul, Germany, Bastarnia, Coele Syria (central Syria) and Idumaea.[138] We actually do not have enough ancient evidence to understand how anyone could have worked out that a king would be born specifically in Judaea in the first century BCE. If we look for a more exclusive, Messiah-focused, Judaean astrological geography, it takes us back to the triple conjunction in Pisces, but this is not attested until we get to the Jewish astrologer Māshā'allāh Ibn Athārī (*c.*640–815) from Basra.[139] So how sure can the date be?

Veracity concerning the star may be hard to come by, but some memory of a star interpreted as indicating royal change is not unlikely. As deployed in Matthew, the story underscores the identity of the expected Anointed as being from the house of David, born in Bethlehem of Judaea, since this birth is now recognised by experts who understand how to read the stars and who also receive messages in dreams (2:12). There *may* be a memory of an actual star being identified by certain *magoi* who came to Jerusalem and then went to Bethlehem – an event that utterly enraged Herod. The core story may not have been that *magoi* came to 'the child' *Jesus*, specifically, but the fact that they came to Jerusalem at all, looking for 'a child' on the basis of a royal horoscope, stirred expectations that a great king had been born, especially as Herod's death seemed imminent.

What then of possible family memories in this case? In this particular story, the focus is not initially on Joseph, and yet somehow the narrative reads as if it is Joseph's perspective, because ultimately it provides a rationale for his actions:

> So when they had got away, look – an angel of the Lord appeared in a dream to Joseph, saying, 'Get up and take the child and his mother, and flee to Egypt, and stay there till I tell you, because Herod is going to search for the child to do away with him.' And he got up, and took the child and his mother by night, and got away to Egypt.
> (Matt. 2:13–14)

Joseph has not been part of the magi story, but now he reappears, as if this is still his memory and telling. The story justifies why Joseph takes his family and leaves. The angel tells him to get up and take his family to Egypt, and stay there, because Herod was going to search out 'the child' and kill him. So Joseph then takes his family away, at night, to Egypt, and they stay there until the death of Herod (2:13–15). At this point, given that Joseph's method of prediction has previously been a combination of a dream (with angel) and a passage of Scripture, it is surprising that we are not in fact given the scriptural passage. We can easily find one, however, in Genesis 46:3 (as spoken to Jacob): 'I am God, the God of your father; do not be afraid to go down to Egypt, for I will make you a great nation there.' While we may be impressed by how many scriptural passages are crammed into Jesus' nativity in Matthew 1 – 2 to explain Joseph's movements, each angelic visitation in a dream should actually be paralleled with Scripture. That is the format.

The massacre of Bethlehem's male children

The story goes on to explain what happened in Bethlehem after Joseph took his family away to safety, again justifying Joseph's actions. We also get a supposed window into Herod's emotions: he feels he has been made to look foolish. This then is more a folk tale than a family memory recounting Joseph's experience. In this story, Herod has all the male children under 2 years old killed (Matt. 2:16–18). This horrific atrocity is linked with Scripture, in this case a somewhat modified form of Jeremiah 31:15. The spirit of Rachel herself is revivified to grieve at the terrible disaster:

> A voice was heard in Ramah,
> weeping and great mourning;
> it is Rachel weeping for her children,
> and she refuses to be comforted
> because they are no more.
> (Matt. 2:18)

This passage connects with a calamity befalling the descendants of Rachel in the vicinity of Bethlehem. While this prophecy was originally written in the context of the Babylonian threat in the sixth century BCE, it is brought into the story of Bethlehem and Herod by reference to the

Tomb of Rachel, as if the environment of Bethlehem was familiar. As we saw, the Tomb of Rachel lay just north of Bethlehem (see Chapter 3).

As we have also already seen, Herod did slaughter Judaeans in the vicinity of Bethlehem (Josephus, *Ant.* 14:359–60; *War* 1:265), in the year 40 BCE, shortly after a Parthian-backed (therefore magi-friendly) king took the throne of Judaea: Antigonus Mattathias. This terrible killing of sons of the town would have created trauma that passed down to the next generations. Studies of how political events are remembered by social groups have traced how people can remember nuggets of the past and shape them in line with their current identity; outright fabrication is rare, but modification is common.[140] In line with a Jewish understanding that Scripture predicted contemporary events, such as we see in the Qumran *pesharim* and Josephus, scriptural passages would have been brought out to make sense of that event, as here.

Josephus does not otherwise tell any story of a massacre of small children in Bethlehem, though he recorded many other horrendous deeds of Herod. This is not to say that it could not have happened, but the ramifications of such an immense atrocity would have been known widely. While we might set aside the precise details of this incident as actual, then, its barbarity is consistent with the memory of Herod, testifying to an understanding that Herod was deeply hostile to the family of David in Bethlehem. All the infants killed, living in Bethlehem, are assumed to be of David's line. But as a story, the implication is that it is told *by Joseph*, showing his skills as an interpreter of dreams and Scripture, and explaining his actions. In this narrative, Herod the king is a threat, a manipulator and an aggressor. It is a story that could well have been told to Jesus and his siblings. Jesus is remembered as having called Herod Antipas 'that fox' (Luke 13:32), after all, which creates a sense of Herod's son being a wily and deceitful predator to his own people.[141]

In the story of the massacre, there is another important allusion to a scriptural predecessor of Jesus: the prophet Moses.[142] In Exodus 1:22, Pharaoh declares that all newborn male Israelite children will be drowned in the Nile, but Moses is saved by being placed in a reed basket and floated in the water, where he is found by Pharaoh's daughter. This story of Pharaoh and the massacre of the Israelite children was told not only in Scripture but also in the later retelling of a surviving midrash, in *Exodus Rabbah*

(1:22). It is also retold in the Aramaic *Targum Pseudo-Jonathan* on Exodus 1:15, and here Pharaoh is informed by 'magi' or priests of a deliverer of the Hebrews. This text was finally redacted in the seventh century, but, as with other such stories, it likely contains traditions from the Second Temple period.[143] Clearly, in the first century, there were similar stories, as shown in the *Biblical Antiquities* in which Miriam, Moses' sister, has a dream in which an angel warns her to save Moses (*LAB* 9:10).[144]

In Josephus's retelling of Exodus, Pharaoh hears from one of the sacred scribes that there will be an Israelite saviour, and so he puts to death all the newborn Israelite boys (*Ant.* 2:205); Moses' father, Amran, has a dream that his son will become the future redeemer and acts to save him.[145] Considering all this imaginative retelling with elements that correspond to Matthew, Vermes attributes the source of Herod's massacre of the innocents to 'Jewish folklore'.[146] But this comparable evidence might also be used differently: the story in Matthew was told by someone absolutely steeped in both Scripture and Jewish folklore, namely a Judaean like Joseph himself. The echoes of Moses are so obvious they must have been presented consciously.

In Raymond Brown's view, such elements show that the infancy narrative of Matthew 1 – 2 can be separated out into 'Matthean' and 'pre-Matthean' strata.[147] He thought that the scriptural proof-texts were Matthean innovations, as these are typical of what is done throughout the Gospel, but there was something not so tidy that pointed to a pre-Matthean tradition. According to Brown, '[i]f a passage in the infancy narrative is almost purely Matthean in vocabulary and style, it is more likely that Matthew has composed the passage himself', but if 'Matthean peculiarities are mixed with neutral or non-Matthean features, the possibility increases that Matthew has edited a pre-Matthean tradition or narrative'.[148] Then, finally, Brown thought that shared material between Matthew and Luke could indicate not Lukan dependence but a pre-Matthean stratum, a core of which could be held to be historically true.[149] In terms of composition, Brown suggested that the author of Matthew edited this pre-Matthean material, but much of it could be discerned as a block.[150]

Brown located the Moses typology in the *pre-Matthean* block: first, Joseph the father of Jesus has dreams, just as Joseph the son of Israel has dreams in Genesis chapters 37, 39 – 48, where Joseph is a 'man of dreams' (Gen. 37:19). Joseph son of Israel is a dreamer like Joseph son of David, who also ends up in Egypt. Joseph son of Israel is involved with a wicked pharaoh in Egypt; Joseph son of David is involved with a wicked king and goes to Egypt. There is then a shift to the pharaoh of Exodus, and the conflict with Moses. In Exodus, Moses enrages Pharaoh by killing an Egyptian slave-master, and Pharaoh seeks to do away with Moses, so Moses flees to Midian (2:15); Pharaoh commands that Hebrew male children be killed (1:22); Pharaoh dies (2:23); God says to Moses in Midian, 'Go back to Egypt, for all those who were seeking your life are dead' (4:19); Moses takes his wife and children and returns to Egypt (4:20). In Matthew, Herod seeks to do away with Jesus, so Joseph takes Jesus and Mary to Egypt (2:13–14); Herod commands that all boys of 2 years of age and under in Bethlehem and environs be killed (2:16); Herod dies (2:19); an angel says to Joseph in Egypt, 'Go back to the land of Israel, for those who were seeking the child's life are dead'; Joseph takes the child and his mother back to the land of Israel (2:20–1).[151]

Brown then went on to consider the Jewish midrashic retellings of the story of Moses' birth and flight to Midian, particularly evidenced in two first-century works: the *Life of Moses* by Philo and Josephus's *Antiquities* (2:205–37). As noted, in the latter, Pharaoh is forewarned of the birth of a Hebrew leader by 'sacred scribes' (*Ant.* 2:205). This fills the Egyptians with dread (2:206, 215); Moses' father is warned in a dream to save his (yet unborn) son, who would deliver the Hebrew people from slavery (2:212, 215–16). In Matthew, Herod is alerted to the birth of a Judaean king by the magi (2:1–2); he and all Jerusalem are troubled (2:3); Joseph is warned to protect his son, 'who would save his people from their sins' (2:13; 1:21).[152]

This was clearly, then, all designed in order to underscore the veracity of events. But this does not mean the events were all entirely untrue. Scripture was supposed to corroborate, not invalidate. But if all this was in the pre-Matthean tradition, who was responsible for it? The clue lies in the figure of Joseph.

The signs of the times

Joseph is the hero and also an expert in prediction. Linking all the individual stories together in Matthew 1 – 2 are a sequence of Joseph's dreams and illuminating scriptural passages used to interpret what is taking place, guiding Joseph's actions. The magi themselves are 'expert' in listening to the Divine. Like Joseph, they can determine divine messages through dreams, and God directly speaks to them (Matt. 2:12). They are directed by Scripture also, in their case through the third party of the chief priests and scribes in Jerusalem, who point to Micah 5:2 (Matt. 2:4–6).

Centrally, the figure is Joseph, working on interpretation in order to understand the divine plan. As the Matthean Jesus would later state, advising his own disciples how to interpret events:

> When evening comes you say, 'The weather will be nice [tomorrow] because the sky is red,' and in the morning [you say], 'Today it will be stormy, because the sky is red and overcast.' You know how to interpret the look of the sky, but not the signs of the times. (Matt. 16:2–3; cf. Luke 12:54–6)

Here, then, we see Joseph fathoming out the signs of the times, because readers knew that dreams plus Scripture spelt revelation. Both dreams and Scripture contained inspiration: an angel, as God's messenger, speaks through a dream, and God speaks through the written word.

As we have seen, this was recognised as a method of reading Scripture in Second Temple Judaism. Events of the past, present and future were believed to be embedded symbolically within Scripture and could be drawn out in order to understand the present age. In the Qumran *pesharim*, which were interpretative readings of the 'signs of the times', we see this working the other way round. The scriptural text is quoted, and then how it relates to real-life events and people (whose names are hidden by sobriquets) is set out, particularly in regard to an esteemed Teacher of Righteousness and his opponent the Man of the Lie. For example, in the Habbakuk *pesher* (1QpHab 1:12–13) we read first a quote from Habbakuk 1:4: 'for the wicked will surround the righteous', and then the interpretation: 'the "wicked" is the Man of the Lie and "the righteous" is the Teacher of Righteousness.'

In Matthew, the fulfilment of Scripture is like a gong striking throughout the narrative. There is a pattern: dream (+ angel) and Scripture = action. As noted above, we are not given the relevant scriptural passage that was read as revealing the need to flee, even though we may find one in Genesis 46:3.[153] However, we *are* given the passage that was read to justify the return: '[Joseph] was there until the death of Herod, so that what was spoken by the Lord through the prophet would be fulfilled, in saying: "Out of Egypt I called my son"' (Matt. 2:15). The passage here is from Hosea 11:1. The 'son' in Hosea is historical Israel,[154] not Moses and not the Messiah. The text does not, therefore, appear to *prove* anything. Out of Hosea 11:1, it seems there is an interpretation about Jesus, like a back-to-front *pesher*. The subject of the sentence is Joseph as the active doer, as he is the active interpreter throughout, which leads to his action: 'he got up and took the child and his mother', 'he got away' and 'he was there' in Egypt, and then – apparently – a son is called back. We might expect Joseph to be called 'son', but there is a sudden shift from Joseph to Jesus, so that the focus is on Joseph protecting and enabling his own son to follow God's command. In this case the passage is detached from the angel's message to return (Matt. 2:19–20) and is found already in 2:15.

The sequence of Joseph's predictions runs as follows:

1 angel of the Lord in a dream + Isaiah 7:14: meaning Joseph should publicly accept Mary as his wife and name him Jesus when he is born, because he would save people from their sins (Matt. 1:20–5);
2 [angel of the Lord in] a dream + (Gen. 46:3?): meaning Joseph should take the child and his mother and flee to Egypt (Matt. 2:13–14);
3 angel of the Lord in a dream + Hosea 11:1: meaning Joseph should go back (Matt. 2:19–20, 15).

That not all elements are included supports Brown's impression that the Gospel-writer is shaping received material rather than inventing everything from scratch. The pre-Matthean tradition is, by implication, Joseph's.

The 'us' and 'them' of this narrative is clear. 'We' as readers are with Joseph, listening to his stories and crediting all he says as true, impressed by his predictions and testimony of angelic encounters in dreams. 'We' as readers know about Herod and the locations of Jerusalem and Bethlehem. The family of Jesus are even directly implied, because in Matthew 1:25 it is said that Joseph 'did not have sex with her (Mary) *until* (*heōs*) she had given birth to a son'. While this shows Joseph's righteousness, in following the principle that sex should only be for procreation,[155] it indicates that he *did* have sex with Mary after Jesus' birth and therefore fathered further children. These siblings of Jesus appear elsewhere in the Gospel: Mary and Jesus' siblings arrive outside a synagogue where Jesus is speaking and ask to talk to him (Matt. 12:46–50) and they appear also in Nazareth (13:53–8), with the brothers of Jesus named as in Mark, though curiously in a slightly different order, with Simon moving forward in sequence.[156]

We need, then, to think of Jesus' own family. As we saw, as fellow descendants of David and siblings of Jesus, the members of this group were remembered as being in leadership positions in the Judaean churches through to the early second century, at a time when belief in the physical paternity of Joseph, in passing on the line of David to Jesus as well as to them, is well attested. They were the ones who could authoritatively retell the memories of their father. Thus, their own testimony may well lie behind these stories and the interpretations given.[157]

Therefore, we should cast some doubt aside. Andrew Lincoln reflects widespread scholarly scepticism in stating that it is 'highly unlikely that there were reliable traditions stemming from Joseph in the case of Matthew . . . that only became accessible at a late date'.[158] But it is worthwhile asking what presuppositions lie behind this scepticism. Given that the relatives of Jesus were still alive and leading churches when the Gospel of Matthew itself was composed, out of *pre-existing* source material, why wouldn't the author have had any access to their stories?

Pantera

As a final matter here, it is important to consider one much later story too. In the middle of the second century there was a counter-narrative to that of Matthew, told in Jewish circles. We know of it from the anti-Christian philosopher Celsus, in his work *On the True Doctrine*, quoted by Origen. Celsus claims to reflect a Jewish source in suggesting that Jesus was illegitimate: 'the mother of Jesus' is described as having been 'turned out by the carpenter who was betrothed to her, as she had been convicted of adultery and had a child by a certain soldier named Panthera' (Origen, *Against Celsus* 1:32; cf. 1:33, 70).[159]

Celsus's story probably reflects accurately what was said in Jewish circles of his era, as it overlaps with a similar story later preserved in the

Babylonian Talmud (fifth century CE; *b.Shabb.* 104b and *b.Sanh.* 67a).[160] The name of this soldier can be found in later rabbinic texts in various forms – Pandera, Panderi, Panthera, Pantera, Pantiri[161] – and it likely results from a joke or pun: *panthera* or *pantera* rejigs the Greek word *parthenos*, 'virgin' (Matt. 1:23, 25), with the letters 'r' and 'n' ingeniously switched around, so that instead of Jesus being 'son of a virgin' he is 'son of [a] Panther', as Eusebius notes.[162] The nickname 'Panthera', meaning 'panther', is found among Roman soldiery in inscriptions.[163] The panther, being a dangerous wild animal, is also then representative of the empire that oppresses Israel, and certainly does not indicate a Jew.[164]

Some scholars of the historical Jesus have been taken by this later counter-story.[165] It is proposed that Jesus was born illegitimate and that the stories of the Gospels were designed to cover this up. However, in the Gospels and in early Christian literature there is never an accusation that Jesus was illegitimate (a *mamzer*) in criticisms from Jesus' opponents; rather, they acknowledge him as 'son of Joseph' (John 6:42). The counter-story is not authentic.[166] Importantly, Peter Schäfer has shown that this counter-story is a parody of Gospel accounts.[167] In fact, it seems particularly focused on Matthew. In this telling, instead of Joseph contemplating putting Mary away secretly, Joseph actually does reject Mary as an adulterous wife. This revision of the story presents what would have been considered a normal reaction for a man who discovers his betrothed bride to be mysteriously pregnant. The story also indicates knowledge that Joseph is a 'carpenter' (*tektōn*, more correctly 'constructor'), as found in Matthew 13:55.

But what is most interesting here is that the story's redirection of Matthew shows how firmly held Matthew's account was among the Christians whom the Jewish sages were most concerned about: those who were Jews themselves. For Greek-speaking Jews in hellenised Syria Phoenicia and Syria Palestina (i.e. in places such as Antioch, Tyre, Sidon, Ptolemais or Caesarea), a pun worked as part of a counter-narrative that was initially passed on to Celsus and was later echoed in Hebrew in the rabbinic circles of the Babylonian Talmud in the fifth century. The story of Jesus' conception and birth as told in Matthew is implicitly acknowledged and reshaped. Instead of the mysterious pregnancy being engineered by God's Spirit, providing reassurance to Joseph that this was nevertheless his son, it was shameful, and a result of an illicit union while Mary was betrothed. Here also the shame falls on Mary, not on Joseph. Joseph repudiates Mary: he stays 'righteous' (Matt. 1:19). There is no moral quandary. Therefore, this story severs Joseph from the way he is presented in Matthew and challenges the idea that Joseph could actually be the source of the story in the Gospel account. Joseph (as son of David?) was not even an adoptive father to Jesus: he abandoned him. Clearly, there is no way Jesus could be credited with being a son of David. The counter-story turns things round but uses a presupposition that Jesus' conception was mysterious and that an issue of shame was part of it. This is designed to assert that there could be a very different spin on the truth. This counter-story, at first told in Jewish circles, was designed to throw doubt in the faces of those who preserved what they believed were accurate recollections stemming from Joseph.

In conclusion, then, historians are generally highly sceptical about any historical actuality being represented in the birth narrative of Matthew. In this chapter, however, we have tested this notion. We have noted that Joseph's paternity of Jesus was commonly accepted in our very earliest sources. It is found reinforced in manuscript variants and in understandings of the birth narrative of the Gospel of Matthew among Christian Jews in Syria. Reading with this interpretation in view, we have tried to probe whether Matthew's story as it stands could indeed be understood in the light of Joseph's paternity. Indeed, we can read it to indicate Jesus' conception (with Joseph's Davidic seed) miraculously engineered by the Holy Spirit, consistent with what would have been credible within a Jewish milieu, where the Holy Spirit of God can act creatively. Here, there is still the presentation of Mary's virginal conception. We have also looked at the stories of the magi, who were thought of as Arabian *magoi*, and the Herodian massacre, and reflected on whether there were genuine memories contained here.

We have situated these stories as being appropriate as compositions that reflect local memories of Bethlehem and its struggles with Herod. There may well have been a memory of an unusual star, which appeared sometime during Herod's reign, even perhaps related to the Parthian installation of Antigonus Mattathias in 40 BCE. The massacre of infants may well reflect the fact that Herod did massacre youths of the

Bethlehem region near to Herodion when the Parthians invaded. The chronology might be off, and the details modified. Yet, Herod's attitude to Bethlehemites and the descendants of David is consistent with what we know from Josephus and archaeology. The geography of Bethlehem is implied, regarding the Tomb of Rachel, the town's proximity to Jerusalem, and the alternative road to Nabataea. The type of interpretation attributed to Joseph, using dreams and Scripture, is consistent with practices known within Second Temple Judaism. The account seems to draw on scriptural retellings of the birth of both David and Moses that have been preserved in later midrashic literature but would not have been known outside the Jewish milieu. These were used to underscore veracity. All this would be consistent with the kinds of stories that were told among the early Jewish followers of Jesus, and indeed his family.

The centrality of Joseph in these stories in which his feelings and actions are reported makes an explicit claim to authentic memory. The fear of Joseph is key. This must be understood within a context in which the family of Jesus exercised leadership and feared for their own lives. They were held in esteem by Jesus' followers and could send authoritative messages to Syria (Gal. 2:11–14). There would have been awareness of their family stories, which would have acted as a check on invention. Jesus' parents' memories would have been filtered through the retellings of their children, and then filtered again through the early churches of Judaea and wider Syria, until they were written down.

As we have them, the stories of Matthew are traced to the memories of a father, Joseph, who was adept at predictive dream and scriptural interpretation, so as to read 'the signs of the times', and who situated himself and his Davidic family as being targeted by a king who was deeply suspicious of all they represented. At its core, the story indicates that Jesus' birth was auspicious and significant at a time of grave danger. If these stories were told by Joseph to his own family, then Jesus would have gained a sense of destiny. He would be brought up with an intense wariness of the Roman client rulers of the house of Herod. He was expected to exercise leadership, indeed even as a prophet. God was with him and would protect him. He was named with hope.

5

Born Jesus: Luke and beyond

We have seen how the Gospel of Matthew's birth and infancy narrative is foundational, grounded in a claim to Joseph's memories. In this chapter, we will think about how stories evolved over the course of time, both in the Gospel of Luke and also in a second-century work known as the *Protevangelium of James*. The aim here is not to become embroiled in a study of literary relationships, however. Ultimately, we will probe these texts and ask if there is anything in the memories they contain that might be significant as we think of Jesus' identity and challenges as a child.

The Lukan nativity and infancy stories

Scholars have long pondered the literary relationship between Mark, Matthew and Luke given the overlaps between these three Gospels. Overall, the scholarly consensus has been that Luke was composed independently of Matthew, but, coincidentally, that it also used Mark as a basis for its narrative[1] as well as Q (or original Matthew), in the same Greek form. The author of Luke additionally used another source.[2] In fact, multiplicity of sources is directly indicated in the prologue to the Gospel itself, which states that 'many have undertaken to compile an account (*diēgēsis*) about the matters brought to completion among us, just as those who were eyewitnesses and servants of the word/teaching from the beginning handed [these matters] on to us'. This suggests a time when these eyewitness accounts were known and respected, but the author does not claim eyewitness status. The work is composed for a particular high-status man, 'most noble Theophilus', who has been instructed in Christian teaching (Luke 1:1–4). Here, also, the author makes an important self-reference: 'it seemed appropriate to me, having followed all for a long time, carefully to write an orderly account for you'.

Given that the author used a range of sources, the view that Luke is totally ignorant of Matthew's Gospel has been increasingly challenged. There are many small agreements between Luke and Matthew when using Mark, and some of these are hard to explain. Indeed, in the 'Two Gospel Hypothesis' it has been proposed that Luke's Gospel is based on that of Matthew; thus the 'Q' material in Luke is actually comprised of non-Markan passages drawn out of Matthew.[3] The author of Luke adapted material from Matthew, and then also wove in other sources.

To make things more complex, the Gospel of Luke is actually Part 1 of a two-part work, with the second part being the Acts of the Apostles. Some have suggested that Luke–Acts might reflect knowledge of historical details found in Josephus's *Antiquities*, written *c*.93 CE.[4] This would then place the Gospel and Acts in the last decade of the first century or early second century.[5] Since there are passages of Acts that refer to the author in the first person, included in the category of 'we' when discussing Paul's mission,[6] these 'we-passages' should really be connected with the Lukan prologue (Luke 1:1–4) and the preface of Acts (1:1) to indicate someone who travelled with Paul in the late 50s,[7] who could indeed have written in the 90s. Tradition ascribes authorship therefore to an obscure physician named Luke (2 Tim. 4:11; Phlm. 24; Col. 4:14), as indicated in the third-century Muratorian Canon (2–9), but this is much disputed.

The matter is made even more complicated by the fact that there were different versions of the Gospel of Luke circulating in the early second century. Cerdo and Marcion, who were active in Rome *c*.138–44 CE, questioned whether Christians should use Jewish Scripture, or whether the God of the Jews was really the Christian God, and apparently used a version of the Gospel of Luke.[8] It may well be that our version of Luke–Acts in its final (canonical) form is designed to answer Marcion.[9] While the case cannot be argued in detail here, there is a plausible suggestion that there was (1) an original Luke–Acts from the 90s, (2) a version of Luke used by Cerdo and Marcion, and then (3) a revised Luke–Acts.[10]

Importantly, the Lukan nativity and infancy narrative (Luke 1:5 – 2:40) did not appear in Marcion's version of the Gospel.[11] If we adopt the three-stage model, we cannot then assume it was found in the original work, unless we insist that Marcion deliberately left it out.

There are literary grounds to consider the birth narrative separately.[12] The Lukan nativity account is highly distinctive stylistically within the text of Luke–Acts. The canonical Gospel is otherwise written in a polished Attic Koine style, evident in the historical prologue of 1:1–4 and then resuming from 3:1 with the baptism of John – which begins with a neat historical positioning (Luke 3:1–2). By contrast, the Lukan nativity is written in a style that mimics the 'Hebraic' Greek of the Septuagint.[13] It is also never referred to in the rest of Luke–Acts. Despite its description of the close relationship between John the Baptist's mother Elizabeth and Jesus' mother Mary, John sends people to Jesus in Luke 7:19 to ask: 'Are you he who is to come, or shall we look for another?', as if he does not know Jesus' significance. In none of the speeches in Acts do any speakers claim that people should believe in Jesus because a heavenly host of angels declared to shepherds minding their flocks that he was the expected Saviour (Luke 2:8–20).[14] When referring back to the 'time that the Lord Jesus went in and out among us', the text refers to a period 'from the baptism of John to the day when he was taken up from us' (Acts 1:21–2).[15]

The Lukan nativity story begins and ends neatly, as one clear unit. It starts with a nice time-signal and introduction to a key character, 'It happened that in the days of Herod, King of Judaea, there was a priest . . .' (Luke 1:5), and ends with an equally satisfying conclusion: 'And the child continued to grow and become strong, increasing in wisdom, and the grace of God was upon him' (2:40). It could be excised from the Gospel so that the flow goes from the prologue (Luke 1:1–4) to the arrival of John the Baptist (Luke 3:1) without a hitch, and that is apparently what was found in Marcion's version.

Given Marcion's separation of the Jewish God and the Christian God, it is striking that there is a strong emphasis in the Lukan nativity on features of Judaism, such as the importance of the Temple, and aspects of Jewish law, gleaned from the Greek Septuagint, as we shall see. The narrative makes sure there is a firm correlation between the God of Judaism and the God of Christianity. As such, it forms a fitting response to those who followed Cerdo and Marcion in Rome and beyond.

In terms of themes, the Lukan nativity ties in with nostalgic notions of the so-called Augustan peace, as Mina Monier has shown. For example, to the shepherds, the angel announces 'good news to you' (*euangelizomai humin*) at the birth of the 'saviour' who will bring peace to the world (Luke

2:10–11). In the 9 BCE calendar inscription of Priene (150:40–1), a city in what is now western Turkey, Augustus's birth is hailed as the beginning of 'good news' (*euangelia*) for the world, and he is the saviour.[16] Phrases in the Lukan nativity cohere with the work of the Christian bishop Clement in his letter written from Rome *c.*96 CE, where a connection is made between the Pax Romana and Christian hope.[17] Furthermore, there are specific themes that overlap: the God of Israel is praised for salvation (Luke 1:54–5, 68b, 71, 77; 2:30 and *1 Clem.* 60:3); there is a new age of peace (Luke 1:7–9; 2:29 and *1 Clem.* 60:4; 61), typified by social justice (Luke 1:51 and *1 Clem.* 59:3) and the messianic reign (Luke 1:34–5, 69; 2:29–32 and *1 Clem.* 20:11; 59:3; 60:30); and a proclamation rooted in antiquity (Luke 1:55, 70 and *1 Clem.* 23:3; 30:7; 60:4).[18] According to Monier, such thematic correspondences link the Lukan nativity with the period of *1 Clement* in Rome.[19]

If the Lukan nativity was originally a detached piece, written around the same time as the first version of Luke–Acts and incorporated into the Gospel later, then our study does not need to address the more difficult question of whether Luke as a whole was based on Matthew; we need only to pose a question about whether the author of the Lukan nativity knew Matthew. As Mark Goodacre has stated, this question concerning knowledge should not be framed in terms of direct usage of words and passages. There are certainly striking correlations of information and Greek language. For example, in regard to naming, in Matthew 1:21 the statement 'She will bear a son and you will call his name Jesus (*texetai de huion kai kaleseis to noma autou Iēsoun*)' is duplicated in Luke 1:31, only with the subject of the initial verb changed from 'she' to 'you' (*texē huion kai kaleseis to onoma autou Iēsoun*).[20] Subsequently, regarding Joseph, we find in Matthew 1:25: 'he called his name Jesus' (*kai ekalesen to onoma autou Iēsoun*), and in Luke 2:21: 'his name was called Jesus' (*kai eklēthē to onoma autou Iēsous*). In regard to Herod, in Matthew 2:1 events are 'in the days of Herod the king' (*en hēmerais Ērōdou tou basileōs*) with 'Bethlehem of Judaea (*Ioudaia*)' just mentioned, while in Luke 1:5 events are 'in the days of Herod king of Judaea' (*en tais hēmerais Ērōdou basileōs tēs Ioudaias*). Scholars have profitably looked for further 'echoes' of Matthew in the Lukan nativity that seem to show knowledge of Matthew's account.[21]

Having a nativity at all might well indicate knowledge of Matthew, since it was by no means a necessary component of a gospel.[22] However,

Andrew Lincoln argues against the notion that Luke knew Matthew, because of the substantial differences and only minor agreements between the two accounts.[23] Lincoln finds all the material left out of Luke's version indicative that Matthew was not used, while the commonalities are put down to wider knowledge. As for these commonalities, he states that

> behind these disparate traditions there does lie a briefer common tradition of an angelic appearance during the period of betrothal between Joseph and Mary in which Jesus' birth was announced, the Spirit's part in his conception stated, his name given and a divinely chosen role within Israel predicted.[24]

These commonalities are actually slightly more than Lincoln defines. In Luke, as in Matthew, Jesus was born at the time of King Herod (Matt. 2:1; Luke 1:6); Joseph was a descendant of David (1:27; 2:4); Jesus' mother was Mary (1:27, 30, etc.); Mary was a virgin at the time of his conception – from the Holy Spirit – and birth (1:27–38; 2:1–7); she was betrothed to Joseph at the time (1:27); the angel indicated Jesus' name (1:31); Jesus will save people (2:11); and Jesus was born in Bethlehem (2:4–20). This is quite a substantial overlap.

Conceptually, Lincoln assumes that the Lukan nativity sought to present one comprehensive nativity story, independently, which *coincidentally* improved and superseded Matthew in incorporating common knowledge. But why should anything have been coincidental, what is this common knowledge, and why should it supersede Matthew?

The scholarly presupposition that each Gospel in the New Testament was written independently as authoritative for one community alone has been challenged of late. Christians shared texts.[25] Works circulated. People could read different Gospels side by side, and sometimes conflate them or create response narratives.[26] People and texts travelled. In an environment, then, where Matthew's nativity was being used as an authoritative text for the birth of Jesus, the Lukan nativity could be read alongside Matthew as a responsive retelling. But we do not need to suppose it was a complete retelling and conflation of common source material, designed as an alternative.

In fact, the Lukan nativity fits together with Matthew's nativity. That it does this quite well is something we know from our Christmas nativity plays. The two narratives, melded together, do not result in complex choices about what to include; rather, one can jump between the two accounts without conflict. Indeed, in Tatian's *Diatessaron*, as evidenced in the Arabic translation[27] and Ephrem,[28] everything runs in a fairly unproblematic sequence: Luke 1:5–80 (annunciation to Zechariah of the birth of John the Baptist, annunciation to the betrothed Mary in Nazareth, Mary's visit to Elizabeth, birth of John); Matthew 1:18–25a (Joseph's quandary and dreams; his acceptance of Mary); Luke 2:1–39 (travel to Bethlehem for census, birth of Jesus, shepherds' visit, presentation in the Temple); Matthew 2:1b–23 (magi's visit to Bethlehem, slaughter of children, flight to Egypt, return and travel to Nazareth); Luke 2:40–52 (older child Jesus in the Temple). No decisions are needed about overlaps apart from in Jesus' naming and the identification of Herod, where Tatian chose to follow Luke. This suggests that the Lukan nativity was constructed to fill in opportune spaces suggested by the narrative in Matthew.

The Lukan nativity as responsive retelling

The notion that our canonical Luke was a final redaction of a prior gospel (with Acts), designed to answer Marcionite theological positions, prompts us to propose a solution to the relationship between the nativity stories of Luke and Matthew, viewing the Lukan nativity as a separate unit incorporated into this final redaction. Luke's nativity can be understood to answer Christian questions directly arising on the basis of a reading of Matthew, while addressing certain other matters as well.[29] We have already noted how spare Matthew's nativity is: we are told nothing about background circumstances, but the Lukan stories give us details of these, satisfying readers' hunger to know more. We have noted how much Matthew's narrative is Joseph's telling; in Luke we are given Mary's. Luke is not aiming to duplicate but rather to fill in new details, and thereby answer key questions, as shown in Table 5.1.

Given the way this story answers questions arising from Matthew, without significant duplication, the Lukan narrative reads well as a companion piece. As a strategy, the Lukan nativity does not seek to rework Matthew but simply to fill in the gaps. The questions appear to arise from a later Christian milieu in a non-Jewish world. It is not part of our current focus to analyse these in great detail, and others have

Table 5.1 Lukan answers to questions raised by Matthew's Gospel

Questions after reading Matthew	Matthew	Luke	Lukan answer
John and Jesus			
Given that John recognises Jesus at his baptism, what was their previous relationship?	3:14–15	1:5–25, 36–80	John, who was from the priestly Abijah division, was the son of Zechariah, and the mothers Elizabeth and Mary were relatives. His birth was all part of the same divine plan as that involving Jesus and was announced by the angel Gabriel to his father in the Temple. So John and Jesus knew each other, but John knew his place as the forerunner to Jesus.
Mary and the Holy Spirit			
Joseph had a dream of an angel, but what about Mary's experience? How did Mary, as a virgin, conceive a baby from Holy Spirit?	1:18, 20	1:26–38	The angel Gabriel came to Mary and told her what would happen: she would conceive a baby by God's power overshadowing her. That's what made Jesus the son of God.
Nazareth and Bethlehem			
Why is Jesus identified as a Nazarene when he was actually born in Bethlehem? And why did Joseph and Mary even go to Nazareth of all places?	2:1, 23	1:26; 2:1–5	Mary and Joseph already lived in Nazareth, but they had to go to Joseph's home town, Bethlehem, the city of David, because of the first census under Quirinius.

Table 5.1 (*continued*)

Questions after reading Matthew	Matthew	Luke	Lukan answer
How Jewish was Jesus, given that only foreigners honoured him at his birth? Magi came from far away, but no Jews?	2:1–12	2:8–20, 25–38	There were local shepherds who received an angelic announcement of Jesus' birth, but he was also honoured in the Temple by two inspired Jewish prophets, Simeon and Anna. The Jewish Temple was a very important place for God's messages.
How Jewish was Jesus? Was Jesus actually circumcised as a Jew?	1:21, 25	2:21–4	He was circumcised. Jesus and his mother were purified after the birth, and Jesus was presented as a firstborn son in the Temple, with sacrifices, in accordance with Jewish custom.
Mary's memories? This is all about Joseph, but what about Mary's memories?	1:1 – 2:23	1:5 – 2:40, esp. 1:46–55; 2:19	This is Mary's story, who was inspired to speak prophetically, as was her kinswoman Elizabeth.

defined how carefully the Lukan nativity has been constructed,[30] but we will briefly review how the questions are answered.

John the Baptist and Jesus

In terms of answering how John the Baptist and Jesus relate, Luke emphasises the character of John as a prophet like Elijah, linked with priestly authority: his father Zechariah (a prophet's name) is a priest in the Abijah division of Temple service (cf. 1 Chr. 24). That Elijah himself was a priest may have been a popular tradition (cf. Epiphanius, *Pan.* 25:3). Here, then, John is presented as a priestly and prophetic forerunner to the royal Messiah, drawing on beliefs that Elijah was expected to return before the Day of the Lord (Mal. 3:1–7; 4:5–6; Sir. 48:10).[31] The prophet Zechariah had seen a vision of two anointed ones in the sanctuary of the Temple (Zech. 4:14), and John's father – aptly named Zechariah – experiences a vision of the angel Gabriel during the hour of prayer when he is serving in the sanctuary.

The links between John and Jesus are repeatedly highlighted: the angel Gabriel comes to both Zechariah and Mary, as if the births of John and Jesus are part of the same divine operation, but John will have 'the spirit and power of Elijah' (Luke 1:13–17); he is not the Messiah. After John's mother Elizabeth becomes pregnant, she is visited by Mary, the mother of Jesus, her 'relative' (1:36), who travels all the way from Nazareth in Galilee to the hill country of Judaea. This fits with an interpretation of Matthew that would have Mary sent away by Joseph (Matt. 1:19) for a period of three months, while he pondered a course of action. Strong links between John and Jesus are emphasised in this setting. When Mary approaches Elizabeth, the unborn John leaps in her womb, and Elizabeth also is filled with the Holy Spirit and prophesies, proclaiming to Mary that she is the 'mother of my Lord'. Following this, in some early Latin manuscripts Elizabeth is given as the speaker of the Magnificat (Luke 1:19–56). Mary stays with Elizabeth for three months, cementing the bond of association between Jesus and John. After Zechariah's affliction of dumbness is lifted, at the time of John's circumcision, Zechariah prophesies concerning both Jesus and John together (Luke 1:67–79). The repeated emphasis on the working of the Holy Spirit on Zechariah, Elizabeth and Mary likely reflects the beginning of the fulfilment of an ancient prophecy in which God states: 'I will pour out my spirit on all flesh; your sons and your daughters shall prophesy, your old people shall dream dreams, and your young people shall see visions' (Joel 3:28).

The conception of John is modelled on those of Samson and Samuel (Judg. 13:2–25; 1 Sam. 1:1–2:11; cf. *m.Naz.* 9:5) in that he is born to aged parents. The predecessor prophets were also lifelong Nazirites, and John is defined as such (Luke 1:15). Jesus' conception and birth is even more miraculous in that he is conceived in the womb of a virgin. Thus, Jesus is in every way outdoing John, and John himself is co-opted as a kind of proto-Christian.[32] Precedents of Scripture are carefully woven together to create a story of John that shows how his birth and Jesus' birth were part of the same divine plan in which the Holy Spirit was breaking out into the world. While it is possible that the narrative supplies some actual information about the names of John's parents, his identity as a priest, and his provenance from the hill country of Judaea, this has been subsumed into a story focusing on explaining his inferior but related status in regard to Jesus.

Mary and the Holy Spirit

Throughout the Lukan nativity the focus is on Mary's experience, and Joseph is marginal. This focus on women's experience continues when Mary visits John's mother, Elizabeth (1:16–56). The angel Gabriel comes to Nazareth, not Bethlehem. Gabriel announces to Mary, who is a virgin betrothed to 'Joseph from the house of David' (1:27), that she would conceive in her womb a child:

> he will be great, and will be called Son of the Most High; the Lord God will give him the throne of his father David; he will rule over the House of Jacob for ever and his kingdom will have no end.
> (Luke 1:32–3)

This balances out the angelic engagement with Joseph, found in Matthew (1:20–1).

As for any question about the means of Jesus' conception, this is given a specific response: '[t]he Holy Spirit will come upon (*epeleusetai*) you, and a Power of the Most High will overshadow (*episkiasei*) you, and so what is begotten will be holy and will be called Son of God' (Luke 1:34–5). In this somewhat technical statement, we are given a description involving a divine entity who acts and 'overshadows' Mary. The verb *epeleusetai* has the sense of a sudden arrival of something powerful, and in the Septuagint it can even be used negatively for an attack (Mic. 5:5–6). In Acts 1:18 it is used of the Holy Spirit suddenly coming upon the disciples of Jesus in the Upper Room, quite forcefully, filling them with divine power.[33] The verb *episkiazō* in the Septuagint has quite a literal meaning: to 'create darkness' (as in Exod. 40:35) or else to 'provide protective shade' (Ps. 140:7),[34] and in Luke 9:34 it is used of the cloud that overshadowed the disciples at the time of the

Transfiguration.[35] It conjures up a sense of a large figure creating a shadow over Mary, blocking out the sun, as if a large male body is looming over her. Thus, this terminology recalls Graeco-Roman stories of impregnations of women by Zeus or other gods, producing demigods such as Heracles or Dionysus. As Plutarch noted, 'a spirit of a [male] god could approach a woman and insert in her certain principles of generation' (*Numa* 4:4).

The maleness of the looming figure is clear. Reference to the 'Most High' (*hupsistos*) is masculine. This term could be applied to the God of the Jews (Mark 5:7; Heb. 7:1) and is found in the Septuagint (Gen. 14:18; Num. 24:16; Deut. 32:8; Mic. 6:6). It is particularly used in the Lukan nativity (1:32, 35, 76) but also elsewhere in Luke–Acts (Luke 6:35; 8:28; Acts 7:48; 16:17). For Gentiles, it was a familiar designation because it was well known as a term for Zeus.[36] This story has therefore been recognised as having something in common with biographical stories told about the birth of Augustus or Alexander, the former likely modelled on the latter, both world leaders allegedly impregnated by the god Apollo.[37] Indeed, it is the 'overshadowing' of God's power that will lead to 'what is begotten' being holy and called son of God (1:35). In the mid-second century, Justin Martyr could interpret this as indicating that the divine *Logos* (Word) became human when, 'as Spirit and Power', he himself came upon Mary (*Apol.* 1:32.10; 33:6), not unlike how Zeus fathered Perseus from Danae (*Apol.* 1.22.5).[38] All this belongs within the conceptual framework of the Graeco-Roman world. This is not so much a divinely engineered conception; it is more a divine impregnation.[39]

Nazareth and Bethlehem

To answer the question of why Jesus was called a Nazarene when he was born in Bethlehem, or why Joseph and Mary went to Nazareth at all, Joseph and Mary are situated in 'their own city of Nazareth' (2:39) and only go to Bethlehem because of a census. Matthew did not provide a location for the conception of Jesus, after all. There is here a great deal of travel, as if the distances are not too great. Mary goes to visit Elizabeth in the hill country (1:39) and returns to Nazareth (1:56), and then goes to Bethlehem (2:4–5), then back to Galilee (2:39), and Joseph and Mary both go to Jerusalem every year for Passover (2:41). Nazareth is 'a city (*polis*)' of Galilee (1:26; cf. 2:39), as it is in Matthew (2:22–3).[40]

Picking up on Matthew, then, it explains that Nazareth is a valid place for the family to go instead of Bethlehem of Judaea because they had lived there already. Mary sees Gabriel in Nazareth (Luke 1:26), regardless of where Joseph was at the time having his own angelic encounter; if she is there, then presumably it is considered her family home. This provides another reason for the family to later settle in Nazareth.

The Matthean flight to Egypt is not referred to, but, as noted, the *Diatessaron*, as evidenced in the Arabic version, shows no difficulty in bouncing between the stories of Matthew and Luke: the census travel, birth, shepherds, circumcision of Jesus, and presentation in the Temple appear in one block (Luke 2:1–39; *Diat.* 2:9–46). Mary and Joseph then go back to Nazareth (as in Luke 2:29), but in the next section they have returned to Bethlehem, where the magi arrive (Matt. 2:1–23; *Diat.* 3:1–23). They are on the road often, so Tatian saw in Luke's presentation the opportunity for the family to make another trip south in time for the magi's arrival, especially given that Herod's decision to kill every male child under the age of 2 would imply the passing of time (Matt. 2:16–18).

E. P. Sanders thought that 'Luke's device is fantastic' in that there was no reason for Joseph to go to his ancestral town [of Bethlehem] for the census.[41] But actually Sanders is reading into Luke that Joseph was himself *always* from Nazareth; there would indeed be a reason for Joseph to go back to Bethlehem if the author of Luke's nativity assumed that Joseph was actually a Bethlehem man (as per Matthew). In Luke, he is 'Joseph of the house of David' (1:27; 2:4). He was in Nazareth with his betrothed bride Mary at the time of the census, but it is never said he is *from* there. The census required everyone to go 'to their own city' (2:3), after all, and so Joseph had to travel because Bethlehem was his own city.

The very fact that Joseph went to Bethlehem as his 'own city' (Luke 2:4) would have indicated, to an audience familiar with how any registration or census would work, a very recent departure from home and property attachment there, not heritage alone. Since Joseph is of the 'house of David', Luke assumes that he has a close connection with Bethlehem as a residence, as if everyone so descended *should* live there, in the city of David, as Scripture indicated. The rationale may be wrong, but that Bethlehem was Joseph's 'own city' is clear.

Nazareth was also 'their own city' for Joseph and Mary, not because they had always lived in Nazareth but because it had become their home. Modern scholarship might force a choice: which town was *really* their home? It imagines stability, when a duality of homes implies disruption. But that is just the point. Mary and Joseph are transient, belonging to two places, in a way that points to instability and emigration. To have two places called home is not an uncommon situation among refugees and emigrants.

As for the census, this has been the subject of intense scholarly debate. Normally, someone would be registered where they were living, as would have been known to the initial audience of the account. It is implied, then, that Joseph and Mary were only temporarily in Nazareth and needed to return to Bethlehem. Actually, Bethlehem is overcrowded with returnees. When Jesus was born, Mary wrapped him in swaddling clothes and laid him in a manger 'because there was no room for them in the lodging (*kataluma*)' (2:7). In Matthew there is mention of an *oikia*, 'household' (2:11), when the magi arrive, but the census in Luke is imagined as creating massive overcrowding.

The census should not have happened at the time of Herod, because Judaea was then a country entirely under his royal authority. A Roman census only took place when taxes were no longer paid to a client king but rather through the direct administration of Roman officials. This did not happen in Judaea until the end of the reign of Herod's son Archelaus, who ruled Judaea as ethnarch (see *War* 2:117–18; *Ant.* 18:1–11) till 6 CE. It has been suggested that 'Herod, king of Judaea' (1:5) might then refer to Archelaus.[42] Even Josephus himself incorrectly calls him 'king' (*Ant.* 18:93).[43] In Luke–Acts, any ruler of the Herodian line could be 'Herod'.[44]

If the author of the Lukan nativity was responding to Matthew, though, this royal figure could not be Archelaus, because he is identified correctly in Matthew 2:22.[45] Yet the census is noted as being the 'first census taken while Quirinius was governor of Syria' (Luke 2:2). The Roman legates of Syria at the time of Herod's final years did not include Quirinius. They were C. Sentius Saturninus (9/8–6 BCE) and then P. Quinctilius Varus (6–4 BCE). Quirinius was governor of Syria from 6 to 9 CE,[46] which would match a census at the time Archelaus was removed, not in the time of Herod.

There is quite good information about Quirinius, and his dates, because being a Roman legate (*legatus Augusti*) was like being a head of state, and Romans kept good records about their leading men. So Quirinius is recorded in inscriptions, and mentioned by the Roman historian Tacitus (*Annals* 3:48) and the Greek writer Strabo (*Geogr.* 12:6:3, 5), as well as by Josephus (*Ant.* 17:355; 18:1–6). There was really only one census that affected Judaea, and it occurred in 6 CE, as a result of Augustus transferring Judaea to direct Roman administration within the province of Syria, under the legate of Syria, with a local governor (prefect) put in post in Caesarea.[47] Indeed, this one-census model ('the census') is the view in Acts 5:37. The Romans registered everyone in order to make them pay taxes to Rome, which was abhorrent to some Judaeans, and the census was an enormous landmark event that we will consider further later on. As such, it would have formed part of the social memory of people. It would have been a story much told. The problem with the Lukan story is not so much that it describes the census under Quirinius, and that it would have affected Mary and Joseph, but that it is directly linked up with Jesus' birth.

Annette Merz has suggested that there is here a combination of two censuses, given that the reference to a census is not local to Judaea: 'Now it happened in those days that a decree went out from Caesar Augustus that a census be taken of *all the world*' (Luke 2:1). The *Res Gestae* of Augustus, outlining his achievements, records three Augustan censuses, which took place in 28 and 8 BCE, and 14 CE, though these were only of Roman citizens of the empire (*Res Gestae* 8).[48] Merz argues that the Lukan census is actually a fusion and that bringing in a memory of Augustus is canny because the nativity story itself is designed to recall the language of Augustan proclamation.[49] That there were three censuses by decree of Augustus also makes sense of the reference to the 'first' one, even though it is anachronistic.

If we put the census on one side, there is a clear articulation of the dating of Jesus' birth elsewhere in Luke–Acts, in a chronological pointer focused on John's arrival on the scene in Judaea as an adult:

In the fifteenth year of the reign of Emperor Tiberius, when Pontius Pilate was governor of Judea, and Herod was ruler of Galilee, and his brother Philip ruler of the region of Ituraea and Trachonitis, and Lysanias ruler of Abilene, during the high priesthood of Annas and Caiaphas, the word of God came to John son of Zechariah in the wilderness. He went into all the region around the Jordan, proclaiming a baptism of repentance for the forgiveness of sins. (Luke 3:1–3)

The fifteenth year of Tiberius gives us the year from 19 August 28 CE.[50] At this point, Jesus was 'about thirty years of age' (Luke 3:23). This by implication indicates that Jesus would have been born c.6–1 BCE, if we allow some vagueness about his age (i.e. he was between 28 and 33 years old). This fits with Jesus being born in the final years of the life of Herod (who probably died in 4 BCE), correlating well with what is stated in Matthew. The problem for the historicity of the Lukan nativity is that there simply was no census at this time.

How Jewish was Jesus?

The Gospel of Matthew has three non-Jews, the magi, coming to honour Jesus at his birth. There is nothing at all about any Judaeans celebrating him with wonder. Therefore, in Luke, to have local people in Bethlehem, and Jewish prophets in Jerusalem, all honouring Jesus serves to emphasise that Jews celebrated him from the very start. The stories of the Lukan nativity work well as an answer to people who distanced themselves from Judaism (such as Cerdo and Marcion), in continually emphasising the importance of Jewish Scripture, and Jewish customs, for the family of Jesus. As Mina Monier has explored, the narrative is strongly focused on the Jewish Temple: it begins here with Zechariah, the father of John the Baptist, serving as a priest (1:5–22), and the Temple features also in a story about Jesus being brought there as a baby (2:22–38): 'the Temple thus functions as the womb of the good news and assures the reader of the continuance of . . . Israelite salvation history.'[51]

The reference to Jewish customs and ancient traditions continues in the story of Jesus' presentation in the Temple, which is 'according to the law of Moses' (2:22), 'the law of the Lord' (2.23, 24, 39) and 'the custom in the law' (2:27). However, in terms of Jewish praxis, the Lukan nativity seems to rely on notions of what might have happened purely on the basis of reading the Septuagint in a Diaspora context, not on actual Jewish praxis. For example, while the circumcision of Jesus is correctly noted as being on the eighth day (Luke 2:21), it is said that after a period in which *both* mother and baby needed to be purified Jesus' parents brought him (from Bethlehem?) to Jerusalem 'to present him to the Lord' (2:22), and to offer the sacrifice (for purification) of a pair of turtledoves or two young pigeons (Lev. 12:8), so purification and presentation are conflated (Luke 2:21–8).

Under the Mosaic law there is a need for the redemption of a firstborn son in the Temple (Exod. 13:2, 12).[52] However, in the time of Jesus the redemption of the firstborn was just a tax payment to the priests, requiring no presence in the Temple: the father paid a tax of five shekels (Josephus, *Ant.* 4:71).[53] While there is a concern to emphasise that the ancient laws of Moses were being followed (Luke 2:22, 23, 24, 27, 39), the baby did not actually need purification: in Jewish praxis only the mother needed purification, after thirty-three days, which traditionally involved a sacrifice (Lev. 12:1–8). In the Second Temple period, the post-partum purification of the mother was done by immersion in water (*m.Eduy.* 5.4), which is not mentioned. While purification could be done by the Eastern Gate of the Temple (*m.Sot.* 1.5), where there were presumably *miqvaot* (immersion pools), women outside Jerusalem did not go to the Temple especially for this but immersed themselves locally and waited until they had an opportunity to present the sacrifice (*m.Ker.* 1:7; 2:4). It looks as if a non-Jewish author has read Scripture but is not familiar with actual Jewish praxis.

In terms of who honoured Jesus, here the holy family are visited by nearby Judaean shepherds who have received the good news of his birth (Luke 2:8–20). There is a description of a heavenly host of angels singing. As we saw, this provides an opportunity to make claims about Jesus in relation to imperial announcements of the Pax Romana, but this motif of shepherds also connects Bethlehem to the memory of David ('city of David', Luke 2:11), who was a shepherd in his youth when he lived in Bethlehem (1 Sam. 16). The local shepherds honour Jesus while he lies in the manger, and go off glorifying and praising God. Jesus' birth is also celebrated by the prophets Simeon and Anna in the Temple, who proclaim his auspicious arrival, with Simeon in particular referencing Isaiah 52:10: Jesus would be 'a light for the revelation to the Gentiles' (Luke 2:32).

Mary's memories

Matthew's nativity was all about Joseph's experiences and actions. In an environment where Mary, the mother of Jesus, was remembered and esteemed (Acts 1:12–14), readers might well ask where her memories were in all this. Thus, the Lukan nativity implies memories passed down from Mary: 'Mary preserved all these things, pondering them in her heart' (2:19). Mary is specifically identified, therefore, as the source of the stories, which she kept to herself and then by implication revealed.

At this point, we may wonder about which elements in such stories might possibly have come from Mary. While the first two chapters of Luke's Gospel are profound and beautiful in terms of both meaning and poetry, we have noted that they seem to be designed for a Gentile Christian audience in the wider Graeco-Roman world: an audience that had Matthew's Gospel but had questions about it. If we dig into possible memories of Mary, it is hard to distinguish much beyond what may have been constructed for particular reasons in the Lukan nativity narrative. The story of Jesus being born marginalised and poor, and being visited by poor shepherds, connects his birth to a central theme of Mary's own prophetic proclamation in the Magnificat (1:46–55): she is in the humble state of a female servant; God has exalted the humble and filled the hungry with good things (Luke 1:52; Ps. 107:9). It situates Mary and Joseph in a low social status. Nevertheless, the description of an overcrowded house in Bethlehem, and how 'she wrapped him in swaddling cloths, and laid him in a manger, because there was no place for them in the lodging (*kataluma*)' (Luke 2:7), does provide remarkable detail and a peculiarity. It is this particular nexus of the story, involving shepherds arriving in what may have been a sheep stall, where Jesus lay, that creates an idiosyncratic picture. We know so little about the actual circumstances of Joseph and Mary in Bethlehem that it would be possible to imagine multiple alternative scenarios to account for this picture. So, if we look for some core material in Mary's story, it is perhaps found here.

The *Protevangelium of James*

The suggestion that the Lukan nativity was designed to answer questions arising from Matthew, with an incorporation of some possible alternative memories, may seem like a very speculative position to take. However, this kind of responsive retelling is precisely what is found in the next stage of nativity development, which we see in a work from the later second century: the *Protevangelium of James*. The *Protevangelium* exists in Greek (some 150 manuscripts) and in translations (e.g. in Syriac, Coptic, Georgian and Armenian), and was massively popular. Though a full critical edition is still to be produced, George Zervos has determined that the earliest extant form of the text can be found only in one early third-century manuscript: Papyrus Bodmer 5, located in the Bodmer Library in Cologny, Switzerland.[54]

As Mark Goodacre states, the *Protevangelium* makes much use of the nativities of Matthew and Luke, sometimes with clear verbatim sequences, but 'the use of source material is seldom predictable, often creative, and usually serves to forge a compelling narrative with an idiosyncratic take on tradition.'[55] In short, it 'omits a lot and adds a lot; sometimes it conflates and sometimes it ignores.'[56] This is by no means a work that considers the previous nativity accounts unmodifiable.

The *Protevangelium* as we have it indicates that it incorporates two previous works: the *Genesis of Mary* and the *Revelation of James* (25:4).[57] The James (or rightly Jacob) in question is identified at the end:

> I, James, [am] the one who wrote this account (*historia*) in Jerusalem, after a disturbance came about when Herod died, after I withdrew myself to the wilderness until the disturbance ceased [in] Jerusalem. I glorify the Master (*Despotēs*), who has given me the wisdom to write this account.
> (*Prot. Jas* 25:1–3)

The implication is that this is James the brother of Jesus,[58] who himself needed to hide from Herod. This work, then, makes a claim to be James's memories.[59] Indeed, the siblings of Jesus appear within it: the children of Joseph are mentioned as accompanying Joseph and Mary, and thus they are implied eyewitnesses (*Prot. Jas* 9:8; 17:2). Exactly where the two source-works end and begin may be debated,[60] but the core part concerning the annunciation through to Herod's massacre is found in chapters 11 – 24: this is the *Revelation of James*.

However, the *Protevangelium* is not a patchwork. There is a stylistic integrity, in that overall the work is written in a somewhat Semitic style, which may indicate a Syriac/Aramaic original.[61] Just as the Lukan nativity answers questions that arise from Matthew, the *Protevangelium* answers questions that particularly revolve around the perpetual virginity and exceptional character of Mary the mother, and resolves issues that arise from reading both Matthew and Luke.[62] In doing this, it does not just fit its story into what preceded it. It does not necessarily choose one or other of the previous accounts to follow, but rather is able to present a new solution, in a creative retelling.

In Matthew (2:13–15), Mary and Joseph's home is in Bethlehem, but Luke makes room for Jesus' conception to take place in Nazareth (Luke 1:26; 2:4). In the *Protevangelium*, the precise location of Joseph's home is not stated, but it is near to the Temple, where Mary grew up. The journey from Jerusalem to Bethlehem is a modest one, not requiring a difficult trek all the way from Galilee, as if objections had arisen about the Lukan presentation given the distances involved (*Prot. Jas* 10 – 11).[63] Objections that there was no worldwide census – surely noted by any educated Christians in the second century who could read the works of Josephus or the Roman historians – are now dealt with by proposing that the registration only concerned Bethlehem itself (*Prot. Jas* 17:1–2). The precise location of Jesus' birth is defined: it was actually a cave (*Prot. Jas* 19 – 21). In response to why any mother would actually lay her baby in a (smelly, dirty) feeding trough for animals (Luke 2:7), there is the answer: 'Mary, hearing that the babies were being killed and afraid, took the child and swaddled him, and laid him in a manger' (*Prot. Jas* 22:2). This directly links the action with the need to hide the baby from Herod's soldiers. Questions arising from how the infant John escaped Herod's wrath are answered with a story about Herod pursuing John, and Elizabeth fleeing to a miraculous rock-cleft in the hill country (*Prot. Jas* 22:3), while his father Zechariah was interrogated and murdered (*Prot. Jas* 23 – 24).[64]

The matter of Jesus' genealogy running through Joseph in the canonical Gospels, when there is a divine impregnation in Luke, is answered by asserting Mary's own Davidic descent (*Prot. Jas* 10:2, 4).[65] The question of whether Mary might really be the mother of Jesus' siblings (Mark 3:31–5//Matt. 12:46//Luke 8:19–21; Mark 6:3//Matt. 13:55–6) is answered by revealing that Jesus' siblings were actually from a previous marriage of Joseph (*Prot. Jas* 9:8; 17:2; 18:1).[66] There is no need to introduce characters, however: it is expected that readers/hearers will know who Elizabeth, Zechariah, Mary, Joseph, James and Simeon are. They would understand the relationships between them.

The *Protevangelium* recounts the visit of the magi, following Matthew 2:1–12, but while in Matthew Herod was disturbed (*etarachthē*) and 'all

Jerusalem with him' (Matt. 2:3), in the *Protevangelium* the 'disturbance' (*thorubos*) is specifically in Bethlehem of Judaea (*Prot. Jas* 21:2). It is never said that Bethlehem is the town of David, or that prophecy identified Bethlehem as the location for the birth of the expected king: everyone simply knows that this location is significant. The magi ask: 'Where is the king of the Judaeans?' (21:3) and claim 'we saw his star in the East, so came to worship him' (21:4), in line with Matthew (2:2), but a little later in the *Protevangelium* it turns out that the magi actually saw *stars* (plural) and 'they [stars] entered the cave and one stood upon the head of the child' (21:12). The holy family are still in the cave after the birth when the magi come.

In his study of the way the *Protevangelium* uses both Matthew and Luke, Goodacre notes the omissions in the account, including the angels' announcement of glad tidings to the shepherds, which is 'surprising',[67] but the *Protevangelium* also does some subtle switches, while assuming knowledge of source material on the part of the readership. Instead of the shepherds' adoration of baby Jesus, there is the story of the doubting midwife Salome, who is sceptical of the testimony of an initial midwife, unnamed, who proclaims that a virgin has given birth and who adores Jesus. The doubting midwife, Salome, puts her hand inside Mary's vagina to examine her and finds her hand falling away with pain, and an angel then announces to her that she should touch the infant Jesus to be healed. While the story strongly recalls John 20:25, the episode of doubting Thomas, it creates an alternative adoration scene that answers questions about the perpetual virginity of Mary. After the midwife acts on the angel's instruction, a miracle of healing takes place, and 'an angel of the Lord was saying with a [loud] voice: "Salome, Salome, proclaim/preach all the wondrous things you saw until the child comes to Jerusalem"' (20:11).[68] In fact, while the arrival of Jesus in Jerusalem is described in the presentation-in-the-Temple sequence of Luke 2:22–8, in the *Protevangelium* we last see Jesus hidden by his mother in a manger in the cave (22:2).

There is a repetition of the name Salome (19:3, 14; 20:3, 4, 11). Repetition of names in direct addresses are found elsewhere (4:1, 4, 9; 8:7; 9:7), but here her name occurs eleven times in a short section. This would have been striking in Aramaic/Syriac, since the name Salome (*Shaloum*) means 'peaceful one' or 'peace'.[69] The repetition of the name, then, would carry the weight of the Lukan angels' announcement to the shepherds: 'Glory to God in the highest heaven, and upon earth *peace* (*eirēnē*) among people of goodwill' (Luke 2:14).

One of the remarkable points made by the *Protevangelium* is that Mary gives birth to Jesus in a cave. In Justin's *Dialogue with Trypho*, written in Rome *c.*160,[70] a cave is also mentioned: 'About the birth of the child in Bethlehem: when Joseph could not find any lodging, he went to a cave near the village, and Mary gave birth to the child there and laid him in a manger' (*Dial.* 78:12). Similarly, in the *Protevangelium* it is Joseph alone who cannot find anywhere else but a cave for Mary to give birth in (17:12; cf. Luke 2:7), and the cave was apparently near (not in) Bethlehem, as in Justin, because he goes towards the town to find a midwife.[71]

A cave may have suggested itself to Justin independently due to the presence of a manger, where animals were fed, since in Palestine caves were often used for animal shelters, even through to modern times.[72] Justin himself was a Palestinian, from Neapolis, who left Palestine and went to Ephesus to study, and there he was converted to Christianity. But the birth of Jesus in a cave near the village of Bethlehem is written about by Justin not as a proposition but as a given piece of knowledge he could rely on his audience to know. It is therefore quite likely that Justin read this either in the *Protevangelium* (and that this should then be dated prior to Justin writing the *Dialogue*) or in the now-lost source document, the *Revelation of James* (*Prot. Jas* 25:4).

In the *Protevangelium*, Mary tells Joseph en route to Bethlehem, in fact midway: 'Take me down from the donkey because the one inside me is pressing me to come out' (17:11). One may note that this is the first appearance of the donkey in Christian tradition. In Luke, Mary accompanies Joseph (2:5), but nothing is said about her riding on any animal. Joseph identifies the country around Bethlehem as 'desolate' with nowhere to cover Mary during childbirth (*Prot. Jas* 17:12). This does not fit well with the actual landscape around Bethlehem in ancient times. In Cyril's *Catechetical Lectures*, written around 348 CE, it is said that 'until recently' the area around Bethlehem was wooded (12:20), as we saw earlier (with reference to *m.Ta'an.* 4:5). The *Protevangelium*'s desolate landscape fits better with the area east of Bethlehem, which stretches into the wilderness and on to the Dead Sea. One may therefore wonder exactly what is being envisaged. Joseph seeks a Hebrew midwife from 'the region of Bethlehem' and finds one 'coming down from the hills' (19:1), meaning that the cave is imagined as being in a valley, which would also match the descending wilderness to the east of Bethlehem. As we saw in Chapter 3, the village of Bethlehem was indeed on two conjoined hills, but the traditional birth-place of Jesus would be remembered on the elevation itself (see below).

Overall, then, the *Protevangelium* presupposes knowledge of the nativities of both Matthew and Luke. There is no aim to produce a comprehensive account designed to set the record straight and replace the previous stories, but rather the story may be seen as a retelling of the previous stories, one which is supposed to sit with them while at the same time answering questions. This technique is quite similar to Jewish midrash, which involved a drawing out of meaning via a reimagining of a scriptural story, thus creating a new story.[73]

The question is whether any authentic memories might be preserved within this work. Clearly, storytelling was a creative occupation within early Christian milieux, and stories could present quite fantastical scenarios. However, as noted, there are constraints on stories the closer they are to the time of the people presented in them. Here, there is an acceptance of fixed characters and details: Jesus' parents were named Mary and Joseph; Jesus had siblings; there were questions about Jesus' paternity and Mary's behaviour at the time of his birth; Jesus was born in the area of Bethlehem of Judaea; magi saw some astrological indications in the east; there was trouble with Herod; there were disturbances; and so on. There is the distinctive element of the baby being laid in a manger, and, as with Justin, there is the cave. All the elements are bent to a different purpose, but such elements appear to be fixed points to which new creative retellings adhere. In the mind of the author, then, there is a subtle differentiation between what may be moulded and what remains constant as a foundation. These elements are not to be confused with historical details, but this shows there was a creative licence that nevertheless accepted the need for some preser-vation of what the author and audience determined to be core memories.

The cave of the nativity

The earliest attestation that Jesus' birthplace was a cave is found in the work of Justin Martyr, when he wrote of a cave near Bethlehem (*Dial.*

78:12–13). It is not at all clear that he knew (or cared) where exactly the birth cave really was, or that anyone had thought to identify it precisely, but it indicates that people knew of a story of a cave. However, in the following century (c.246 CE), a cave was indeed identified. We find this evidenced in the work of Origen, arguing against attacks on Christianity by the philosopher Celsus, when he mentions that

> in accordance with the story in the Gospel about [Jesus'] birth, the cave *in Bethlehem* is shown where he was born and the manger in the cave where he was wrapped in swaddling clothes. What is shown there is famous in these parts even among people alien to the faith, because it was in this cave that the Jesus who is worshipped and admired by Christians was born.
> (*Against Celsus* 1:51)[74]

Origen wrongly suggests here that 'the Gospel' itself indicates that Jesus was born in a cave, but he did also know the *Protevangelium*.[75] Clearly, the idea of the cave as being the location of Jesus' birth was firmly stuck in his mind, and he might well have gone to Bethlehem, as elsewhere in his writings it is indicated that he had travelled around Palestine.[76]

Initially commissioned by the empress Helena c.325 CE, the Basilica of the Nativity was built over this cave on the orders of the emperor Constantine, and the resplendent church was dedicated in 339 CE. Thus, the cave became extremely famous and much mentioned by Christian scholars of the fourth and fifth centuries, as well as by pilgrims.[77] Archaeology has revealed the layout, with an octagonal structure at the eastern end of the basilica, enclosing the sacred cave (12.3 × 3.5 m wide), accessed by stairways on the west leading from the building's side aisles and nave. In the centre of this octagon a 4-metre-wide hole allowed a view of the cave and manger-altar. Archaeology and other studies have shown how the cave in question is actually one of a network of caves and passages, the dating of which is uncertain (see Fig. 3.3).[78]

In Eusebius's *Demonstration of the Gospel*, written after Constantine's work had begun and indebted to Origen in certain places, he states (echoing Origen) that it is 'agreed by all that Jesus Christ was born in Bethlehem, as even a cave is shown by the local inhabitants there to those who come from elsewhere for a look' (3:2:47). These people have the tradition handed down 'from their ancestors' (7:2:14) and bear witness to those who come from far away to Bethlehem for the sake of an enquiry into Gospel places (1:1:2). However, prior to the emperor's developments, Eusebius makes no mention of a cave in Bethlehem when he refers to the town (*Onom.* 42:10–14; 82:10–14). Furthermore, according to Jerome, the cave had formerly been used as a pagan cult site for the worship of the Syro-Palestinian god Tammuz-Adonis, located within a sacred grove of trees (*Ep.* 58:3).[79]

Was the cave remembered by Judaean Bethlehemites as being where Jesus was born, or was this a convenient cave venerated by the Syro-Palestinians which they happened to point out to visiting Christians? Did they conflate the dying-and-rising god Tammuz-Adonis with Jesus? This raises questions of continuity of memory, which we have already explored,[80] and we need to remember that there are many caves in the region of Bethlehem. Origen may well reflect the words of the local (pagan) inhabitants, attested by Jerome: they pointed out where 'the one who is worshipped and admired by Christians was born'. They venerated the place as a holy site for the dying-and-rising god Tammuz-Adonis, and suggested that the Christians should venerate it as the birth cave for the one they worshipped and admired.[81] The question is then: which memory came first, the pagan or the Jewish(-Christian)?

The tradition of the *Protevangelium* and other stories clearly fed into what visitors expected at the site, the cave being a central feature, even though the cave of the Basilica of the Nativity does not match the cave as defined in the *Protevangelium* (halfway between Jerusalem and Bethlehem in a desolate valley in the wilderness). For all his adherence to canonical Gospel writings, Jerome (*Ep.* 108:10:2) wrote that the pilgrim Paula saw *inside* the cave 'with the eye of faith' the swaddled child in the manger, the magi, the attentive mother and foster father, shepherds, 'the star shining above', and the ox and the ass. While in Matthew the star remained outside (2:9–11), in the Papyrus Bodmer 5 of the *Protevangelium* (and some later Greek manuscripts and translations) the star entered the cave and 'stood over the head of the child' (*este epi tēn kephalēn tou paidiou*).[82] The ox and the ass are not in fact found in the *Protevangelium*, but neither are they present in the canonical Gospels. They are woven into Christian memory by reference to Isaiah 1:3: 'The ox knows his owner, and the ass his master's crib: but Israel has not known me, and my people have not understood.' Shown in a carved relief of a nativity scene (side-facing the apse) from the 'sarcophagus' of Stilicho in S. Ambroglio in Milan, dated to 400 CE, these animals are part of the expansive and responsive story-telling tradition that the *Protevangelium* illustrates.[83]

A cave, then, may well once have been a real location where Jesus was born, and a location remembered in stories, but it became (again) an actual location embedded in the earth, a material location that could be visited. This actual location provides in turn a space for the remembering and retelling of the stories.

The troubles

Matthew mentions that Herod and all Jerusalem were 'troubled' (*etarachthē*) by the magi's visit, and this implies more than mild concern: the verb *tarasso* means 'to stir up' or 'agitate', and would imply civil unrest (see Acts 17:8, 13). Luke does not reinforce any story of disturbances under Herod in the final years of his reign, and passes over the story of the magi, the massacre and the flight, and yet there are peculiarities in the Lukan account that likewise indicate trouble. The census, which called for registration (for taxes on property and earnings), leads to a situation in which there is no room in a lodging (*kataluma*) for a newborn, so that Mary lays her baby in a place where there is a manger, a feeding trough (Luke 2:7). Any birth should require a midwife and privacy, an expectation answered in the calling of a midwife in the *Protevangelium* (19). The idea that there is 'no room' in the lodging is not explained, but what kind of circumstances could have led to this? Were there too many Davidic descendants pushed together to house them all in one place? One thinks of the refugee experience, where large groups are forced into small places of shelter, or other precarious situations where persecuted groups are herded together out of their safe spaces.

Houses in nineteenth- and twentieth-century Palestine could be built with a lower part reserved for animals, as Gustaf Dalman well documented,[84] and one might read this as showing that Mary and Joseph then went to this zone. However, as we saw, Justin (*Dial.* 78:5) located the birthplace of Jesus in a cave near the village, separate from any houses, because Joseph himself could not find a lodging (for the birth?) there.

The location is detached from where people were normally living. The family are removed from a normal home at a critical time.

That a baby was put in a manger is actually indicated as extremely unusual in Luke's own telling of the story, since the 'sign' to the shepherds is that they will find a baby wrapped up and laid in a manger – of all places (Luke 2:12, 16).[85] The people around at the time of the birth are therefore not family members but rather strangers, local shepherds ('in the same region', 2:8), who easily find a newborn infant in a Bethlehem animal shelter (Luke 2:7–20).

Crisis and instability is reflected also in the *Protevangelium*. In this work, the census is not worldwide but very specifically targeting the people of Bethlehem (17:1), the descendants of David. But the holy family (inclusive of Joseph's previous Davidic children) never actually arrive in Bethlehem. The cave is imagined in a wilderness (17:3), in a valley below Bethlehem. After the birth, 'Joseph prepared to go out [from the cave] in Judaea and a great disturbance (*thorubos*) came about in Bethlehem of Judaea' (21:1–2). The slaughter of the infants takes place, but Mary hunkers down in the cave, and for safety's sake she hides her child in the manger (22:2), as we saw. Mary's hiding of the infant Jesus in the manger creates a much more dramatic scene than a simple use of a manger as if it were a cot. At the end of the story in the *Protevangelium*, the family are still in the cave. The family (inclusive of Joseph's other children) never leave the cave, never actually arrive in Bethlehem, where there is a disturbance caused by the magi.

In Luke, even without specific mention of a cave, there is an implication that the place where there was a manger was not actually where animals were located, as a normal part of a house: it was empty, as would perhaps be appropriate during summer when shepherds watched their flocks by night and didn't shelter with them in a cave. To say there was a 'manger' in a cave may imply there was a carved stone trough for water or food, or a trough made of clay mixed with straw or stones. But still, this circumstance implies disruption and difficulty. As Gustaf Dalman concluded, the 'peculiar couch of the new-born Child was due to the circumstance that his parents were on a journey and had no home in the strange place'.[86] Yet in Luke, Joseph has come 'home' to Bethlehem; it is not a strange place: this is his 'own city' (Luke 2:3). Since Davidic family members are nowhere to be seen, the narrative reads as if everyone who could be supportive has scattered. If there was no room in the lodging, who was filling it? Should this isolation of Joseph and Mary be connected to the social shame that he feared in Matthew 1:19–20? In terms of memory, then, there are elements of disruption embedded in the Lukan story.

The desolate location of the cave in a valley is extremely suggestive. As archaeology has amply shown, east of Bethlehem there were caves in the wilderness to which Judaean refugees fled to hide as a result of both the First and the Second Revolt in Judaea (in 68–73 CE and 135–6 CE respectively), and during other times of trouble as well. Refugee caves from these rebellions have been discovered and excavated, particularly in the region by the Dead Sea where the extremely hot and arid environment has preserved the refugees' clothing, wool, wooden plates, cosmetics, papyri and other organic remains (see Plate 6), along with the more commonly found hard materials of pottery and metal, and, tragically, these surviving remains can include the skeletons of the refugees themselves.[87] For example, in the coincidentally titled 'Christmas Cave' located 12 miles (20 km) east of Bethlehem in the Wadi en-Nar (Nahal Qidron), excavated in the 1960s, investigations have now determined multiple periods of cave inhabitation.[88] Thermoluminescence testing of pottery sherds determined that there were two pieces of Hasmonean–Herodian pottery here,[89] and overall both radiocarbon and this thermoluminescence dating have shown that this location was likely used as a refugee hideout at several points in time when people fled from settlements on the eastern and southern sides of Jerusalem, including Bethlehem. The dry environment of this cave preserved clusters of their possessions for over 2,000 years.

To hide in a cave in the wilderness was what Judaeans did in times of crisis, and the archaeology of these caves painfully demonstrates the kinds of things people found precious enough to bring with them, often carried in baskets or waterskins. These items were not only useful; they were often also identity-markers: in terms of jewellery or cosmetics, for example, or vital documents in terms of property.[90] Fleeing to the hills (to caves) was how people hoped to survive the threat of massacre or other forms of violence: Josephus states that the entire population of Jericho fled to the hills ahead of the arrival of Vespasian's forces in 68 CE (*War* 4:451). Jesus himself would warn his own followers that when they saw the sign of end-time trouble, 'let those who are in Judaea flee to the hills' (Mark 13:14//Matt. 24:16//Luke 21:21). He knew where to flee.

So, for those already familiar with the Gospel of Matthew, the Lukan nativity formed a companion piece that served as a responsive retelling and purported to tell Mary's stories rather than Joseph's. At the outset, the family of Jesus are already settled in Nazareth, not in Bethlehem. In the 'days of King Herod of Judaea' we find Mary betrothed to Joseph there, and *she* is told by an angel that she will conceive a child by the Holy Spirit. Joseph and Mary travel to Joseph's town, Bethlehem, because of a Roman census during the time when the Roman legate Quirinius is governor of Syria. Finding no room in a lodging (*kataluma*), the baby Jesus is laid in a manger, a feeding trough for animals. Jewish shepherds of the region see angels while watching their flocks, and come to honour the baby. Jesus is named, circumcised and presented in the Jewish Temple, where there are prophetic utterances from Jewish seers. The narrative may include some elements of actual stories told by Jesus' family, but they appear in embellished retellings with clear themes focusing on the centrality of the Temple, 'Jewish customs' (via the Septuagint) and the championing of Christian peace in Roman terms.

The *Protevangelium* employed a similar strategy in using both Matthew and Luke, in a new interpretative retelling, to answer further questions arising in the later second century, though it also incorporated a previous work about Jesus' birth, the *Revelation of James*. In both cases, these retellings likely include material circulating orally, but the question is: how old was this oral storytelling tradition? Both the cave and the manger within it are certainly curious inclusions, considering how little they help any messianic claims known to us. As such, given their anomalous character, there may be some basis to these in actuality.

What repeats in all the nativity stories, as preserved, are motifs of vulnerability, displacement, disruption and (social) marginality. All of the stories imply or indicate trauma in some way, whether persecution caused by a vicious ruler, or lack of decent lodging for a birth, and they tell of God's hand in directing and protecting the holy family. It is that core, in terms of recounted memory, that is perhaps most important. In the next chapter, in order to explore this more deeply, we will return to the foundational narrative of Matthew and contextualise it within what we know of history.

6

Refugee: into Egypt

The Gospel of Matthew follows the story of the arrival and departure of the magi (Matt. 2:1–12) with another angelic dream appearance to Joseph: this time it is a warning to flee with his family. He is told to 'take the child and his mother, and flee to Egypt, and stay there till I tell you, because Herod is going to search for the child to destroy him'. Indeed, Joseph 'got up, and took the child and his mother by night, and got away to Egypt' (Matt. 2:13–14). The sudden flight to Egypt is related succinctly, and nothing is said of what happened there. Rather, the story focuses on what happens in Bethlehem when Herod orders his soldiers to kill any male child under 2 years of age (Matt. 2:16–18). It is all about showing how the dream angel's warning was proven very right.

In Chapter 3 we investigated the tensions between Herod and the Davidic dynasty, and it was suggested that, as a memory, the massacre of the infants in Bethlehem could in part have had its origins in an attested massacre of (young?) men around Bethlehem who were opposed to Herod's rule. At the time, they had joined the Parthians in supporting a rival king, Antigonus Mattathias, when he temporarily took over Judaea in 40 BCE. Some hint of this earlier incident may well be found in the fact that Herod kills the infants not only in the town of Bethlehem itself but also 'in all its borders' (so Matt. 2:16), as if there was a wide circle drawn with Bethlehem at the centre. A story of why Joseph fled seems to have been boiled down and encapsulated in this one event. As previously noted, the attack on Herod and its aftermath must have been a continuing trauma to the people of this area, especially given the fact that the palace-fortress of Herodion, built to glorify Herod's success in this massacre, was visible from Bethlehem. The story as presented in Matthew relies on a memory of Herod as a threat, which is verifiable by reference to Josephus. As Robert Myles notes, 'Jesus' displacement comes to life against this backdrop of Herodian tyranny, which is woven into the historical intertexture of the text.'[1]

144

Figure 6.1 Map of region from Syria to Egypt, 6 BCE
(Drawing by Joan Taylor)

In Matthew the massacre of infants happens after Joseph flees, and it justifies the family's flight. The family become a paradigm for the experience of refugees: in danger, they suddenly have to drop everything and flee, and they do so in the middle of the night.[2] They leave for Egypt, far to the south-west. There is an implied journey of at least 140 miles (225 km) (see Fig. 6.1).

To be a refugee is one of the most profoundly challenging things that can happen in terms of someone's identity, when all the ties to normal life, work, relationships, place and future are taken away. Loss of identity is one of the most common experiences refugees have.[3] Refugees in today's world are prone to a range of mental health issues (identity diffusion, negative affectivity, detachment, antagonism and disinhibition), including post-traumatic stress disorder.[4] The identity crisis of the refugee experience can haunt families and be received as a trauma even into the next generation.

Scholars have long been highly suspicious about the flight of the holy family as an actual historical event. However, if we think further about the attested events in Judaea before and around the time of the death of Herod, especially as told by Josephus, there was clearly a great deal to fear if you were a descendant of David. There would have been very good reasons for people with Davidic heritage to lie low or flee. Given what happened, it is very likely that many stories were told of instability and danger. We must, then, be fully aware of this wider context.

Trouble with Herod

In the years leading up to Jesus' birth, Herod was increasingly paranoid and at risk of acting with great cruelty towards those he considered disloyal. He killed his own sons, and had few qualms about killing anyone else's. As Augustus quipped: 'I would rather be Herod's pig than his son' (Macrobius, *Saturnalia* 2:4): an ironic statement, since pigs are not butchered by Jews.

We know about Herod's actions largely from Josephus, drawing from the eyewitness narration of Nicolaus of Damascus, who was part of Herod's court,[5] and therefore there are good reasons to think of this narrative as reflecting Nicolaus's first-hand observations. It is retold in highly dramatic form in the pages of Josephus's *Judaean War* (*c.*73 CE) and *Antiquities* (*c.*93 CE), but these were written in part for the elite of Rome and Judaea, and therefore Josephus would have been aware of their own memories (and knowledge of Nicolaus) in terms of his historical details. These included descendants of Herod himself, including his great-grandson Agrippa II (*Apion* 1:50; *Life* 364–5), Roman client king of various regions and cities of Judaea/Syria Palestina (*c.*50–100 CE), who would have had access to many memories and reports. Agrippa also would have well known what it meant to be a Roman client ruler.[6] Josephus therefore needed to keep his facts correct.

The story is important here because events affecting the house of Herod affected everyone. Josephus indicates that what happened in palaces was widely known. At several points also, *ekklēsiai*, or group assemblies of leading (elite) Judaean men chosen by Herod, were summoned to witness and rubber-stamp Herod's decisions, an exercise founded on a Hellenistic ideal of consultation with the population.[7] The story of Herod is therefore the story of current events as they would have affected Jesus' family.

In Josephus's description, Herod quashed any whiff of insurrection among his own family and close associates.[8] He had married Mariamme, the granddaughter of the Hasmonean high priest Hyrcanus (*War* 1:435), in 37 BCE, and they had five children together, but Herod had also executed her for treason at the end of the year 29 BCE (*Ant.* 15:218–39; *War* 1:438–44), and soon afterwards other family members and friends fell foul of the king (*Ant.* 15:247–66). At some point a group of ten men attempted to kill Herod as a lawbreaker, knowing the nation would be behind them, but they were caught by a spy and tortured to death. The spy was then killed by their supporters, and Herod rounded up the culprits and their entire families and had them all killed, strengthening himself against the people of the nation in every way in order to curb any further rebellion (*Ant.* 15:280–91).

Around the year 23 BCE, Mariamme's two eldest sons, Alexander and Aristobulus, were sent off for their education in Rome, even residing in Caesar's palace (*Ant.* 15:342). They returned to Jerusalem on completion of their studies *c.*17 BCE, but the young princes were apparently not liked by others at court. Herod by this time favoured Antipater, his elder son by another wife, Doris, as his successor. Mariamme's sons were considered a threat, and vilified by Antipater, so much so that Herod brought them for judgement all the way to the emperor Augustus, then in Aquileia, who ostensibly settled the dispute (*Ant.* 16:87–135; *War* 1:452–66).[9]

On return from the trip to Italy sometime in 12 BCE, Herod apparently 'assembled the people' in the Jerusalem Temple and presented his three sons. He made a speech in praise of Caesar, which Josephus duly records as if verbatim, and ended this performance with a fond embrace of each of his eldest sons in full view of the multitude (*War* 1:457). Notwithstanding this, Herod soon resorted to torturing and murdering his household staff to discover any signs of treason (*Ant.* 16:229–60; *War* 1:488–97).

In 10 BCE Herod turned his mind to the pesky memory of David, and violated his tomb, as we have seen, but something happened that gave him a fright. When he and his men went deep inside to where the actual body of David lay, there was a strange burst of fire that injured two guards; thereafter, he built a fabulous white monument at the mouth of the tomb (*Ant.* 16:179–83).[10] Whatever Herod thought he was doing by this, Josephus identifies it as a desecration leading to divinely wrought consequences (*Ant.* 16:188) which, for our purposes, provide the immediate background to Jesus' birth story.

In the same year as this desecration and looting, Herod's son Alexander somewhat foolishly wrote a four-part treatise denouncing his various enemies at court, and only managed to survive the backlash thanks to the intervention of his diplomatic father-in-law, the king of Cappadocia (*War* 1:498–512; *Ant.* 16:261–70). However, with the machinations of another visitor, a Spartan named Eurycles who connived against Alexander, this reconciliation turned to custard. Eurycles spoke to Herod about Alexander's criticisms of his management of the nation, which was apparently bled dry by taxation, and praised Antipater. There was a forged letter impugning Alexander and Aristobulus for plotting Herod's death, and Herod duly put further people to torture for the purpose of extracting confessions (*War* 1:513–31; *Ant.* 16:313–14). After additional conniving from the young men's aunt, Salome, Herod shackled the princes in irons, separately, and requested authority from Augustus to decide their fates.

The judicious emperor counselled that the brothers should be put on trial before a royal court composed of Roman client rulers. This was assembled in Berytus (modern-day Beirut) with Alexander and Aristobulus absent: imprisoned and not able to represent themselves.

At this point, says Josephus, 'all of Syria and all of the Judaean people (*Ioudaikon*) waited' (*War* 1:543), signalling again that this was not something kept private, as a royal matter, but instead was publicly known: it was headline news. What happened in the palaces was the top story in the marketplaces and synagogues. This is exactly the kind of thing, then, that feeds into social memory.

The decision of this royal court was that the young men should be executed. The nation of Judaea was outraged at this sentence. An old soldier named Tiro, whose son was a friend of Alexander, openly denounced Herod and proclaimed that many of the army pitied the princes. Not surprisingly, he, his son and all those in the army whom he named were arrested, tortured, condemned by another assembly (*ekklēsia*) that Herod had summoned, then promptly executed by stoning (*War* 1:544–50). Alexander and Aristobulus were taken to Sebaste, a city built by Herod in Samaria in honour of the emperor, with a temple to Augustus and Roma at its centre, and there they were strangled to death. They were not permitted to be buried in Herodion; their bodies were instead taken to Alexandrion in the Jordan Valley (*War* 1:538–51; *Ant.* 16:361–94).

The effect of this execution on the nation is simply stated by Josephus: people not only hated Herod but also blamed Antipater (*War* 1:552, 560, 567; *Ant.* 17:1–3), who subsequently departed to visit Rome, and Augustus Caesar. There, he presented himself as the magnificently resourced heir to the throne of Judaea.

Josephus presents Antipater as mulling over the hatred of his subjects and how much everyone in Judaea loved his dead (half-)brothers. This hatred brewed intensely also in the royal house. In Antipater's absence, Herod sniffed out any whiff of conspiracy, including among the senior women at court,[11] and identified the (unnamed) wife of his brother Pheroras, who was tetrarch of Peraea (east of the River Jordan; see Fig. 1.1), as the ringleader. He also accused her of supporting the influential legal school of the Pharisees against him, and summarily executed some of the leading Pharisees along with further members of his own family and two handsome attendants: Bagoas the eunuch and Carus, whom Herod kept for sexual pleasures (*Ant.* 17:41–5). Pheroras's wife was accused of opposing him, alienating him from his brother and bewitching Pheroras with drugs (*War* 1:568–74, 78–80).[12] Pheroras and his wife sensibly fled to Peraea, their own territory, likely to the palace-fortress Machaerus, with Pheroras vowing never to see Herod again, even on his deathbed. Unfortunately, Pheroras then took ill. Herod visited him in a grand act of brotherly love, and Pheroras suddenly died. Not surprisingly, as Josephus reports, it was said that Herod had poisoned his brother (*War* 1:581). However, as a result of further tittle-tattle, Herod then tortured women – servants and ladies both – and many others at court, who now revealed treasonous plots on the part of Antipater (*War* 1:582–603; *Ant.* 17:61–78).

The drama, worthy of the popular TV fantasy series *Game of Thrones*, played out in various palaces of Herod, not just in Jerusalem, thus including Herodion. The court of Herod was sometimes on the move through the country as Herod and his retinue decamped from one palace to another. This court was constructed on a Hellenistic model comprising Herod's family, attendants, officials, bureaucrats, visiting elite (kings, princes, ambassadors, Roman officials), slaves and bodyguards. Herod ruled with an advisory bureaucratic body of 'friends' (*philoi*, including the chronicler Nicolaus) who enacted Herod's wishes militarily, judicially, administratively and personally, and could number as many as 500 people.[13]

Herod's paranoia is shown by archaeology as well. Corroborating Josephus's presentation of Herod's mentality, Eyal Regev has examined the spatial dimensions in the archaeology of Herod's palaces in Jericho, Masada and Caesarea, where the court personnel were housed, and noted how in the last period of his reign (from 15 BCE) his structures are marked by segregated sections, different from the more open-plan forms preceding them, and are devoid of central courtyards. Thus, '[i]n the Third Palace in Jericho Herod sat in his relatively secluded throne room and his guests were scattered in several peristyle courts and reception rooms'.[14] The promontory palace in Caesarea was expanded with an upper wing (*c.*10 BCE) that made the lower wing, with its large pool, more remote to visitors. Herod's architecture therefore reflects the king's detachment from his friends and family.

These events concerning Antipater took place within the two years prior to Herod's death in 4 BCE, and thus they form the direct background to the events of Jesus' birth as Matthew describes them. Antipater's story would have been in the air, and it acts as a kind of warning. At this time the ageing Herod (nearing 70 years old) was in a state of extreme paranoia about conspiracies and death threats, and willing to torture anyone – family member or friend included – to reveal secret information about individuals who might be against him.

When Antipater finally returned from Rome to Judaea, arriving at the port of Caesarea, he did not apparently suspect that his father's thoughts had turned against him, though he was somewhat perplexed by the fact that Herod had exiled his mother, Doris. His mother's letter warning him of events had been intercepted, so Antipater was completely in the dark. He was confused by the icy reception he encountered at the port and along the way. Again, Josephus indicates how the royal drama was playing out in discussions among the population: everyone avoided him, and hated him, but people were also extremely afraid of Herod (*War* 1:614): 'every city now was full of the talk about Antipater'.

The new Roman governor of Syria, P. Quinctilius Varus,[15] was coincidentally visiting the palace in Jerusalem from his base in Antioch. Herod received his son Antipater with furious rage, and assembled a council (*sunedrion*) of his relatives and friends, presided over by himself and Varus. Herod launched into a tirade accusing Antipater of treachery, aided by the first-hand witness to all this: the chronicler Nicolaus of Damascus himself. Antipater responded, tearfully imploring his father to recognise his loyalty, appealing for him not to believe evidence extracted from torture, but to no avail. His final statement was: 'God is witness I have done no wrong.' As some form of warning, a random prisoner under sentence of death was forced to drink poison to see if it was still potent, and died in front of everyone. Antipater was put in iron shackles. Varus wrote a full report for Caesar in order to obtain Augustus's judgement on the situation, sent it off and left the next day (*War* 1:608–40; *Ant.* 83–145).

Herod changed his will to name another son as heir to the throne: Antipas, son of his Samaritan wife Malthace. Then Herod's health began to fail, as he succumbed to an unspecified illness. There was talk that the king was dying. At this cue, there was a popular insurrection (*epanastasis*) and brazen action in the heart of the judiciary and the cult: the Temple itself. Two leading and very popular scholars (*sophistai*), named Judas son of Sepphoraeus and Matthias son of Margalus, had a large body of keen young students. Emboldened by news of Herod's illness, Judas and Matthias indicated to their students that Herod's erection of a grand golden eagle, symbol of Rome, over the 'great gate' of the Temple had long been utterly unlawful: a terrible contradiction of Mosaic law prohibiting graven images (Exod. 20:4–6; Deut. 4:13), and it should be pulled down by those who had courage enough to be martyred.

At noon, when there were a huge number of people in the Temple, the most eager of the students swung themselves by ropes down from the roof and began hacking off the Roman eagle with hatchets. The captain of the king's guard sent in troops to stop this and arrested about forty young men, who were then brought before Herod, apparently now in his winter palace in Jericho. Apoplectic with rage, Herod summoned an assembly (*ekklēsia*) of leading men in Jericho and denounced the perpetrators. Appeals for clemency from those assembled only resulted in changes in the high priesthood: Herod swiftly deposed his previous appointee Matthias, and appointed Matthias's brother-in-law Joazar in his place. He had the scholars Judas and Matthias and the forty students who had taken the action in the Temple burned alive, while others arrested were executed in other ways (*War* 1:647–55; *Ant.* 17:149–67). Again, here is another massacre of young men by Herod, now at the very time that Matthew records the massacre of the infants in Bethlehem. This is surely another element of social memory that has informed what is told: Herod massacred youth.

Subsequent to this horrific bloodbath, Herod was not sated. Beset by illness, and still in Jericho or at his spa complex of Callirrhoe by the Dead Sea, Herod issued a horrendous order. Village and town leaders from throughout Judaea, who had come to Jericho in regard to the judgement about the insurrection, seem to have been staying on for Herod's death, but the king lingered. Herod then ordered that when he died they should all be assembled in the Jericho hippodrome and massacred by his soldiers so that Judaeans would not celebrate his death with a festival (*War* 2:659–60).

In a case of tragic timing, Herod then received a letter from the emperor Augustus, advising that he could either banish or execute Antipater at his discretion. Herod, after certain theatrics, had his guards execute Antipater there and then. As with his other murdered sons, Antipater was not allowed to be buried in Herodion; his body was instead sent to the fortress of Hyrcania, ignominiously far away in the Judaean wilderness (see Figs 1.1; 3.1).[16] Herod then altered his will again, naming Archelaus, another son of Malthace, as his heir to the throne of Judaea, with Antipas and Herod Philip now tetrarchs over lesser territory, and his sister Salome appointed ruler (gaining taxation revenue) of certain individual cities in his domains (*War* 1:661–4; *Ant.* 17:182–90).

At this point, everyone was waiting for Herod to die. From the looting of David's tomb in 10 BCE to the end of his reign six years later, Herod's reign was one of terror, torture and murder. This then provides a fitting historical situation to justify Joseph's intense fear. Myles observes rightly that the very phrase 'in the days of Herod the king' (Matt. 2:1) 'evokes for the reader the repressive regime and intensifies the political instability surrounding the narrative of displacement'.[17]

Refugee in Egypt

Josephus indicates throughout his telling of the story that the nation took sides and was seriously disturbed, which explains the insurrection in the Temple against Herod and the subsequent ugly retribution. This too brings to mind mention, in Matthew's account, of how the whole of Jerusalem was stirred up by the arrival of magi (Matt. 2:3). The terrible executions of the students and their teachers would have made anyone in the firing line of Herod's suspicions extremely nervous, especially those from the house of David. The desecration of the tomb of their ancestor David[18] would have sent a strong signal, implying a threat even beyond the building of Herodion overlooking Bethlehem. It would have been a period of great stress when many, not only Joseph, would be turning to ways of reading the 'signs of the times'. To desecrate a grave of an ancestor is to wish harm on that person's descendants. Fleeing to Egypt to avoid danger was a reasonable idea, and Joseph was probably not the only man in Judaea who decided on this path. While scripturally Egypt was a place of enslavement, it had long been a place of refuge and settlement for Judaeans. Papyri, epitaphs and inscriptions, as well as our literary sources, testify to a thriving Jewish expatriate community in Egypt, originally made up of both Jewish mercenaries and earlier refugees.[19] There was a large Jewish community in Alexandria, where in fact the philosopher Philo himself would be a child at just this time. It would have been possible, then, for refugees from Bethlehem to flee there. Josephus notes that Judaean revolutionaries (and their children) fled to Alexandria after the Roman quashing of the First Jewish Revolt (*War* 7:407–19) in the year 73 CE.

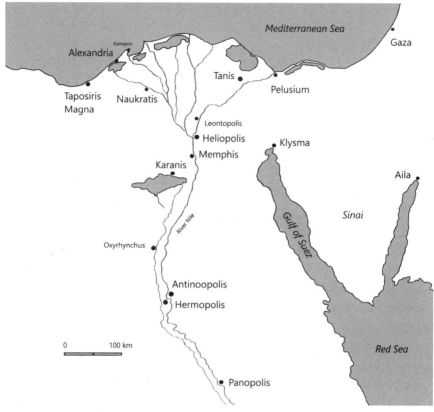

Figure 6.2 Roman Egypt
(Drawing by Joan Taylor)

However, just like today, new refugees were not necessarily welcome, and the Jewish emigrant community itself existed in a precarious position. A letter of the emperor Claudius, written in 41 CE, states that Jews in Alexandria lived in 'a city not their own' in which they were 'not to bring in or invite Judaeans who sail down to Alexandria from Syria[-Palaestina]' (P.London 1912; CPJ I:151). Thus, from the perspective of the Roman overlords, trouble in Judaea could lead to trouble in Alexandria. This letter also shows that the usual route to Egypt was by sea: most likely from the port of Joppa (now Jaffa), not overland on a highway. Road travel was largely reserved for camel caravans, heading along the Via Maris, which skirted the Syro-Palestinian coastal cities. From Bethlehem to Gaza was about 45 miles (75 km). From Gaza to the Egyptian port city of Pelusium (see Fig. 6.2) was 75 miles (120 km), and that was only on the eastern edge of Egypt. To get to Tanis, on the Nile Delta, was another 20 miles (30 km). In total, a journey to Tanis from Bethlehem was, on the ground, some 140 miles (225 km). Even with a very good day's journey of 12 miles (20 km) per day, that would have taken some eleven days. But to go from Tanis to Alexandria was another 160 miles (260 km). To go by boat from Jaffa to the port of Alexandria covered a distance of 290 miles (465 km), though it was a much faster journey. But a sea passage would have cost money, and assembling cash takes time. Desperate refugees, fleeing in a hurry, walk.

One of the most magnificent cities of the Roman Empire, Alexandria had been established in honour of Alexander the Great in 331 BCE as a Hellenic colony, and was ruled by his heirs, the Ptolemaic dynasty, for about two centuries, but it had fallen under direct Roman governance after the failure of the war waged by Antony and Cleopatra in 31 BCE. Diodorus Siculus (*Bibl. Hist.* 17:52:6) reports that Alexandria had around 300,000 citizens, divided into five areas, one mainly inhabited by (indigenous) Egyptians, two largely populated by Jews, with 'Hellenes' (people of Greek heritage) in the remaining two.[20]

Judaeans had arrived early on in the history of Alexandria through providing military support to the Ptolemaic rulers (Josephus, *Apion* 1:186–9; *Ant.* 12: 8).[21] Eventually, the leaders of the Jewish community in Alexandria also provided support for the Romans, gaining privileges as a result.[22] Perhaps due to a complex shift in allegiance, the relationship between the Ptolemaic rulers and the Jewish population could be remembered as both positive and negative. In the second-century BCE *Letter of Aristeas*, Jews astound the king, Ptolemy II Philadelphus, with their wisdom (*Arist.* 200–1, 293–4, 312). The Jewish philosopher Aristobulus is described in the second-century BCE narrative of 2 Maccabees as the teacher of King Ptolemy VI Philometor (2 Macc. 1:10).[23] In a story of 3 Maccabees, however, composed in the late first century CE, the king Ptolemy IV Philopator coerces Jews into the hippodrome, where they are threatened with trampling by elephants (3 Macc. 5). By the time of Philo, most Jews were strongly loyal to Rome, while bewailing poor government by Rome's representatives. Under the Roman prefect Flaccus (38–9 CE) there was little protection; indeed the opposite. In 38 CE, tensions would explode, resulting in riots and pogroms against the Jewish population of the city.[24]

The attitude of the Jews of Alexandria to uprisings in Judaea was diffi-dent.[25] Alexandrian Jews seem not to have supported any uprising against Rome, and when the flood of Judaean refugees arrived in 73 CE they denounced them, so that 600 men, along with their families, were horrif-ically tortured and killed by the Roman authorities for not confessing 'Caesar as their lord (*despotēs*)' (*War* 7:409–19). The implication is that loyal Jews would do so, and in fact Philo is keen to demonstrate the loyalty of the Jewish community in his writings (see *Flacc.* 49–50). To what extent Alexandria was a safe place for those of Davidic descent, who were not in favour with Herod (the Roman client king of the Judaeans), may then be questionable, even though Alexandria was often the Judaean refugee's location of choice. Moreover, the city's official Roman name was Alexandrium ad Aegyptum (Alexandria by Egypt),[26] not Egypt proper, strictly speaking. Josephus writes that the refugee revolutionaries fled from Alexandria 'into Egypt' (*War* 7:416).

There were indeed other places where Jews lived in Egypt proper, most particularly in the Heliopolis nome, where there was a Jewish temple (or large synagogue) at a site named Leontopolis (Tell el-Yehoudieh).[27] In Josephus's *War* he begins and ends with the story of this temple, which also included a 'small town resembling Jerusalem' (*War* 2:33). This had been built by a refugee high priest, Onias, in the second century BCE when civil war took him from Jerusalem, and the Jewish community there was distinctively different from that of Alexandria. In due course, this community did not sit well with the Romans. The temple was shut down (*War* 7:421–36) after the Romans had done their worst with the Judaean refugee revolutionaries they tracked down there.

Perhaps, then, fleeing Judaeans from Bethlehem did not go to Alexandria but rather found safety in Leontopolis, but they could have sought refuge anywhere in Egypt where there were enough Jews who would protect them. For new refugees, as anywhere, life would have been very hard. Debt could result in enslavement (Matt. 18:23; Philo, *Spec.* 2:82). Presumably, Jewish charity and voluntary giving through the synagogue would have helped a struggling refugee family, but they would also have been reliant on the kindness of strangers.

Whatever happened, we see a curious awareness of the vicissitudes of transience and precariousness in Jesus' later teaching. When he set off on his mission, he seems to have consciously taken up the life of a displaced person with 'nowhere to lay his head' (Matt. 8:20; Luke 9:58).[28] His mode was itinerant, looking for kindness. He asked those who acted for him to go out without a bag or a change of clothing, essentially to walk along the road like destitute refugees who had suddenly fled, relying on the generosity and hospitality of ordinary people whose villages they entered (Matt. 10:9–11; Mark 6:8–11; Luke 9:3). And it was precisely the villagers' welcome or not to such poor wanderers that showed what side they were on: 'And if any place will not receive you and refuse to hear you, shake off the dust on your feet when you leave, for a testimony to them' (Mark 6:11). In turn, this welcome, or offer of hospitality, is defined as the most important action Jesus expects of his disciples in relation to other displaced persons. Identifying himself with them, Jesus says: 'I was hungry and you gave me food; I was thirsty and you gave me something to drink; I was a stranger and you welcomed me' (Matt. 25:35).

In his study of the homelessness theme in the Gospel of Matthew, Robert Myles has identified how a sense of forced displacement is embedded not only in the flight to Egypt story but also elsewhere in the Gospel. For example, the word *anachōreō*, meaning to 'get away' or 'withdraw', is used four times in the flight-to-Egypt story (2:12, 13, 14, 22) and is used six other times in Matthew (4:12; 9:24; 12:15; 14:13; 15:21; 27:5; cf. 8:20), when it is only used once in Mark (3:7), once in John (6:15), twice in Acts (23:19; 26:31) and not at all in Luke. This word does not just refer to moving from place to place. In Egyptian papyri, the world *anachōrēsis* refers to poor people fleeing to the hills or desert to avoid punishing taxes.[29] As Myles notes, the 'repetition [of this word] within the flight to Egypt, in particular, draws attention to the plight of Joseph, Mary and Jesus in their encounter of imperial sanctioned violence, and the displacement caused thereafter'.[30] Even in the genealogy, Myles suggests there are names associated with forced displacement, such as Abraham.[31] David himself is often on the move, and he needs to ask the king of Moab for his parents' protection (1 Sam. 22:3–4). In sum, as Myles notes, Jesus' social location in Matthew is one of 'displacement and marginality'. The echoes of displacement in Matthew's infancy narrative present 'a marginalized and displaced individual, who later comes into significant conflict with institutions of power in Galilee and, especially, in Judea at the culmination of the gospel narrative'.[32]

Remembering Egypt

The earliest Christian memory of Jesus' childhood life as a refugee is vestigial. However, in the second century the pagan philosopher Celsus claimed that Jesus, on account of poverty, worked for hire in Egypt, and there he experimented with Egyptian magic (Origen, *Against Celsus* 1:28). This suggests that by the time he wrote, in the second century, there were some tales of the destitute child Jesus engaging in wonder-working, and indeed the link with Egypt is a trope in later memories of Jesus as a magician.[33] In the writing of Hippolytus of Rome, early in the third century, there is mention that the family stayed in Egypt for three years and six months (*Comm. Matt.* 24:22).[34]

The stories developed further. As the Lukan nativity answered questions arising from Matthew, and the *Protevangelium* answered questions arising from both canonical Gospels, further questions about what happened to the holy family in Egypt were answered by later stories, largely told among the Christian communities of Egypt, often by reference to Old Testament texts. These stories were particularly attached to sites that became monastic centres in the later fourth and fifth centuries, frequently associated with water miracles and healing.[35] In terms of the earliest location for the family in Egypt, before the development of the holy family 'tour', we encounter the city of Hermopolis as a key place. This city is mentioned in the *Historia monachorum in Aegypto* (*Inquiry about the Monks in Egypt*), an anonymous Greek work by a Palestinian monk who travelled around Egyptian monasteries in a party of six others in the late fourth century and recorded what he was told by people he met. The monk writes of how he arrived in Hermopolis,[36] which was a major city on the border of Upper and Middle Egypt, located today near el-Ashmunein. Here he met a holy man named Apollos, who claimed that Mary, Joseph and Jesus came there from Judaea in accordance with Isaiah 19:1: 'Behold, the Lord is seated on a swift cloud and will come to Egypt, and the manmade idols of the Egyptians will be shaken at his presence and will fall to the ground.'[37] In line with Second Temple Jewish practice, here a scriptural verse is matched with an event. The decommissioning and destruction of a temple, in this case the famous temple of the god Thoth, has been matched with Isaiah 19:1. As the visitor states: 'We saw there also the very temple in which they say all the idols tumbled over and were shattered after the Saviour entered it' (*Hist. mon.* 8:1). Archaeology shows that a church was built here in the fourth century.[38] Soon after, in Sozomen's *Ecclesiastical History* (5:21:8–11), there is mention of a tree named Persis which bent down and worshipped the young Jesus, and was rewarded with healing powers. This was also located in Hermopolis.[39]

The monk Apollos was first to 'reveal' an association between the holy family's time in Egypt and a specific place, and this may have been on his own initiative rather than something based on any tradition. Nevertheless, intriguingly, there was indeed a Jewish community here in the first century BCE. Inscriptions from this time indicate Judaean (Idumaean) soldiers serving the Ptolemaic rulers.[40] In a letter written by a Roman soldier *c.*115 CE, there is even a reference to Jewish rebellion (P.Brem. 1; CPJ 2:438). There was a 'Jewish lane' in this city, noted at the end of the second century CE (CPJ 3:468, l.9).[41] One might conclude, then, that it would have been an appropriate place for a Judaean family to flee to. But nothing more can be said.

Whatever happened, and wherever they went, it does not seem implausible that Joseph took his family away from Judaea, given what he would have heard of Herod's dangerous actions in the years leading up to Jesus' birth.

The stories of Matthew are Joseph's stories, as we have seen, and they tell of his earnest attempts to interpret the 'signs of the times' in order to preserve his family. But all the stories of Jesus' birth tell of strife and dislocation. This fits well with what we know of the historical context. Herod's actions at this time would have been understood by those descended from David as extremely threatening. The horrific deaths of people in Herod's family and circle, and anyone else who dared to counter him, would have been terrifying. It was a wise idea to flee.

While the flight of the family has long been doubted as mere invention, any supposition that the family's circumstances in Jesus' early years were completely peaceful and ordinary relies on suppositions, not on what is actually stated in *any* early Christian literature. If we accept that the widespread testimony of Jesus' Davidic descent is true, then from the point where Herod desecrated the tomb of David and completed his palace (and tomb) complex on Herodion, overlooking Bethlehem, through to his quashing of threats in his own court and the savage retribution meted out on those who rebelled against him in the Temple, Herod's actions must have been viewed as extremely threatening to anyone of that line. A common place of refuge was Egypt, and this would have been a likely place for the family to go to.

The earliest attested location for their refuge is Hermopolis in the middle of the country: the heartland of Egypt. Wherever Joseph took his family, they did not in the end stay in a place of transient settlement. Like many refugees, they hoped that their flight would be temporary and they would go home. But home was not where they went. Whatever happened in Bethlehem that provoked flight, and wherever the family actually went in Egypt, Jesus as an adult was remembered as being from Nazareth. But, as it turned out, this place too was not one of peace and stability in Jesus' early years.

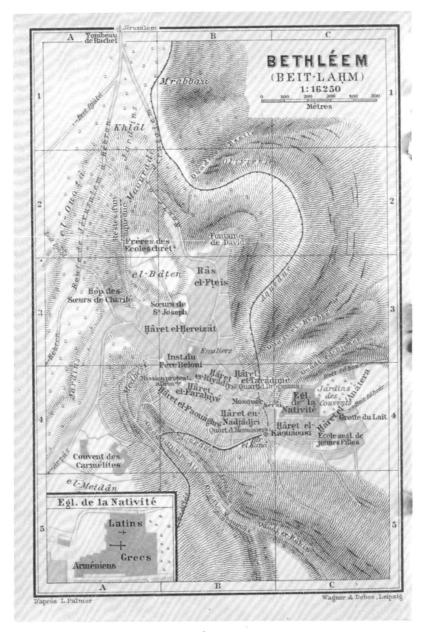

Plate 1

The ancient Lower Aqueduct running through Bethlehem in a French plan from Baedeker's guide 1912. The aqueduct leads from the south to a pool just south-west of the Church of the Nativity, called Bir el-Kana. It then runs under the town and out to the valley in the north

(Plan after L. Palmer, in Albert Socin, Immanuel Benzinger and John P. Peters, *Palestine and Syria, with routes through Mesopotamia and Babylonia and the Island of Cyprus: Handbook for travellers* (Leipzig: Karl Baedeker, 1912), plan opposite page 101. Public domain)

Plate 2

A view of Bethlehem in 1867 from the hill beyond it to the north, with Herodion on the horizon at the extreme left and aqueduct right

(Photograph by Henry Phillips, 1867. Courtesy of the Palestine Exploration Fund, London. PEF-P19-964, slightly cropped)

Plate 3

View from Bethlehem to Herodion, with Herod's tomb on the left side of the hill, zoom setting

(© Joan Taylor)

Plate 4
View from Herodion hill to Bethlehem, with Bethlehem in the distance
(© Joan Taylor)

Plate 5
The Holy Spirit imagined as a feminine divine manifestation in Ezekiel's vision
of the revivification of Israel in the Valley of Dry Bones: 'I will put my Spirit
in you and you will live' (Ezek. 37:14). The figure of Ezekiel appears twice,
in different dress, on either side of the Spirit. She is connected to Ezekiel
(on right) by two thin ribbons

(Photograph of wall painting from the third-century synagogue of Dura Europos, Syria. Section
B, scenes 1–2. From Carl H. Kraeling, 'The Synagogue', in A. R. Bellinger et al. (eds), *The
Excavations at Dura-Europos: Final Report 8, Part 1* (New Haven, CT: Yale University Press,
1956), plate 70. National Museum of Damascus. Public domain.)

Plate 6
Artefacts from Judaean refugees in the Christmas Cave in the Judaean
wilderness east of Bethlehem, dating from the Bar Kokhba Revolt (*c.*136 CE):
coins, wooden plates, kohl sticks, pottery bowls and spindle whorls
(© John Allegro. Reproduced with permission from the Allegro estate)

Plate 7
Coin of Herod showing *pilos* cap (left) and *tau-rho* ⳨ abbreviation (right)
(Wikimedia Commons, Staatliche Museen zu Berlin. Creative Commons Public Domain Mark 1.0)

Plate 8
Coins of Herod showing X in diadem
(Wikimedia Commons from Glyphmark. Creative Commons Attribution-Share Alike 4.0
International License)

Plate 9
The Temple and Antonia Fortress – model in the Israel Museum, Jerusalem
(© Joan Taylor)

Plate 10
View over upper Sepphoris south-west towards Nazareth
(© Joan Taylor)

Plate 11

Panoramic view of Nazareth and its vicinity, 1866. In the nineteenth century the village of Nazareth lay on the slope of the hill, but archaeological remains indicate that the Roman–Byzantine settlement in part lay under and adjacent to the Church of the Annunciation, which is the large building at the centre of the photograph in the valley

Plate 12

Entrance to triple silo pit complex (hiding place) in first-century house, Mary of Nazareth International Centre, Nazareth

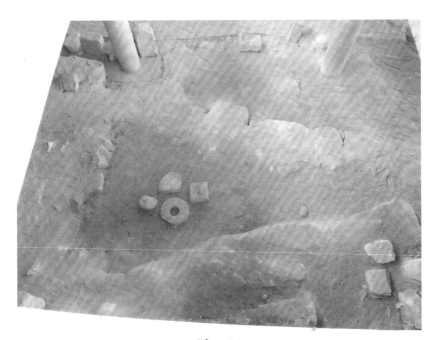

Plate 13

Remains of building foundations, cuttings for structures, agricultural troughs and grinding stones, in area outside the Church of the Annunciation, Nazareth

(© Joan Taylor)

Plate 14

Holy Caves of Nazareth, Greek Orthodox property, Nazareth

(© Joan Taylor)

Plate 15
Woodworker in the Tower of Babel mosaic panel, Huqoq synagogue
(*c*.400 CE), Israel
(Photograph by Jim Haberman; courtesy of Jodi Magness)

Plate 16
The courtyard of the Mosque of al-Azhar, built in 970–2, Cairo, Egypt
(Albumen print by Felix Bonfils, late 1800s. Accession number: 909-1917 © Victoria and
Albert Museum, London)

7

Return: a time of hope

According to the Gospel of Matthew, Joseph decided to return from the place of refuge in Egypt, but the duration of the family's stay in Egypt is not given. There is no indication of the age of Jesus at the time of return, though second-century stories would make him a child old enough to work and learn magic, as we saw. However, at some point the family do make their way back. Nothing is said of the historical circumstances, and – without knowing anything of the context – one might presume that everything in Judaea was reasonably peaceful. Nothing could be further from the truth. We now, then, need to set the return of the family from Egypt against the backdrop of what we know took place in the region at this time. Just the backdrop itself, as we will see, explains some intriguing details in Matthew's brief statements.

Hope: the Land of Israel

In Matthew we read that when Herod died, an angel (in another dream) said to Joseph in Egypt: 'Go back to the Land of Israel, for those who were seeking the child's life are dead.' And we see Joseph's reaction: 'So he got up and took the child and his mother and came into the Land of Israel' (Matt. 2:20–1). There is suddenly a note of hope.

The term 'the Land of Israel' is distinctive usage, and is repeated over two verses. In Scripture it is rarely found. The 'Land' is the country promised to Abraham, and then to Isaac and Jacob (also known as Israel), and the concept flows through Scripture from Genesis, but the particular term 'the Land of Israel' ('*Erets Israel*) does not appear until 1 Samuel 13:19 where it is the territory occupied by the Israelite tribes ruled over by Saul, which will ultimately be under the authority of David. In 1 Chronicles 22:2, David gives orders in regard to 'the Land of Israel'.[1]

The phrase refers here to the scope of his kingdom. This terminology of royal rule took on a different meaning when the lands of the Israelite tribes were eroded by conquests from the eighth to the sixth century BCE. In Judah's exilic context, the prophet Ezekiel saw 'the Land of Israel' in a wide sense (Ezek. 27:17; 40:2; 47:18), as a place of promise: the place where the reconstituted tribes of Israel would return and live (including 'Joseph with two portions', Ezek. 47:13–23). In Ezekiel 20:36–8, the land of Egypt and the land of Israel are juxtaposed.[2] But 'the Land of Israel' is the *Davidic* kingdom: it is under the rule of 'my servant David' (Ezek. 34:24; 37:24–5).[3] The term 'the Land of Israel' also appears in a fragment of Pseudo-Ezekiel found among the Dead Sea Scrolls (4Q386 1 ii 1). At the end of the second century, in the Mishnah, the phrase 'the Land of Israel' is vitally important in terms of the historic and present enactment of Jewish law,[4] but it is not an expression used by Josephus,[5] and it appears nowhere else in the New Testament.[6]

Reading Matthew's account as reflecting memories of Joseph about the decisions he made, the return of Jesus' family to the Davidic 'Land of Israel' at the time of Herod's death can be understood as a statement of hope: something would change. Safety would return. The Land, without Herod, would be different. This parallels the hope shown in the revolt by the students of Judas and Matthias in the Temple when they mistakenly believed that Herod was dying (*War* 1:648–53; *Ant.* 17:149–58). It was then time to take down the golden eagle from the front of the Temple: Rome's power would be shaken off. Hope in 'the Land of Israel' therefore correlates with what we know of historical actuality.

Why was there so much hope? Josephus does not provide much of a rationale as he follows Nicolaus of Damascus's interest in the shifting candidates for the succession in Judaea. He prefers to tell the court drama, with only an occasional mention of Herod's broader cruelties, but there are signals of widespread upset, as we saw. There are also clues that indicate that in the latter part of the first century BCE Jewish scholars were undertaking a kind of intellectual resistance in the face of Roman power, in seeking out Scripture to work out the signs of the times, and discerning what would follow. They were engineering hope through interpretation. In order to understand this activity, and explain the hope of return to the Land of Israel, we need to be technical again and solve a puzzle.

Reading Scripture as prediction

We saw in Chapter 3 how Herod's rationale for his right to rule was that he was king by divine will (*Ant.* 15:384, 387). We can actually see this claim reflected in his coinage. Herod was allowed to issue bronze coins in Judaea, and there were eleven types during the course of his reign (40–4 BCE). A group of four denominations have the date 'Year 3'. Victory is a theme of the first coin type, which depicts on the obverse a pointy *pilos* cap of one of the Graeco-Roman mythological heroes, the Dioscuri (Castor and Pollux), surmounted by a star, in between two palm branches (see Plate 7).[7] This is indicative of Herod's self-representation as a hero.

More strikingly, there is another coin (see Plate 8) in which inside the circle of the inscription BASILEŌS ĒRŌDOU ('[coin] of King Herod') there is a diadem, with trailing ribbons, with the shape of a Greek letter *chi* (X).[8] Another coin type also gives us a *chi* inside the diadem, in the form of two palm branches crossed over.[9] It has been noted by coin expert Ya'akov Meshorer that this diadem with a *chi* was a symbol of kingship, in that, according to the Babylonian Talmud's instructions regarding coronation anointing (*b.Ker.* 5b): 'In anointing kings one draws the figure of a crown [around his head], and with the priest [one anoints] in the shape of the letter *chi*.'[10] Anointing was part of the ceremony of kingship (1 Sam. 24:7; Pss 2:2; 18:51; 20:7; 28:8; 84:10; 89:39, 52; 132:10, 17).[11] This coin, then, presents a view from above, looking down on the head of King Herod, encircled with a crown. The *chi* could itself indicate the anointing, because *chi* is the first letter of the Greek word *christos*, 'anointed'. Likewise, the two crossed palms are another symbol of victory, yet they are also presented as a *chi* for *christos*, creating a dual message. The *chi* of *christos* would signify Herod's anointing as king: Herod was the rightful, anointed king.

It is worthwhile examining this claim more closely to determine what exactly made Herod so confident. This involves analysing various historical accounts. The first account is found in Josephus. He describes how when Herod took charge in 37 BCE he had insisted on an oath of loyalty from his subjects, but the legal school of the Essenes were exempted because Herod held them in great honour (*Ant.* 15:368–71). This was because one of them, a man named 'Menaemos', or rather Menahem, had made a prediction that foretold that Herod would be king

(*Ant.* 15:373–6; cf. *War* 2:159). When Herod was a boy, on his way to a teacher (in Jerusalem?), Menahem suddenly addressed him as 'King of the Judaeans'. When Herod protested, Menahem spanked him 'with his hand on his buttocks' to make Herod remember the changes wrought by Fortune (= God). He said: 'You will rule, for God has deemed you worthy.' As a result, because of this prediction, Herod 'continued to honour all the Essenes'.[12] Certainly, Herod was soon thrust into extraordinary responsibility. He was probably only 15 when he was appointed as governor of Galilee (*Ant.* 14:58).[13] He was amazingly protected from harm: he survived a house collapsing in Jericho and emerged unscathed after an attack by Antigonus's supporters while he was taking a bath.[14] Such stories could only have been told as truth by Herod himself.[15] The point is that such stories were told. This prediction by Menahem connects well with Herod's affirmation that he ruled by 'the will of God' (*Ant.* 15:384, 387).

Herod owed his claim of divine support to Menahem, but no explanation is given as to why Menahem made such a prediction. Interestingly, the Essene prophecy was a bit of a mixed blessing. Menahem foretold also that Herod would not love justice, or show piety to God or decency to the citizens of Judaea, and that these things would not be forgotten by God at the end of Herod's life. So Menahem apparently indicated that God had chosen someone who would be less than virtuous to rule as king, and he would be punished. Understandably, Herod was unsettled by this. It truly was a very strange prediction. Even Josephus notes that it seems 'paradoxical' or 'unbelievably strange' (*Ant.* 15:379). While Josephus considers the Essenes extremely good and pious, they also somehow validated Herod's unrighteous rule as the will of God.[16] Menahem had basically endorsed Herod's right to rule as a bad king by divine determination.

According to Josephus, the Essenes were fatalistic in thinking that everything was in the hands of God (or Fortune; *Ant.* 13:171–3; 18:18) and that all rulers were placed in authority by God (*War* 2:140), so if you predicted that someone would rule Judaea, then you were predicting God's will. In order to predict the future, the Essenes could use dreams, and often the sacred books and sayings of the prophets (*War* 2:159), namely Scripture, which they esteemed greatly (*War* 2:119) and interpreted to find hidden meaning (*Ant.* 18:11, 20), as we see in the Qumran *pesharim*. Apart from Menahem, Josephus mentions two other Essenes who were expert predicters (*War* 2:112–13; *Ant.* 15:371–9; 17:345–8).[17]

Well born himself, Josephus as a young man went through education in the three legal schools (Sadducees, Pharisees, Essenes) for thorough training as a potential future leader, before deciding which school he would follow (*Life* 10–11). This means that he himself learned something about how the Essenes interpreted Scripture to understand 'the signs of the times' and what would soon come to pass. He is full of admiration for them and represents their predictions as inevitably sound (*War* 1:78; 2:159; *Ant.* 13:310–14; 17:345).[18] What they said counted a great deal.

Our second piece of evidence to explain Herod's confidence is found in the experience of Josephus. Remarkably, Josephus himself used his knowledge of Essene prediction, because he too made a prediction about someone who would become a future ruler. This happened during the Great Revolt. At a time of incredible carnage, in July 67 CE, and in fear of his own life as a Judaean rebel leader when Jotapata was taken by the Roman forces, Josephus hailed Vespasian, then a Roman general, as the future emperor.

Josephus claims that he 'was himself one to interpret concerning the discernment of dreams and ambiguous (*amphibolos*) sayings of God . . . in the prophecies in the sacred books' (*War* 3:352). This gives us a strong clue to the predictive method in question involving both a dream and an interpretation of Scripture, as we see in Joseph's methods (in Matt. 1 – 2). With his life in danger, it seems that Josephus suddenly had a moment of inspiration. Like the Essenes, he was able to understand the sacred books and 'read their meaning', helped by dreams, and he offered a prayer to God, asking that he might be his minister (*War* 3:353–4). He delivered the message to Vespasian that he would be emperor and honoured (*War* 3:399–408; see also Suetonius, *Vesp.* 5). But in this part of the story, too, nothing is said of how exactly Josephus made this prediction and which passage of Scripture he used.

Fortunately, hailed as a future emperor, Vespasian spared Josephus's life. Two years later, Vespasian did indeed become emperor (Suetonius, *Vesp.* 12), and Josephus – like the Essenes – was honoured for it, including being given land (*Life* 414, 422–3, 428–9). Thus, strangely, Menahem's prediction of Herod's rule and Josephus's own prediction of Vespasian's rule function as a parallel.

Later on in his *War*, Josephus reveals something more about what he did when he states that there was an 'ambiguous' (*amphibolos*) passage in the sacred writings that indicated to Judaeans that 'about that time one from their country would become ruler of the habitable earth'. The Judaeans thought this referred to one of themselves, but many 'wise men' (*sophoi*) were wrong in their interpretation, because actually this text denoted Vespasian, who was appointed emperor in Judaea (*War* 6:312–15). Thus, Josephus used the ambiguous but key passage of Scripture to predict that Vespasian would rule, and it was interpreted by others as indicating a future *Judaean* ruler. We are in the world of messianic expectation.

For this 'ambiguous' passage used by Josephus, various proposals have been offered,[19] but the one that seems most likely is Genesis 49:9–10,[20] which reads (in a literal translation from the unstable Hebrew):

Judah is a lion cub; my son, you have gone up from the prey. Crouched, he lay down like a lion, and like a lioness, and who dares to rouse him? The sceptre (*shebet*) shall not depart from Judah, nor staff [of office] from between his loins, until Shiloh [or: tribute; or: *shai lo*, to whom it belongs] comes; and to him is the obedience of the nations.

In the context in which it is found, this is a prophecy delivered by Jacob (Israel) concerning what is to come (Gen. 49:1), and it occurs in the first book of Scripture, Genesis, which was believed to have been written by Moses. The passage has multiple ambiguities.[21] Much depends on how you interpret 'until', in Hebrew *ad ki*. Does it mean there will be no failing of Judahites on the throne all the way through to the arrival of the Messiah? Or does it mean there will be a disruption of Judahite royal rule, and then the Messiah comes?

The Greek text of the Septuagint reads:

Judah is a lion cub; my son, you have risen up from the bud (*blastos*). Crouched, you lie down like a lion, and like a cub; and who will rouse him? A ruler shall not fail from Judah, nor a leader from his loins, until (*heōs ean*) there come the things reserved for him; and he (*autos*) is the expectation of nations/Gentiles.[22]
(Gen. 49:9–10 LXX)

The Greek then identifies a 'he', so there is an expected figure who will arrive subsequent to some disruption of Judahite/Judaean leadership.

To interpret it as he did, it seems that Josephus's special insight was that this figure would be Vespasian, then a general, soon to be the ruler of the world as the emperor of Rome. In his understanding, this would mean there would be a Judahite/Judaean ruler until the arrival of 'Shiloh': a *Gentile* who would rule Judaea and gain the obedience of the Gentile nations as well.

But, prior to its appropriation by Josephus for Rome, this passage gave Judaeans hope for Rome's overthrow: this is clearly what Josephus's 'wise men' thought. This interpretation can be seen in an early text from the Dead Sea Scrolls, where Shiloh or the 'one to whom it belongs' is definitely the Davidic Messiah. This interpretative text (*pesher*) reads:

(1) [he] 'will not cease from the tribe of Judah' a ruler for Israel; (2) [nor will] 'one sitting' on the seat of David be 'cut off', because the 'staff' is the covenant of kingship (3) [. . . and thousands] of Israel are the 'loins' 'until' the Anointed of righteousness comes, the sprout of (4) David, for to him and to his descendants has been given the covenant of kingship of his people for all everlasting generations, which (5) has kept [. . .] the Law with the people of the union (*yahad*) for (6) [. . . the 'obedience of the people]s' is the assembly of the people of (7) [. . .] he gave . . .[23]
(4Q252 [or *4QCommGen A*] 5: frag. 6)

Here, to make the identity of the expected ruler clear, there is a reference to Jeremiah 33:17: 'there shall not be cut off for/to David a man sitting upon the throne of the house of Israel'.[24] It is predicted that there will be rulers from Judah (= Judaeans) on the 'seat of David' (the throne) *until* the arrival of the Messiah/Anointed of righteousness,[25] who is the returned Davidic descendant, the 'sprout of David', who will sit on his rightful throne.[26] There will be an unbroken chain of rulers leading Israel, coming from the 'loins' of the thousands of Israel.

Such a reading of Genesis 49:10 is, then, what Josephus directly spurned; he instead interpreted the passage as indicating there would be a Gentile ruler, *not* the Judaean Messiah. The wise men of Judaea were misguided. This came as very good news to the Romans, and both Suetonius and Tacitus, as Roman historians, seized on Josephus's interpretation. Suetonius notes that there was a belief that men from Judaea would rule the world but actually this referred to the Roman emperor. How wrong those Judaeans were! Tacitus identifies that this reference meant Vespasian and Titus.[27]

Josephus therefore implicitly provides evidence of three different interpretations of Genesis 49:10:

1 the interpretation by 'wise men' that there would be a Judaean ruler: the Davidic Messiah (*War* 6:312–15), which correlates with 4Q252;
2 the interpretation by Menahem that Herod would rule (*Ant.* 15:373–6; *War* 2:159);[28]
3 the interpretation by Josephus that Vespasian would rule (*War* 3:399–408).

As for Menahem's prediction, Herod was not a Judahite by descent, but as king he came to rule not only over Judaeans and Samaritans but over Gentiles as well. He fits with the prediction. This also makes sense of why Herod issued the 'Year 3' coins. The *pilos* coins (see Plate 7) include on the reverse a mysterious *tau-rho* monogram, ⳨, which should be shorthand for a word beginning with the Greek letters *tau* (T) and *rho* (R), or represent a word having these letters prominently within it. There have been many suggestions as to what this symbol could refer to, but the most plausible solution is offered by David Jacobson. He has noted that, when the Ituraean client king Zenodorus died, Augustus gave all of his territory, comprising Ituraea and Trachonitis, to Herod as tetrarch (*War* 1:400; *Ant.* 15:359–60).[29] Augustus assigned this territory to Herod in 23 BCE, and further territory was handed over three years later, in 20 BCE, when Augustus visited Syria;[30] thus, 'Year 3' celebrated Herod being three years as tetrarch, in 20 BCE.[31] The *tau-rho* may well also refer to *Trachonitis*, since this territory could be referred to as 'Trachonitis' alone (*War* 3:510; *Ant.* 18:137; Strabo, *Geogr.* 16:2:20). Later, in the year 10 BCE, Herod allegedly quashed banditry there by settling Judaean (Idumaean) mercenaries (*Ant.* 16:271–5).[32] This was Gentile territory.

Our third piece of evidence is found in the writings of Julius Africanus from the second century. He states specifically that Genesis 49:10 was read to affirm the rule of Herod (Eusebius, *Hist. Eccles.* 1:6–7):[33]

At this time Herod became the first foreigner to become king of the nation of the Judaeans, so fulfilling the words of Moses: 'A ruler shall not fail from Judah, nor a leader from his loins,' he says, 'until the reserved things come for him; and this man is the expectation of nations.' There could be no fulfilment of the prophecy as long as they [= Judaeans] were free to live under rulers of their own people, starting with Moses himself and lasting to the reign of Augustus, at which time the first foreigner, Herod, was entrusted by the Romans with rule.

(*Hist. Eccles.* 1:6:1–2)

The Roman intervention to place Herod as king of the Judaeans was therefore read as the disruption of Judahite rule (Eusebius, *Hist. Eccles.* 1:6:3–5). Herod was not a Judahite, but rather his father Antipater was the son of a certain Herod from Ascalon, who was a Gentile temple-servant of Apollo, brought up in Idumaea after being taken prisoner (*Hist. Eccles.* 1:6:3). Africanus indicates that 'when to such a man the kingdom of the Judaeans came, already the one who was really the expectation of nations, following the prophecy, was present at the gates (*epi thurais . . . parēn*)' (*Hist. Eccles.* 1:6:4). Herod was just one step. After the rupture of Gentile rule, *then* the Messiah would come (*Hist. Eccles.* 1:6:7–8).[34]

All this indicates how Herod was able to point to divine will in terms of his right to rule. We have

1 a prediction ascribed to Menahem the Essene of Herod's rule without a scriptural passage;
2 a prediction by Josephus of Vespasian's rule that appears to use Genesis 49:9–10;
3 a prediction as recorded by Africanus of Herod's rule ascribed to Genesis 49:9–10.

We can plausibly propose that the same scriptural passage as used by Josephus and Africanus was also used by Menahem. Africanus's interpretation greatly helps us to make sense of the complexity of Menahem's interpretation. Despite Menahem endorsing Herod's rule as a Gentile, he was not in the end endorsing Herod as a righteous king, and certainly not as the Messiah. But, since Essenes believed all rulers were put in place by God (*War* 2:140), it was *necessary* for Herod to rule. Even though the prediction was complex, Herod could well use this prediction to claim that he was king by divine will. He was not of the loins of Judah, indeed, and yet was a Judaean king, and he ruled over Gentiles as Genesis 49:9–10 predicted.

Yet, for others, Herod had become king by divine mandate, fulfilling the expectation of the Gentiles, but the true Messiah would apparently follow after his rule ended. This explains why Herod was particularly vigilant, and this may also explain his savage behaviour towards his sons. It would also explain why people were hopeful. And it explains why the students of Judah and Matthias took the bold step of tearing down the Roman eagle from the front of the Temple on hearing news that Herod was dying: the end of Roman rule was coming. The same hope can be seen in three revolts which exploded throughout Judaea after Herod's death, each one headed, apparently, by a would-be messiah.

The memory of this turmoil upon Herod's death was so acute it is found even as late as the *Protevangelium of James*. The Papyrus Bodmer 5 version correctly reflects the situation at the end of its text: 'I, James, [am] the one who wrote this account (*historia*) in Jerusalem, after a disturbance (*thorubos*) came about *when Herod died*, after I withdrew myself *to the wilderness* until the disturbance ceased [in] Jerusalem' (25:1–3, italics mine). The ending of the *Protevangelium* here provides detail that can be correlated with historical events, as told by Josephus. This is detail not found in the Gospels of Matthew and Luke: that there were revolts when Herod died, just at the time when Joseph gets a hopeful message to return to the Land of Israel (Matt. 2:20–1). But this detail is vital.

The War of Varus

The period in history immediately following Herod's death is rarely discussed fully as being immensely significant, but in many ways the turmoil of that time was a prequel of the First Revolt of 66–70 CE, and it demonstrates the deep feelings of the population of Judaea.[35] According to Josephus, when Archelaus was finally named as his father's successor, and Herod's army in Jericho went to place the diadem on his head, he cannily declined to accept it until his role had been ratified by the emperor Augustus in Rome. Given the weight of expectation and the recent killing of his brother Antipater, to be reticent was probably wise in terms of the public mood, and it also showed his deference to the emperor's decision.

Herod's body was placed on a solid golden bier covered with a superb purple cloth, and taken from Jericho to Herodion (a route which would have passed by Bethlehem) in a solemn procession with family, household staff and armed regiments, including a guard of Thracians, Germans and Gauls (*War* 1:670–3; *Ant.* 17:198–9).[36] He was buried in his monumental tomb in Herodion (overlooking Bethlehem), and seven days of public mourning were decreed. Then Archelaus came to Jerusalem to make a sacrifice at the Temple. He released prisoners, gave a speech announcing his goodwill and attempted to be conciliatory. But he was met with protests. One group demanded tax reductions, another group demanded a reduction in sales tax, and another group demanded the release of prisoners. Archelaus apparently agreed to all demands (*War* 2:1–7; *Ant.* 17:200–5).[37]

However, Archelaus had to deal with the fallout from the horrific execution of Judas, Matthias and their students, and all the fury at Herod in general. A massive rally ensued in the Temple. Huge numbers of people shrieked and wailed in mourning at what had happened to the students and their teachers, who were martyrs for the laws of the nation and the Temple itself. They demanded the immediate removal of the replacement high priest, Joazar (see *Ant.* 17:164–5), and called for a proper method to choose his successor. Archelaus, initially aiming to show clemency and patience, sent various representatives to them, including his general, to try to appease the crowd, and they all were met with hails of stones. This 'Jerusalem Spring' moment ran to the Passover in April 4 BCE, with the protest rally continuing in the Temple and more people joining it as many came in from the regions for the festival (*War* 2:8–10; *Ant.* 17:208–12).[38] We remember here Joseph's signal from the angel to return to 'the Land of Israel' now that Herod was dead. News of his death would have quickly spread to Jewish communities beyond Judaea. There surely was hope. Archelaus was not yet confirmed as king.

But this hope turned to violence. Archelaus decided to act as an authoritative kingly ruler, willy-nilly, even without official endorsement, and finally lost his patience. A military presence was stationed hard by the Temple in a fortress built by Herod and named in honour of Mark Antony, who had enabled him to take Jerusalem in 37 BCE. Known as the Antonia, it allowed soldiers to keep a close eye on whatever happened below in the huge Temple courts (see Plate 9), and they could spring into action from this location with no warning. Archelaus sent in a cohort (*speira*) of 1,000 troops to arrest the ringleaders. This caused an enormous clash. The troops were set upon and pelted with stones, and many were killed. Archelaus then sent in his entire large army, including cavalry, which stormed the Temple and allegedly killed 3,000 people. Anyone remaining in the Temple precincts was told to go home, and people fled to the hills, namely to shelter in caves there (*War* 2:12–13; *Ant.* 17:213–18), as James is represented as doing in the *Protevangelium*, and Jesus would advise people to do in a future period of tribulation (Matt. 24:16). It is hard to imagine the horror and terror of the clampdown on this great protest rally, and the carnage, taking place as it did at the time of celebration of Passover, commemorating the people's liberation from bondage in Egypt. It would also have been a crushing disappointment. Archelaus was no better than his father, and Archelaus intended to rule as king.[39] Where was the Messiah?

Josephus tells of how Archelaus then went to the port of Caesarea Maritima with his entourage, including Salome the sister of Herod,[40] and proceeded to sail for Rome to be confirmed as ruler of Judaea, leaving his brother Philip in charge. Perhaps he thought he had conclusively quashed the rebellion, but clearly the legate of Syria, Publius Quinctilius Varus,[41] thought otherwise. Marching down from Antioch with three legions (*War* 2:40),[42] some 15,000 men, he arrived in Jerusalem to take charge, and posted Philip off to Rome as well (*War* 2:83), along with a party of fifty leading Judaean representatives (see below). Varus then left, after installing the Roman procurator (*epitropos*) for the province of Syria (*War* 2:16), Sabinus, in the royal palace in Jerusalem with control over all the Herodian palace-fortresses (implicitly including Herodion; *War* 2:14–19; *Ant.* 17:219–23). Not to be outdone, Archelaus's brother Antipas also sailed for Rome to stake his own claims (*War* 2:20–38; *Ant.* 17:224–8).[43]

While the Herodian heirs were overseas disputing about their succession in Rome, and Judaea was under direct Roman control, there was open revolt. At the Feast of Pentecost, seven weeks after the bloodbath of Passover (i.e. June 4 BCE), Judaean fighters assembled in the Temple, spread out and surrounded the 5,000-strong Roman legion left in Jerusalem, and attacked the Romans in the Phasael tower adjacent to the royal palace. The Roman legionaries fought back, the Judaean fighters retreated to the Temple, and then the Romans set fire to the Temple porticoes. The fighters – who had come from Galilee, Idumaea, Jericho, Peraea, and beyond – were burned to death, or fell from heights, or killed themselves to avoid capture, after which the Romans plundered the Temple treasury, with the remainder of the funds (of 400 silver talents) collected by Sabinus (*War* 2:39–50; *Ant.* 17:249–64).[44]

The Judaean fighters elsewhere were then even more enraged and motivated. A large group of the royal troops of Herod deserted and joined the insurrection, while others (the Sebasteni) fought on the side of the Romans.[45] The fighters, no doubt bolstered by the defection of many Herodian troops to their cause, managed to surround the royal palace in Jerusalem, and promised Sabinus and his men safety if they surrendered (*War* 2:51–4; *Ant.* 17:265–8). Now they wanted 'national/ancestral autonomy' (*tēn patrion autonomian*, *War* 2:53), 'national/ancestral freedom' (*eleutherian tēn patrion*, *Ant.* 17:267).[46] This is the language of revolution, and indeed in both the First (66–70 CE) and the Second Revolt (132–6 CE) the revolutionaries would issue coinage proclaiming 'for the freedom of Zion' (*kherut Tsion*), or 'for the freedom of Jerusalem' (*lekherut Yerushalem*), and date documents from a point of liberation.[47]

In Rome, the fifty leading Judaeans who had followed Archelaus and journeyed to Rome with Varus's blessing 'before the revolt' (*pro tēs apostaseōs*, *War* 2:80) also pleaded for Judaean autonomy.[48] There was a face-off between them and the royal claimants in a council convened by the emperor in the temple of Palatine Apollo in Rome.[49] The deputation from Judaea spoke of Herod's terrible tyranny. He had killed and tortured, and wrecked towns, and sunk the nation into poverty, and now his son Archelaus had killed 3,000 people in the Temple at a festival. This group sought Roman help: to do away with dodgy client rulers in Judaea and have Judaea joined to the rest of Syria under the administration of the Syrian legate (Varus) with *Judaean* governors (*War* 2:80–5; *Ant.* 17:304–14).[50]

But the emperor Augustus ruled in favour of the royal client rulers of the house of Herod, not conceding anything to this group. The kingdom of Herod would be divided into four parts: the territory of Idumaea, traditional Judaea and Samaria would be collectively ruled by Archelaus as ethnarch; Galilee and Peraea would be ruled by Antipas; Philip would rule Batanaea, Trachonitis and Auranitis; while Salome, the sister of Herod, was given Jamnia, Azotus and Phasaelis as independent cities. Each region and city would provide revenue for the royal house by taxation. However, some Syro-Palestinian Hellenic cities which had been attached to Herod's kingdom would be joined to Syria: Gaza, Gadara and Hippos (*War* 2:80-100; *Ant.* 17:317-23).[51] This solution would have been a crushing blow to those Judaeans who had sought a moderate and more independent outcome.

Meanwhile, during the time the deputations were in Rome, the Judaean fighters' occupation of Jerusalem continued, and revolts in support of the liberation of Judaea broke out in other places, sometimes led – according to Josephus – by various men who considered themselves to be rightful royal rulers.[52] His account is of course selective, and dependent on Nicolaus of Damascus, who was staunchly opposed to all of these, and there are additional overlays of Josephus's own pro-Roman perspective. One can nevertheless get some sense of the extreme turbulence and what took place.

In Idumaea, 2,000 of Herod's veteran troops fought against the royal guard (under Herod's cousin Achiab), though the leader of these troops is not named and the details are not provided. The fight was so fierce, however, that Achiab was driven to the hills, to the wilderness (*War* 2:54; *Ant.* 17:269-70), most likely the Negev Desert.

This war was probably not about kingship, but a number of rebellions clearly were (so *War* 2:55). A man named Judas son of Hezekiah assembled fighters 'around (*peri*) Sepphoris of Galilee', stormed the royal palace and broke into the arsenal (*War* 2:56; *Ant.* 17:271-2). Hezekiah is defined in Josephus's writings as a bandit chief (*War* 1:204; *Ant.* 14:159-60; 17:271), with his son now seizing the opportunity to gain control of the central part of Galilee,[53] though Josephus indicates that Judas wanted kingship and attacked other claimants (*War* 2:56), and this suggests much grander aims than theft. Sepphoris, the capital of Galilee, lay only 4 miles (6 km) away from Nazareth. It was originally a Syro-Phoenician city built on a hill overlooking the Beth Netofa Valley and was occupied by Judaean forces at the time of Alexander Jannaeus in the early first century BCE (*Ant.* 13:338). When the Romans occupied the area in the wake of Pompey's invasion (*c.*57-55 BCE), one of the regional councils was set up there (*Ant.* 14:90). Importantly, it had been a stronghold of Antigonus Mattathias, Herod's rival, and Herod and his Roman forces had taken it in 37 BCE (*Ant.* 17:289). It may well have been that some of the population stayed loyal to Antigonus and supported

Judas's initiative to reject Herodian rule. Sepphoris was strategically important, commanding good views, and overseeing multiple villages.[54]

In Peraea, a man named Simon who had been a slave within Herod's court – apparently tall and handsome – flagrantly wore the diadem of kingship, and attacked and burned the royal palace of Jericho and other Herodian mansions, while another group of associated Peraeans burned the palace of Betharamatha (Amathus), near the River Jordan. Josephus states that two Roman officers, Rufus and Gratus, led the royal infantry, along with archers from Trachonitis and the three cohorts of Sebasteni, and gained victory over Simon and his Peraean fighters. Simon was caught while fleeing along a steep ravine and subsequently beheaded (*War* 2:57–9; *Ant.* 17:273–7). This Simon was widely known, so much so that he is mentioned by Tacitus (*Hist.* 5:9) as usurping royal rule. He proclaimed himself king without waiting on Augustus's decision regarding Archelaus, and Tacitus attributes the suppression of his revolt to the actions of the legate of Syria, Varus (see below).

Another man, a shepherd named Athronges, strong and tall, also claimed kingship. He was supported by four brothers and a leadership council, and he too wore the diadem of kingship. He attracted Judaean fighters who attacked both Romans and other Judaeans. He seems to have operated in traditional Judaea. His forces ambushed a Roman convoy near Emmaus that was carrying grain and arms to the legion (in Jerusalem), killing the centurion, Arius, and forty men. Athronges' own fate is not mentioned, but the four brothers continued fighting. They were nevertheless eventually defeated by Archelaus's generals Gratus and Ptolemy, employing the might of the Sebasteni. Archelaus took the eldest brother prisoner, and the last brother surrendered, but, as Josephus says, this rebellion lasted a long time (*War* 2:60–5; *Ant.* 17:278–84).

In terms of the basis for any claims to rule, in no case does Josephus indicate that these men who donned the diadem were from the line of David, but Josephus carefully avoids mention of the expectation of a messiah of the line of David in any of his works. After all, for him Judaean kingship was related to the Hasmonean priestly dynasty, his own line. Furthermore, he thought that a key passage interpreted by 'wise men' as pointing to the Messiah actually pointed to Vespasian, as we have seen.[55] He never mentions David in connection with the belief in a future ruler. When he paraphrases scriptural passages that were used to point to a messiah of David's line, he even makes changes to ensure this meaning is hidden. While in 1 Chronicles 17:12 it is said that David's throne would endure for ever, Josephus states that David's house would be glorious and renowned and David rejoiced that his descendants would rule, but there is no mention of 'for ever' (*Ant.* 7:94). Overall, as Louis Feldman has explored, he de-emphasises David in his narrative of Judaean history and concentrates on his virtues.[56] Therefore, absence of any specific mention of Davidic lineage for someone claiming kingly rule in Josephus cannot mean they were *not* of the house of David. The Romans later targeted David's descendants for a reason (see Chapter 2).

According to Josephus, the insurrections in general lasted a long time (*Ant.* 17:285) and the royal claimants 'filled the whole of Judaea with piratical war' (*War* 2:65). This means that we should not assume that the Romans quickly sorted everything out.[57] But they did act, in what was remembered by Josephus as a military incursion paralleling the huge invasions of the Seleucid king Antiochus Epiphanes in 170–168 BCE, the Roman Pompey in 63 BCE, and Vespasian and Titus in 66–70 CE (*Apion* 1:34).[58] In scholarly discussions, the revolts of 4 BCE have often been configured as a cluster of random rebellions, or even riots,[59] rather than a national revolt as such. Thus, in Schürer's influential presentation, they are defined quite briefly as 'Disturbances after Herod's Death'.[60] But in the *Seder Olam*, a little-known work of Jewish historiography attributed to Rabbi Yose from the late second century,[61] what took place was a huge post-Herod rebellion, involving multiple elements, recognised as the 'War of Varus'. It was a benchmark of Judaean history, along with the First Revolt (the 'War of Vespasian', 68–70 CE), the 'War of Quietus' (*c.*115 CE) and the Second Revolt (the 'War of Ben Koziba', 132–6 CE).[62] Judaea in 4 BCE was in revolution.

Josephus states that Varus, on receiving messages from Sabinus asking for aid, then mobilised two legions (10,000 soldiers) and four cavalry regiments of 2,000 men and marched them down to Ptolemais on the coast, where further auxiliary troops from client kings and powerful people were assembled. The massive mobilisation also brought in support from Aretas IV, the king of Nabataea, who supplied a large contingent. This operation would have taken time to arrange, the aim being to ensure there was a force of colossal strength. From Ptolemais the Romans and their allies marched into Galilee under the command of the general Gaius.

The Romans duly arrived with incredible force at Sepphoris, burned the town and enslaved the inhabitants. Varus then led some of his troops through Samaria and torched various villages, an action that indicates Josephus did not include all the details of the rebellion in his narrative, because no reason is given for this destruction, apart from attributing cruelty to the Arab Nabataeans, who were settling old scores with Herod. They marched through to Emmaus (Nicopolis), which in this case was burned in revenge for the murder of Arius and his forty soldiers. Reaching Jerusalem, which was now independently ruled by Judaeans (since Sabinus had eventually managed to escape for the coast), Varus and his legions met the client kings' armies and their commanders and the Sebasteni outside the city. On seeing the might of the Romans and their allies, the Judaean fighters fled, while the remaining Jerusalemites themselves swore loyalty to Rome rather than standing with them (no doubt mindful of what had happened in Sepphoris). Those fighters who fled were, however, hunted down. Some were imprisoned, but Varus crucified *two thousand* of these men (*War* 2:66–75; *Ant.* 17:286–95).[63] It is hard to imagine the horror. Crucifixion was the most agonising and terrorising method the Romans had devised to torture someone to death as both a punishment and a public deterrent. It was expected that the bodies of those nailed to wood would be subject to utter humiliation, including after death, when they could be left to be eaten by birds of prey and dogs.[64]

Turning to Idumaea, Varus sent the Nabataeans away and went with his own Roman legions to quash the revolt there. The leaders were seized and sent to Rome for trial. Varus then left a legion in Jerusalem and returned to Antioch, perhaps hopeful that the moderate group of Judaeans he had sent to Rome would prevail (*War* 2:76–9; *Ant.* 17:296–9). At some point, when it was safe enough, Herod's sons Archelaus, Antipas and Philip, along with all their retinue, returned and took up their rule. Their indebtedness to Roman military might would have been absolutely clear.

While these events at the death of Herod have long been documented and discussed, the reasons why the revolts occurred with such ferocity upon Herod's death have not been fully explained.[65] Certainly, they can be understood as a release of fury after the injustices of the reign of Herod, the killings of the students and teachers, and the appalling massacre in the Temple by Archelaus. But, given the hopeful interpretation of Genesis 49:9–10 in the air, they would also have been fuelled by messianic prediction. Instead of looking to restore the Hasmonean house (from which Josephus himself claimed descent) or establish another kind of priestly rule (as perhaps the moderates in Rome were suggesting), the populace looked for an alternative *king* who would shake off Roman rule entirely: the royal diadem is explicitly mentioned in regard to the leaders of different Judaean armed forces.

Furthermore, while Josephus presents Varus as heroically marching through the land with all the might of the Roman legions and their allies to restore Roman control, he also indicates that the revolts continued for a long time, especially that of Athronges and his brothers. He does not say that the Roman legate Varus and his troops put down that particular rebellion but rather that it was defeated by Gratus and Ptolemy. While this seems to imply it was done prior to Varus's arrival, it could have been afterwards. He doesn't mention Judas son of Hezekiah actually being captured or killed by Varus. It was the population of Sepphoris that was killed or enslaved; there is no mention of what happened to Judas himself.[66]

Josephus is, then, not interested in telling a comprehensive story, and he is limited by what he found recorded by Herod's chronicler, Nicolaus. He does not care to portray the effect on the people of Judaea of this enormous Roman invasion and all the abuse, bloodshed and terror that resulted from it. In line with his Roman-friendly perspective (and tone of aristocratic superiority), he presents it as a case of the Romans properly sorting out a troublesome nation, subduing the problematic masses and restoring order. The significance of it is nevertheless reflected in that the 'War of Varus' is included as one of the above-mentioned 'benchmark' events Josephus acknowledges in his work *Against Apion*, as it is also included in the rabbinic *Seder Olam* a century later.

In addition, in a first-century work known as the *Assumption of Moses* or *Testament of Moses*, there is a statement of prediction, as if stated by Moses, that is meant to strike chords of deep recognition in its readers, while asking them to reflect on how their own sins have contributed to God's willingness to afflict them with cruel rulers:

And a wanton king, who will not be of a priestly family, will follow them. He will be a rash man and perverse, and he will judge them as they deserve. He will shatter their leaders with the sword, and he will (exterminate them) in secret places so that no one will know where their bodies are. He will kill both old and young, showing mercy to none.

Then fear of him will be heaped upon them in their land, and for thirty-four years he will impose judgements upon them as did the Egyptians, and he will punish them. And he will beget heirs who will reign after him for shorter periods of time. After his death there will come into their land a powerful king of the West who will subdue them; and he will take away captives, and a part of their temple he will burn with fire. He will crucify some of them around their city.

When this has taken place, the times will quickly come to an end . . .'[67]
(*Test. Mos.* 6:2 – 7:1)

This prediction is designed to correlate with recent events: the reign of Herod, leading to the rule of Herod's sons. As a 'wanton king', Herod's rule lasted for thirty-four years, from 37 to 4 BCE. Here, the statement about his wickedness interestingly correlates with Menahem's prediction (*Ant.* 15:373–6; cf. *War* 2:159), which we have connected with the prophecy of Genesis 49:9–10. There is mention of Herod's heirs, who are noted as ruling for shorter periods of time.[68] The 'powerful king of the West', who arrives after the king's death, clearly indicates the Roman emperor, acting via representatives; thus, Sabinus's troops' burning of part of the Temple and Varus's crucifixions are the actions of the same powerful individual. What is particularly striking here is the claim that 'the times will quickly come to an end' following all this; this links with the interpretation of Genesis 49:9–10 in Julius Africanus, which suggested that the Messiah would come hot on the heels of Herod. However, here this event is pushed back to a point following the rule of Herod's sons.

This statement shows that hope had not ceased, but scriptural interpretation was reconfigured. The *Testament of Moses* reassures readers that God's eschatological interventions are close at hand: the messenger of God will be sent, the kingdom (of God) will appear throughout all creation, the devil and sorrow will be removed, and the heavenly one will go from his throne in heaven with indignation and wrath to destroy the nations that have oppressed and abused Israel, and bring Israel to safety in the heavens (10:1–12). Here we see again an intellectual resistance, and one that represents the profound anger that the Roman action left behind in Judaea. This, then, encapsulates the prevailing mood after Varus, during the childhood of Jesus.

The archaeology of the revolt

A word needs to be said about the archaeology of this rebellion and its defeat in the War of Varus. Excavations in Sepphoris have not found a clear burnt layer across the site. It is likely that the city of this time would have been on the acropolis, and no ashy stratum can be distinguished,[69] though the royal palace and arsenal have not actually been identified precisely either. If some burning happened on upper storeys and reconstruction work was thorough, then it would not be easily found. Indeed, it seems that much of the post-revolt construction was on bedrock, indicating a total clearance.

Some evidence in refugee caves in the Judaean wilderness could very well be attributed to the time when Judaean fighters (and their families) fled there in 4 BCE, but the dating of artefacts in the caves is often imprecise, and archaeologists have tended to think more of the more famous revolts of 70 CE (First Revolt) and 132–6 CE (Second or Bar Kokhba Revolt). More positively, destruction of the part of the Jericho palatial complex has been attributed to the actions of Simon's troops.[70]

In 2000, a limestone tablet came to light, apparently found by a Bedouin man somewhere east of the Dead Sea, which may relate to this time if it is authentic.[71] Now dubbed the Gabriel Revelation, it contains eighty-seven lines of a fragmentary Hebrew text written in ink. Dated to the late first century BCE, it is a series of short predictions in the first-person singular by a figure named Gabriel, surely the angel: it is as if the angel is directly speaking to a recipient, who is addressed in the second-person singular. The recipient then records this message on stone. In terms of form, the content seems remarkably like the kind of angelic revelations interwoven with scriptural allusions or quotations that one might well imagine were received by Essenes in dreams, but there is no precise interpretation provided, as in a *pesher*, to link these with events that can be determined exactly.[72] The text has references to an attack on Jerusalem (line 57) and the Messiah as 'my servant David' (lines 16, 72), yet there is a great deal of ambiguity. There are several controversies about its reading, but Israel

Knohl has suggested that this relates to the failed uprising led by Simon, who was killed in the ravine after his army was routed by Gratus.[73] Further work on this tablet in the future will benefit from new technologies, which may well also settle the question of its authenticity.

Joseph's revelations

At any rate, when we look at the historical background of the post-Herod revolt, the War of Varus, this makes sense of what is written in Matthew 2 regarding Joseph's decisions about returning from Egypt to 'the Land of Israel'. There are different stages in terms of the events as told. At first, Joseph, again using his method of prediction, gets news from an angel:

> [19]After the death of Herod, look, an angel of the Lord appeared to Joseph in Egypt in a dream [20]saying, 'Get up, take the child and his mother and go back to the Land of Israel, for those who were seeking the child's life are dead.' [21]So he got up and took the child and his mother and came into the Land of Israel.

There is a curious note struck in the plural 'those' here, as if it was not just Herod who was the enemy: in fact, Antipater had just been killed by his father as well. This may hint that what we have is condensed from a fuller source account. The Davidic 'Land of Israel' concept carries the hope of restoration, as we saw. Joseph hoped for someone other than a son of Herod to rule. This would be the moment of liberation. But then he gets bad news:

> [22]But hearing that Archelaus was reigning as ruler of Judaea instead of his father Herod, he was afraid to go out (*apelthein*) there. Warned in a dream, he departed into the region of Galilee, [23]and came and resided in a city named Nazareth, so that what was spoken through the prophets would be fulfilled: 'he shall be called *Nazōraios*.'

Joseph got to the Land of Israel, journeying to Bethlehem, perhaps buoyed by the 'Jerusalem Spring' of people gathering in the Temple demanding justice, only to find that Archelaus was now very much taking up a position of reigning as ruler in Judaea and ready to throw his weight around. So much for change. Depending on the exact timing, Joseph would surely have learned much more as well: details of the horrific massacre in the Temple, for example. Therefore, the double movement of being called back to the Land of Israel upon Herod's death (hopeful of better times) and making the journey but then moving off to Nazareth in Galilee (worried about Archelaus) correlates well with the events leading up to the War of Varus.

The above scenario modifies what Raymond Brown proposed in terms of the source text and the Matthean redaction. As we saw in Chapter 4, Brown thought that the nativity, the story of the magi, the massacre, the flight to Egypt and the return to 'the Land of Israel' were all part of the pre-Matthean stratum. This stratum itself utilised a typology of correspondence with the scriptural and midrashic retellings of the story of Moses, illuminated by angels in dreams. However, he did not understand the shift in movement. In Matthew 2:19–23 he noted two straightforward geographical thrusts: first, one to go to Egypt and then to go back to the Land of Israel; and then a second one to go to the region of Galilee. He detached the second one from the pre-Matthean stratum, which would thus conclude with the statement that Joseph 'got up and took the child and his mother and came into the Land of Israel' (Matt. 2:21).[74]

The doubling of returning to 'the Land of Israel', and then getting a second command to go to Galilee, seemed odd to Brown. Why didn't the angel simply tell Joseph in the first dream to go straight to Galilee?[75] He determined that the passage of Matthew 2:22–3 about Joseph going to Nazareth in Galilee was very similar to Matthew 4:12–16 in language, hence Matthean style, and – since there are two distinct geographical parts – that meant that Matthew was not the creator of 2:19–21 but was the creator of 2:22–3. This could be confirmed by the fact that Luke has the story originally set in Nazareth, which Brown thought of as a separate tradition. There was, therefore, no pre-Matthean story explaining the move between Bethlehem and Nazareth: each evangelist had worked it out for himself how to place Jesus in Nazareth (in due course) despite having been born in Bethlehem.[76]

However, given historical circumstances, the geographical movement in Matthew makes good sense. The Lukan nativity, as we have seen, does work things out differently by creating a preceding period of residence in Nazareth where the annunciation to Mary and the divine conception takes place, but since this is actually a responsive retelling of Matthew, it is Matthew that holds greater weight for actuality.

For Joseph, or anyone of the Davidic line, there was a very good reason in 4 BCE to be extremely frightened, once Archelaus was ruling. He was no better than his predecessor. We remember here that the tomb of Archelaus, as built, is recorded by Jerome as existing on the very edge of Bethlehem, just at the bottom of the hill below where the Basilica of the Nativity and the monks' cells would be in the fourth century (see Figs 3.1, 3.2). If so, in building his tomb there, Archelaus would make a claim even bolder than that of his father against the descendants of David, and the implications for the people of Bethlehem (and whoever remained of the Davidic house) would have been huge. The location of his tomb in fact raises significant questions about the role of the descendants of David in regard to any of these revolts. Josephus states that Athronges the shepherd[77] did not have any noble lineage, but that begs a question about the other would-be kings. Simon might have been reduced to the role of a slave, serving in the house of Herod, but that does not mean all his forebears were slaves.

Given the reign of Archelaus, and his frightening actions, Joseph chooses not to return to Bethlehem or to stay in (traditional) Judaea at all, but he also decides not to return to the safety of Egypt. Amazingly, he chooses to go to Galilee. There is no indication that this was because Antipas had been appointed as tetrarch and he was much milder than his brother. Rather, we can situate this decision before the formal beginning of Antipas's rule. This decision seems to express a hope that the region of Galilee was, at the time of the decision, *free of danger* from the house of Herod. From Josephus, we learn that it was precisely at this time in Galilee that Judas son of Hezekiah had stormed the royal palace of Sepphoris and was ruling there independently, and bringing in people from around the city. At that very time, while the succession was still in doubt and rebels held this area, Joseph chooses to go to Nazareth, a neighbouring village to Sepphoris.

However, after Joseph and his family were settled there, the liberating insurgency was utterly crushed by Varus and the mighty legions and cavalry of the Roman army, supported by the auxiliary troops of others, including a large contingent of Nabataean soldiers. What then, in terms of Joseph's decision? From the point where Joseph takes his family to Nazareth, Matthew falls completely silent. The story of Jesus is then picked up from the narrative of the Gospel of Mark, where Jesus comes to the River Jordan to see John the Baptist, who is proclaiming a coming heavenly figure (Matt. 3:1–6 //Mark 1:1–6). There is nothing about Varus, or what it was like in Nazareth during Jesus' early years. Joseph is presented as having completed his job of keeping Jesus safe, out of the reach of Herod and his son Archelaus, with the help of angelic instruction in dreams and Scripture. He has read the signs of the times accurately. The mere fact that Jesus survived, and grew to adulthood, is a measure of his success and loving care.

What we have, then, in Matthew 1 – 2 overall is at core Joseph's story during the final years of Herod's reign and the first year of Archelaus, *c*.6–4 BCE. Many verbs are in the third-person singular: this is all about Joseph, what he experienced and what he did in order to protect the child: Jesus. It is written as if Joseph's voice lies behind it. This account can be understood as having been retold, filtered through retellings in the early Judaean churches led by Jesus' siblings, retold further in wider Syria, and finally edited by the author of Matthew, probably in Syria. However, what it indicates about Jesus' early childhood relies in part on a wider cultural memory of what happened in Judaea. It provides a pointer to sociopolitical turbulence, terrible pain and suffering, extreme violence, revolution, atrocities and disaster for those who fought against the Roman Empire.

Jesus in these early years was taken from home as his family sought safety while foreigners from the West clobbered the country and defended their client ruler, foreigners who massacred those who stood up for ancestral customs and law in the holy city of Jerusalem. The story in Matthew implies the messianic hopes of a large swathe of the population. It demonstrates forms of prediction and interpretation based on serious scriptural knowledge and training. It shows us Joseph as a father who was deeply concerned to protect his wife and son from harm, and would make bold and courageous decisions. Just as he had taken his family to safety in Egypt, he would again take them to safety far from Bethlehem and traditional Judaea itself. They would need to emigrate to Galilee.

8

Growing up Galilean

Despite being born in Bethlehem, Jesus was remembered as a man from Nazareth. This was known as his specific home town, his *patris*.[1] Yet, in Matthew's Gospel, Nazareth is initially a place in which Joseph and his family arrive after being forced to flee from their real ancestral home. Now – unlike in Egypt – they stay and put down roots. They become immigrants.[2]

In general, as we have seen, scholars of the historical Jesus have tended to make Nazareth foundational, with the move to Bethlehem for Jesus' birth deemed a completely invented notion. E. P. Sanders used the very movement between Nazareth and Bethlehem to conclude that this story was invented.[3] As he sets it out, in Matthew 1:18 – 2:23 Mary and Joseph live in Bethlehem, go to Egypt, return to Bethlehem, then move to Nazareth; in Luke 2:1–39 Joseph and Mary live in Nazareth, go to Bethlehem (for the census) and return 'to their home in Nazareth'. He states that it is not possible for both of these stories to be accurate and it 'is improbable that either is', in that they agree on only two sets of 'facts': 'in real history, Jesus was from Nazareth; in salvation history, he must have been born in Bethlehem.'[4] Apparently, it is necessary to choose either one place or another for Jesus' family's home town, and people certainly cannot be torn between two locations.

However, as we have explored in Chapter 5, if we read Luke 1 – 2 as responsive to Matthew's story, as a midrashic and creative retelling (yet with certain memory snippets embedded), there is a solution. The Lukan placement of Nazareth answers the valid question that might arise from reading Matthew: why did the family go to Nazareth – of all places? In the next stage of development, however, the author of the *Protevangelium* actually rejected Nazareth completely as an option in their story. Nazareth is not a place where anything happens. No one is Galilean. In this, the *Protevangelium* follows through on the Matthean (or pre-Matthean) story and appears to 'correct' an impression one may get from Luke.

'He will be called *Nazōraios*'

Following Matthew as our basic historical source, then, Jesus was brought to settle in Nazareth as a small child, as a refugee from (traditional) Judaea. He grew up there and gained his identity from Nazareth, rather than Bethlehem (his father's home). In this, his identity is typical of second-generation immigrants, who do not continue the identity of their parents in terms of their provenance, even if born in their parents' home town. It is growing up in a place that forms you in terms of how you speak and how you see the world, even though you can look to a heritage somewhere else. Jesus grew up in Nazareth. He was known as coming from Nazareth, not Bethlehem. In Mark, Jesus is said to have arrived 'from Nazareth in Galilee' (1:9) to be baptised by John. Given the messianic predictions concerned with Bethlehem (John 7:40–3, 52), one might well ask what good could come from Nazareth (John 1:46).

Joseph's interpretation remains crucial here: in Matthew the verbs continue to be in the third-person singular, not plural: 'he', not 'they'. The family's arrival in Nazareth is then a result of Joseph's decision, stemming from his final dream:

> Being warned [by an angel] in a dream, he got away (*anechōrēsen*) to the region of Galilee, and coming (*elthōn*) [there] he resided (*katōkēsen*) in a city[5] called Nazareth, so that what was spoken through the prophets would be fulfilled: 'He will be called *Nazōraios*.' (Matt. 2:22–3)

As Robert Myles notes, 'Nazareth's insignificance makes it a suitable hiding place for the exiled. Escaping to a small village far from the political centre of Judea means that Jesus will be "off the radar" of the ruling aristocracy.'[6]

The term *Nazōraios* is usually translated as 'Nazarene'. It is certainly connected with the place. Joseph understands that it is necessary to live in Nazareth, in particular, to fulfil a prophecy regarding his son: someone who lived in Nazareth would be called *Nazōraios*. However, fulfilment of Scripture, in this case, would have been oddly unclear to a Greek-reading audience, who would find the quotation 'he will be called *Nazōraios*' nowhere in the Greek Septuagint. They would have found the single word *Nazōraios* nowhere either; no one would be identified as being called by this term.

To explain this puzzle, Jerome recognised that Matthew 2:23 follows the Hebrew text of Scripture (Jerome, *Vir. Ill.* 3), as he found it in the Aramaic version of Matthew, 'the gospel of the Hebrews/Nazarenes', that he consulted in the Caesarea library (*Adv. Pel.* 3:2),[7] but he does not identify precisely which scriptural passage is meant. Various solutions have been offered,[8] especially given that the introduction of something spoken 'through the prophets' is vague, but the prediction seems to relate best to the Hebrew text of Isaiah 11:1: 'A sprout/rod (*khoter*) will come forth from the stem of Jesse, and a shoot/branch (*netser*) from his roots will bear fruit.'[9] The term *netser* in itself is messianic in the *Hymns* (*Hodayot*) of the Dead Sea Scrolls (1QH 6:15; 7:19; 8:6, 8, 10). This word is connected to the Davidic ancestor Jesse and to messianic hopes.

In the Greek Septuagint form of Isaiah 11:1 the term for *netser*, 'shoot' is *anthos* (more often meaning 'blossom'), and the verse reads: 'A rod (*rhabdos*) will come forth from the root (*rhiza*) of Jesse, and a shoot/blossom (*anthos*) from the root will rise up.' Jesus is called *anthos* by Justin Martyr (*Dial.* 126), which shows that Christians were linking this text with him.[10]

That Hebrew Scripture is foundational here is important to note in terms of the interpretation linked to Joseph's dream. Isaiah 11:1 would not have sprung immediately to mind in Aramaic, the most prevalent language of Galilee,[11] since the Hebrew word *netser* is not the same as the Aramaic word for 'shoot'.[12] In Syriac (a later form of Aramaic) there is a verb *nuts* or *nats*, meaning 'to shoot'.[13] But the letter *resh* (r) in the word *Nazōraios* suggests *netser*, which is Hebrew.[14] We are therefore in the world of Hebrew language and interpretation, with the implication that the angel himself spoke Hebrew, and Joseph understood it. This connects to a notion in Second Temple Judaism that indeed Hebrew was the heavenly language spoken by angels.[15]

The proclamation that 'he will be called *Nazōraios*' seems, therefore, to be an interpretation of Hebrew Scripture. Yet, even if we track down the source text to Isaiah 11:1, this still does not exactly give us the prediction verbatim. It seems, therefore, to echo what would have been the angel's Hebrew words rather than Scripture itself. One would expect the scriptural passage to be stated, and then 'he will be called *Nazōraios*' given as the interpretation. Again, this might well have been the case in the source material, but it is not how it appears in canonical Matthew. At any rate, the interpretation indicated that Jesus was the shoot from the roots of Jesse – of the Davidic line – and this identity is then connected with living in a particular place named Nazareth. This place is named in the Gospels as Nazara,[16] Nazareth[17] or Nazaret.[18] The -eth or -et feminine ending is an Aramaic form that can attach to certain sites. The unvoiced 'ts' sound (e.g. in *netser*) is found in Greek as a voiced 'z' (a *zayin*), when usually in Greek that would be transliterated with an 's' (*sigma*). But there are parallels: for example, Hebrew *Tso'ar*, the name of a place south of the Dead Sea, is found in Greek as Zoara.[19]

The word *Nazōraios* could have been explained just as the Hebrew term *Immanuel* is explained in Matthew 1:23, but in 2:23 *Nazōraios* was left untranslated, probably because the members of Matthew's community, and early readers in the area of wider Syria, knew what it meant. This was because Jesus' disciples in this area were known as *Nazōraioi* themselves ('Nazarenes') on the basis of Jesus' epithet.[20] They were the followers of the 'Nazarene' (Acts 24:5). In Mishnaic Hebrew this designation became the word *Notsrim*, the standard way of referring to Christians.[21] This term, and its cognates, also became the normative one in the East: in Persia, Arabia, Armenia and Syria as a whole,[22] and oddly meant that the followers of Jesus were named in the same way as people from his home town. There was very likely, then, a wide knowledge base that understood the term as not only connected to the founder of the movement but also connected to his *patris*, a place that meant 'shoot' (and thus both its inhabitants and Jesus' followers were known as 'shoot-people').[23]

The epithet *Nazōraios* as a transcription is largely found in Matthew, Luke–Acts and John,[24] but *Nazarēnos* appears in the Gospel of Mark.[25] *Nazarēnos*, with an -*ēnos* ending, is more correct as a Greek term that could indicate someone coming from a place: a Nazarene. *Nazōraios* is more Aramaic in form and seems to reflect local Galilean pronunciation, because in Galilean Aramaic verbs were pronounced in a more open way; so, for example, *magdal* ('tower') could even become *mugdal* or *mogdal* with an addition letter *waw* (sounded as 'u' or 'o').[26] Jesus' epithet in Syriac is *Natserayya*; in Mishnaic Hebrew it is *ha-Notsri*.[27] In short, the name of the Galilean town was *Natsara* or *Natsareth*,[28] but it

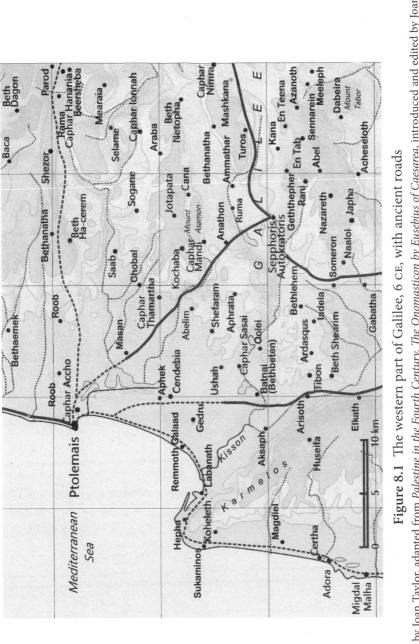

Figure 8.1 The western part of Galilee, 6 CE, with ancient roads

(Drawing by Joan Taylor, adapted from *Palestine in the Fourth Century. The Onomasticon by Eusebius of Caesarea*, introduced and edited by Joan E. Taylor, translated by Greville Freeman-Grenville, and indexed by Rupert Chapman III (Jerusalem: Carta, 2003), plate 1, detail)

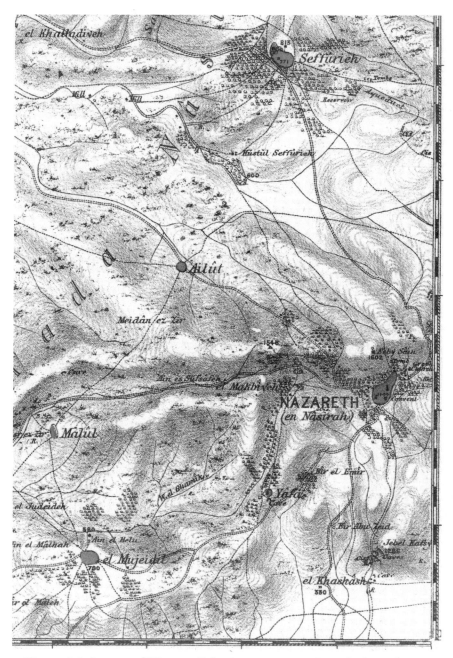

Figure 8.2 Survey of Western Palestine map 1880. Detail of Sepphoris, Nazareth and Japhia

(Courtesy of the Palestine Exploration Fund, London)

was pronounced by Galileans as *Natsora* or *Natsoreth*, giving the transliteration into Greek of *Nazōraios*.

The name of the town itself is, then, in Joseph's interpretation, suggestive of prophecy, but perhaps he was not alone in this recognition. Africanus notes that there were actually two 'Jewish/Judaean towns' where the *desposunoi*, the 'nobles', recognised as descendants of David, lived: one was Nazareth and the other was Kochaba. This is interesting, because the names of both are significant. While the association of Nazareth, 'shoot', connects with Isaiah 11:1, the name Kochaba means 'star'.[29] This connects the place with another messianic prophecy: 'A star will come out of Jacob; a sceptre will rise out of Israel. He will crush the foreheads of Moab, the skulls of all the people of Sheth' (Num. 24:17). Here the 'star' is the great military king who will destroy all of Israel's enemies. Kochaba was also close to Sepphoris, about 9 miles (15 km) to the north (see Fig. 8.1).[30]

So some of the *desposunoi*, the descendants of David, relocated themselves in Galilee in two towns with messianic scriptural associations built into their names. We can reflect on the hopes of the Davidic clan. It may well be that these towns, not just any old village, were particularly chosen by refugees from Bethlehem.

Galilee

Nazareth was established in the late second century or early first century BCE on a ruined site from the eighth century BCE.[31] It was located in the heart of Galilee (ha-Galil in Hebrew), a region north of the traditional homeland of Judaea, and north of Samaria. From the seminal work of Sean Freyne in 1980[32] to the present, there has been much archaeological and historical work done on Galilee, and a clearer picture is emerging.[33] In more ancient times it had once been the location of Israelite settlement, in that the tribes of Naphtali, Zebulun and Dan lived in the area. However, after the Assyrian invasion of the eighth century and the deportation of the population, the area was not largely occupied by Israelites but rather by Syro-Phoenicians. Thus Isaiah 9:1, dated from this time, refers to 'Galilee of the Gentiles'.

This region had been included under Hasmonean rule as the result of expansionist Judaean conquests at the beginning of the first century BCE, with the existing Israelite and Syro-Phoenician/Palestinian population then being converted to Judaism, the national religion, and assimilated, or moving to Hellenic towns, such as Panias, Tyre or Sidon to the north, Ptolemais to the west, Hippos to the east or Scythopolis to the south. Both archaeological and literary evidence suggests that there was extensive settlement of Galilee by Judaeans in the early first century BCE, with numerous new villages created from scratch.[34] It was a region therefore colonised by Judaeans, who would have intermarried with converts in the area, so that by Jesus' time it was predominantly Jewish.[35]

Galilee was small in area. Josephus defines Jewish Galilee quite precisely in terms of its borders (*War* 3:35–41). Surrounded by other nations, it had two administrative areas (Upper and Lower), and was (in the north) bounded by Phoenicia and Syria (Syro-Phoenicia), including the cities of Ptolemais and Carmel, belonging to Tyre, situated on the coast on the west. In the south the region was bordered by the territory of Samaria and the independent Syro-Palestinian city of Scythopolis, extending to the River Jordan (*War* 3:37). It encompassed Lake Gennesareth (the Sea of Galilee), since the eastern border began at the territory of the cities of Hippos and Gadara (*War* 3:38). As Josephus sketches it, Galilee was only 42 miles (69 km) in length from north to south and 30 miles (49 km) wide at its maximum (see Fig. 1.1).[36]

Growing up in Nazareth was not a case of growing up in an environment of bucolic peace and quiet, full of contented, well-fed and healthy people, with green rolling hills to the horizon and a lot of space to play. The 'Sunday school' image of Galilee does not correlate with what Josephus describes. Josephus presents the Galileans as tough, courageous and *machimoi*, 'warrior-like' (*War* 3:42).[37] While this partly explains to his Roman audience why the Galileans were prone to revolt, it also speaks to their hard lives. Given how easily Josephus could recruit fighting men when he was a general in Galilee, it seems also quite likely that boys and young men were expected to learn the basic methods of fighting, using swords, daggers and other weaponry. It would have been a skill needed for survival.

This small area was extremely densely populated.[38] In *War* 3:42–3, Josephus states that every inch of soil in Galilee is cultivated, with no wasteland. There 'the cities are close-packed (*puknai*)' and 'a majority of the villages/towns everywhere are much-populated because of the [agricultural] abundance, so that the smallest [of this majority is said] to have over 15,000 inhabitants (*War* 3:43)'.[39] Many scholars suspect that Josephus is exaggerating.[40] But other figures that Josephus gives for population are equally huge. When in 52 BCE the Roman general Cassius sacked the city of Tarichaea, on the western shore of the Sea of Galilee, he enslaved 30,000 people (*Ant.* 14:120; *War* 1:180). Josephus reports that the total population of Galilee was more than 3 million (*War* 6:420), and he himself mustered either 60,000 ('six myriads of') men for infantry or 100,000 ('ten myriads of') fighters for the war against Rome in 67–68 CE (*War* 2:583, 576). Josephus describes Japha as the 'largest village in Galilee' (*Life* 230), indeed a 'city' (*War* 3:289), where 12,000 fighters were killed (*War* 3:298).

Japha was actually just 2 miles (3 km) from Nazareth, and would have been far more important as a neighbouring town than Sepphoris (see Fig 8.1). One can see the proximity and closeness reflected well in the Palestine Exploration Fund's *Survey of Western Palestine* map, printed in 1880 (see Fig. 8:2), where Japha's name is retained in the small village of Yafa (Sepphoris is Seffurieh) and the old pathways between the settlements remain. Japha was a short walk away from Nazareth along the winding valley, though Nazareth lay behind a hill. Its close presence as a large population centre would have been important for trade and social interactions.

Josephus made his assessments as a military commander with access to accurate information about fortifications and populations. He knew this region very well (*War* 3:35–44). It used to be thought that Josephus exaggerated in stating that there were 204 villages and cities (*Life* 235), but recent archaeological surveys have indicated that this assessment is actually reasonably likely.[41] Josephus's measurements of distance and size have largely been verified by archaeological investigations.[42] He apparently used not only his own recollections but also the imperial *hupomnēmata* (records) of Vespasian and Titus for his information (*Life* 342, 358; *Apion* 1:56). This being so, had Josephus got factual information about numbers drastically wrong, he would have risked serious chastisement from his readership in Rome. There were significant constraints on him, given that he was writing for an audience that had had direct experience of the Judaean revolt of 66–70 CE.

In short, a main point Josephus makes is just how very densely populated Galilee was. He was not alone in claiming this. That the area of Galilee and wider Judaea was very highly populated in the first century is found also in the works of Philo of Alexandria: 'For the Judaeans have such a large population (*poluanthrōpia*) that no one country can hold them' (*Flacc.* 45, as also *Mos.* 2:232; and see *Spec.* 1:141; *Legat.* 214). The nation of the Judaeans is 'highly populous' (*poluanthrōpos*) (*Deus* 148, 178; *Spec.* 1:7, 78); it is the 'most populous of all nations' (*Congr.* 3), or the 'most populous of all nations anywhere' (*Virt.* 64). Syria Palestina is where most of the 'highly populous nation of the Jews' live (*Prob.* 75), and so many people give their first-fruits to the Jerusalem priests that they are overwhelmed with plenty (*Spec.* 1:321). For Philo, the huge population of Judaea was striking *even in the ancient world*: (Syro-)Phoenicians were astonished at how many Judaeans arrived at their border to protest when the Roman legate Petronius came to place a statue of Gaius Caligula in the Jerusalem Temple in 39 CE, because they had no idea how populous the nation was (*Legat.* 226).

With this kind of consistent literary attestation, current archaeological assessments made of populations in Galilean villages and towns are likely erring on the side of being drastically too small, using irrelevant population ratios from other places. In terms of making assessments of ancient population density on the basis of archaeology, it is indeed acknowledged to be extremely difficult, as pointed out by Uri Leibner, who presents a range of possible populations in ancient Galilean settlements in his extensive survey.[43] The whole of Judaea (or Syria Palestina) has more recently been estimated as having between 2,265,000 and a mere 500,000 inhabitants.[44] There has been a strong tendency to minimise sizes.[45] As for rural settlements, 16–25 people per dunam has been considered a standard model. But in the Old City of Jerusalem today, which in many ways is comparable to ancient walled cities with multi-storey structures, the population density for residential areas is 90 persons per dunam, that is, 900 persons per hectare.[46] Even that may reflect too roomy a sense of space. While it is not a city at all, today about 160,000 people are living in Rocinha, Brazil's largest favela, which has largely two-level structures and a total area of just 143.5 hectares,[47] giving a population density of 1,115 people per hectare. Given that ancient villages and towns could have mudbrick and other impermanent structures and superstructures hidden from the archaeological record, overreliance on stone remains for population estimates is problematic; but, even using assessments based on stone remains alone, we do not know how many people managed to squeeze into the space between such existing walls.

As Leibner states, during the period of Judaean settlement from the beginning of the first century BCE to the mid-first century CE:

> settlement in the region underwent a dramatic change; numerous settlements were established; unsettled or sparsely settled areas, such as the eastern portion of the region or hilly areas with *limited agricultural potential*, experienced a wave of settlement; and the size of the settled area doubled.[48]

If people came and built a settlement in an area with limited agricultural potential, this means that people were prepared to establish themselves even when the arable land was poor, indicating the need for housing despite the likelihood of agricultural poverty.

Josephus indicates that this population density was caused by Galilee being so fertile and abundant, seeming to imply that there was enough food, so that people didn't die of starvation. But the huge sociopolitical disturbances of Jerusalem and wider Judaea would also have played a part. With population density came problems, especially intermittent food shortages, or indeed there could be famine (Acts 11:27–8; Josephus, *Ant.* 20:49–53, 101).[49] Any environment reaches a breaking point when faced with unfettered human population growth, despite the fertility of the land and sea. From modern analyses, it is clear that in an overpopulated environment there would have been a significant rise in the likelihood of disease spread, additional stress economically and practically, and an increase in the chances of falling into poverty through lack of work;[50] the waged day-labourers of Jesus' parables (e.g. Matt. 20:1–16) clearly reflect a social situation that people knew. Unemployment is paired with pressure on the environment, and again, if comparable models in today's world are applied, there would have been significant demand for food. Josephus mentions varieties of vegetation (*War* 3:42), but it is likely that much of Galilee was deforested along with the expansion of village settlements in the first century BCE.

With expanding human population and settlements, the environment is also degraded and polluted. Evidence of a huge impact on the environment at this time can be found in the results of sedimentation analysis in the Tarichaea (Migdal) harbour area.[51] The researchers note that during the period of harbour activity, accompanying massive development in the first century, trace metals were found, 'which is consistent with anthropogenic pollution of the environment, probably linked to shipbuilding and boat insulation.'[52]

Social circumstances

Scholars have shown Galilee in the time of Jesus to be a place beset by social inequalities and terrible poverty.[53] People struggled under the weight of high taxation levied by Herod Antipas,[54] and also with debt.[55] One question has been whether there was rapid social change for the worse in the early first century.[56] Not everyone has sung from this song sheet; some have suggested that there was *more* economic comfort in Jesus' Galilee.[57] Overall, however, the former assessment is winning in the battle for scholarly consensus, for good reason: most of the evidence for a more prosperous Galilee comes from the second to fourth centuries, and even when one can now identify fine building works by Herod Antipas in Tiberias or Sepphoris, and city affluence,[58] this does not necessarily translate to prosperity in the general population. The inhabitants are likely to have been taxed hard to fund such constructions.[59] No household structure datable to the first century in Capernaum looks anything but poor, given that the compounds are often largely constructed out of unhewn basalt fieldstones, without so much as plastered walls.[60]

In this environment there was also crime, especially in the form of banditry. Identifying it can be tricky, because Josephus can sweep independence fighters, rivals and would-be kings into the bracket of 'bandits' and 'thieves' as a smear tactic. Josephus describes how in the early days of Herod in Galilee (c.38 BCE) 'bandits' were based in the inaccessible caves of Arbela (*War* 1:304–13), and archaeology has indeed brought to light a large number of caves in Mount Arbel and Mount Nitai, close to ancient Tarichaea.[61] However, Josephus indicates that these 'bandits' (*lēstai*) were evicted and massacred, along with their families, as part of Herod's campaign against Antigonus Mattathias, which means they were actually his enemies in the civil war.[62] Richard Horsley has nevertheless defined 'social banditry' as endemic in the rural society of first-century Galilee, where there were massive social inequalities between a small, rich, land-owning elite and a vast, poor population of subsistence farmers and landless workers.[63] There were likely bandits of all kinds: from self-serving gangs, to Robin Hoods, to partisan forces and ideologically driven militias.

There are certainly instances in which robbery seems to have had no particular political motive: bandits who raided in Trachonitis (*Ant.* 15:343–8; *War* 1:398–400), for example.[64] Bandits seem to have been hired as mercenaries for the purposes of revolution. When Josephus himself arrived in Galilee to take charge in 66 CE, he summoned bandit leaders to stop their raids, and he got people to pay them as mercenaries instead (*Life* 77), yet the raids were 'on the Romans or their neighbours', and there is a sense that banditry was targeted against the elite. There were highway robberies of convoys that belonged to or supported either the Romans or their client royals. For example, a convoy of expensive clothes, silver and gold belonging to Agrippa II en route to Caesarea was attacked on the Plain of Jezreel (*Life* 126–7; *War* 2:595–6), but this again furnished resources for the revolt against Rome.[65]

Still, if you were a hapless slave, servant or labourer working for the elite, you would be in the line of fire, and low-level robbery that would strip you bare also seems to have been rife. Jesus' own teaching portrays a world in which people could be attacked on the road by thieves, robbed of clothing and left for dead (Luke 10:30–6), and he describes a situation where someone would slap you and take your mantle (Matt. 5:39–40// Luke 6:29). When he called those in charge of the Temple in Jerusalem a 'den/cave of thieves' (Mark 11:17//Matt. 21:13//Luke 19:46), he drew the image from Jeremiah 7:11, but he would have expected it to be recognisable to his hearers. Jesus can even, perhaps jokingly, respond to critics who scorn his exorcistic healing work by using an image from the perspective of the bandits: 'No one can enter a strong man's house and plunder his possessions unless he ties up the strong man first – and then he can plunder his house' (Mark 3:27//Matt. 12:29//Luke 11:21–2).

In a place of high population density and poverty there was very likely to have been high mortality and disease. Josephus writes of a plague, *c.*24 BCE, in the thirteenth year of Herod's reign, which he ascribes to famine

(*Ant.* 15:300–1).[66] As Jonathan Reed has noted, on the basis of analyses of skeletal remains:

> Life in first-century Galilee – though not necessarily dissimilar to other parts of the Mediterranean – was substantially different from the modern world and cannot be characterized as stable. Chronic and seasonal disease, especially malaria, cut down significant segments of the population and left even the healthy quite often ill.[67]

Reed notes that the inhabitants of Galilee, in common with people in other places in the Mediterranean, would have suffered from 'a plethora of quick-killing gastrointestinal and respiratory diseases such as dysentery, typhus, tuberculosis, plague and especially malaria',[68] and that indeed 'Josephus at one point describes the areas south of the lake as pestilent and disease ridden'.[69] The existence of such a pestilential area (*War* 4:456) was put down to bad air (see Vitruvius, *Arch.* 1:4:1; Diodorus Siculus, *Bibl. Hist.* 2:47:1; 5:19:5).[70] But people still lived in such places, presumably because they had little choice.

Given the high population of Galilee, the huge number of villages crammed into a limited area, and the stress this would have caused for people eking out their living there, a new immigrant family might not have been entirely welcome. There would have been some negotiations with the inhabitants of Nazareth to accept incomers. A new family would have needed to be careful in their approach, and grateful for being accepted.

The remaining Archelaus years

We explored in the previous chapter how Joseph took his family to Nazareth after a short period of hope following the death of Herod when there was something of a hiatus, and that during this time a massive protest took shape in the Temple in Jerusalem. When Archelaus showed his hand as ruler in Judaea after the death of his father, he dispersed the Temple protest by perpetrating a massacre, and shattered the hopes of many who had dreamt of a new order. Archelaus, his brothers and other elites went to Rome to gain confirmation of their rule. There was now a period of extreme societal instability when different insurgencies broke out in Idumaea, in Jericho and Peraea, in central Judaea around Emmaus, and in

Galilee, and likely elsewhere as well. This was a period of revolution, and it was dangerous. Returning to 'the Land of Israel' on Herod's death, and avoiding Herod's son Archelaus, Joseph then turned north, where Judas son of Hezekiah had taken over Sepphoris, the district capital of Galilee. But Varus, the Roman legate of Syria, marched a massive force south from Antioch to quash this resistance, and did so with great ferocity.[71]

Josephus indicates that some aspects of the rebellion lasted for a long time, as we saw (*Ant.* 17:285), even after Varus had ostensibly crushed all opposition. Nevertheless, what we seem to have is Jesus' family arriving in Nazareth not very long before the full might of Rome bore down on Judas's resistance fighters in Sepphoris and the population who supported them. Josephus tells the story all too briefly in *War* 2:68 (and see *Ant.* 17:288–9): 'Varus sent a part of his army straight into the region of Galilee adjoining Ptolemais, commanded by one of his friends, Gaius. Gaius defeated those resisting him and captured the city Sepphoris, burnt it, and enslaved the inhabitants.' Jesus, as a small child, would have witnessed this.

While Nazareth was hidden behind a hill and away from any main roads (see Fig. 8.1), it would not have felt safe there when the Roman army occupied the heart of Galilee. Sepphoris was only a few miles away (see Plate 10). From the hills above Nazareth, the whole horror could have been watched. Loud noises would have carried. The smoke from burning buildings would have been seen, and smelt. The inhabitants of Nazareth would have known that the Roman army was inflicting terrible things on the nearby city. Some inhabitants would have managed to escape to tell the tale.

Sepphoris, after Varus and his army took the town, then became a centre of Roman control, and, when Antipas arrived back from Rome as tetrarch of Galilee, he would remake it as a fine district capital. After the work was completed sometime in the period 6–9 CE, he renamed the city Autokratoris, and it was acclaimed as the 'ornament of all Galilee' (*Ant.* 18:27).[72] The Greek term *autokrator*, 'sole ruler', was a Greek translation of Latin *imperator*, 'emperor'; thus, this city was rebuilt in honour of the emperor.[73] Hope for independence was clearly dashed among the population. Having Roman forces so close by, meting out terrible harm to people who had briefly celebrated freedom, would have sent a powerful message about the futility of armed resistance for those with ears to hear.

Galilee was thus 'subdued', in Roman terms. While Antipas concentrated on developing Autokratoris as an architectural gem, likely using the slave labour that had recently become available, Archelaus, it seems, continued to oppress Judaea in the south. His reign ran from 4 BCE to 6 CE, from the time when Jesus was 2 or 3 to when he was 12 or 13 years old. For a descendant of David, Galilee was still less dangerous than Judaea. Josephus does not give details, but he suggests that Archelaus's rule was extremely harsh. He notes that Archelaus did eventually remove Joazar the son of Boethus from the high priesthood, but he did not go back to traditional methods of letting the high priest be chosen by lot (so 1 Chr. 24:31). Rather, he himself selected the next high priests: the men in charge of the judiciary, which operated according to religious law. After the defeat of Simon, Archelaus worked on rebuilding the palace of Jericho that had been damaged, and constructed the hilltop village of Archelais nearby (*Ant.* 17:339–40), but such construction work would have required levels of taxation similar to those that had supported his father's building programme. In fact, the fabulous third palace excavated in Jericho, usually attributed to the last phase of Herod's building programme, would also have been the palace of Archelaus.[74]

Archelaus continued to crack down hard on people. According to Josephus, he remembered old differences and treated both Judaeans and Samaritans 'savagely' (*ōmos*, *War* 2:111). By implication, the descendants of David in his territory would not have fared well. We are given no details, but both Judaeans and Samaritans eventually sent elders to the emperor to complain of his abuses, and his royal brothers went too. This action indicates that there was some incredibly serious incident, or series of incidents, but Josephus gives us no specifics. Indeed, Archelaus was eventually summoned for trial, removed, and banished to Vienne[75] in Gaul. All his property (palace-forts such as Herodion included) was confiscated by the Roman imperial treasury (*War* 2:212–13; *Ant.* 17:342–4). The tomb Archelaus had constructed for himself in Bethlehem would have been left empty.[76]

In this case, what Josephus says is corroborated by Roman sources, because the removal and banishment of a client king by the emperor was a very serious matter. Cassius Dio mentions the removal of 'Herod' of Palestine, who was 'accused by his brothers' and then banished beyond the Alps (*Hist. Rom.* 55:27:6). Strabo writes of all Herod's sons (plural) being publicly accused (*Geogr.* 16:2:46): while one died in exile among the 'Allobroges Gauls', where Vienne was located, the others, with pleadings and difficulty, were eventually allowed to return to their own country, each with their tetrarchy restored. Therefore, the deputations in Rome in 6 CE would have been similar to those of 4 BCE, with different elite groups contesting for power and accusing one another as a result of disturbances and atrocities at home. All this speaks volumes for understanding Jesus as a young boy growing up in Galilee during an extremely turbulent and insecure time when the nation's rulers were violent and oppressive.

Interestingly, Josephus indicates that in 6 CE, when Archelaus was removed, there was again hope for independence, or semi-independence, after years of fear. At this point, Jesus would have heard many stories about what prompted the deputation of Judaean elders and the two tetrarchs. He would have heard accounts – first-hand perhaps – of what had happened to people who fell foul of Archelaus, and perhaps Antipas as well.

These were Jesus' formative childhood years. The descendants of David would have existed under continued threat, additionally suspect after the recent post-Herod revolt. To be safe, it would have been necessary to lie low and take very great care when it came to the authorities. They would have understood themselves to be persecuted, living as survivors in a very dangerous world.

The census rebellion

As had occurred when Herod was removed, there was a flare-up at Archelaus's departure. Judaea was divided, and everything not ruled by Herod's sons Antipas and Philip was now finally joined to Syria, becoming the Roman province of Judaea, administered under the new legate, Quirinius (*War* 2:433; 7:253).[77] This territory of Judaea, designated as a province, comprised Idumaea, Samaria and (traditional) Judaea, all lying on the west side of the Jordan Rift Valley, and edging the independent Hellenic Syro-Palestinian cities of the coast, but with ports at Joppa and Caesarea (see Fig 1.1). While the moderates might still have hoped for Judaean priestly governance in Judaea of some kind, under the overall auspices of Rome, what they got as a governor was a military prefect sent from Rome (one Coponius, now installed in Herod's fabulous palace in Caesarea),[78] a battalion of auxiliary troops, and direct Roman taxation.

So a census was required (*War* 2:117–18; *Ant.* 18:1–10). Even though Galilee itself would have remained under the taxation system of Herod Antipas, Josephus reports that a Galilean, Judas, incited people to revolt (*War* 2:118). More precisely, Judas hailed from Gamala, a city in Gaulanitis (in the territory of Philip, *Ant.* 18:4), but his remembered epithet was the *Galilaios*, 'Galilean' (*War* 2:118, 433; *Ant.* 18:23; 20:102; Acts 5:37).[79] This may have been because Gamala was conceptually included in Galilee; certainly it was in the First Revolt (*War* 2:568).[80] It may also have been because Judaeans recognised Galileans as being the main revolutionary element that arrived in Judaea to object to what was happening.

Some have argued that this Judas was the same Judas son of Hezekiah who attacked and burned the palace of Sepphoris in 4 BCE, and that Josephus failed to connect the dots when using a different source.[81] However, 'Judas' was a very common name, and Judas the Galilean is described as more an inciter of revolt than a man who claimed kingship and commanded an armed force. He was a *sophistēs* (sophist) and a *didaskalos* (teacher) who asserted that people were cowards for accepting that tribute must be paid to the Romans, indeed for allowing anyone to rule as lord (*despotēs*) other than God (*War* 2:118, 433; cf. 7:410), and he is never associated with Hezekiah.[82] He and his adherents were in line with the interpretations of the Pharisees, except they held that only God should rule as lord (*Ant.* 18:23), and indeed a Pharisee, Saddok, is associated with Judas (*Ant.* 18:4, 9).[83] Judas's call for rule by God would in practical terms mean that Judaea would have a priestly hierocracy administering religious law in the country autonomously, without ceding any separate jurisdiction to a foreign power. He and his followers wanted 'freedom' (*eleutheria*, *Ant.* 18:4).

As for Roman rule, Josephus indicates that the prefect Coponius was granted authority by the emperor *mechri tou kteinein*, 'through to ordering death' (*War* 2:117). That meant Roman judicial decisions in Judaea, not even ones made by client rulers, and that was totally unacceptable. The followers of Judas the Galilean believed they had God on their side: they would be aided by God in their purpose and be rewarded with well-being (*eudaimon*) once they had gained freedom (*Ant.* 18:5). Described in this way, Judas has much in common with the teachers Matthias and Judas of Jerusalem, who incited their students to tear down the Roman eagle from the front of the Temple in order to maintain the traditional laws of the country, and so met horrific deaths.[84]

In due course, Josephus would identify that the revolutionaries who later led the First Revolt of 66–70 CE against Rome had Judas as the founder of their particular legal school or party (*hairesis*); therefore at that time they became a 'fourth philosophy', in addition to that of the previous three: the Sadducees, Pharisees and Essenes (*Ant.* 18:9, 23–5).[85] They were deemed such because they held juridical power over Judaea during the period of the revolt and appointed their own high priests (*War* 7:262–70),[86] now employing the traditional practice of choosing the high priest by lot. They seem not to have accepted Hasmonean priestly authority, much to Josephus's disapproval.[87] This shows what their concept of 'no lord but God' entailed.

However, at the time of Jesus' childhood the ideology that would lead to this 'fourth philosophy' is difficult to assess in terms of its influence.[88] As Josephus tells it, the incitement of Judas and his teaching led the population of Judaea to resist the census, initially, but the majority at least were persuaded by the high priest Joazar son of Boethus (*Ant.* 18:3), who seems to have been reinstated after Archelaus deposed him (*Ant.* 17:339). Joazar could no doubt draw on recent memory of the cataclysm of the 'War of Varus' nine years earlier to urge the population to be calm: resisting the Romans was an act of self-harm. In Acts 5:37 it is stated that Judas was executed and his followers were scattered,[89] but Josephus himself does not record this.

It is interesting, then, that the author of the Lukan nativity (Luke 1:5 – 2:40) positions Joseph – as a Bethlehemite – as complying with the census (Luke 2:1–5), thereby *not* joining in any anti-Roman actions. We may ask if there is some memory nugget contained in the story. The census is located as taking place during the time when Quirinius was governor of Syria (2:2), that is, from 6 to 9 CE.[90] However, as we saw in Chapter 5, it is likely that the Lukan census is a fusion: one component was one of the Augustan censuses of Roman citizens, likely that of 8 BCE, given that the census took place by order of 'Caesar Augustus' and was a directive that 'all the world' should be taxed (2:1);[91] the other component was the census that took place when the region became a Roman province proper and no longer a client kingdom, when Quirinius was indeed legate of Syria, in 6 CE. So, might there then be a chronological displacement in the association of Joseph and Mary's travel to Bethlehem for the census? They did make this journey, but in 6 CE? If so, this story would actually tell of Joseph and Mary's ongoing association with the town and their property there. Given Mary's travel, the implication would be that she too had property. We know of a comparable census where a married Jewish woman declared her property: in the census of Arabia of 127 CE: 'I Bab[a]tha [daughter] of Simon Mahozene in the Zoarene district of Petra, living in my own private property in the same Mahoza, register what I possess' (P.Yadin 16:13–15), namely four date groves.[92]

If we trust the report of the census in Luke, but not the timing, it tells of Bethlehem's continuing significance for the family. The census itself would not have stretched to Galilee, but Joseph and Mary were still connected to Bethlehem because of property. Neither of them may have had much property left behind in Bethlehem, and – given their absence – they would not have been able to benefit from it. Refugees invariably resign themselves to loss of property and possessions in order to seek safety, and this itself can cause ongoing trauma. But there are also cases where refugees attempt to return to recover what is lost.[93] Given that Archelaus was now removed, and in Matthew he was the reason why Joseph took his family to Galilee in the first place (Matt. 2:22), it would make sense if Joseph and Mary felt safe enough to return to Bethlehem once he was gone, if only to state claims.

It may well be that descendants of David did in general comply with the Roman census and were resistant to the calls from Judas and his supporters, not only because of past catastrophes but also because Judas's vision did not include a place for a Judaean king ruling from the line of David. There are some ambiguous things said by Josephus of Judas the Galilean's descendants in terms of royal aspirations: he describes how in 66 CE, during the First Revolt, Menahem, the son of Judas, broke into the armoury of Masada to equip his men, returned to Jerusalem with bodyguards 'such as befits a king' (*oia dē basileus*) and donned royal robes,[94] but he never states that Menahem donned the *diadem*. The robes, presumably long, fancy and purple, would suggest authority but not necessarily kingship. Another revolutionary of this later time also put on a royal, purple robe over a white tunic, but again not the diadem.[95] At no point do the revolutionaries of the First Revolt crown a king or place him on the throne, and their affirmation to call no one 'lord' but God alone actually ties in better with a rejection of kingship as a concept.

While we can only contextualise and probe here, the actions of Judas and the census rebellion in 6 CE would definitely have been part of what Jesus and his family experienced. At this time, Jesus was around 12 or 13 years old (if born c.6–5 BCE). The quashing of the rebellion would have led to many stories of slaughter, and much fear. Men and boys would have honed their fighting skills. In the public discussion there would have been supporters and detractors. Judas's rebellion seems not to have been a messianic movement, but some of the 'warrior-like' Galileans had clearly rallied around a cause. And it was dangerous. Jesus would later tell his disciples: 'Beware of the false prophets, who come to you in sheep's clothing but inwardly are ravenous wolves' (Matt. 7:15).

Thus, the move to Nazareth would give Jesus his adult identity and shape his world view. Bethlehem would have been remembered as the ancestral home that was no longer safe. In Nazareth there were probably other descendants of David, perhaps because there was significance in terms of the naming of the village. In Nazareth, Jesus as a small child would have witnessed the might of the Roman army as it came to destroy the hopes of those who had occupied Sepphoris, and its region, in the cause of independence. The brutality of what happened there would have lived on in memory, and quite visibly in the physical destruction. Following on from it, the Roman client ruler Antipas, son of Herod, would see to it that the city was reconstructed gloriously, as the district capital, at great expense. Its resplendent buildings would be erected in honour of the emperor, using revenue harvested from taxes on the people of his territories. Everything that Varus had done would be celebrated.

Antipas himself may not have been a particularly harsh ruler, apart from his economic oppression, but in Judaea, to the south, Archelaus his brother clearly was far more hard-line, so much so that he was evicted and banished by his Roman overlords, with this region now falling straight into direct Roman administration. With this came a revolt by another Judas, who, while hailing from across the Lake of Gennesaret, in Gamala, led a primarily Galilean band of insurgents who fomented resistance against Rome at the time of the census. As such, Jesus grew up in an environment where fear, revolt and resentment were in the air, in a region where life was fraught, and pressured by overpopulation, poor health, banditry and poverty. People may well have wondered what had happened to hope, and God's care for his people.

9

Growing up Jesus

We turn, then, to what we might know about Nazareth and Jesus' life as a child there. We have seen that it is important to recognise the wider sociopolitical circumstances of Galilee and Judaea as a whole, and the effect these would have had on Jesus' life and identity. We cannot know many details for sure, but we can still contextualise his life as a child in this particular place and time.

There has not been a huge amount of work done on Jesus as a child in his context, but scholars of the historical Jesus have at times dipped their toes into this subject matter, thinking about what it was like for him, growing up in Nazareth. Sometimes this has been done with an idea that he was born and brought up in a relatively peaceful, small agricultural village, and that he was, as John Meier put it, 'insufferably ordinary'.[1] However, the circumstances of Judaea as a whole at the time of Jesus' birth and early years were, as we have seen, unstable, and Galilean life was difficult. It was a place where stories of atrocities were circulating. There was powerful foreign intervention, and a great deal to fear from authorities.

In terms of Jesus' family and personal circumstances, being a child with an unusual conception and naming story would have marked Jesus out. Being a refugee and an immigrant child would have made him different from others who were long settled in Galilee. Jesus was a Judaean Jew who had arrived in Galilee, rather than a Galilean Jew, and his heritage as Davidic would have marked him out even more as different. He may also have suffered from post-traumatic stress, depending on what he himself witnessed and remembered from his early years, and also intergenerational or inherited trauma on the basis of the stories told to him by his parents and other relatives.[2] We now look at Nazareth as the context for all this in his childhood.

Nazareth

Nazareth was located within a very populous and challenging Galilee. No village was very far from any other, and many had been founded or refounded in the century prior to Jesus' arrival as part of a colonising process from Judaea in the wake of Hasmonean conquests. Jesus as an immigrant child grew up in a place where there were no very ancient tombs of ancestors, but rather more recent ones of others. This landscape did not have the same stories embedded into it as Judaea. Jerusalem was far away.

As we have seen, Nazareth's name meant 'shoot' in Hebrew, and here and in nearby Kochaba ('star') descendants of David from Judaea had established themselves, perhaps attracted by the place names (Matt. 2:23). Thus, these two towns might well be considered quite specific colonies of Bethlehem of Judaea. There was also a village named Bethlehem in Galilee,[3] lying in between Kochaba and Nazareth, west of Sepphoris (see Fig. 8.1). Perhaps those with a Davidic heritage were attracted by this name too.

There was something else attractive about Nazareth for people who had been persecuted and who feared the governing authorities: the town was nestled around and on a flat valley (measuring 2 × 1 miles [3 × 1.5 km]) between hills, and somewhat up the slopes. At the top of these surrounding hills, people could see from afar whether there were any incoming troops. On the south-east, you could walk a couple of miles up to a spur (Mount Precipice) and look out over the wide expanse of the Jezreel Valley and to the road where Roman troops from Caesarea would march inland. The nearby town of Japha (*Life* 230; *War* 3:289) also looked south over the Jezreel Valley (see Fig. 8.2). From the hilltops to the north of Nazareth, you could look towards Sepphoris and see the road where Roman troops would come from Ptolemais. But Nazareth itself was hidden.

Nazareth was well served in terms of water.[4] It had a perennial spring, now called Mary's Well,[5] with another well further north, situated under the present Greek Orthodox Church of St Gabriel, and probably a further seasonal spring further south.[6] Through the centre of Nazareth ran a seasonal stream, a wadi.[7] Around the town the hills were terraced for growing grapes, fruit and vegetables, and watchtowers were built. One later pilgrim, from the sixth century CE, mentions Nazareth's excellent

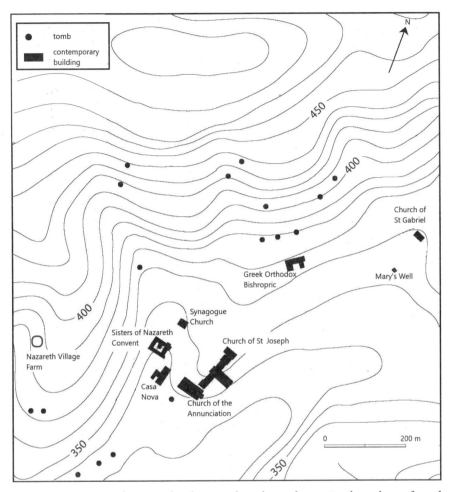

Figure 9.1 Areas of Nazareth where archaeological remains have been found
(Drawing by Joan Taylor, adapted from Ken Dark, *Roman-Period and Byzantine Nazareth and Its Hinterland* (London: Routledge, 2020), fig. 7.1)

grain, wine, oil and apples (Piacenza Pilgrim, *Itin.* 5). The agricultural life of the town has in fact been recreated in the Nazareth Village Farm centre, located in an area where landscape archaeology undertaken by the University of the Holy Land has revealed cultivations and installations.[8] Archaeological excavations on the western hill have brought to light Roman-period quarries, terrace walls and field towers.[9] While a 'town built on a hill cannot be hidden' (Matt. 5:14), like Bethlehem, whose night-time lights and fires would be seen from a distance, a town built in a valley tucked in between hills might well be hidden, and stand more of a chance against aggressors.

Today, Nazareth is a substantial town, but the shapes of the hills and the valley remain. One can mentally 'photoshop' modern buildings away to imagine what things would have looked like in the first century, especially when aided by photographs taken in the nineteenth century when the village was very small and confined to the slope of the western hill (see Plate 11). Basing ourselves on such old photographs of the landscape, we actually need to add further houses, because at this time Galilee was not as densely settled as it was in Jesus' era. Houses in the Roman period would have been built up along the lower reaches of rocky hillsides and around the water sources, likely leaving most of the flat, soil-rich valley (which could flood in heavy rain running down from the hills) for farming, but no one knows the full extent of the settlement of Jesus' time. It would have been bounded by many tombs; several from the Roman period have been discovered to the north-west and south-west and also on the eastern hill (see Fig. 9.1).[10] Some of these tombs are quite grand, not befitting at all the concept of Nazareth as a tiny, insignificant village,[11] but these likely date from a period later on, in the second and third centuries.[12] At this time Nazareth seems to have been designated as a location with special status: in an inscription found in Caesarea it is named as a place where priests could live.[13]

Interestingly, Nazareth in the early Roman period appears to have been *larger* than in the period following 70 CE, because later tombs were built into disused domestic and agricultural spaces dating from an earlier time.[14] Earlier homes and installations had been abandoned. This is evident from remains discovered underneath the Sisters of Nazareth Convent (see below). Two tombs superseded agricultural installations and a domestic building (c.4 BCE – 8 CE) from the time of Jesus' childhood here.[15] One of these tombs had a round-headed niche and was sealed by a large round rolling stone.[16] This type of niche and large round rolling stone went out of use before the second century CE, so it would be dated sometime in the late first century. In fact, there is another tomb very close by, just 30 m south-west from the Church of the Annunciation, comprising a rock-cut chamber with loculi (*kokhim*) closed by a large round rolling stone, which held objects dating from the (late?) first century.[17]

Nazareth is not mentioned by Josephus, but he only records the names of a tiny fraction of the 204 villages and towns of Galilee, largely if they were directly involved in military or bandit actions, or formed boundaries of districts.

Archaeological excavations in central Nazareth have not been extensive.[18] However, in addition to salvage excavations in recent times, some evidence was revealed by exploratory digging in various Christian churches and monasteries in the nineteenth and twentieth centuries: in the Sisters of Nazareth Convent, the Church of the Annunciation and the Church of St Joseph area,[19] and at the Church of St Gabriel.[20] These have brought to light important ancient evidence.

Explorations beginning in 1884 through to 1963 uncovered ancient remains in the Sisters of Nazareth Convent, south-west of the Church

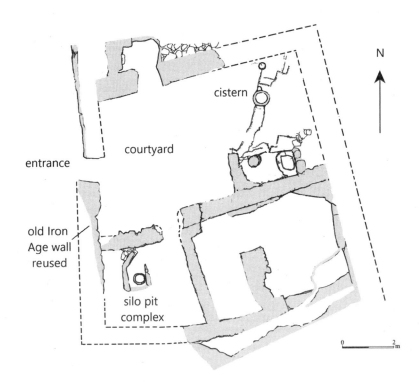

Figure 9.2 Remaining walls of lower level of first-century house, excavated in the Mary of Nazareth International Centre, Nazareth

(Drawing by Joan Taylor, adapted from Yardenna Alexandre, 'The Settlement History of Nazareth in the Iron Age and Early Roman Period', *'Atiqot* 98 (2020): pp. 25–92, plan 1, p. 30)

of the Annunciation. The investigations revealed walls, cisterns, basins, many Roman-period artefacts and tombs, and an ancient house.[21] Details of these remained largely unpublished,[22] but from 2006 British archaeologist Ken Dark worked on reinvestigating them and publishing the results, and traced the features of a house, built partly on rock and extending into a pre-existing cave. The walls of this house were plastered and it had a compacted limestone floor.[23] Datable remains from the early Roman period, from the time of Jesus, included pottery, stone vessels (used to ensure Jewish ritual purity),[24] a spindle whorl and glass fragments.

In 2009 and 2011, excavations took place nearby, prior to a building redevelopment for the Mary of Nazareth International Centre across from the Church of the Annunciation in central Nazareth. The excavation, led by Yardenna Alexandre of the Israel Antiquities Authority, uncovered the remains of an Iron Age house, and then the lower area of a house from the Hasmonean–Roman period, the time of Jesus' childhood (see Fig. 9.2).

This house is built on the creamy-coloured limestone rock of the area, which has a softness that allows you to sculpt cavities into it, unlike the dark basalt around the Sea of Galilee and the Golan. The excavated house had been built on top of a long-abandoned building from the Iron Age and constructed afresh. But this house built on rock – with small rooms surrounding a courtyard (only partially exposed) – had a peculiar feature. In room 3, under a stone structure that would have concealed its opening, there was a pit complex, cut down into the rock 6 m deep. This consisted of three levels of a bell-shaped cavity, each level accessed by a small circular opening topped with a stone lid.[25] On the edge of each pit was a niche for a lamp. The pottery was from the mid-first century BCE to the first century CE, testifying to its use at the time of Jesus. Alexandre suggested that these pits served as cisterns, storage silos or underground hideouts.[26] While the top pit could have been originally dug for storage, in favour of the latter interpretation is the fact that the two lower pits appear to have been dug out later and more hurriedly (with rougher carving), and the passage to the pits was intentionally camouflaged (see Fig. 9.3; Plate 12).[27]

This is not the only place in Nazareth where a possible hiding place has come to light. While storage silos, cisterns and other pits cut into the rock are common features within agricultural villages, and have utilitarian uses, hidden dugouts and tunnels not specifically connected with agricultural

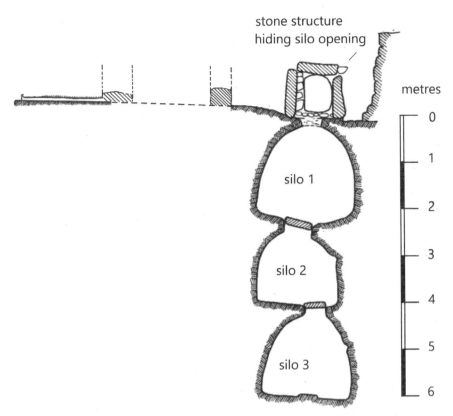

Figure 9.3 Triple silo pit complex (hiding place) in the first-century house in the Mary of Nazareth International Centre, Nazareth. View looking to the south across three rooms

(Drawing by Joan Taylor, adapted from Alexandre, 'Settlement History', plan 1-1, p. 31)

production and storage suggest different concerns. Underneath the Church of St Joseph a four-level pit (silo) complex was exposed in excavations of 1890 and 1909–10,[28] in association with a cave identified traditionally as Joseph's workshop.[29] This was itself located within a larger agricultural complex containing cisterns and silos adjacent to a set of collecting vats for wine.[30]

Alexandre suggests that these hiding places could be connected to the events of the First Revolt, since it is said by Josephus that in Jotapata the Roman army 'searched out and attacked those in underground places (*hupomenoi*) and caverns (*spēlaioi*)' when they took the city (*War* 3:336). During the First Revolt, people are mentioned as hiding in or fleeing to underground places and caverns in Jerusalem (e.g. *War*

2:428; 5:102, 104; 6:370). At this time, too, Gamala was strengthened 'by underground places (*hupomenoi*) and trenches (*diōruxes*)' (*War* 4:9), and these underground places could have been tunnels that allowed for escape (*War* 4:52). Considering what happened when Vespasian's troops attacked, slaughtered and enslaved the population of nearby Japha (*War* 3:289–306), the people of Nazareth would have been very wise to create safe rooms. However, the practice of an army or persecutor searching out hiding places is and was widespread. Given what we have reviewed here, and the ongoing threats, storage spaces could have been configured as safe rooms at various times. The pottery found in the pit complex of the excavated house ties in better with the early first century CE than later, since late Hasmonean (first-century BCE) forms are included with first-century types. We must always remember the War of Varus in 4 BCE, and its consequences, when dating such subterranean features.

Caves, cuttings and indications of housing have been found in other places in Nazareth. Nearby, to the east, excavations during the rebuilding of the Church of the Annunciation in the 1950s and 1960s revealed a large area of agricultural installations (75 × 85 m), including collecting vats for wine, silos, an olive-press, a sloping grape-treading area, a fermenting vat and bell-shaped cisterns (see Plate 13).[31] There are also tunnels, and locking and blocking devices, suggestive of a network of hiding places. The grotto identified as the Cave of the Annunciation might also have provided a hiding place, since there is a tunnel connected to it.[32]

There was at least one original cave in the Sisters of Nazareth Convent area.[33] There was a cave under the Church of St Gabriel, north of Mary's Well.[34] Tourists in Nazareth today can visit what is presented as 'The Holy Caves of Nazareth' (see Plate 14), located about halfway between the Church of the Annunciation and the Church of St Gabriel,[35] where, a guide will tell you, Joseph and Mary sheltered from the Romans, though much later use is also evidenced in the form of a rock-cut Christian chapel known as the Chapel of the Forty Martyrs. These caves were found under the Greek Orthodox Bishopric compound in 1863, and only part of this complex has been explored. Tunnels led south and north from a main cave and have yet to be investigated. There are installations, including a wine vat, that suggest this cave was put to agricultural processing use, but the tunnels could also suggest a hiding complex.

As one headline runs in the publication *Nazareth Today*, there is 'a world hidden underground' in the town.[36] The tunnels and deep pits seem to tell of a particular defensive attitude among the inhabitants at some point(s) in time. As noted previously, the extent of the town shrank sometime in the late first century, so that tombs were built in former domestic and agricultural structures. This suggests a catastrophe, after which the population declined.

We need to remember here that there were multiple catastrophes for the descendants of David that were specific to them alone. Herod's actions imply persecution, as we have seen. According to Eusebius, after the First Revolt Vespasian ordered that those of David's lineage should be killed, so that 'none of the royal tribe should be left among the Judaeans' (Eusebius, *Hist. Eccles.* 3:12). In the *Letter to Aristides* by Julius Africanus, quoted by Eusebius (*Hist. Eccles.* 1:7:11–14), there is mention of the *desposunoi*, the Davidic 'lords' or 'nobles', who could recite their genealogy, even though Herod had burned the written records of such noble families. In the time of Domitian (81–96 CE), the Roman authorities looked for those with Davidic descent and interrogated the grandnephews of Jesus, sons of Jude, as descendants of David in Nazareth (*Hist. Eccles.* 3:19 – 20:5). They assured the authorities that their very moderate landholdings gave no reason for anyone to think they could raise an army, and they were left alone (Eusebius, *Hist. Eccles.* 3:32:6; 3:20:6). Simeon the son of Clopas survived earlier persecutions, only to be horribly executed for being a descendant of David and a Christian in the reign of Trajan (*Hist. Eccles.* 3:32:1–6), likely *c.*115 CE. Some hiding places might, then, fit with specific times when the descendants of David were attacked in Nazareth. The shrinking of the town after 68 CE correlates well with Vespasian's targeted persecution.

It seems that the hiding places were carefully constructed in and around and inside both houses and agricultural installations, and may well have served dual purposes. What is apparent, though, is that the soft rock of Nazareth provided the opportunity to create additional or expanded caves and tunnels that would be helpful in times of trouble. There were already a number of natural caves here, conveniently located close to the perennial spring and wadi, that were in use from very ancient times.[37] This would mean, for those who settled here in both the Iron Age and in the Hasmonean–Roman period, that there were grottoes that could be used and built around, affording natural locations for safety, as well as useful places for shelter, house-building and agricultural installations.

Carpenter

In the Gospels, Jesus is defined as a *tektōn* (Mark 6:3), and 'son of a *tektōn*' (Matt. 13:55), which literally means a 'constructor', though 'carpenter' is the common translation.[38] This was Joseph's profession, and Jesus as Joseph's son would have been trained in it, learning the skills of his father. While a *tektōn*'s work mainly involved wood, it could also involve other materials, such as stone, though it could be distinguished from the work of a mason (a *lithologos*) or a stone-cutter (*lithoxoos*).[39] Early Christian writings provide some clues about how the term was understood in ancient times. In the *Protevangelium of James* it is written that Joseph 'threw aside his *skeparnon*' (9:1), a woodworking adze-plane (see below), and later on he 'came from his buildings' (13:1), implying he was constructing them. In the *Paidika* (see below) Joseph, being a *tektōn*, used to make (wooden) ploughs and yokes. He also received a commission to make a wooden bed (13:1). In the *Acts of Thomas* (1 – 3), a work dating from the mid-fourth century CE, a slave carpenter is sought, and Judas Thomas (here understood as the twin brother of Jesus) states that he has the required skills: 'In wood I have learned to make ploughs, and yokes, and ox-goads, and oars for ferry-boats, and masts for ships; and in stone, tombstones and monuments, and temples and palaces for kings.'[40]

This sweep of skills reflects what a *tektōn* might do, including smoothing stone, and shows that such 'constructors' were supposed to be multi-skilled and adaptable. Their skills would have been connected to the range of tools they were competent in using. However, there was more of a connection to woodworking than stone-working, and hence carpentry. Celsus, the second-century pagan philosopher, scoffs that Christians talk of a 'tree of life' because resurrection comes from the wooden cross on which Jesus the carpenter was nailed: if Jesus had had some other trade – that of 'a leather-cutter (*skutotomos*), or stone-cutter (*lithoxoos*) or iron-worker (*sidēreus*)' – and been executed by some other means, such as hanging, Christians would have to talk of the 'cord of immortality' (Origen, *Against Celsus* 6:34). In listing these trades, Celsus provides comparable occupations: they are all lowly.[41]

In a remarkable mosaic recently excavated in the Galilean synagogue at Huqoq (*c.*400 CE),[42] a carpenter wielding a *skeparnon*, as mentioned in the *Protevangelium*, is depicted in some detail (see Plate 15). He appears with other manual workers in an illustration of the construction of the Tower of Babel (Gen. 11:1–8) in the panel of the south nave. We see here a bearded man with short hair using his *skeparnon* to smooth a plank of wood,[43] which he holds upright in his left hand. Small bits of wood chips are shown flying off as he works, seated on the ground, with his eyes focused on the task. He is wearing a greyish-blue *exomis*-style tunic, a garment that allowed easy room to move. He is barefoot. Over his right ear there is another implement, ready for use. In the mosaic a variety of carpentry processes and implements are shown: two men sawing a block of wood, for example, and a man planing timber. This woodworker and his associates provide us with a good idea of what Joseph would have looked like in his labours. This was the work Jesus would have been trained to do.

While any village or town would have required the skills of carpenters and tradespeople of all kinds, there has been some speculation about whether those in Nazareth might have gone to Sepphoris for work, given that the city was being actively resettled and rebuilt by Herod Antipas.[44] Since Sepphoris was close by, it is suggested that there would surely have been interaction between Nazareth and Sepphoris.

However, Sepphoris was known as Autokratoris (Josephus, *Ant.* 18:27), essentially 'emperor city', built on rock after clearing away the destruction of the previous town[45] following the quashing of Judas son of Hezekiah's rebellion, when Varus enslaved the inhabitants (*Ant.* 17:288–9). This enslavement was a useful means of supplying free labour for rebuilding. Romans otherwise could deal much more harshly with insurgents. In nearby Japha in 68 CE the Romans actually killed all the men and boys, with only the women and young children spared to be sold as slaves (*War* 3:289–306). Antipas clearly engaged in a large building and resettlement programme, but it seems unlikely that building a city in honour of an emperor who had inflicted suffering on Galileans would be attractive to the descendants of David. It is also unlikely that any people of Nazareth would have wished to be involved in construction work for the Roman client ruler Herod Antipas, 'that fox' (Luke 13:32).

Cities also had a very different culture from that of the villages and towns in Galilee. Inherently, cities were projects of the ruling class, residences of the land-owning elite, attracting trade and wealth. As the district capital, Sepphoris-Autokratoris housed the royal bank and archives (Josephus, *Life* 39) and remained staunchly loyal to Rome (*Life* 346). Given this loyalty, and the city's wealth, Galilean villagers responded to the outbreak of the revolt in 66 CE by pillaging it (*Life* 30, 373–80): their attitude was one of *misos*, 'hatred' (*Life* 374). Perhaps the source of this hatred was the fact that the cities gained their revenue for building projects from the taxation of villages that lay within their city territory.[46] Later on in his mission, Jesus is said to go through towns and villages (e.g. Mark 6:6//Matt. 9:35) but is never said to go to any of the large cities of Galilee: Tiberias, Sepphoris, Tarichaea.

The different culture of the cities can be seen in material remains. A fieldwalking survey in the valley lying between Sepphoris and Nazareth, led by Ken Dark, revealed at least twenty-three sites within a 3 × 2 mile (5 × 3 km) strip. What they are exactly has yet to be determined by excavations, but one might expect a mix of villages, villas, and agricultural structures (including towers) and installations.[47] Dark noted that there was a difference between the remains relating to the two places: the objects found near Sepphoris were different from the ones near Nazareth in having finer ware and Roman imports in the pottery assemblage. This fineware profile of pottery correlates with what has been found in Sepphoris itself. The archaeology suggests that Sepphoris was a richer place in which there was considerable trade, with more of a Roman overlay culturally.[48] Jesus certainly knew of royal palaces and those who lived in them, who dressed beautifully (Matt. 11:8//Luke 7:25). Features of cities, the activities of powerful kings and wealthy landowners, and the slaves and labourers who served them, are drawn on frequently in his parables (e.g. Matt. 22:1–11),[49] but while Jesus would likely have visited Sepphoris, it is another thing to say that he, or his father Joseph, took employment there.

Being a carpenter situated Jesus and his family in a particular social class, very different from the wealthy elite. This also meant he was quite different from educated scribes and teachers. As Chris Keith has explored,[50] they would have looked down on Jesus as effectively illiterate. In the book of Sirach (38:24–34), written from the perspective of the priestly educated elite, it is affirmed that the wisdom of a scribe requires leisure time, but someone doing manual labour or a tradesman does not have this required time. The author asks: 'How can he be wise . . . one who is occupied in labours . . . so every *tektōn* and *architektōn* who labours night and day?' (38:25, 27). The author of this work admits that such tradesmen 'trust in their hands and each one is wise in his own work' (38:31). However, as Sirach states, they are not sought out for their public counsel, nor do they sit high in the public assembly. They are not judges, nor do they understand court decisions. They cannot expound discipline or judgement. They are not city rulers. As James Crossley and Robert Myles note, from the perspective of the elite, 'someone like Jesus should not be involved in intellectual matters and should know his place as a rural manual worker'.[51]

There is one incident recorded concerning Jesus' mission that has a bearing on how we see him as a child in Nazareth in terms of his education, knowledge and authority. According to Mark 6:1–6 (//Matt. 13:53–8; cf. Luke 4:16–19), Jesus comes to his *patris*, his home town, with his disciples. The context suggests this is Nazareth, but it is not actually said;[52] only in Luke's retelling is it stated that this was 'Nazareth, where he had been raised' (Luke 4:16). At any rate, on the Sabbath, he teaches in the synagogue, and 'many' people there are said to be 'astonished' and ask:

> Where did this [man] get these [ideas]? And what's [with] the wisdom given to him? And how are such wonder-workings he does happening? Isn't this the carpenter, the son of Mary, and brother of James, Joset, Judas and Simon? And aren't his sisters here with us?

People in Nazareth are offended. They do not accept him as a prophet.

The town's residents use the fact that Jesus is a carpenter to question the validity of his interpretation of Scripture. They are by implication noting that interpretation of Scripture is the usual realm of the scribal elite, as presented in Sirach 38, not a carpenter (Mark 6:3),[53] though the members of this scribal elite are apparently not themselves around. Indeed, one would not expect to see them in a rural synagogue in Nazareth. In Mark, Jesus teaches with divine authority (*exousia*), as a prophet, 'not as the scribes' (Mark 1:22), and thus Jesus responds by telling his disciples that 'a prophet is not without honour except in his own home town (*patris*), and among his own relatives (*sungeneis*), and in his own household (*oikia*)' (Mark 6:4). Jesus is shown as expecting people of his own home town to accept the transformation he had experienced, to accept him as a prophet with an ability to proclaim God's purpose in regard to the coming kingdom. Therefore, pre-transformation, there had been no reason to see him as having any inspired insight or special learning.

In the Gospel of John, the divide between Jesus and the scribal elite is made explicit: 'How is it this man has learning, when he hasn't studied?' (John 7:15). We see here a social stigma, despite Jesus' heritage as a descendant of David. To be a tradesman, working with his hands for a living, meant he belonged to a class that was well below that of the men who claimed true learning and authority: those who sat on 'Moses' seat' (Matt. 23:1–3).

Education

Despite his status as a manual worker, Jesus was not without any education. The synagogue context in Nazareth, as described in Mark, implies that teaching is what was expected in this space (Mark 6:2). It was just not the kind of teaching that Jesus presented. Sirach was written *c.*200 BCE, but, in the centuries that followed, the institution of the synagogue grew in both Judaea and the Jewish Diaspora, and part of the synagogue's raison d'être appears to have been education. For example, Philo of Alexandria set great store on synagogues being 'schools' (*didaskaleia*) whereby all Israel would be taught the Mosaic law.[54] After all, Moses commanded Israel to teach the precepts of God to children 'so that you and your children may live long in the land that Yahweh swore to your ancestors' (Deut. 11:16–21; and see 6:1–3). This was a particular responsibility placed on fathers.[55] Josephus writes of how Moses' form of education was by means of precepts and praxis, words and actions, the latter beginning with eating kosher food and resting on the Sabbath. This was a pattern established early in life, along with regular assemblies (in the synagogue) to listen to the law and gain a full knowledge of it, so that people could repeat the laws by heart, having them 'inscribed on [their] souls': (male) children had to learn to follow the law so as not to use ignorance as an excuse for transgression, and to know the actions of their ancestors and imitate them (*Apion* 2:171–204).[56] This method of education therefore entailed memorisation of Scripture.[57] Synagogues were comprised of a main hall for the assembly of the community over the course of the Sabbath day (men, women and children) but also other rooms, including a Beth ha-Sepher, the 'book house',[58] where learning letters and reading would take place, and also the

Beth Midrash, the 'study house',[59] where there was Torah study for men and older boys. Such rooms within synagogue complexes, such as in Magdala and Gamala, can be distinguished in the archaeological remains.[60]

Therefore, it seems likely that training in Scripture within the synagogue was an essential part of growing up as a Jewish boy, though memorisation cannot be considered advanced literacy as such, and in rural synagogues there may have been little time or encouragement for much Torah study. At any rate, from around the age of 13 Jesus would have been supposed to know the basics of the law of Moses; at this point any vows he made would be considered valid (*m.Nid.* 5:6; *m.'Abot* 5:21). There was no coming-of-age Bar Mitzvah ceremony and celebration at this time.[61]

In addition, however, if we accept Matthew's presentation of Joseph's expertise in dream and scriptural interpretation, Joseph would surely have passed this expertise on to his sons, at least, bringing them to a higher standard of literacy than would be usual. Education at home would have complemented the formal education received in the Nazareth synagogue. Indeed, confidence in scriptural interpretation became a mainstay of Christian scholarship, as is evident throughout early Christian writings, and the source of this confidence rests on the way Jesus taught his own disciples to interpret Scripture. No one teaches who is not first taught. As Jesus said: 'The student is not superior to the teacher, nor a servant superior to their master. It is sufficient for students to be like their teachers, and servants like their masters' (Matt. 10:24–5). Becoming like your teacher, in knowledge and praxis, was what education was about.

In the *Infancy Gospel of Thomas* (*IGT*) or *Paidika*,[62] a Gentile Christian work dating from the second century,[63] there are a number of stories about (fruitless) attempts to educate Jesus, who, as a divine child, is assumed to have already a godlike mind, encompassing knowledge of everything; he also, however, has a serious lack of restraint and kindness.[64] As Stephen Davis has explored, the work draws on the cultural memory of how children learned with a teacher in the context of Hellenic education: Jesus learns Greek letters. It shows how young students were expected to memorise, and also that they would be physically punished for their failures.[65] It represents the memorisation system when the teacher, Zacchaeus (*Paidika* 6), writes out the alphabet and then reads out each letter over and over; the young Jesus proves he knows the letters by reciting them back, from *alpha* to *omega*. In *Paidika* 13 a second teacher repeats the process and tells Jesus: 'Say *alpha*.'[66] Jesus is insolent and talks back. The teacher hits him, and Jesus strikes him dead. Joseph is presented as the one with the responsibility for Jesus' education, as his father, but in the end he tells Mary to keep Jesus at home until everyone who angers him is dead. In *Paidika* 14 another attempt is successful, at which point the teacher basically affirms that Jesus is already full of 'grace and wisdom', and the former teacher is restored to life.

As Davis shows, all this illustrates a great deal of animus towards teachers in the ancient world. They were known for their physical punishment of children, and a divine Jesus who turns the tables and strikes back would have been appreciated by readers/hearers.[67] Certainly, the usual classroom of the ancient world was not a site of ease and joy. We can know how (elite) children in antiquity learned literacy skills on the basis of a body of literature known as the *Hermeneumata*.[68] These texts show that, in elementary learning, children would be drilled, with an older student pronouncing letters and syllables aloud and the smaller children writing them down.[69] The youngest pupils would learn 'letters and syllables', as Davis notes.[70] Quintilian (*Institutiones* 10:2:2) mentions that 'boys copy the shapes of letters that they may learn to write' and provides prescriptions on ideal learning.[71] Mistakes were met with chastisement, which could include beating.

There was a similar process in Judaism for Hebrew letter learning for reading. A teacher wrote down alphabetic exercises for the pupils,[72] but there is very little in rabbinic sources about students actually learning to write.[73] Nevertheless, Josephus states that Moses 'commands [children] to learn letters (*grammata*)' (*Apion* 2:204), which implies more than just reading.[74] Yet, even with basic literacy (in Hebrew?) provided through the synagogue, sophisticated analyses of scriptural texts, or interpretation, required skills that would have been beyond most people. This is where initiatives at home would have counted for a great deal, and they would likely have involved a gentler learning environment.[75]

In the *Paidika*, however, the stories of Jesus' childhood present us with a Hellenic demigod who zaps any foes in his way. Young Jesus' hapless teachers risk death in attempting to teach him letters. Given the popularity of this work, when Christian pilgrims came to Nazareth from the fourth century onwards these stories in the *Paidika* found a home in what became known as the Synagogue-Church (or, in Arabic, *al-Madrasat-al-Masih*, the 'Messiah's School'), located north of the Sisters of Nazareth Convent. It was here, according to the Piacenza Pilgrim of 570 CE, that 'the Lord wrote his ABC' and where he sat with other children (*Itin.* 5).[76] This building in its present form is a Crusader church and it is simply a question to be asked whether it sits on the site of a synagogue from the first century.[77] The actual first-century synagogue of Nazareth has not yet been located, but four column bases of white calcite with Hebrew/Aramaic mason's marks (showing the letters *lamed, dalet, mem* and *tet*), appropriate for a public building, were long ago retrieved from a location in central Nazareth, likely from the Greek Orthodox property.[78]

Joseph in the *Paidika* also educates Jesus in household work, including sowing seeds in the family field (*Paidika* 12) and gathering firewood (*Paidika* 16). In addition, the *Paidika* indicates something of young Jesus' help with his mother's tasks, and this alerts us to the education he would have received from his mother Mary as well. He would have taken part in various household duties undertaken by his mother, since these were the preserve of the women, girls and younger male children. Thus, in *Paidika* 11, Jesus is sent by Mary to draw water (and he miraculously brings it back in his cloak). The labour of both Jesus' father and mother, and other members of the wider family and community, along with the agricultural work of people in Nazareth, is also reflected in numerous stories and images of Jesus' teaching in the canonical Gospels. He has seen women working to mill grain at a grinding stone (Matt. 24:41). He has seen women making bread, using leaven to make it rise (Matt. 13:33; 16:6, 12). He would have seen his mother, sisters and other women spinning, weaving and sewing, for example, and he has learned some basic rules about mending old clothing: 'No one sews a piece of unshrunk cloth on an old garment, or else the new piece will pull away from the old, making the tear worse' (Mark 2:21).[79] This in itself speaks to the economic situation of his family: they were mending old clothes with new woven pieces. Jesus was not a boy often dressed in new clothes.

In Matthew, we noted that the comment that Joseph did not have sex with Mary until Jesus was born (Matt. 1:25) indicates that he did then have sex with her, which points to the existence of Jesus' siblings.

Mary can be seen as a mother of many children, busy in the household, supporting her husband's trade, working with wool and cloth to make clothing, preparing food, looking after family members during times of illness, grieving and engaging in burial rituals, and doing all that was normative for women at this time in this place. One can imagine countless ways in which Mary influenced her son: telling stories, singing songs, teaching him how to behave.[80]

Jesus grew up as part of a family, with brothers and sisters, understanding fully all the dynamics of family life, including the loyalty and love that siblings would have for one another. We think again of what Jesus was remembered as saying to the Syro-Phoenician woman: 'Let the children be fed first, for it's not right to take the children's food and throw it to the dogs' (Mark 7:27). There is an image of many hungry children sitting around a table, ready to receive the prepared food: an image perhaps of Jesus' own family table, in which he was the eldest son looking after the younger children.

Jesus' family

The story of Mark 6:1–6 is significant in terms of how Jesus viewed himself in relation to his fellow townsfolk, at least as Mark would present this. In the narrative, Jesus arrives one day in his home town, where he attends the synagogue on the Sabbath and starts teaching the local people. As we have seen, faced with their opposition, he says: 'A prophet is not without honour except in his own home town (*patris*), and among his own relatives (*sungeneis*), and in his own household (*oikia*)' (Mark 6:4). The sceptical people of the town, who do not believe what Jesus is saying or doing, are, then, his 'relatives' (Mark 6:4). Interestingly, Matthew (13:57) drops mention of 'relatives', as does Luke (4:24), but Mark's saying of Jesus is clearly the most original. However, the 'relatives' are not Jesus' immediate family but are pointing towards Mary and Jesus' siblings, who seem to be standing by, watching mutely. His mother and siblings are said to be 'here with us' (Mark 6:3), but the 'us' are the doubting relatives. Jesus' immediate family is distinguished from them.

These relatives are portrayed as taking offence that Jesus, as a tradesman (like them?), is attempting to trump the teaching of the educated scribal elite with a claim to prophecy; but they might well be upset by his *message* too. If we wish to think about the kinds of things Jesus might have said in such a synagogue, we get a good indication from Mark, who has already stated exactly what Jesus was teaching; for example: 'The time is completed. The Kingdom of God is coming. Repent and believe the good news' (Mark 1:15), or 'I came not to call the righteous, but wrong-doers' (Mark 2:17), or 'The Sabbath was made for humanity, and not humanity for the Sabbath' (Mark 2:27). He would have announced that the kingdom of God had already been planted (Mark 4:3–20, 26–32). It is not surprising that the townspeople reacted to such pronouncements with cutting remarks about the 'wisdom' (*sophia*) Jesus was displaying. There would actually be very good reasons for them to be upset, given what had happened recently to other would-be revolutionaries who anticipated the end of Roman rule and the beginning of God's. There was also the issue of the prevailing attitude of the authorities towards the house of David. Jesus would be putting them all in danger.

Jesus, however, 'was amazed at their unbelief' (Mark 6:6). Jesus' amazement here, then, suggests that he thought he *would* be welcomed home and that he would find support. It suggests a prior sense that he had previously been safe and supported in his own home town, among his own relatives and in his own household. Given what we have already explored in our discussion of Joseph's story about Jesus' auspicious birth, which set him up to take on some kind of leadership role, Jesus might well have expected more trust that what his father had said – presumably to his wider family – was true. Here, Jesus had now embraced the role of prophet, and had returned to Nazareth only to find that whatever his father had said was not believed.

Jesus' fellow Nazarenes' lack of faith is indicated in Mark and Matthew as the reason Jesus could not do any significant works of the Spirit's power in Nazareth: 'He could do no wonder there, except he laid his hands on a few sick people and healed them' (Mark 6:5//Matt. 13:58). It is as if the stuffing is knocked out of him by their reaction. The Spirit withdraws. We can get a sense of Jesus' emotion: it is all incredibly disappointing.

We can note also that in Luke the story is developed in a way that has far more vehemence: all the people in the synagogue get up, 'filled with fury', throw Jesus out of the city and take him to the 'projection (*ophrus*, literally 'eyebrow') of the hill upon which their city was built in order to hurl him down' (Luke 4:29). This is the incident later associated with Mount Precipice, a hill south of Nazareth and closer to Japha. Nazareth itself was not built on top of a hill, but mainly on the western slope of an elevated valley. This story seems to point forward to the death of Jesus' brother James, who was thrown from the height of the Temple parapet – as told by Hegesippus (*Hist. Eccles.* 2:23:4–20). The developed story oddly recalls also the antagonistic tales of the *Paidika*: we find that Jesus, in the end, after miraculously 'passing through the midst of them, went away' (Luke 4:30).

But in Mark and Matthew there is less drama, and more a sense of Jesus' personal pain. It is not only that he is not believed; he is now without his father Joseph for support. Notably, the local people of Nazareth point to Jesus' mother, Mary, but not to his father, Joseph. She is here with Jesus' siblings. In Matthew, Jesus is known as the 'son of the carpenter' (13:55), which might imply Joseph's continuing presence, and in Luke Jesus is identified as the 'son of Joseph' (Luke 4:22). In the Gospel of John, the *Ioudaioi* (Judaeans) at one point say: 'Isn't this Jesus, the son of Joseph, whose mother and father we know?' (John 6:42). But, despite playing an extremely important role in the birth narratives, particularly that of Matthew, Joseph is completely absent from the story of Jesus' mission as an adult. For this reason, it is very likely that Joseph had died before Jesus' mission began. Unfortunately, there is no indication about *when* exactly he died.

Jesus was remembered as knowing about the plight of widows. He tells a story of a widow who is persistent in appealing before a corrupt judge (Luke 18:1–5). A widow gives two small coins to Temple charity, even though it is all she has (Mark 12:41–4; Luke 21:1–4). Heartless scribes 'devour widows' houses' (Mark 12:40 and parallels), presumably using legal technicalities relating to inheritance. Jesus was filled with compassion at the death of a widow's only son in Nain (Luke 7:11–17).

Andries van Aarde has explored what being fatherless would have meant for Jesus as a child, born in Galilee, with his mother Mary as a solo parent of an illegitimate child who would have been an outcast.[81] In van Aarde's view, Joseph in reality was not the father of Jesus, and the Gospel stories about Joseph are inventions designed to counter the kinds of attacks on Jesus that are found in Celsus and later rabbinic tradition.[82] Jesus' lack of known paternity would have put him in a vulnerable and marginalised position, and would have involved a certain psychological profile in which there is a status envy of those with a father, identification with the mother and female-gendered characteristics (such as gentleness and lack of aggression), and also a compensatory adoption of God as his heavenly Father (*Abba*).[83] This portrait of Jesus as illegitimate, with Joseph not adopting him, has been taken up by Donald Capps, who also examines Jesus' psychology as a boy during the 'hidden years' as a result of the social stigma attached to being illegitimate.[84]

However, this portrait requires an erasure of what is actually said about Jesus' family connections, as well as Joseph. Even if Joseph did die when Jesus was still a child, there was apparently a brother of Joseph in the picture: Clopas. As Jesus' uncle (Eusebius, *Hist. Eccles.* 3:11), Clopas could have taken on responsibility for Mary, Jesus and his siblings as a guardian until Jesus came of age.[85] However, there is no evidence of this arrangement. There is also no indication in the earliest Christian literature that Jesus' siblings were born of a wife of Joseph prior to Mary, even though this became a common view from the *Protevangelium* onwards, in line with the concept of the perpetual virginity of Mary. Six siblings are indicated (Mark 6:3//Matt. 4:55–6). By implication, Joseph lived for some time to father them.[86] If we assume a two- to three-year spacing between the children,[87] it would mean a birth schedule something like this:

4 BCE   James
2 BCE   sister (Salome)
2 CE   Joset
5 CE   sister (Mary)
7 CE   Judas
10 CE   Simon

In addition, there might well have been children who did not survive, making the span of ages wider. Infant and child mortality was high. In her study of Jewish childhood in the Roman world, Hagith Sivan notes that in the cemeteries of Hellenistic–Roman Jerusalem and Jericho 'skeletal remains belonging to individuals younger than twelve years old formed about 30 percent of the identifiable material'.[88]

Joseph, then, must have lived through to at least 10 CE. There seems no good reason to doubt that Joseph played an important role in Jesus' upbringing. Surely, it was precisely because Jesus had a model of a loving, forgiving and understanding father that he could insist on this model for God.[89]

Jesus, as the eldest son, would have inherited a double portion of his father's estate[90] and been responsible for his mother and siblings after his father's death. Indeed, this responsibility seems to be implied in an exchange between Jesus and the 'beloved disciple' in the Gospel of John 19:26, where Jesus seems to commit Mary's care to this disciple. As John Miller has noted, it may be that Jesus' lack of marriage was partly related to Jesus losing his father before a marriage could be arranged, since it was the father's responsibility towards his son 'to circumcise him, redeem him as firstborn son, teach him Torah, teach him a trade and find him a wife' (j.Qidd. 1:7).[91]

The responsibility of Jesus to look after his family may be hinted at elsewhere. In terms of how Mark portrays Jesus' siblings, they are not forefronted, however. Jesus is portrayed in Mark as apparently prioritising his disciples above his immediate family. When his mother and siblings arrive in Capernaum, and stand outside the house (of Peter?) where Jesus was staying, 'calling (kalountes) him', his response is: 'Who are my mother and my siblings?' He looks to those who are listening to him and says: 'Behold, my mother and my siblings. Whoever does the will of God – that person is my brother, my sister and my mother' (Mark 3:31–5). This is clearly designed to endorse the concept of the 'fictive kinship group' of the community of disciples,[92] who would indeed consider themselves brothers and sisters (adelphoi) together, and for Mark this group of the disciples was the key one. But this should not mean we should minimise the historical importance of Jesus' actual siblings 'according to the flesh', or Jesus' responsibility towards them. Mark does not provide many names of figures who interact with Jesus, and the fact that the names of Mary and the brothers are given, one after another, may well imply that the readers/hearers are expected to recognise them. In the same way, it can be said that Simon of Cyrene was 'the father of Alexander and Rufus' (Mark 15:21), as if people would know who they were.[93]

In the story of Mark 3:31–5 we are not told what motivated Mary and the siblings to be in Capernaum and 'call' him. Are they summoning him as a group in authority, in dependence, or in deference? Copying Mark, Matthew softens what they say to make them more polite: they are 'seeking to speak to him' (*zētountes autō lalēsai*, Matt. 12:46) rather than calling him. There is an expectation that Jesus would respond. The siblings are not portrayed with any spouses or children, and that may make us wonder whether they are younger, and again all unmarried, at this stage, all needing Jesus for help.

Jesus' help then would be to include them in his mission, supported along with all his other disciple 'brothers and sisters' out of common funds. And they trusted Jesus. In the Gospel of John, Jesus' mother Mary and his siblings are presented as being part of his mission right from the outset. Jesus' mother urges him to act in the wedding at Cana, apparently knowing he has wonder-working powers (John 2:1–11). He travels with his 'mother and his siblings and his disciples' to Capernaum (John 2:12).[94] His siblings urge him to go from Galilee to (old) Judaea, to Jerusalem, for the Feast of Tabernacles, so that 'your disciples [there] can see [all] the works you are doing, because no one does anything in secret when he seeks to be publicly known. If you are doing these things, show yourself to the world!' (John 7:2–4). It is said at one point that 'his siblings did not trust in him (*oude . . . hoi adelphoi autou episteuon eis auton*)' (7:5), but it is not that they did not believe he was the *Messiah*; rather, they did not trust in him on the specific point that 'the Judaeans [i.e. Judaean authorities] were seeking to kill him' (John 7:1) and that he would die if he went to Jerusalem right then, in the same way that Simon Peter in Mark 8:31–3 did not believe that would happen. They naively thought Jesus would go to Jerusalem and prove himself (as Messiah) by his works of wonder. However, because Jesus knew he would be killed there, he told them: 'My time is not yet come, but your time is always ready.' They are pushing him, as if the time is always ready, when it is not. He testifies against the world, and cannot be hailed within the world, as they seem to want him to be (John 7:6–7). This presents the siblings of Jesus as more worldly-focused than Jesus, in not understanding everything and seeking to have him publicly acclaimed as king, but they are completely on his side in thinking of his capabilities and messiahship.

Indeed, in John, unlike in the other Gospels, after his miracle of the multiplication of loaves and fish (John 6:1–14) Jesus realises that certain people (unspecified) 'were about to come, to seize him (*harpazein*) so as to make him king'. Because of this, and resisting it, he withdraws again to the mountain,[95] 'alone by himself' (6:15). The Greek word *harpazein* indicates that Jesus would be seized by force, but 'they' who would do the seizing are only loosely hinted at. Jesus goes off into the wilderness away from everyone.[96] But in portraying this, the story in John emphasises the deep divide between what Jesus believed and what some of his supporters, including perhaps his siblings, thought. Jesus rejects the idea of worldly kingship, a role that would befit a 'Son of David', but not him. Indeed, in Matthew and Luke this prospect is even presented as the lure of Satan (Matt. 4:8–10//Luke 4:5–8). Given what is said of the attitude of Jesus' siblings in John, that in Jerusalem he should show himself to the world, perhaps even his siblings would be included in those who might 'seize' Jesus, against his will, and make him king. Jesus' siblings are, then, both his supporters and also misguided in their ambitions for him.

The family of Jesus might otherwise have tried to protect him at times. In Mark 3:20–1 there is mention of people who grab Jesus in a house in the midst of an extremely pressing crowd, and the Greek wording is often translated as indicating that his family seized him, thinking he was out of his mind.[97] However, the language is ambiguous. The Greek phrase read as 'family' literally means 'those from him' (*hoi par' autou*), and in Mark 4:10 a similar phrase, *hoi peri auton*, 'those with him', refers to his disciples. Nevertheless, idiomatically, this phrase can refer to a household (Prov. 31:21 LXX; Josephus, *Ant.* 1:193), as well as to friends (Sus. 33 LXX), so we may translate 'those from him' as 'his people'. In the narrative, Jesus has just chosen the Twelve and sent them out to proclaim his message (3:14), whereas his blood family has not yet been mentioned.

If they are his family, though, they hear news (from whom?) and go off to grab (*kratēsai*) Jesus, as an intervention, and explain themselves by saying '*exestē*'. This is often translated as 'he is out of his mind'. But the verb *existēmi* really means 'to be beside oneself', and elsewhere in Mark means 'amazed' or 'astonished' in a way that is flabbergasting and overwhelming (2:12; 5:42; 6:51). One can be 'beside oneself' with wonderment, or in an exorcistic trance. So is Jesus so astonished by the needs of the pressing crowd that he doesn't move? Or is Jesus really overwhelmed? Or is he in an altered state? In this case, whoever is doing the grabbing of Jesus may well have thought they were rescuing him from the crowd for his own good. After all, 'they' (Jesus and the crowd?) cannot eat.

So Mark 3:20–1 can be translated as:

And he came to a house, and a crowd assembled again, such that it was not possible for them even to eat bread. So, after hearing this, his people (*hoi par' autou*) went off to grab (*kratēsai*) him, for they said, 'He's beside himself (*exestē*)!'

If this does refer to Jesus' family, then they can be seen to rescue him from a crowded house in which he and others have no space to eat. It does not indicate opposition; it indicates protection. Interestingly, it is also a story that the early church did not want to repeat: it is not found in Matthew or Luke, and is even modified textually, perhaps because it shows Jesus' vulnerability.[98]

In the variants of the Aramaic Matthew, used by 'Hebrews/Nazarenes' of the third to fourth centuries, the immediate family of Jesus are on his side and are proactive in pushing him in a particular direction. Jerome provides an interesting snippet of what this gospel contained:

Behold, the mother of the Lord and his siblings were saying to him: 'John the Baptist baptises for the remission of sins. Let's also be baptised by him.' But he said to them, 'In what way have I sinned, that I should go and be baptised by him – unless perhaps this very thing I said is ignorance?'
(*Adv. Pel.* 3:2)

This piece seems to have a place just after Matthew 3:12, before Jesus does go to John for baptism, and it introduces Jesus as having a supportive mother and siblings (and no living father) who are themselves determined to heed John's call.[99] While Jerome does not provide it here, it would likely have been followed by some reply from Mary and Jesus' siblings to Jesus' query, indicating that it is necessary to fulfil all right-eousness (cf. Matt. 3:14–15).

This prepares the reader for what follows in Matthew:

Then Jesus came from Galilee to the Jordan to John to be baptised by him; John would have prevented him, saying 'I need to be baptised by you, but you come to me?' but Jesus answered him, 'Let it be so now, for it is appropriate for us to fulfil all righteousness.' (Matt. 3:13–15)

The prompting of Mary and the siblings of Jesus in the additional section of Aramaic Matthew seems to show full cognisance of the interpretations by Joseph in our canonical Matthew 1 and 2, and pushes the mother and siblings of Jesus into further prominence in his mission: Jesus was of the royal line of David (Matt. 1:1–17); conceived miraculously, as revealed to Joseph (1:18–21); to be named Jesus, who is Immanuel ('God with us'), as revealed to Joseph (1:22–5); shown as a king by the star, as understood by the magi (Matt. 2:1–12); protected by God in Egypt, as revealed to Joseph (2:13–15); called back to 'the Land of Israel', as revealed to Joseph (2:19–21), and then to Nazareth in Galilee, again as revealed to Joseph (2:22–3). Then, according to Aramaic Matthew, John the Baptist came proclaiming that the kingdom of heaven would be coming soon, so that Jesus' mother and siblings quite naturally suggest they all go to repent, and be baptised in the River Jordan as they confess their sins (Matt. 3:1–6). Jesus asks why he should do so. An angel states that this is to fulfil all righteousness and that the whole fount of the Holy Spirit would descend upon him there, and provide 'freedom'. Mary and Jesus' siblings are part of the same trajectory that would ultimately launch Jesus. Notably, Joseph is absent by the time John arrives.

As we saw in Chapter 4, the Holy Spirit is in Aramaic Matthew a divine Mother to Jesus.[100] Jesus' baptism would have been shown to set him quite apart from his siblings and to fulfil prophecy about his destiny. In this version, then, there was an earthly mother and father, Mary and Joseph, and a spiritual Mother and Father, the Holy Spirit and heavenly Father. Jesus' disciples were his spiritual brothers and sisters (Mark 3:31–5//Matt. 12:46–50; cf. Luke 8:19–21). But Jesus had physical brothers and sisters too.

In terms of James's significance, we also noted that Paul mentions how Jesus 'appeared to James' (1 Cor. 15:7). None of our canonical Gospels record this appearance to James. However, Jerome reports this passage in the Aramaic Matthew, the gospel 'according to the Hebrews':

But when the Lord had given the linen cloth (*sindon*) to the servant of the priest, he went to James and appeared to him. For James had

taken a vow not to eat bread from the hour he drank the cup of
the Lord until he should see him raised from those who sleep . . .
The Lord said, 'Bring a table and bread' . . . He took the bread and
blessed it, broke it, gave it to James the Righteous, and said to him,
'My brother, eat your bread, for this son of humanity is risen from
those who sleep.'
(Jerome, *Vir. Ill.* 2)

This implies a previous story also: a linen cloth (*sindon*), mentioned as
being wrapped around Jesus (Matt. 27:59), being given to 'a servant of a
priest' (*servo sacerdotis*; Joseph of Arimathea? Matt. 27:57). James is also
indicated as being previously present at the last supper (Matt. 26:20–30)
when he ate bread and drank from the Lord's cup, as a disciple. There is
an appearance of the risen Christ to James, which can be inserted into
canonical Matthew at the point after the arrival of the women at the
tomb and Jesus' encounter with them (Matt. 28:1–10), and before the
discussion among the chief priests (Matt. 28:11–15). In this way, James –
Jesus' brother – is made an early recipient of a resurrection appearance.[101]
This again emphasises the important place of Jesus' siblings among
certain Christian Jews of Syria (including those of Syria-Palestina).

It might be asked at this stage why all this was not more widely known
and influential in mainstream Christian tradition. But of course we must
remember what happened to the Judaean churches, led by the relatives of
Jesus, and reflect on their capacity to pass on memories, given the disastrous consequences of the Bar Kokhba Revolt (132–6 CE).[102] There is no
indication that Jesus' family survived in Galilee. As we saw, Jerome and
others note that Christian Jews were in southern Syria and elsewhere in
the fourth century but they were a minority.[103]

In the New Testament, James goes from a score of near zero to 100 in
terms of his significance. In the Synoptic Gospels (Mark, Matthew and
Luke) James is mentioned only within the sweep of Jesus' siblings: 'James,
Joset, Judas and Simon? And . . . his sisters . . .' (Mark 6:3//Matt. 13:56;
implied in Mark 3:35//Matt. 12:46//Luke 8:19); but he plays no particularly
important role. In John he is by implication less in the shadows because
the mother and siblings of Jesus are more obvious. But in the Acts of the
Apostles, in the letters of Paul and in early Christian tradition, James is

233

clearly in charge in Jerusalem and has very significant authority elsewhere, as John Painter has well explored.[104] How did James, then, fill the person specifications for this job? It seems that our sources are content with identifying him as 'the Lord's brother', as if that meant it was obvious he should lead. But why would being a brother of Jesus have counted for so much? Being a descendant of David was surely significant, and a reason for the Judaean churches to esteem him. However, added to that, James seems known as a disciple, one who saw the risen Jesus. It is taken for granted that Jesus' family always supported him. Thus, as Painter notes: 'an intertwining of the Davidic family and his distinctive relationship as the brother of the Lord underpinned [James's] leadership of the Jerusalem church.'[105]

Our stories do nevertheless point to some difference between Jesus' vision of the kingdom and that of his siblings, and these show how Jesus went his own way. In terms of his identity and heritage, Jesus would have heard stories about his birth, as provided by his father Joseph. There would have been the weight of heritage and expectation on his shoulders. This would prompt him to think that he was destined to be the 'salvation' of Israel. But Jesus would as an adult problematise what it meant to be a 'prophet', hailed as the Messiah, the Son of David, who would liberate the nation.

If Jesus was identified by his parents as a special child, with an auspicious birth, destined for an important role in the future, his childhood in Nazareth would have been one in which he reflected on what that role might entail. Given what had happened to would-be kings in the recent past, and the terrible violence that followed their bids for power in the face of the huge military might of Rome, might he already have thought about another way? With the legacy of trauma in his own family, and among his own people, and the difficulties of life for the ordinary inhabitants of Galilee, where was real hope to be found? How was God's love for his people and justice actually going to be shown? What did it mean to lead Israel in these circumstances, when to be esteemed as a leader – as Son of David – was likely also to end in death?

Perhaps the only way was to build a community living out an ideal of justice and fellowship, of healing, of egalitarianism, sharing resources, caring for the vulnerable, providing a utopian vision of a world that would soon be transformed, where God would truly rule and all would be well. This was the true rule of God: the dominion, the power and the glory. Perhaps this community would bring a hope that would ultimately cause the oppressive powers of this world to crumble, if enough people joined together as spiritual brothers and sisters with the same vision, founded on the gift of the Spirit to heal and bring life, in an embrace of love and compassion, standing up against the mighty elites that now held sway. Even as a boy, growing up with the weight of expectation on his shoulders, perhaps Jesus began to think this way.

Overall, then, we can imagine Jesus in Nazareth as a child grappling with identity, heritage, trauma and hope. Mary was likely a mother of many children, hard at work with their care and household labours. Joseph, who died before Jesus' mission, would have played an important, vital role in his upbringing, including teaching him the skills of both carpentry, 'righteousness' and scriptural interpretation, demonstrating what being a loving father should mean. There were consequences of losing a father in terms of guardianship for the family: this role would normally pass to the eldest adult son. Jesus would have had to look after his mother and younger siblings. In his later mission he would pass this care on to the wider group of disciples, whom he would call his 'mother and brothers and sisters' (Mark 3:31–5). By this, he integrated a loving standard of household care into a wider community, and integrated his physical family into it too, so deeply that his brother James would come to lead it.

10

Boy Jesus in the Temple

When Christian artists have imagined Jesus as a boy, they have at times portrayed him helping his father in his carpentry workshop in Nazareth,[1] or as a miracle-working child.[2] However, for many artists an incident described in the Gospel of Luke has been the key paradigm: in Luke 2:41–52 Jesus comes to the Temple in Jerusalem with his parents, stays behind when they have started to journey home, and amazes the teachers there with his incredible learning.

This is the one vignette within the New Testament that provides an apparent glimpse of Jesus at around the age of 12.[3] In this final, short chapter, then, we will probe this story to see whether it might contain some authentic memory.

In the Temple

In the Lukan nativity story, after the presentation of Jesus in the Temple, we are told that the family returned to 'their own city Nazareth' and 'the child continued to grow and become strong, increasing in wisdom (*sophia*), and the grace of God was upon him' (Luke 2:39–40). The phrase 'increasing in wisdom' probably implies education.[4] This statement reads as a conclusion, paralleling what has been said of John the Baptist (Luke 1:80), and so the Lukan nativity seems to finish here as a responsive retelling of Matthew 1 – 2. However, there is an additional story of Jesus, aged 12, in the Temple (Luke 2:41–52). This piece was viewed by Raymond Brown as being a separate element within the structure of Luke 1 – 2, added 'in a second stage of composition'.[5] Brown noted how Joseph and Mary seem to have strangely forgotten everything miraculous concerning Jesus' conception and the associated proclamations, just recounted. They appear to be ordinary parents who have no idea about the true identity of Jesus as Son of God.

The reason for the inclusion of the additional story is clear. If the Lukan nativity did end with Jesus still very young, as with Matthew, it left a huge lacuna in the story of Jesus for readers/hearers, who may well have wanted to know more about his wondrous childhood. In ancient biographies there was a wealth of stories of the childhoods of exemplary men, from Homer to Plato to Augustus,[6] and people would have expected to have at least *something*. After all, the emperor Augustus, at the age of 4, could command noisy frogs to be silent (Suetonius, *Div. Aug.* 94:7) and at the age of 12 could give an impressive funeral oration for his grandmother (Suetonius, *Div. Aug.* 8:1). The element of the precocious high-achieving child is a trope of ancient biography.[7] Where were the similar anecdotes about boy Jesus?

So we have a story in which Jesus has phenomenal insights into Scripture in the Temple of Jerusalem (Luke 2:41–52). Tantalisingly, in this case, the story is found in a very similar form in the *Paidika*.[8] We can view the two versions side by side. As a second-century text, we would expect it to be a responsive retelling of canonical accounts. In many ways the *Paidika* follows on from where the *Protevangelium* leaves off, and in later apocryphal works, such as the *Gospel of Pseudo-Matthew*, the two works were indeed combined. Nevertheless, given what we have noted previously about the independence of the Lukan nativity and its inclusion only in the final redaction of the Gospel of Luke, as late as the early second century itself, if the story of boy Jesus in the Temple is secondary to this nativity, we should ask which is earlier: Luke or the *Paidika*? Or are both based on a prior story? It is therefore worthwhile looking at these two versions side by side (see Table 10.1 overleaf).

The two accounts are very similar in Greek, though each has slight variations and distinctive features.[9] For example, in Luke the mention that Joseph and Mary went to Jerusalem every year for the Passover (Luke 2:41) continues a Lukan emphasis on the careful following of Jewish custom, so that might suggest that at this point the *Paidika* replicates an original story more authentically. But one clue to the *Paidika*'s dependence on the Lukan nativity is the way it repositions a statement found within it: when Elizabeth greets Mary she says: 'Blessed among women are you, and blessed the fruit of your womb' (Luke 1:42). In the *Paidika*, this statement is found in a similar way on the lips of the 'scribes

Table 10.1 The story of the boy Jesus in the Temple as told in Luke's Gospel and the *Paidika*

Luke 2:41–52	*Paidika 19:1–5*
[41]His parents journeyed every year to Jerusalem for the festival of the Passover. [42]When he was twelve years old, they went up according to the custom for the festival. [43]After completing the days, while they were returning [home], the child Jesus remained in Jerusalem, and his parents did not know.	[1]When Jesus was twelve years old, his parents journeyed to Jerusalem according to custom for the festival of the Passover. While they were returning [home], Jesus remained in Jerusalem, and his parents did not know.
[44]Thinking he was in the company, they came a day's journey and [then] they looked around for him among their relatives and friends, [45]and when they did not find him, they returned to Jerusalem to look around for him. [46]And it so happened that after three days they found him in the Temple sitting in the midst of the teachers, listening to them and asking them questions. [47]All those hearing him were amazed by his understanding and answers. [48]Seeing him, they were astonished.	[2]Thinking he was in the company, they went a day's journey and [then] began looking for him among their relatives and friends. When they did not find him, they returned to Jerusalem, searching for him. After three days they found him sitting in the Temple in the midst of the teachers, listening to them and asking questions. Those hearing him were amazed at how he posed questions to the elders and solved the main points of the law, and the riddles and parables of the prophets.

238

Table 10.1 (*continued*)

Luke 2:41–52	Paidika 19:1–5
His mother said to him, 'Child, why have you done this to us – look, your father and I have been searching for you in great anxiety.' And he said to them: 'Why were you searching for me? Did you not know that I must be in my Father's places?' And they did not understand the statement that he spoke to them.	³His mother said to him, 'Child, why did you do this to us? Look, we have been searching for you pained and distressed.' Jesus said to them, 'Why were you searching for me? Did you not know that I must be in my Father's places?'
	⁴And the scribes and the Pharisees said to Mary, 'Are you the mother of this child?' And she said, 'I am.' And they said to her, 'Blessed are you, because the Lord God has blessed the fruit of your womb. For we have never seen nor heard such present wisdom and glory of virtue.'
⁵¹He went down with them and came to Nazareth and was obedient to them. His mother kept safe all these words in her heart, ⁵²and Jesus increased in wisdom and growth and grace before God and people.	⁵Jesus rose from there and followed his mother and was obedient to his parents. And she kept safe all these things, pondering them in her heart. And Jesus increased in wisdom and in age and in grace before God and people.

and Pharisees' (17:4), as if the reader/hearer is supposed to be reminded of this affirmation. The expression 'scribes and Pharisees' is not in the Lukan version, which just has 'teachers' in the Temple; however, this expression is found elsewhere in Luke (e.g. 5:21; 6:7, 11; 7:30; 11:23; 15:2), so the *Paidika* author may have used Luke here. Here the *Paidika* has a strong endorsement of the perception of the 'scribes and Pharisees', when elsewhere in the *Paidika* (6 – 8; 13 – 14) the teachers of Jesus are confounded and things do not go well.

In Luke, Jesus listens to the teachers and asks them questions, and the teachers of Jerusalem are amazed by his 'understanding and answers', while in the *Paidika*, the teachers are amazed by how he 'he posed questions to the elders and solved the main points of the law, and the riddles and parables (*ta skolia kai tas parabolas*) of the prophets'. The *Paidika* therefore makes Jesus more impressive. As Tony Burke notes: 'In Luke, Jesus sits engrossed as an attentive, curious student' while in the *Paidika* 'Jesus explains *to them* the main points of the Law'.[10] However, the mention of riddles and parables in the Prophets indicates an understanding that Scripture was a puzzle that should be solved. This was indeed a view found within Second Temple Judaism, as we have seen, where Scripture could be understood as a collection of *razim*, 'mysteries'.[11]

In Luke, the comment that 'his mother kept safe (*dietērei*) all these things in her heart' (2:51) is meant to indicate that this story of the 12-year-old Jesus is Mary's memory (echoing Luke 2:19), but the *Paidika* makes the same claim for its entire account of Jesus' childhood as well, here and in *Paidika* 11:2.[12] Both accounts, then, show an awareness that there needs to be a line of memory for readers to believe what they present: they are both claimed as mother's stories.

Elsewhere, the *Paidika* appears to weave into Luke some of John's Christology in which Jesus is the divine, pre-existent *Logos*.[13] Jesus fashions new eyes for a man born blind (John 9:1–41); thus, Jesus fashions living birds out of clay (*Paidika* 2). Joseph appears as Jesus' father (*Paidika* 4:1–2; 6:1; 11:2; 12:1), but Joseph is also firmly contrasted with Jesus' divine Father (*Paidika* 5:1; 17:3). So it is likely that the *Paidika* author knows the Gospels of Luke and John.[14] Its entire narrative seems to springboard off Luke 2:40, where the family return to Nazareth, filling in a gap about Jesus' childhood there. The story then explains how Jesus could read Scripture so well in the Temple.[15] In its concluding lines, therefore, the story in the Temple is retold. But we cannot rule out the possibility that the *Paidika* had access to an independent tradition of boy Jesus in the Temple.

It is not an inherently implausible childhood story at core: in the flurry of departure, Jesus was left behind. Stories of parental slips are commonly told by parents, shared among family members and friends. Stories of a child's exceptional ability are and were also much told. Josephus presents himself as a child who was so brilliant in his understanding that the chief priests asked him for advice (*Life* 8–9). Since in Luke (not in the *Paidika*) the parents of Jesus are baffled by Jesus' response that he was 'in his Father's places' (Luke 2:49), Brown suggested that the original story 'or a form of it may well have first circulated in circles ignorant of the annunciation story and ignorant of the virginal conception',[16] and some scholars have suggested it circulated among Jewish-Christians who thought of Jesus' parents as being Joseph and Mary.[17]

In both Luke and the *Paidika*, the story involves Jesus being forgotten when a company of 'relatives and friends' from Nazareth, who have come to Jerusalem for Passover, set off back home. In the midst of the busy departure, his parents leave without him, not realising he is not in the group. This correlates with what we have explored in the previous chapter: that in Nazareth there were several relatives of Jesus, who would later on not accept his proclamation.

So what about this story of leaving a child behind? It is not unbelievable. It represents accurately the hurly-burly of the Passover feast in Jerusalem, where there were throngs of pilgrims and, in this case, a company of townspeople travelling together. Josephus indicates there could be 2,700,000 people present in Jerusalem at this time of year, not including Gentiles (*War* 6:420–7). A caravan would have been made up of walkers, donkeys and/or camels laden with luggage, and perhaps carts, and it could comprise many people: possibly the one from Nazareth included half the population of the town itself. Jesus could have been thought to be at the front or the back. In extended family groups, the older children might not be supervised only by their parents, but by other responsible adults too. It was only when they stopped, after a day's journey, perhaps in the area of Jericho, that Joseph and Mary realised Jesus was not there.

Missing his cue to leave with the Nazareth caravan, Jesus goes to the Temple. Given the numbers of people departing from the Jerusalem environs to different villages, there would have been a constant stream of hordes of pilgrims on the roads. It would have been almost impossible to push through and catch up with the Nazareth party. So Jesus stays put, sits with other students and asks questions of the teachers, who would provide a certain amount of education for free. In Acts (3:11; 5:12; and see John 10:23), this zone where teachers spoke is called Solomon's Portico. Roofed and protected, it lay within the vast precincts of the outer court, on the eastern side. The portico was very long, and immensely grand, with a double row of large white columns (Josephus, *War* 5:185; *Ant.* 15:401–2; 20:221). There would have been distinct areas for different teachers, chairs for the speakers, rugs for those listening, food and drink. You could roll up in your mantle and sleep there, as we see shown in old photographs of Cairo's al-Azhar Mosque, where traditional teaching practices continued through to the nineteenth century (see Plate 16).

Joseph and Mary then have to struggle back through the flow of pilgrims departing from Jerusalem to find their lost son. They search everywhere 'for three days' (Luke 2:46; *Paidika* 19:2). In Luke, as Mary says, they are 'anxious', but in the *Paidika* they are 'pained and distressed' (Luke 2:48; *Paidika* 19:2), reflecting well how any parent would feel searching for a lost child. But if the story contains elements of a family reminiscence of Jesus' youth, we need to situate it in time. Jesus was taken by his parents, as a 12-year-old, to the Passover in Jerusalem. As we saw, Jesus would have been that age in 6 CE (if he was born c.6–5 BCE). This would be just before, or just after, Archelaus was removed by the Roman emperor Augustus and exiled in Vienne in Gaul. The memory of what Archelaus had done in the Temple, at Passover, and the horrendous consequences of the War of Varus just a decade earlier would have been in the minds of all who came to Jerusalem. Passover, the festival commemorating the liberation of Israel from bondage in Egypt, the actions of the heroic prophet Moses who led the people into freedom, and the loving care of God for the nation at that time, would have been the main subject taught by the teachers here. The contrast between then and now would have been acute.

The response of Jesus to his parents, namely that he is in 'my Father's places', is clearly told to indicate his divine sonship, which is a Lukan theme,[18] as in the *Paidika* also. The plural 'places' for the Temple precincts is interesting in that it encompasses not just the Sanctuary of the Temple but also the wider Court of the Gentiles and the columned portico itself.

Yet this statement about the fatherhood of God is also part of the Passover story. In Exodus 4:22–3, Moses says to Pharaoh: 'This is what the Lord says: Israel is my firstborn son, and I told you, "Let my son go, so he may worship me."' Moses says to Israel, 'You are the children of the Lord your God . . .' (Deut. 14:1).[19] In the Song of Moses, after the crossing of the sea, there is: 'Is he not your Father, your Creator, who made you and formed you?' (Deut. 32:6). In the Amidah, the central Jewish prayer that dates to the Second Temple period, God is directly addressed as 'Father': 'Cause us to return, our Father, to your Torah . . . Forgive us, our Father, for we have sinned . . . Merciful Father, have compassion upon us and accept our prayers . . . Bless us, our Father, all of us as one . . .' Jesus had learned well.

Therefore, the story of boy Jesus in the Temple makes a claim to memory from Jesus' parents, particularly from his mother (2:31), and this memory has been communicated in a form that has ultimately been recorded and then slotted into Luke to fill in a gap, just as the *Paidika* later slots in a much-developed sequence of childhood tales. Actuality may well have been different. But in its presentation of Joseph and Mary as ordinary parents who mistakenly depart from Jerusalem without their son, and return to find him among teachers in the Temple and saying things they do not understand, this is not an implausible tale. The story says something about the way the family would remember Jesus: he could go his own way, work out how to be safe in a strange environment, exhibit remarkable insight and intelligence, understand Scripture deeply, and not necessarily do his parents' bidding. It was no wonder that this story is followed by the assurance: 'He went down [from Jerusalem] with them and came to Nazareth, and was obedient to them' (Luke 2:51; cf. *Paidika* 19:5). Despite everything, Jesus was in the end a good boy.

Ultimately, we are left with some reflections on memories. We need to ask why stories are told, who by, for whom, in what context? There would have been many possible stories about Jesus as a child, told among his family, and yet we have only this one snippet as possibly representative of actuality, albeit in an evolved version. Underlying it is a sense of expectation. This story fits with a family sense of hope. Jesus would have carried this hope: that he would be a leader, in some way, at a time when survival meant keeping very quiet.

Conclusions

This book has explored what we might know of Jesus as a child by turning over the evidence of literature and archaeology. We can travel with this evidence on a journey through the world of the past. Written works preserve certain memories of individuals, families and communities at different times and places, and we have looked to the earliest ones, and thought also about how these memories could have been shaped and retold. The writings of Josephus, much based on those of Herod's eyewitness chronicler Nicolaus of Damascus, illuminate through his own lens the very troubled social landscape of Jesus' early years. This was a time of revolution, already erupting in the final days of Herod, followed by the terrible quashing of national hopes by the Romans in the War of Varus, and further suppressions in the census rebellion. We have seen that in terms of his identity Jesus was a Jew, a Judahite and a Judaean, living in a land with a particular history and culture, where there was wariness about the other peoples within the region of Syria Palestina and Syria Phoenicia, and a deep sense of heritage. As a Judaean child, he would have been told of the events that Josephus relates.

We have seen that there is generally a great scepticism among historians that anything much can be known about Jesus prior to his mission as an adult. There is a frequent assertion that Jesus was born in Nazareth, when no early Christian source states this. Likewise, there is also a common assumption that Jesus was not a descendant of David, despite this being very widely recorded in the earliest Christian literature. Here, this scepticism is contested.

The stories of Jesus' birth in Matthew have been looked at as arising within the family of Jesus. All this speaks to Jesus' siblings playing a greater role in Jesus' mission from the outset than is generally recognised. It is too extreme to sweep everything in Matthew aside as mere invention. Given the powerful positions of Jesus' relatives in the early Judaean churches, such stories would have been told within their circles and among those who knew them. A sceptical view would assert that all such stories were made up in order to increase the family's own status, that such birth and childhood stories were ubiquitous elements when talking of the lives of great men and great prophets.

However, this was a world in which people looked for auspicious signs, where they believed that the Divine shed light on events through portents of all kinds and could communicate with human beings through their dreams and interpretations of Scripture. Whatever might have actually happened, the stories tell us that a particular family of Davidic descendants, originating in Bethlehem, fleeing in a time of danger and resettling in Nazareth in Galilee, had a son whose unusual conception and early childhood indicated that he would in some way lead and free Israel. The family thought this at a time when resistance to the Roman client rulers of Judaea had been put down by acts of extreme violence, backed by the imperial armies of the West, quashing any glimmer of hope for national independence. This was their belief – whether their stories were entirely true or not – and there is no reason to suppose it was not already their belief when Jesus was growing up.

We have looked at Luke and other responsive retellings, seeking to find memory nuggets within these stories, and contextualised Jesus' early life within the historical circumstances of his time. It seems in the end that Jesus was surely a child with a weight on his shoulders. This was a weight of the past in terms of his identity as a Judaean, as a descendant of David, as a Bethlehemite who had been ripped from the ancestral home, as a refugee in Egypt and an emigrant in Galilee, conscious of persecution. He grew up within a region recently injured by Rome in a context of overpopulation, poverty and resentment against the ruling class. He was taught a trade, and he was educated in Scripture so as to be skilled in tools of interpretation, like his father Joseph, in order to read the 'signs of the times'. In terms of the latter skill, he would in due course teach what he had learned to his own disciples: those he gathered in the wake of the arrest of John the Baptist, when the son of Herod, the tetrarch Antipas, had quashed potential rebellion by capturing him and putting him to death.

Yet, embracing his role in a way that was somehow surprising, Jesus would eventually also teach his family. Whatever they expected in terms of his ability to work wonders and liberate Israel, he would reveal that his path was far more complicated.

But that is another story.

Abbreviations

Ancient texts

Acts. Thom.	*Acts of Thomas*
Adomnan	
Loc. Sanct.	*On Holy Places*
Arist.	*Letter of Aristeas*
Aristotle	
Hist. Anim.	*History of Animals*
Met.	*Metaphysics*
Pol.	*Politics*
Bordeaux Pilgrim	
Itin.	*Itinerary*
Cassius Dio	
Hist. Rom.	*Epitome Historiae Romanae*
Cicero	
Tusc.	*Tusculan Disputations*
Clement of Alexandria	
Exc. Theod.	*Excerpts from Theodotus*
Clement of Rome	
1 Clem.	*1 Clement*
Cyril of Jerusalem	
Cat.	*Catechetical Lectures*
Dead Sea Scrolls	
1QH	*Hodayot* (*Hymns*)
1QpHab	*Pesher Habakkuk*
1QS	*Rule of the Community*
CD	Cairo Genizah copy of the *Damascus Document*
Did.	*Didache*
Diodorus Siculus	

Bibl. Hist.	*The Library of History*
Diogenes Laertius	
Lives	*Lives and Opinions of Eminent Philosophers*
Egeria	
Itin.	*Itinerary*
Epiphanius	
Pan.	*Refutation of All Heresies*
Eucherius	
Ep. Faust.	*Letter to Faustus*
Eusebius	
Adv. Haer.	*Against Heresies*
Dem. Evang.	*Demonstration of the Gospel*
Hist. Eccles.	*Ecclesiastical History*
Mart. Pal.	*The Martyrs of Palestine*
Onom.	*Onomasticon*
Quaest. Steph.	*Questions to Stephanus*
Vita Const.	*Life of Constantine*
Gos. Phil.	*Gospel of Philip*
Gos. Thom.	*Gospel of Thomas*
Herodotus	
Hist.	*Histories*
Hippolytus	
Comm. Matt.	*Commentary on Matthew*
Ref.	*Refutation of All Heresies*
Hist. mon.	*Inquiry about the Monks in Egypt*
Horace	
Ep.	*Epistles*
Iamblichus	
Vit. Pyth.	*Life of Pythagoras*
Ignatius of Antioch	
Ephes.	*Letter to the Ephesians*
Smyrn.	*Letter to the Smyrnaeans*
Trall.	*Letter to the Trallians*

IGT	*Infancy Gospel of Thomas*
Irenaeus	
Adv. Haer.	*Against Heresies*
Jerome	
Adv. Jov.	*Against Jovinianus*
Adv. Lucifer.	*Against the Luciferians*
Adv. Pel.	*Against the Pelagians*
Comm. Isa.	*Commentary on Isaiah*
Comm. Matt.	*Commentary on Matthew*
Comm. Micah	*Commentary on Micah*
Ep.	*Epistles*
Lib. Loc.	*On the Locations and Names of Hebrew Places*
Tract. Ps.	*Tractates on the Psalms*
Vir. Ill.	*Illustrious Men*
Josephus	
Ant.	*Jewish Antiquities*
Apion	*Against Apion*
Life	*The Life of Flavius Josephus*
War	*The Judaean War*
Jub.	*Jubilees*
Julius Africanus	
Let. Arist.	*Letter to Aristides*
Justin Martyr	
Apol.	*Apology*
Dial.	*Dialogue with Trypho*
LAB	*Biblical Antiquities*
LXX	Septuagint version of the Old Testament
Nicephorus Kallistos	
Hist. Eccles.	*Ecclesiastical History*
Origen	
Comm. Matt.	*Commentary on Matthew*
Comm. Joh.	*Commentary on John*
De Princ.	*First Principles*

Hom. Jer.	*Homilies on Jeremiah*
Hom. Num.	*Homilies on Numbers*

Philo of Alexandria

Abr.	*On the Life of Abraham*
Cher.	*On the Cherubim*
Congr.	*On the Preliminary Studies*
Contempl.	*On the Contemplative Life*
Deus	*That God Is Unchangeable*
Ebr.	*On Drunkenness*
Flacc.	*Against Flaccus*
Fug.	*On Flight and Finding*
Jos.	*On the Life of Joseph*
Legat.	*On the Embassy to Gaius*
Migr.	*On the Migration of Abraham*
Mos.	*On the Life of Moses*
Mut.	*On the Change of Names*
Praem.	*On Rewards and Punishments*
Prob.	*That Every Good Person Is Free*
Quaest. Gen.	*Questions and Answers on Genesis*
Spec.	*On the Special Laws*
Virt.	*On the Virtues*

Piacenza Pilgrim

Itin.	*Itinerary*

Pliny the Elder

Nat. Hist.	*Natural History*
Prot. Jas	*Protevangelium of James*

Pseudo-Phocylides

Sent.	*The Sentences*

Pseudo-Tertullian

Adv. Omn. Haer.	*Against All Heresies*
Pss Sol.	*Psalms of Solomon*

Rabbinic literature

'Abot	*Pirkei 'Abot*

'Abot R. Nat.	*'Abot of Rabbi Nathan*
AZ	*Avodah Zarah*
b.	Babylonian Talmud
BB	*Bava Batra*
Bekh.	*Bekhorot*
Ber.	*Berakhot*
Betz.	*Betzah*
BQ	*Bava Qamma*
Dem.	*Demai*
Eduy.	*Eduyyot*
Gen. Rab.	*Genesis Rabbah*
Git.	*Gittin*
Hag.	*Hagigah*
Hor.	*Horayot*
j.	Jerusalem Talmud
Ker.	*Kerithot*
Ket.	*Ketubbot*
Kil.	*Kil'ayim*
m.	Mishnah
Makk.	*Makkot*
Meg.	*Megillah*
Men.	*Menahot*
Naz.	*Nazir*
Ned.	*Nedarim*
Nid.	*Niddah*
Pes.	*Pesahim*
Qidd.	*Qiddushin*
Qod.	*Qodashim*
Sanh.	*Sanhedrin*
Shabb.	*Shabbat*
Sot.	*Sotah*
Ta'an.	*Ta'anit*
Ter.	*Terumot*

Yad.	*Yadayim*
Yev.	*Yevamot*

Socrates of Constantinople

Hist. Eccles.	*Ecclesiastical History*

Sozomen

Hist. Eccles.	*Ecclesiastical History*

Strabo

Geogr.	*Geography*

Suetonius

Div. Aug.	*The Divine Augustus*
Vesp.	*Life of Vespasian*
Vit.	*Life of Vitellius*

Tacitus

Hist.	*Histories*

Tatian

Diat.	*Diatessaron*

Tertullian

Adv. Jud.	*Against the Jews*
Adv. Marc.	*Against Marcion*
Carn.	*The Flesh of Christ*
De Virg.	*The Veiling of Virgins*
Test. Jud.	*Testament of Judah*
Test. Mos.	*Testament of Moses*

Theophylact

In Gal.	*Commentary on Galatians*
In Matth.	*Commentary on Matthew*

Vitruvius

Arch.	*On Architecture*

Journals, lexica etc.

ANRW	Wolfgang Haase and Hildegard Temporini (eds), *Aufstieg und Niedergang der römischen Welt: Geschichte und Kultur Roms im Spiegel der neueren Forschung* (Berlin and New York, NY: De Gruyter, 1972–).

251

BAIAS	*Bulletin of the Anglo-Israel Archaeological Society*
BASOR	*Bulletin of the American Schools of Oriental Research*
BDAG	Bauer, Walter, Frederick W. Danker, William F. Arndt and F. Wilbur Gingrich, *A Greek-English Lexicon of the New Testament and Other Early Christian Literature*, 3rd edn (Chicago, IL, and London: University of Chicago Press, 2000).
BJS	Brown Judaic Studies
CBQ	*Catholic Biblical Quarterly*
CCSA	Corpus Christianorum Series Apocryphorum
CPJ	Corpus Papyrorum Judaicarum
DSD	*Dead Sea Discoveries*
HTS	*Harvard Theological Studies*
HUCA	*Harvard Union College Annual*
IAA	Israel Antiquities Authority
IEJ	*Israel Exploration Journal*
JAAR	*Journal of the American Academy of Religion*
JAJ	*Journal of Ancient Judaism*
JANES	*Journal of the Ancient Near Eastern Society*
JAOS	*Journal of the American Oriental Society*
JBL	*Journal of Biblical Literature*
JEH	*Journal of Ecclesiastical History*
JFSR	*Journal of Feminist Studies in Religion*
JHA	*Journal for the History of Astronomy*
JJS	*Journal of Jewish Studies*
JQR	*Jewish Quarterly Review*
JRA	*Journal of Roman Archaeology*
JRS	*Journal of Roman Studies*
JSHJ	*Journal for the Study of the Historical Jesus*
JSJ	*Journal for the Study of Judaism in the Persian, Hellenistic and Roman Periods*
JSNT	*Journal for the Study of the New Testament*
JSOT	*Journal for the Study of the Old Testament*
JSQ	*Jewish Studies Quarterly*

JSS	*Journal of Semitic Studies*
JTS	*Journal of Theological Studies*
LNTS	Library of New Testament Studies
LSJ	Henry George Liddell, Robert Scott and H. Stuart Jones, *A Greek-English Lexicon*, 9th edn with supplement (Oxford: Clarendon, 1968).
NIGTC	New International Greek Testament Commentary
NT	*Novum Testamentum*
NTS	*New Testament Studies*
PEFQSt	*Palestine Exploration Fund Quarterly Statement*
PEQ	*Palestine Exploration Quarterly*
PG	Jacques-Paul Migne (ed.), Patrologia Graeca (Paris: Imprimerie Catholique, 1844–66).
RB	*Revue Biblique*
RPC	*Roman Provincial Coinage*
RQ	*Revue de Qumran*
SBL	Society of Biblical Literature
SBS	Stuttgarter Biblische Studienbeiträge
SCM	Student Christian Movement
SNTS	Society for New Testament Studies
SPCK	Society for Promoting Christian Knowledge
STDJ	Studies in the Texts of the Desert of Judah
SVTP	Studia in Veteris Testamenti Pseudepigrapha
TZ	*Theologische Zeitschrift*
VC	*Vigiliae Christianae*
WUNT	Wissenschaftliche Untersuchungen zum Neuen Testament
ZDPV	*Zeitschrift des deutschen Palästina-Vereins*
ZNW	*Zeitschrift für die neutestamentliche Wissenschaft und die Kunde der älteren Kirche*
ZPE	*Zeitschrift für Papyrologie und Epigraphik*

Notes

1 Identity: Jew, Judahite, Judaean

1 The term 'Syria Palestina' is found in Herodotus (*Hist.* 1:105; 2:104, 106; 3:5, 91; 4:39; 7:89) and Aristotle (*Met.* 2:3) but also in the work of Jewish writers (e.g. Philo, *Prob.* 75). See Joan E. Taylor, *The Essenes, the Scrolls and the Dead Sea* (Oxford: Oxford University Press, 2012), pp. 146–7; David M. Jacobson, 'Palestine and Israel', *BASOR* 313 (1999): pp. 65–74.

2 Josephus, *War* 2:234–5; *Ant.* 20:118; cf. Tacitus, *Annals* 12:54. See Gary N. Knoppers, *Jews and Samaritans: The origins and history of their early relations* (Oxford: Oxford University Press, 2013), p. 221.

3 Num. 15:38; Deut. 22:12. For Jesus' appearance see Joan E. Taylor, *What Did Jesus Look Like?* (London: Bloomsbury T&T Clark, 2018), pp. 155–68.

4 For the meaning of social 'identity', see Peter Burke, 'Identity', in Peter Kivisto (ed.), *The Cambridge Handbook of Social Theory: Volume 2: Contemporary Theories and Issues* (Cambridge: Cambridge University Press, 2020), pp. 63–78.

5 Among many important studies, see Urban C. von Wahlde, 'The Johannine "Jews": A Critical Survey', *NTS* 28 (1982): pp. 33–60; John Ashton, 'The Identity and Function of the *Ioudaioi* in the Fourth Gospel', *NT* 27 (1985): pp. 40–75; Cornelis Bennema, 'The Identity and Composition of OI IOUDAIOI in the Gospel of John', *Tyndale Bulletin* 60 (2009): pp. 239–63; Ruth Sheridan, 'Issues in the Translation of οἱ ᾽Ιουδαῖοι in the Fourth Gospel', *JBL* 132 (2013): pp. 671–95; Adele Reinhartz, *Cast out of the Covenant: Jews and anti-Judaism in the Gospel of John* (Philadelphia, PA: Fortress, 2018).

6 Christians believed that the blessings of God would flow out from Israel to the Gentiles (non-Judaeans) in accordance with prophecies in the book of Isaiah (2:2–4; 49:6; see Rom. 1:16), and in Mark the story was probably included to show how the spread of these blessings began in Jesus' own mission. See Richard France, *The Gospel of Mark* (NIGTC; Grand Rapids, MI: Eerdmans, 2002), p. 298.

7 For further discussion see Rebecca Harrocks, 'Jesus' Gentile Healings: The Absence of Bodily Contact and the Requirement of Faith', in Joan E. Taylor (ed.), *The Body in Biblical, Christian and Jewish Texts* (London: Bloomsbury T&T Clark, 2014), pp. 83–101.

8 In Matthew (15:21–8), the woman is described as a 'Canaanite', thereby referencing the scriptural narrative in which God intends to drive out the enemy Canaanites from the land that would be the territory of the tribes of Israel (see Exod. 34:11; Josh. 3:10). This somewhat explains Jesus' hostility. The story is additionally redesigned to point towards the important place of non-Judaeans (Gentiles) in the mission for Israel (cf. Matt. 28:19). See Craig S. Keener, *A Commentary on the Gospel of Matthew* (Grand Rapids, MI: Eerdmans, 1999), pp. 414–15.

9 Erik Erikson, *Identity: Youth and crisis* (New York, NY: Norton, 1968); James E. Marcia, 'Development and Validation of Ego Identity Status', *Journal of Personality and Social Psychology* 5 (1966): pp. 551–8. I am grateful to Emily Taylor Hunt for these references.

10 This creates 'survivor identity': see Steven L. Berman, 'Identity and Trauma', *Journal of Traumatic Stress Disorders and Treatment* 5/2 (2016): doi:10.4172/2324-8947.1000e108.

11 For further discussion see Shaye J. D. Cohen, *The Beginnings of Jewishness: Boundaries, varieties, uncertainties* (Berkeley, CA: University of California Press, 1999); Daniel R. Schwartz, 'Judeans, Jews, and Their Neighbors: Jewish Identity in the Second Temple Period', in Rainer Albertz and Jakob Wöhrle (eds), *Between Cooperation and Hostility: Multiple identities in ancient Judaism and the interaction with foreign powers* (Journal of Ancient Judaism Supplements 11; Göttingen: Vandenhoeck & Ruprecht, 2013), pp. 13–31; Sean Freyne, 'Behind the Names: Samaritans, *Ioudaioi*, Galileans', in Stephen G. Wilson and Michel Desjardins (eds), *Text and Artifact in the Religions of Mediterranean Antiquity* (Studies in Christianity and Judaism 9; Waterloo: Wilfred Laurier University Press, 2000), pp. 393–8; Larry Wills, 'Jew, Judean, Judaism in the Ancient Period: An Alternative Argument', *JAJ* 7 (2016): pp. 169–93. The following draws on Joan Taylor, '"Judean" and "Jew", Jesus and Paul', *Marginalia Review of Books*, 26 August 2014: http://marginalia.lareviewofbooks.org/judean-jew-jesus-paul/ (accessed 18 August 2024).

12 See *patria*, BDAG 788: 2. 'a relatively large body of people existing as a totality at a given moment and linked through ancestry and sociopolitical interests'. The use of the alternative term *ethnos* is complicated by the fact that Jews distinguished themselves from the *ethnoi* (nations, Gentiles).

13 See BDAG 459: 'expression of devotion to transcendent beings, esp. as it expresses itself in cultic rites, *worship*'.

14 See also Jas 1:26. By Greek definitions, a *thrēskeia* is essentially '[cultic] worship', as we find in Col. 2:18: 'the *thrēskeia* of angels'.

15 See Victor P. Furnish, *Jesus According to Paul* (Cambridge: Cambridge University

Press, 1993); Mogens Muller, 'Paul: The Oldest Witness to the Historical Jesus', in Thomas L. Thompson and Thomas S. Verenna (eds), *'Is This Not the Carpenter?': The question of the historicity of the figure of Jesus* (Bristol: Acumen, 2013), pp. 117–30.

16 Gal. 1:11–24; Acts 9:1–19; 22:6–21; 26:12–18.

17 The key exception is Luke Timothy Johnson, *The Real Jesus: The misguided quest for the historical Jesus and the truth of the traditional Gospels* (San Francisco, CA: HarperCollins, 1996), esp. pp. 117–22; see also Furnish, *Jesus According to Paul*, pp. 19–20.

18 For more on this see Joan E. Taylor, 'Two by Two: The Ark-etypal Language of Mark's Apostolic Pairings', in Taylor (ed.), *The Body in Biblical, Christian and Jewish Texts*, pp. 58–82.

19 As explored by E. P. Sanders, *Paul and Palestinian Judaism: A comparison of patterns of religion* (Philadelphia, PA: Fortress, 1977).

20 Lysias, *Against Simon* 3:6–7; Philo, *Spec.* 3:169; *Flacc.* 89; cf. 2 Macc. 3:19; 4 Macc. 18:7.

21 See the Babylonian Talmud, *b.Qod.* 66b. For Philo, the Jewish identity of the mother was critical in defining a child as Jewish; see Maren Niehoff, *Philo on Jewish Identity and Culture* (Tübingen: Mohr Siebeck, 2001), pp. 75–80. Note, however, that the biblical pattern of ethnicity was patrilineal, despite Lev. 24:10–23; see Cohen, *Beginnings of Jewishness*, pp. 241–307.

22 Steve Mason prefers the term 'Judaeans' for the Greek term *Ioudaioi* in ancient writings. Thus, for Josephus's work *Bellum Judaicarum*, Mason adopts the title *The Judaean War*: Steve Mason, *Flavius Josephus: Translation and commentary, vol. 1b: Judean War 2* (Leiden: Brill, 2009). For his argument see Steve Mason, *Josephus, Judea, and Christian Origins: Methods and categories* (Peabody, MA: Hendrickson, 2009), ch. 5: 'Jews, Judeans, Judaizing, Judaism: Problems of Categorization in Ancient History', pp. 141–84; and also Steve Mason and Philip F. Esler, 'Judaean and Christ-Follower Identities: Grounds for a Distinction', *NTS* 63 (2017): pp. 493–515, at pp. 500–4.

23 The concept of ethnic identity is both a modern and an ancient category, but the nuances of both need to be understood in terms of the group in question. See, for discussion, Mason and Esler, 'Judaean and Christ-Follower Identities', pp. 498–504.

24 James L. O'Neil, 'Royal Authority and City Law under Alexander and His Hellenistic Successors', *Classical Quarterly* 50 (2000): pp. 424–31.

25 Erwin R. Goodenough, *The Jurisprudence of the Jewish Courts in Egypt: Legal administration by the Jews under the early Roman Empire as described by Philo*

Judaeus (New Haven, CT: Yale University Press, 1929). On the limits, see Markus Oehler, 'The Punishment of Thirty-nine Lashes (2 Corinthians 11:24) and the Place of Paul in Judaism', *JBL* 140 (2021): pp. 623–40. For the punishment, see Deut. 25:1–3; Josephus, *Ant.* 4:238; Mishnah, *Makk.* 3.

26 The editorial comment found in Mark 7:19b is unlikely to be original as it is not found in the parallel passage in Matthew, and in Acts 10:14 Peter vehemently affirms that he has never eaten anything 'unholy and unclean'.

27 Other Jews too were willing to let go of some of the distinctive laws of Judaism while professing to be Jews, valuing the deeper meaning of Scripture. Philo stated: 'There are some who, regarding the words of the laws as symbols of things of the mind, are scrupulous about the latter, while they carelessly neglect the former' (*Migr.* 89; my translation from the Greek text of G. H. Whitaker, *Philo IV* (Loeb Classical Library; Cambridge, MA: Heinemann/Harvard University Press, 1958), p. 183.

28 Ben Witherington, *The Jesus Quest: The third quest for the Jew of Nazareth*, 2nd edn (Downers Grove, IL: InterVarsity Press, 1997).

29 See Amy-Jill Levine, *The Misunderstood Jew: The Church and the scandal of the Jewish Jesus* (New York, NY: HarperOne, 2006), pp. 17–52.

30 T. W. Manson, *The Teaching of Jesus: Studies in form and content*, 2nd edn (Cambridge: Cambridge University Press, 1935), pp. 307–8.

31 See also Isa. 1:14–17; 58:6, 9–10.

32 Geza Vermes, *Jesus the Jew* (London: SCM Press, 1973), p. 7.

33 See also Joseph Klausner, *Jesus of Nazareth: His life, times and teaching* (New York, NY: Macmillan, 1925): Jesus is presented as a great teacher of morality and an artist, with the mystical and miraculous elements seen as encrustations that could be removed.

34 David Flusser, *Jesus* (New York, NY: Herder & Herder, 1969).

35 The importance of the charismatic dimensions of Jesus and his early disciples was further explored by James Dunn, in *Jesus and the Spirit: A study of the religious and charismatic experience of Jesus and the first Christians as reflected in the New Testament* (Philadelphia, PA: Westminster, 1975).

36 E. P. Sanders, *Paul and Palestinian Judaism: A comparison of patterns of religion* (Philadelphia, PA: Fortress, 1977); *Judaism: Practice and belief, 63 BCE to 66 CE* (London: SCM Press, 1992); *The Historical Figure of Jesus* (London: Allen Lane/ Penguin, 1993), pp. 33–48.

37 See Josephus, *Ant.* 11:340–4, though one also could be a 'half-Jew' like Herod in terms of an ethnic category (*Ant.* 14:403): James D. G. Dunn, *The Partings of the Ways: Between Christianity and Judaism and their significance for the character*

of Christianity (London: SCM Press, 1991), pp. 24–48; and his 'The Question of Anti-Semitism in the New Testament Writings of the Period', in James D. G. Dunn (ed.), *Jews and Christians: The parting of the ways, A.D. 70 to 135*, 3rd edn (Grand Rapids, MI: Eerdmans, 1999), pp. 177–212, at p. 181.

38 The parameters are 538 BCE to 136 CE. In 136 CE, Judaea as a homeland of Jews was eradicated by Rome; see Joan E. Taylor, 'Parting in Palestine', in Hershel Shanks (ed), *Partings: How Judaism and Christianity became two* (Washington, DC: Biblical Archaeology Society, 2013), pp. 87–104.

39 John J. Collins, *Between Athens and Jerusalem: Jewish identity in the Hellenistic Diaspora*, 2nd edn (Grand Rapids, MI: Eerdmans), pp. 273–5.

40 Josephus, *Ant.* 20:34–53.

41 Following Jacob Neusner, 'Varieties of Judaism in the Formative Age', in *Formative Judaism: Religious, historical, and literary studies* (Second Series, BJS 41; Chico, CA: Scholars, 1983), pp. 59–89.

42 See the classic study by Arthur D. Nock, *Conversion: The old and the new in religion from Alexander the Great to Augustine of Hippo* (Oxford: Oxford University Press, 1933); also Steve Mason, '*Philosophiai*: Graeco-Roman, Judean and Christian', in John S. Kloppenborg and Stephen G. Wilson (eds), *Voluntary Associations in the Graeco-Roman World* (London and New York, NY: Routledge, 1996), pp. 31–58; and for more see Joan E. Taylor, *Jewish Women Philosophers of First-Century Alexandria: Philo's 'Therapeutae' reconsidered* (Oxford: Oxford University Press, 2003), pp. 107–13.

43 John G. Gager, *Moses in Greco-Roman Paganism* (Nashville, TN: Abingdon, 1972).

44 Jutta Leonhardt-Balzer, 'What Were They Doing in Second Temple Synagogues? Philo and the προσευχή', in Lutz Doering and Andrew R. Krause (eds), *Synagogues in the Hellenistic and Roman Periods: Archaeological finds, new methods, new theories* (Göttingen: Vandenhoeck & Ruprecht, 2020), pp. 215–38.

45 Michael Stausberg, *Zarathustra and Zoroastrianism: A short introduction* (London: Equinox, 2008).

46 James Barr, 'The Question of Religious Influence: The Case of Zoroastrianism, Judaism and Christianity', *JAAR* 53 (1985): pp. 201–35; Stausberg, *Zarathustra*, pp. 101–12.

47 E.g. Matt. 13:36–43.

48 For comprehensive guides to Second Temple Judaism, see Sanders, *Judaism*, and Lester L. Grabbe, *An Introduction to Second Temple Judaism* (London: Bloomsbury T&T Clark, 2010).

49 Halvor Moxnes, *Memories of Jesus: A journey through time* (Eugene, OR: Cascade, 2021), pp. 155–8.

50 Paula Fredriksen, *Jesus of Nazareth, King of the Jews: A Jewish life and the emergence of Christianity* (New York, NY: Vintage, 2000); Bart D. Ehrman, *Jesus: Apocalyptic prophet of the new millennium* (New York, NY: Oxford University Press, 1999); Dale C. Allison, *Jesus of Nazareth: Millenarian prophet* (Minneapolis, MN: Fortress, 1998).

51 John Dominic Crossan, *The Historical Jesus: The life of a Mediterranean Jewish peasant* (San Francisco, CA: HarperSanFrancisco, 1991). John Dominic Crossan focuses on ancient Mediterranean sociological categories of analysis rather than distinctively Jewish ones, and removes the apocalyptic elements of Jesus' teaching: Jesus is a social revolutionary championing the peasant class.

52 Elisabeth Schüssler Fiorenza, *Jesus: Miriam's Child, Sophia's Prophet: Critical issues in feminist Christology*, 2nd edn (London: Bloomsbury T&T Clark, 2015).

53 Reza Aslan, *Zealot: The life and times of Jesus of Nazareth* (New York, NY: Random House, 2013).

54 Exceptionally, it has to be said, John Meier defines him as 'marginal': *A Marginal Jew: Rethinking the historical Jesus*, 4 vols (Anchor Yale Bible Reference Library; New Haven, CT: Yale University Press / New York, NY: Doubleday, 1991–2009); John H. Elliot has argued that in terms of Jesus' identity *Ioudaios* should be understood as 'Judaean' but not as 'Jew': 'Jesus the Israelite Was Neither a "Jew" Nor a "Christian": On Correcting Misleading Nomenclature', *JSHJ* 5 (2007): pp. 119–54.

55 BDAG 788: 1. 'people linked over a relatively long period of time by line of descent to a common progenitor, *family, clan, relationship*'.

56 See discussion in Andrew Tobolowsky, *The Myth of the Twelve Tribes of Israel: New identities across time and space* (Cambridge: Cambridge University Press, 2022), pp. 22–65.

57 Gen. 14:13 (LXX). The term probably means 'migrants'; see Derek R. G. Beattie and Philip R. Davies, 'What Does "Hebrew" Mean?', *JSS* 56 (2011): pp. 71–83.

58 See particularly how this close association is portrayed in the book of Chronicles: Benjamin D. Giffone, *'Sit at My Right Hand': The Chronicler's portrait of the tribe of Benjamin in the social context of Yehud* (London: Bloomsbury T&T Clark, 2016).

59 Two Samaritan inscriptions with the self-definition of 'Israelites' were found in 1979 by the École française d'Athènes, one dated between 150 and 50 BCE and the other 250–175 BCE: Philippe Bruneau, 'Les Israélites de Délos et la juiverie délienne', *Bulletin de Correspondance Hellénique* 106 (1982): pp. 465–504. See also Alan D. Crown, *The Samaritans* (Tübingen: Mohr Siebeck, 1989), pp. 150–1; David Noy, Alexander Panayotov and Hanswulf Bloedhorn, *Inscriptiones Judaicae Orientis, vol. 1: Eastern Europe* (Tübingen: Mohr Siebeck, 2004), Ach66,

pp. 229–32; and for further context see Lidia Matassa, 'Unravelling the Myth of the Synagogue on Delos', *BAIAS* 25 (2007): pp. 81–115.

60 Yitzakh Magen, 'The Dating of the First Phase of the Samaritan Temple on Mt Gerizim in Light of Archaeological Evidence', in Oded Lipschits, Gary N. Knoppers and Rainer Albertz (eds), *Judah and the Judeans in the Fourth Century B.C.E.* (Winona Lake, IN: Eisenbrauns, 2007), pp. 157–212.

61 See 2 Kgs 17:24–41; Sir. 50:25–6; Josephus, *Ant.* 9:277–91.

62 Notoriously, Ernst Renan, in his book *Vie de Jésus* (1863), saw Jesus as fundamentally a Galilean, and noted that Galilee was a region of ethnic mixing so that Jesus' 'blood' would be difficult to determine; see the translation into English of his work as *The Life of Jesus* (London: Watts and Co., 1935), p. 37.

63 See Tobolowsky, *Myth of the Twelve Tribes*, pp. 57–8. Paul also uses the term 'Hebrew' (*Ebraios*) for his own identity, likely indicative that he was Hebrew-speaking (see Acts 6:1; 22:2; 26:14). Nevertheless, Paul was seen by others as a Diaspora *Jew* (Acts 22:3; cf. 21:39).

64 David M. Jacobson, 'The Plan of the Ancient Ramat el-Khalil at Hebron', *PEQ* 113 (1981): pp. 73–80.

65 John P. Meier, 'Jesus, the Twelve and the Restoration of Israel', in James M. Scott (ed.), *Restoration: Old Testament, Jewish and Christian perspectives* (JSJ Supplement 72; Leiden: Brill, 2001), pp. 365–404.

66 BDAG 788: 1. 'a relatively large geographical area associated with one's familial connections and personal life, fatherland, homeland'.

67 E.g. Vermes, *Jesus the Jew*; Crossan, *The Historical Jesus*; Sean Freyne, *Jesus, a Jewish Galilean: A new reading of the Jesus story* (London: T&T Clark International, 2010); Pieter Craffert, *The Life of a Galilean Shaman: Jesus of Nazareth in anthropological-historical perspective* (Cambridge: James Clarke, 2008); and also in Jean-Pierre Isbouts, *Young Jesus: Restoring the 'lost years' of a social activist and religious dissident* (New York, NY: Sterling, 2008).

68 For Jerusalem as *metropolis*, see Philo, *Virt.* 64.

69 See Michael Avi-Yonah, 'Historical Geography', in Shemuel Safrai and Menahem Stern, with David Flusser and Willem Cornelis van Unnik (eds), *The Jewish People in the First Century: Historical geography, political history, social, cultural and religious life and institutions*, vol. 1 (Assen: Van Gorcum, 1974), pp. 95–115.

70 Dalit Regev, 'The Power of the Written Evidence: A Hellenistic Burial Cave at Marisa', *Mediterranean Archaeology* 30 (2017): pp. 19–50; David M. Jacobson, 'Marisa Tomb Paintings: Recently Discovered Photos Show Long-Lost Details', *BAR* 30/2 (2004): pp. 24–39.

71 This model has been challenged by Katell Berthelot, *In Search of the Promised*

Land? The Hasmonean dynasty between biblical models and Hellenistic diplomacy, tr. Margaret Rigaud (Journal of Ancient Judaism Supplements 24; Göttingen: Vandenhoeck & Ruprecht, 2018); but see Kenneth Atkinson's review of Berthelot in 'The Hasmonean State and the Promised Land?' *Histos* (2019): pp. i–x.

72 Magen, 'Dating of First Phase of Samaritan Temple', p. 183.

73 See Kenneth Atkinson, *A History of the Hasmonean State: Josephus and beyond* (London: Bloomsbury T&T Clark, 2016).

74 See 1 Macc. 5:9–23.

75 See Pliny, *Nat. Hist.* 5:4:13–16 [66–74].

76 So Josephus could write of the Roman governor of Syria, Cassius Longinus, coming to 'Judaea' and sacking the city of Tarichaea in Galilee (*War* 1:180). Suetonius (*Titus* 4:3) also identifies this as a city of Judaea. Pliny states, 'Judaea . . . extends far and wide', and Galilee is included within it (*Nat. Hist.* 5:15:70).

77 See Josephus, *War* 3:41.

78 Joan E. Taylor, 'Pontius Pilate and the Imperial Cult in Roman Judaea', *NTS* 52 (2006): pp. 555–82.

79 Corinne Bonnet, *Melqart: Cultes et mythes de l'Héraclès tyrien en Méditerranée* (Leuven: Peeters, 1988). Curiously, though, the Tyrian silver shekel, depicting Melkart, was the standard currency of the Jerusalem Temple.

80 See Ze'ev W. Falk, 'Private Law', in Safrai and Stern (eds), *Jewish People*, vol. 1, pp. 504–33; Ze'ev W. Falk, *Introduction to the Law of the Second Commonwealth* (Leiden: Brill, 1972).

81 Martin Goodman, *The Ruling Class of Judaea: The origins of the Jewish revolt against Rome A.D. 66–70* (Cambridge: Cambridge University Press, 1993).

82 Seth Schwartz, 'Language, Power and Identity in Ancient Palestine', *Past and Present* 148 (1995): pp. 3–47, at pp. 21–31. It is a common belief that Hebrew was not a spoken language in the first century, but this has repeatedly been shown to be erroneous on the basis of rabbinic evidence, inscriptions and Josephus: Moses H. Segal, 'Mishnaic Hebrew and Its Relation to Biblical Hebrew and to Aramaic', *JQR* 20 (1908): pp. 647–737; William Chomsky, 'What Was the Jewish Vernacular during the Second Commonwealth?', *JQR* 42 (1951): pp. 193–212; Jehoshua M. Grintz, 'Hebrew as the Spoken and Written Language in the Last Days of the Second Temple Period', *JBL* 79 (1960): pp. 32–47. The overwhelming majority of non-biblical manuscripts found in or near Qumran are written in Hebrew, which also points to an ideology in which Hebrew was to be employed as an eschatological ideal, since the Qumran fragment 4Q464:8 refers to the 'holy tongue' that will be restored in the Eschaton (end times) when the people become again 'pure of speech' (line 9). This is linked with the *Testament of Judah*

(25:1–3) where the one people of the Lord will speak one language, and in *Jub.* 12:25–7 Hebrew is the 'language of the creation': Michael Stone and Esther Eshel, 'The Holy Language at the End of Days in Light of a Qumran Fragment', *Tarbiz* 62 (1993–4): pp. 169–77 (Hebrew); Steve Weitzman, 'Why Did the Qumran Community Write in Hebrew?', *JAOS* 119 (1999): pp. 35–45.

83 See Steven E. Fassberg, 'Which Semitic Language Did Jesus and Other Contemporary Jews Speak?' *CBQ* 74 (2012): pp. 263–80; and see the studies in Randall Buth and R. Steven Notley (eds), *The Language Environment of First Century Judaea* (Leiden: Brill, 2014).

84 Katherine Southwood, '"And They Could Not Understand Jewish Speech": Language, Ethnicity and Nehemiah's Intermarriage Crisis', *JTS* 62 (2011): pp. 1–19.

85 Abraham Tal, 'Samaritan Aramaic', in Stefan Weninger et al. (eds), *The Semitic Languages: An international handbook* (Berlin: De Gruyter Mouton, 2012), pp. 619–28.

86 Taylor, *What Did Jesus Look Like?*, pp. 169–92.

2 Heritage: seed of David

1 Matt. 1:1; 9:27; 12:23; 15:22; 20:30–1; 21:9, 15; 22:41–5. For a review of discussions see Nathan C. Johnson, *The Suffering Son of David in Matthew's Passion Narrative* (SNTS Monograph Series 183; Cambridge: Cambridge University Press, 2023), pp. 4–28.

2 For the characteristics of David and an exploration of Jesus' identity as son of David in Luke–Acts, see Yuzuru Miura, *David in Luke–Acts: His portrayal in the light of early Judaism* (WUNT 2/232; Tübingen: Mohr Siebeck, 2007).

3 See Andrew Lincoln, *Born of a Virgin? Reconceiving Jesus in the Bible, tradition and theology* (London: SCM Press, 2013), pp. 26–8; James D. Tabor, *The Jesus Dynasty: Stunning new evidence about the hidden history of Jesus* (London: HarperElement, 2006), pp. 50–5.

4 See Yigal Levin, 'Jesus "Son of God" and "Son of David": The Adoption of Jesus into the Davidic Line', *JSNT* 28 (2006): pp. 415–42; Markus Bockmuehl, 'The Son of David and His Mother', *JTS* 62 (2011): pp. 476–93, at pp. 478–9.

5 'This is my blood of the covenant'; so Mark 14:24 and parallels; 1 Cor. 11:25.

6 The *Didache* goes on to proclaim: 'Hosanna to the God of David' (*Did.* 10:6). The vine is perhaps both the physical line of David and also Israel as a whole viewed as the kingdom of David. See Jonathan A. Draper, 'Ritual Process and Ritual Symbol in Didache 7–10', *VC* 54 (2000): pp. 121–58, esp. pp. 148–50; 'Eschatology in the Didache', in Jan G. van der Watt (ed.), *Eschatology of the New Testament*

and *Some Related Documents* (WUNT 2/315; Tübingen: Mohr Siebeck, 2011), pp. 569–70.

7 Unlike many, John Meier holds that the Davidic lineage of Jesus is quite likely: *A Marginal Jew: Rethinking the historical Jesus, vol. 1: The Roots of the Problem and the Person* (New Haven, CT: Yale University Press, 1991), pp. 216–19.

8 *J.Kil.* 32b, and via Hillel his maternal line (*j.Ta'an.* 68a; *Gen. Rab.* 98:8; *b.Ket.* 62b (referring to Judah ha-Nasi); *b.Sanh.* 5a; *b.Hor.* 11b); Origen, *De Princ.* 4:3; see Geza Vermes, *Jesus the Jew* (London: SCM Press, 1973), p. 157.

9 Jens Schröter, 'Memory, Theories of History, and the Reception of Jesus', *JSHJ* 16 (2018): pp. 85–107.

10 Reza Aslan, *Zealot: The life and times of Jesus of Nazareth* (New York, NY: Random House, 2013), p. 227; this agnostic position is also adopted by Jean-Pierre Isbouts, *Young Jesus: Restoring the 'lost years' of a social activist and religious dissident* (New York, NY: Sterling, 2008), pp. 42–4.

11 For social/cultural memory theory and the historical Jesus see Chris Keith, 'Social Memory Theory and Gospels Research: The First Decade (Part One)', *Early Christianity* 6 (2015): pp. 354–76, and 'Social Memory Theory and Gospels Research: The First Decade (Part Two)', *Early Christianity* 6 (2015): pp. 517–42; Alan Kirk, *Memory and the Jesus Tradition* (Reception of Jesus in the First Three Centuries 2; London: Bloomsbury T&T Clark, 2018).

12 Pss 3 – 9; 11 – 32; 34 – 41; 51 – 65; 68 – 70; 86; 101; 103; 108 – 110; 122; 124; 131; 133; 138 – 145.

13 The questions about actuality throughout this account are acute. Archaeologists and historians, looking at the material record and the biblical accounts together, try to discern how they might be correlated, and argue fiercely about how they can be. See in particular Israel Finkelstein, 'The Rise of Jerusalem and Judah: The Missing Link', *Levant* 22 (2001): pp. 105–15.

14 James B. Pritchard, *Ancient Near Eastern Texts Relating to the Old Testament* (Princeton, NJ: Princeton University Press, 1969), p. 308.

15 André Lemaire, 'La dynastie Davidique (*byt dwd*) dans deux inscriptions ouest-semitique du IXe s. av. J.-C.', *Studie Epigrafici e Linguistici* 11 (1994): pp. 17–19; Michael Langois, 'The Kings, the City and the House of David on the Mesha Stele in Light of New Imaging Techniques', *Semitica* 61 (2019): pp. 23–47.

16 Avraham Biran and Joseph Naveh, 'An Aramaic Stele Fragment from Tel Dan', *IEJ* 43 (1993): pp. 81–98.

17 It measures 61 cm high, 68 cm wide, and has a depth of 28 cm. IAA inventory number 1971–410. David Flusser, '"The House of David" on an Ossuary', *The Israel Museum Journal* 5 (1986): pp. 37–40; Craig A. Evans, *Jesus and the Ossuaries*

(Waco, TX: Baylor University Press, 2003), pp. 103–4; Hannah M. Cotton, Werner Eck, Leah Di Segni et al. (eds), *Corpus Inscriptionum Iudaeae/Palaestinae* 1/1 (Berlin: De Gruyter, 2010), pp. 88–9, no. 45.

18 See Kenneth E. Pomykala, *The Davidic Dynasty Tradition in Early Judaism: Its history and significance for messianism* (Atlanta, GA: Scholars, 1995); John J. Collins, *The Sceptre and the Star: Messianism in light of the Dead Sea Scrolls*, 2nd edn (Grand Rapids, MI: Eerdmans, 2010), pp. 24–31, 52–78, 154–72; Emil Schürer, *The History of the Jewish People in the Age of Jesus Christ (175 B.C.–A.D. 135)*, vol. 2, rev. and ed. Geza Vermes, Fergus Millar and Matthew Black (Edinburgh: T&T Clark, 1979), pp. 518–19.

19 There were three other types of messianic figures: a prophet (like Moses), particularly hoped for by Samaritans; a priestly figure; and a heavenly Son of Humanity; see Collins, *Sceptre and Star*, p. 18.

20 This might well originally indicate that this king would not be from the main royal line, as that had been cut down, and Jer. 22:24–30 indicates that no seed of Jeconiah would rule in future; see Richard Bauckham, *Jude and the Relatives of Jesus in the Early Church* (Edinburgh: T&T Clark, 1990), pp. 334–40. However, such subtleties could be interpreted in multiple ways.

21 The designation of 'servant' was significant in that David was understood to have been guided by the Spirit as a prophet. David is often called the servant of God (2 Sam. 3:18; 1 Kgs 11:13, 34, 36, 38; 2 Kgs 19:34; 20:6; 1 Chr. 17:4; Ps. 89:3, 20; Jer. 33:21–2, 26; Ezek. 37:24–5), and see among the Dead Sea Scrolls 11QPs^a. The prophets were understood to be God's servants: 1QpHab 7:4–5; 4Q504 3:12; 5:14 (Moses); 4Q390 frag. 2; 4Q166–7 2:5–6.

22 See for the complexities Matthew V. Novenson, *The Grammar of Messianism: An ancient Jewish political idiom and its users* (Oxford: Oxford University Press, 2017).

23 Gerhard von Rad, *The Problem of the Hexateuch and Other Essays*, tr. E. W. Trueman (London: SCM Press, 1967), pp. 222–31.

24 Kenneth Atkinson, 'The Militant Davidic Messiah and Violence against Rome: The Influence of Pompey on the Development of Jewish and Christian Messianism', *Scripta Judaica Cracoviensa* 9 (2011): pp. 7–19.

25 A high priest was also anointed as part of the appointment ceremony; see Exod. 30:22–5.

26 Kenneth Atkinson, 'On the Herodian Origin of Militant Davidic Messianism at Qumran: New Light from Psalm of Solomon 17', *JBL* 118 (1999): pp. 435–60.

27 Emile Puech, 'Une apocalypse messianique (4Q521)', *RQ* 15 (1992): pp. 475–519. Stephen Hultgren, '4Q521, the Second Benediction of the Tefilla, the Hasidim,

and the Development of Royal Messianism', *RQ* 23 (2008): pp. 313–40, argues strongly that this figure is the Davidic King. For further discussion see Michael Knibb, 'Apocalypticism and Messianism', in Timothy H. Lim and John J. Collins (eds), *The Oxford Handbook of the Dead Sea Scrolls* (Oxford: Oxford University Press, 2010), pp. 403–32.

28 For the new kingdom see Isa. 2:21–6; Jer. 23:5–8; 33:14–18.

29 In Acts 4:25, the disciples proclaim that God spoke by the Holy Spirit through the mouth of 'our father David', then quoting Ps. 118:22.

30 The wording of the crowd's call is slightly different. Ps. 118:26 is placed in a secondary position to 'Hosanna to the son of David!' (Matt. 21:9).

31 See also Luke 13:35 where Jesus predicts that his coming to Jerusalem will involve people quoting Ps. 118:26.

32 Vermes thinks this title 'son of David' on the lips of Bartimaeus was a *captatio benevolentiae*, an address designed to capture the goodwill of the hearer. Mention of Ps. 118:26 is dismissed as inauthentic: Vermes, *Jesus the Jew*, pp. 156–7.

33 I prefer this title to the more archaic 'Son of Man'. See my discussion in Joan E. Taylor, '*Ho Huios tou Anthropou*, "The Son of Man": Some Remarks on an Androcentric Convention of Translation', *The Bible Translator* 48/1 (1997): pp. 101–9.

34 Matthew (20:17–28) follows the same sequence with the words 'and as they went out of Jericho'.

35 Collins, *Sceptre and Star*, pp. 191–214.

36 Darrell L. Bock, 'Dating the *Parables of Enoch*: A Forschungsbericht', in Darrell L. Bock and James H. Charlesworth (eds), *Parables of Enoch: A paradigm shift* (London: Bloomsbury T&T Clark, 2013), pp. 58–113; and also see, in the same work, James H. Charlesworth, 'Did Jesus Know the Traditions in the *Parables of Enoch*?', pp. 173–217.

37 Max Botner, *Jesus Christ as the Son of David in the Gospel of Mark* (Cambridge: Cambridge University Press, 2019), pp. 74–173.

38 Botner shows also how, when a demon identifies Jesus as 'the holy one of God' in Mark 1:24, this too is a Davidic reference, e.g. 'holy one' is a term for the king in the Syriac Psalms (152:4; 153:2). See further discussion on Markan Christology in Jack Dean Kingsbury, *The Christology of Mark's Gospel* (Philadelphia, PA: Fortress, 1989); Simon Gathercole, *The Pre-Existent Son: Recovering the Christologies of Matthew, Mark and Luke* (Grand Rapids, MI: Eerdmans, 2006).

39 Botner, *Jesus Christ as Son of David*, p. 194.

40 In Acts 2:29–36, the psalm is interpreted to mean that David foresaw the resurrection of the Christ, and his exaltation to sit at the right hand of God.

41 Bauckham, *Jude*, p. 365: 'we know of no group who denied it'.

42 France, *Gospel of Mark*, pp. 484–5; and see Botner, *Jesus Christ as Son of David*, pp. 162–72. See also Anthony Le Donne, *The Historiographical Jesus: Memory, typology, and the son of David* (Waco, TX: Baylor University Press, 2009), pp. 260–1: the Markan version 'is hinged on the agenda to show Jesus' authority over the temple and the priesthood', but this typological interpretation 'originated in historical memory and not by literary invention' (p. 268).

43 This reading is affirmed in the Markan narrative when Jesus predicts the coming of the Son of Humanity in clouds with great power and glory (13:26, quoting Dan. 7:13), and in his answer to the high priest's question 'Are you the Christ, the Son of the Blessed One?' with the words: 'I am, and you shall see the Son of Humanity sitting at the right hand of Power, and coming with the clouds of heaven' (14:62, quoting Ps. 110:1 and Dan. 7:13). The interpretation that it was Jesus' divine sonship that was important is found also in the *Letter of Barnabas* 12:10–11, but here the author distinguishes between the physical nature of Jesus as 'Son of Humanity' and Jesus' divine identity as Son of God. Later on, distinction between the two natures of Jesus, human and divine, became common in patristic literature, with the 'Son of Humanity' linked with his humanity rather than his divinity.

44 Jens Schröter states: 'his origin from Galilee is put forward even as an argument against his messiahship by the Jews': *Jesus of Nazareth: Jew from Galilee, savior of the world* (Waco, TX: Baylor University Press, 2014), p. 43.

45 Lincoln, *Born of a Virgin?*, p. 29, thinks this indicates that Jesus does not come from Bethlehem: 'John's Gospel is a clear witness to Jesus' place of origin being Nazareth', and thus he rejects any 'ironic' reading here.

46 Mark Goodacre, 'Parallel Traditions or Parallel Gospels? John's Gospel as a Re-imagining of Mark', in Eve-Marie Becker, Helen K. Bond and Catrin H. Williams (eds), *John's Transformation of Mark* (London: Bloomsbury T&T Clark, 2021), pp. 77–90, esp. pp. 83–9.

47 Assuming 'Son of God' to be original, as it is present in nearly all ancient manuscripts. For discussion see France, *Gospel of Mark*, p. 49.

48 Helen Bond, *The First Biography of Jesus: Genre and meaning in Mark's Gospel* (Grand Rapids, MI: Eerdmans, 2020), p. 91.

49 This was a memory strongly maintained even to the end of the second century by Jewish-Christian Ebionites; see Irenaeus, *Adv. Haer.* 5:1:3.

50 Julius Africanus, *Letter to Aristides*, in Eusebius, *Hist. Eccles.* 1:7:13–14. For this text in full, as reconstructed, see Christophe Guignard, *La lettre de Julius Africanus à Aristide sur la généalogie du Christ: Analyse de la tradition textuelle,*

édition, traduction et étude critique (Texte und Untersuchungen zur Geschichte der altchristlichen Literatur 167; Berlin: De Gruyter, 2011).

51 Tabor, *Jesus Dynasty*, pp. 55–63, thinks that Luke's genealogy is that of Mary and notes that females could also have a 'seed' (Gen. 3:15; Lev. 12:2). However, since the royal lineage is only traced through the male line, it has to go via Joseph.

52 Zerubbabel is one of two 'sons of oil' in Zech. 4:14 and thus an 'anointed one' in *Targum Zechariah* 4:7; see Novenson, *Grammar of Messianism*, pp. 69–72.

53 In the arithmetic, it seems David is counted as the last person in the first section, but Jeconiah is counted as both the last of the second section and the first of the third. Note also that there is explicit mention of the exile, more precisely the 'deportation to Babylon', with an affirmation that the line continues beyond this, embedding a hope of restoration; see Mervyn Eloff, 'Exile, Restoration and Matthew's Genealogy of Jesus', *Neotestimentica* 38 (2004): pp. 75–87. As Robert Myles observes, the phrase 'deportation to Babylon' is used four times in Matt. 1:1–18; see Robert J. Myles, 'Echoes of Displacement in Matthew's Genealogy of Jesus', *Colloquium* 45 (2013): pp. 31–41, at p. 39; *The Homeless Jesus in the Gospel of Matthew* (Sheffield: Sheffield Phoenix, 2014), p. 60.

54 See William D. Davies and Dale C. Allison, *A Critical and Exegetical Commentary on the Gospel According to Saint Matthew*, vol. 1 (Edinburgh, T&T Clark, 1988), pp. 161–5; Raymond E. Brown, *The Birth of the Messiah: A commentary on the infancy narratives in Matthew and Luke* (London: Chapman, 1977), p. 80.

55 The genealogy skips from Joram to Uzziah, missing the kings Ahaziah, Jehoash and Amaziah (2 Kgs 8 – 13).

56 Bauckham, *Jude*, pp. 315–73, sees Jude 6, which quotes *1 Enoch* 10:12, as providing an important link with the Davidic relatives of Jesus.

57 Vermes, *Jesus the Jew*, p. 156.

58 Vermes, *Jesus the Jew*, p. 157.

59 Geza Vermes, *The Nativity: History and legend* (London: Penguin, 2006), p. 43.

60 Phoebe Garrett, '*Sit in Medio*: Family and Status in Suetonius' *Vitellius*', *Acta Classica* 61 (2018): pp. 53–68.

61 Wayne Manaaki Rihari Te Kaawa, 'Re-visioning Christology through a Maori Lens', thesis submitted in fulfilment of the requirements for the degree of Doctor of Philosophy, University of Otago (Dunedin, 2020).

62 As noted by Craig S. Keener, *A Commentary on the Gospel of Matthew* (Grand Rapids, MI: Eerdmans, 1999), p. 76: 'If Luke travelled with Paul . . . and could have interviewed James the Lord's brother in Jerusalem, he would likely have had access to the family's tradition.'

63 John Painter, *Just James: The brother of Jesus in history and tradition*, 2nd edn (Columbia, SC: University of South Carolina Press, 2004), p. 136.

64 Joan E. Taylor, 'Paul's Significant Other in the "We" Passages', in Craig A. Evans and Aaron W. White (eds), *Who Created Christianity? Fresh approaches to the relationship between Paul and Jesus* (Grand Rapids, MI: Hendrickson, 2020), pp. 125–56.

65 See Bauckham, *Jude*, pp. 6–44; Tabor, *Jesus Dynasty*, pp. 81–92, 307–32.

66 See also the story of Jesus' resurrection appearance to James in *The Gospel According to the Hebrews* as quoted by Jerome, *Vir. Ill.* 2 and below pp. 232–3.

67 Eusebius states that here he relies on Clement of Alexandria (later second century); see Painter, *Just James*, pp. 113–17.

68 For further discussion see Painter, *Just James*, pp. 119–30; Joan E. Taylor, *The Essenes, the Scrolls and the Dead Sea* (Oxford: Oxford University Press, 2012), pp. 175–6. This account is complicated by the fact that Hegesippus seems to mix up James with a high priest who had taken Nazirite vows and lived the austere life of an Essene. Tabor, however, thinks James was also a priest: *Jesus Dynasty*, pp. 325–6.

69 For an analysis of all the material related to James in Eusebius, see Painter, *Just James*, pp. 105–58.

70 Some ancient manuscripts, such as the Codex Alexandrinus (fifth century CE), read 'Jose', and the Sinaiticus of the fourth century has 'Joseph', but 'Joset' is attested early on in the Vaticanus (also fourth century) and a range of others.

71 Jesus is called the 'son of Mary' in Mark 6:3, but both the parallel accounts of Matthew (13:55) and Luke (4:22), basing themselves on Mark, indicate Joseph's paternity, likely meaning they read this in their version of Mark. For Mark 6:3 in fact the reading 'son of Mary' in the manuscripts is by no means certain. The Old Latin versions have 'the son of the carpenter and of Mary's family', as do the f13 family of Greek manuscripts and several others, the Old Latin a, aur, b, c, i, r¹, and the Coptic Bohairic, Armenian and Georgian 2. The early papyrus P45 and also manuscript 565 read 'son of the carpenter, of Mary', while 1253 and 2148 have 'son of a carpenter, of Mary'. Given that the second-century *Protevangelium of James* 10:1 and Justin, *Dial.* 100, derive Jesus' Davidic descent through Mary, a reading of 'son of Mary' was perhaps a scribal modification to correlate with this later view. To be called 'son of Mary' does not constitute a metronym, but it is an acknowledgement of Mary.

72 See Bauckham, *Jude*, pp. 37–41; Josef Blinzler, *Die Brüder und Schwestern Jesu* (SBS 21; Stuttgart: Katholisches Bibelwerk, 1976), pp. 36–8; Anastasius Sinaita, *Quaestio* 153, PG 89:812; Sophronius of Jerusalem, *Encomium on St. John*,

PG 87:3364; Theophylact, *In Matth.* 27, PG 123:473; *In Gal.* 1:19, PG 124:968; Nicephorus Kallistos, *Hist. Eccles.* 2:3, PG 145:759. In the Coptic *History of Joseph the Carpenter* (2:3), however, they are called Lydia and Lysia.

73 Hugh Jackson Lawlor, *Eusebiana: Essays on the Ecclesiastical History of Eusebius, bishop of Caesarea* (Oxford: Clarendon, 1912), p. 14.

74 Bauckham, *Jude*, p. 38, notes the textual irregularity here whereby there is mention of 'her sister' rather than 'his sister' in a second mention of Mary, likely harmonising with John 19:25, and suggests: 'if the two lists of three women are to be made consistent, then "her sister" in the first line must be corrected to "his sister", as in the second list.'

75 See Bauckham, *Jude*, pp. 37–44.

76 See also *Didascalia Apostolorum* 24; *Apostolic Constitutions* 8:35:1; cf. 2:63; 7:46.

77 The very wide reach of these memories about James has been well documented by James Painter, *Just James*, pp. 159–81, in his comprehensive survey, which clearly demonstrates how diverse Christian groups would account for his significance.

78 Bart D. Ehrman and Zlatko Pleše, *The Apocryphal Gospels: Texts and translations* (New York, NY: Oxford University Press, 2011), pp. 40–70; Lily C. Vuong, *The Protevangelium of James* (Westar Tools and Translations: Early Christian Apocrypha; Eugene, OR: Cascade, 2018); George T. Zervos, *The Protevangelium of James: Critical questions of the text and full collations of the Greek manuscripts*, vols 1 and 2 (London: Bloomsbury T&T Clark, 2019, 2022).

79 Christophe Guignard, 'Jesus' Family and Their Genealogy According to the Testimony of Julius Africanus', in Claire Clivaz, Andreas Dettwiler, Luc Devillers and Enrico Norelli (eds), *Infancy Gospels: Stories and identities* (WUNT 281; Tübingen: Mohr Siebeck, 2011), pp. 67–93. For discussion of this passage and others concerning Jesus' family see Bauckham, *Jude*, pp. 315–73.

80 See Bauckham, *Jude*, pp. 60–3, 302–7; Tabor, *Jesus Dynasty*, pp. 341–3.

81 See discussion in Joan E. Taylor, *Christians and the Holy Places: The myth of Jewish-Christian origins* (Oxford: Clarendon, 1993), pp. 31–3.

82 William Wright and Norman McLean, with Adalbert Merx, *The Ecclesiastical History of Eusebius in Syriac* (Cambridge: Cambridge University Press, 1898), p. 36. A sixth-century copy of this Syriac version of Eusebius's *Historia Ecclesiastica* (*Ecclesiastical History*) exists in the British Museum, BM 14639.

83 Jessie Payne Smith, *A Compendious Syriac Dictionary* (Oxford: Clarendon, 1903), p. 298.

84 Michael Sokoloff, *A Dictionary of Jewish Palestinian Aramaic*, rev. edn (Ramat Gan: Bar Ilan University Press, 2017), pp. 364–5. *Marutha* means 'dominion', 'authority'. See also Marcus Jastrow, *Dictionary of the Targumim, the Talmud Babli*

and Yerushalmi and the Midrashic Literature (New York, NY: Title, 1943), pp. 834, 840. Jesus is called *despotēs* in Jude 2 and 2 Pet. 2:1.

85 Probably Chronicles (called 'Book of Days' by Jerome, *Adv. Jov.* 2:4; *Comm. Isa.* 1:21); see Guignard, 'Jesus' Family', pp. 81–3. Matt. 1:12–13 seems to use 1 Chr. 3:17–18, but Matthew corrects Chronicles in line with all other scriptural citations to have Shealtiel as the father of Zerubbabel, rather than Pedaiah; see Guignard, 'Jesus' Family', pp. 90–1.

86 Greek text in Eusebius, *The Ecclesiastical History, vols 1–2: Eusebius of Caesarea*, ed. Kirsopp Lake, J. E. L. Oulton and H. J. Lawlor (Loeb Classical Library; Cambridge, MA: Harvard University Press, 1926–32).

87 Guignard, 'Jesus' Family', p. 78, translates this phrase *to sōtērion genos* as 'the family of the Saviour', but *sōtērion* is an adjective, not a noun in the genitive case. He thinks (n. 36) that they were Christians and were travelling around as part of a Christian mission in the mid-first century, and that the importance of the 'brothers of the Lord' in the early church would have made that clear to readers. However, Africanus does not present them in relationship with the church at all, and the 'noble descent' is not from Jesus but from David, as Guignard also realises (p. 87). See Taylor, *Christians and the Holy Places*, pp. 32–4.

88 See Bauckham, *Jude*, pp. 94–106.

89 Painter, *Just James*, pp. 147–9.

90 Eusebius, *Hist. Eccles.* 2:25:5; 3:11:1; 4:5:3–4, 22; Epiphanius, *Pan.* 66:21–2; see Bauckham, *Jude*, pp. 45–133, for discussion, including of the list of Jerusalem leaders (pp. 70–9); also Tabor, *Jesus Dynasty*, pp. 330–1.

91 Miriam Pucci Ben Zeev, 'The Uprisings in the Jewish Diaspora, 116–117', in Steven T. Katz (ed.), *The Cambridge History of Judaism, vol. 4: The Late Roman–Rabbinic Period* (Cambridge: Cambridge University Press, 2006), pp. 93–104. However, Tiberius Claudius Atticus Herodes was governor of Judaea from 99/100 to 102–13 CE; see E. Mary Smallwood, 'Atticus, Legate of Judaea under Trajan', *JRS* 52 (1962): pp. 131–3.

92 Painter, *Just James*, pp. 149–51.

3 Location: Bethlehem

1 Harold M. Proshansky, 'The City and Self-Identity', *Environment and Behavior* 10 (1978): pp. 147–69; Anssi Paasi, *Territories, Boundaries and Consciousness* (Chichester: Wiley, 1996). Paasi's work has largely focused on regional identity. For an overview of research on this subject see Jianchao Peng, Dirk Strijker and Qun Wu, 'Place Identity: How Far Have We Come in Exploring Its Meanings?', *Frontiers in Psychology* 11 (2020): https://doi.org/10.3389/fpsyg.2020.00294.

2 Justin Martyr, *Dial.* 78:1–8; 102:2; 103:3 (mid-second century).

3 Likely also in the Babylonian Talmud, *b.Bekh.* 22a, where a type of 'Bethlehem jug' is mentioned.

4 Though the Galilean Bethlehem has been suggested as Jesus' birthplace by Bruce Chilton, 'Recovering Jesus' Mamzerut', in James H. Charlesworth (ed.), *Jesus and Archaeology* (Grand Rapids, MI: Eerdmans, 2006), pp. 84–110, at pp. 95–6.

5 E.g. E. P. Sanders, *The Historical Figure of Jesus* (London: Allen Lane/Penguin, 1993), pp. 85–6.

6 This would go beyond a 'criterion of dissimilarity', and see for critique Dagmar Winter, 'Saving the Quest for Authenticity from the Criterion of Dissimilarity: History and Plausibility', in Chris Keith and Anthony Le Donne (eds), *Jesus, Criteria, and the Demise of Authenticity* (London: Bloomsbury T&T Clark, 2012), pp. 115–31.

7 From my enquiries, I understand that Roman-period pottery has at times been found in the course of building works in the present old market area.

8 *Ant.* 5:271, 318; 6:166, 227; 7:312.

9 See Amihai Mazar, 'The Aqueducts of Jerusalem', in Yigael Yadin (ed.), *Jerusalem Revealed: Archaeology in the Holy City 1968–1974* (Israel Exploration Society, 1975), pp. 79–84; Amihai Mazar, 'A Survey of the Aqueducts to Jerusalem', in David Amit, Yitzhar Hirschfeld and Yosef Patrich (eds), *The Aqueducts of Israel* (Journal of Roman Archaeology Supplementary Series 46; Portsmouth, RI: 2002), pp. 210–44; Ya'akov Billig, 'The Low-Level Aqueduct to Jerusalem: Recent Discoveries', in Amit, Hirschfeld and Patrich (eds), *Aqueducts*, pp. 245–52; David Amit, 'New Data for Dating the High-level Aqueduct and the Wadi el-Biyar Aqueduct, and the Herodion Aqueduct', in Amit, Hirschfeld and Patrich (eds), *Aqueducts*, pp. 253–66; Kay Prag, 'R. W. Hamilton, D. C. Baramki and the Lower Aqueduct at Bethlehem', *PEQ* 140 (2008): pp. 27–38.

10 There is a section of the Lower Aqueduct incorporated within a souvenir shop on Manger Street; so Lorenzo Nigro, Daria Montanari, Alessandra Guari, Maria Tamburrini, Pierfrancesco Izzo, Mohammed Ghayyada, Iman Titi and Jehad Yasine, 'New Archaeological Features in Bethlehem (Palestine): The Italian-Palestinian Rescue Season of November 2016', *Vicino Oriente* 21 (2017): pp. 5–57, at p. 8.

11 Gen. 35:19 has 'Ephrathah, now Bethlehem'; Jeroboam is called an 'Ephrathite of Zereda' in 1 Kgs 11:26.

12 Josephus, *Ant.* 8:236.

13 Josephus, *Ant.* 5:271. In *b.Ber.* 91a, Ibzan is identified with Boaz.

14 Josephus, *Ant.* 5:136.

15 Josephus, *Ant.* 5:318, 323; *j.Ber.* 9:5; *j.Yev.* 4:2; *b.Ber.* 54a; *b.Makk.* 23b; *b.BB* 91b.

16 See *b.Sot.* 11b.

17 Josephus, *Ant.* 6:156.

18 Josephus, *Ant.* 7:19.

19 This is the numeration of the LXX. It is 5:1 in the Masoretic Text (in Hebrew).

20 The Aramaic *Targum of Pseudo-Jonathan* Gen. 35:21 has the Messiah coming from just outside Bethlehem, from Migdal Eder. Alternatively, John indicates that some in Jerusalem held that 'when the Messiah appears, no one will know where he comes from' (see John 7:25–7). As Matthew Novenson notes: 'John includes in his narrative a hodgepodge of popular opinion about the messiah': *The Grammar of Messianism: An ancient Jewish political idiom and its users* (Oxford: Oxford University Press, 2017), p. 88.

21 Jonathan Rowlands, 'On Chickens, Eggs and the Birthplace of Jesus', *JSHJ* 20 (2022): pp. 218–38.

22 Neh. 10:34; Josephus, *War* 2:425.

23 Shmarya Gutman and Ariel Berman, 'Bethléem', *RB* 77 (1970): pp. 583–5, found Iron Age sherds east of the church and around the Milk Grotto, and also in the south. See also Kay Prag, 'Bethlehem: A Site Assessment', *PEQ* 132 (2000): pp. 169–81.

24 Pottery from one of the Iron Age II tombs was received as a result of a gift by Revd Joseph Barclay in 1865: Jonathan Tubb, *An Iron Age II Tomb Group from the Bethlehem Region* (British Museum Occasional Paper 14; London: British Museum, 1980); for others see Prag, 'Bethlehem', pp. 170–1.

25 Gutman and Berman, 'Bethléem', fig. 3.

26 Lorenzo Nigro et al., 'New Archaeological Features in Bethlehem (Palestine): The Italian-Palestinian Rescue Season of November 2016', *Vicino Oriente* 21 (2017): pp. 5–57, at pp. 10–16; and also Lorenzo Nigro, Daria Montanari, Mohammed Ghayyada and Jehad Yasine, 'Khalet al-Jam'a: A Middle Bronze and Iron Age Necropolis near Bethlehem (Palestine)', *Vicino Oriente* 19 (2015): pp. 185–218. Also to be noted is that a bulla with an inscription mentioning Bethlehem was found in Jerusalem in 2012; see Ronny Reich, 'A Fiscal Bulla from the City of David, Jerusalem', *IEJ* 62 (2012): pp. 200–5.

27 See Bellarmino Bagatti, 'Recenti scavi a Betlemme (Grotte di S. Girolamo; Cisterne di David)', *Liber Annuus* 18 (1968): pp. 181–237, figs 27–8. Bagatti suggested there were tombs here. In Armenian Patriarchate investigations conducted in 2014 to 2015 in the twelfth-century (Crusader) hospital building known as Jerome's Hall, rock-cut caves were found, along with first-century pottery and part of an ossuary lid: Shimon Gibson, 'Fourth Report on Archaeological Work in Armenian Monastery in Church of the Nativity,

Bethlehem', unpublished paper for the Armenian Patriarchate (2015). I am grateful to the Armenian Patriarchate for the invitation to myself and Shimon Gibson to collaborate on a further excavation in the Armenian monastery garden in 2015, where building fragments, nails, pottery and mosaic tesserae dating from the Byzantine to modern periods were recovered, along with indications that the area was used as the cemetery of the Crusader hospital.

28 For the date of this work see Greville S. P. Freeman-Grenville, Rupert L. Chapman and Joan E. Taylor, *The Onomasticon by Eusebius of Caesarea: Palestine in the fourth century AD* (Jerusalem: Carta, 2003), pp. 3–4.

29 Jerome, *Ep.* 58:3; Cyril of Jerusalem, *Cat.* 12:20. The curious association between the term 'Tammuz' and wood (as in the Mishnah, *Ta'an.* 4:5) may be noted.

30 Eusebius, *Hist. Eccles.* 4:5:1–4; 4:6; *Dem. Evang.* 3:5; *j.Ned.* 38a; Tertullian, *Adv. Jud.* 13; Justin Martyr, *Dial.* 16; *Apol.* 1:77.

31 Amos Kloner and Boaz Zissu, 'Hiding Complexes in Judaea: An Archaeological and Geographical Update on the Area of the Bar Kochba Revolt', in Peter Schäfer (ed.), *The Bar Kokhba Revolt Reconsidered* (Tübingen: Mohr Siebeck, 2003), pp. 181–216, at pp. 181–2; Dvir Raviv and Chaim Ben David, 'Cassius Dio's figures for the Demographic Consequences of the Bar Kokhba War: Exaggeration or Reliable Account?', *JRA* 34 (2021): pp. 585–607.

32 Tertullian, *Adv. Jud.* 13; Justin Martyr, *Dial.* 16; *Apol.* 1:77; Eusebius, *Hist. Eccles.* 4:6; Midrash *Lamentations Rabbah* 2:2. For discussion see Benjamin Isaac, 'Cassius Dio on the Revolt of Bar Kokhba', in *The Near East under Roman Rule: Selected papers* (Leiden: Brill, 1998), pp. 211–19. For the period following see Joan E. Taylor, *Christians and the Holy Places: The myth of Jewish-Christian origins* (Oxford: Clarendon, 1993), pp. 48–85; and Michael Avi-Yonah, *The Jews of Palestine: A political history from the Bar Kochba Revolt to the Arab conquest* (Oxford: Basil Blackwell, 1976), pp. 50–1, map p. 17 for the exclusion zone.

33 See Fergus Millar, *The Roman Near East 31 BC to AD 337* (Cambridge, MA: Harvard University Press, 1993), pp. 374–86.

34 Yohanon Aharoni, *Excavations at Ramat Rahel: Seasons 1959 and 1960* (Rome: Università degli studi, Centro di studi semitici, 1962), pp. 24–7; *Excavations at Ramat Rahel: Seasons 1961 and 1962* (Rome: Università degli studi, Centro di studi semitici, 1964), pp. 38–40, 60–82; Oded Lipschits et al., 'Palace and Village, Paradise and Oblivion: Unraveling the Riddles of Ramat Raḥel', *Near Eastern Archaeology* 74 (2011): pp. 1–49, at pp. 42–3. These are shaft graves, similar to other earlier Jewish types.

35 It was recorded as being marked by a pillar 'seen to this day' in Gen. 35:19–20, as also in the Aramaic *Targum of Pseudo-Jonathan* Gen. 35:20.

36 See also Justin, *Dial.* 78:19, and the Bordeaux Pilgrim of 333 CE (*Itin.* 598). Jerome
(*Lib. Loc.* 83:14) modifies Eusebius's identification of four milestones to five (and
see *Ep.* 108:10:1). Later Christians appropriated the site: the Piacenza Pilgrim of
570 CE (*Itin.* 28) mentions the tomb as a place where a church has been built.
Jachintus the Presbyter (*Itin.* 8) notes the presence of a Christian cemetery.

37 Orit Peleg-Barkat, 'The Relative Chronology of Tomb Façades in Early Roman
Jerusalem and Power Displays by the Elite', *JRA* 25 (2012): pp. 403–18 at pp. 404–5.

38 See below, pp. 136–40, and also Michael Avi Yonah, 'Bethlehem', in *The New
Encyclopedia of Archaeological Excavations in the Holy Land*, vol. 1, ed. Ephraim
Stern (New York, NY: Simon & Schuster, 1993); Greville S. P. Freeman-Grenville,
The Basilica of the Nativity in Bethlehem (Jerusalem: Carta, 1993); Robert W.
Hamilton, *The Church of the Nativity, Bethlehem: A guide* (Jerusalem: Government
of Palestine, Dept of Antiquities, 1947, repr. 1968); William Harvey, *Structural
Survey of the Church of the Nativity, Bethlehem* (London: Oxford University Press,
1935); Louis-Hugues Vincent, *Bethléem, le sanctuaire de la nativité* (Paris: J.
Gabalda, 1914); Taylor, *Christians and the Holy Places*, pp. 96–112; Joan E. Taylor,
'The Church of the Nativity: A Byzantine Treasure in Bethlehem', *Minerva* (Jan./
Feb. 2007), pp. 26–8.

39 Leah Di Segni, 'On the Development of Christian Cult Sites on Tombs of the
Second Temple Period', *ARAM Periodical* 18–19 (2007): pp. 381–401.

40 Taylor, *Christians and the Holy Places*, pp. 295–332. Memories (e.g. of the site of
Gethsemane) could endure for a long time. See also Ken Dark, 'Returning to the
Caves of Mystery: Texts, Archaeology and the Origins of Christian Topography
and Pilgrimage in the Holy Land', *Strata* 38 (2020): pp. 103–24.

41 John Wilkinson, *Egeria's Travels to the Holy Land* (Warminster: Aris & Phillips,
1981), p. 162.

42 Translated from Paul Geyer and Otto Cuntz (eds), *Itinerarium Burdigalense*
(Corpus Christianorum, Series Latina 175; Turnhout: Brepols, 1965), p. 25.

43 John Wilkinson, *Jerusalem Pilgrims before the Crusades* (Warminster: Aris &
Phillips, 2002), p. 143.

44 In later years, during the time of the Crusaders, the Tomb of David was identified
by Christians in Jerusalem, in a corner of the ruined Byzantine Church of Holy
Zion; see Taylor, *Christians and the Holy Places*, pp. 213–19; David Christian
Clausen, *The Upper Room and Tomb of David: The history, art and archaeology of
the Cenacle on Mount Zion* (Jefferson, NC: McFarland, 2016).

45 In the accounts of the burials of the kings of Judah, there is a common formula
that the king 'rested with his ancestors in the City of David' (1 Kgs 11:43; 14:31;
15:8, 24; 22:50; 2 Kgs 8:24; 9:28; 12:21; 14:20; 15:7, 38; 16:20; 1 Chr. 9:31; 12:16;

14:1; 16:14; 21:1, 20; 24:16, 25; 25:28; 27:9; 28:27). There are actually only a couple of instances where there is specific mention of Jerusalem. Ahaziah was brought back from Megiddo to Jerusalem in a chariot and then 'buried with his ancestors in his tomb in the city of David' (2 Kgs 9:28), but the language does not actually indicate that the tomb was in Jerusalem as such, only that Ahaziah was brought back to Jerusalem, to the palace, before he was buried. In the case of Amaziah, the Masoretic Text reads that he was buried 'in Jerusalem with his ancestors in the city of David' (2 Kgs 14:20), but the parallel in 2 Chr. 25:28 has him buried rather vaguely in 'the city of Judah'. At any rate, for the early Christians to have identified the royal tombs where they did, in Bethlehem, they read all these references as not referring to the City of David in Jerusalem at all.

46 Hamdan Taha, Director of the Palestinian Department of Antiquities and Cultural Heritage, has excavated the remains of a Byzantine public building, including a large mosaic, two cisterns and two water tunnels. One cistern held a collection of Byzantine plates and five or six lamps. The mosaic has red, black and white geometric designs and extends for about 5.5 m² over the sloping ground. This raises questions about how extensive Byzantine developments were in the region of the church (Hamdan Taha, personal communication).

47 So also Eucherius, *Ep. Faust.* 11.

48 Wilkinson, *Jerusalem Pilgrims*, p. 185.

49 Bellarmino Bagatti and Eugenio Alliata, 'Scavo ai "Pozzi di Davide" a Betlemme', *Liber Annuus* 30 (1980): pp. 259–62, fig. 4, nos 1–2; and see Lorenzo Nigro, 'Bethlehem in the Bronze and Iron Ages in the Light of Recent Discoveries by the Palestinian MOTA-DACH', *Vicino Oriente* 19 (2015): pp. 1–24, at p. 7, and fig. 17, p. 23.

50 Maria Teresa Petrozzi, *Bethlehem* (Jerusalem: Franciscan Printing Press, 1971), pp. 138–40.

51 Nigro et al., 'New Archaeological Features in Bethlehem', pp. 23–4; Nigro et al. note regarding the tombs to the west that they lie in St Joseph Street and St Joseph Church in the property of the Sisters of Saint Joseph of the Apparition (Baten).

52 There is a view of this valley looking up to the hill of the town of Bethlehem shown in Leiven de Hamme's guide, *Guide-Indicateur des sanctuaries des lieux historiques de la Terre Sainte*, 4th edn (Jerusalem: Franciscan Printing Press, 1897), plate 1.

53 Nigro, 'Bethlehem in the Bronze and Iron Ages', p. 4.

54 Ward Goodenough, 'Rethinking "Status" and "Role": Towards a General Model of the Cultural Organization of Social Relationships', in Michael Banton (ed.), *The Relevance of Models to Social Anthropology* (London: Tavistock, 1965), pp. 1–24.

55 Byron R. McCane, *Roll Back the Stone: Death and burial in the world of Jesus* (Harrisburg, PA: Trinity Press International, 2003).

56 For example, see Chris Fowler, 'Identities in Transformation: Identities, Funerary Rites, and the Mortuary Process', in Liv Nilsson Stutz and Sarah Tarlow (eds), *The Oxford Handbook of the Archaeology of Death and Ritual* (Oxford: Oxford University Press, 2013), pp. 511–26.

57 See above, p. 31. It has been suggested that a tomb discovered in East Talpiot in 1980 is Jesus' family tomb on the basis of ossuary inscriptions showing a range of names that duplicates the names of his family members: Jesus (Yeshua) son of Joseph, Mariam, Mara, Marya, Judas (Yehuda) son of Jesus, Josē and Matthew (Matya); see James D. Tabor, *The Jesus Dynasty: Stunning new evidence about the hidden history of Jesus* (London: HarperElement, 2006), pp. 25–36, 363–78; Simcha Jacobovici and Charles Pellegrino, *The Jesus Family Tomb* (New York, NY: HarperCollins, 2007). This tomb was originally part of a salvage excavation and no great significance was attributed to it: see Amos Kloner, 'A Tomb with Inscribed Ossuaries in East Talpiyot, Jerusalem', *'Atiqot* 29 (1996): pp. 15–22. The difficulty in identifying it as being connected to Jesus' family is the commonality of these names; see Taylor, *Christians and the Holy Places*, pp. 5–12; and for a thorough assessment see Shimon Gibson, 'Is the Talpiot Tomb Really the Family Tomb of Jesus?', *Near Eastern Archaeology* 69/3–4 (2006): pp. 118–24. Talpiot is located between Bethlehem and Jerusalem, therefore further away from Bethlehem than would be appropriate for a Davidic sepulchral complex.

58 Among the many studies of Herod and the dynasty he founded see Emil Schürer, *The History of the Jewish People in the Age of Jesus Christ (175 B.C.–A.D. 135)*, vol. 1, rev. and ed. Geza Vermes, Fergus Millar and Matthew Black (Edinburgh: T&T Clark, 1973), pp. 287–329; Nikos Kokkinos, *The Herodian Dynasty: Origins, role in society and eclipse* (Journal for the Study of the Pseudepigrapha Supplement 30; Sheffield: Sheffield Academic Press, 1998); Peter Richardson and Amy Marie Fisher, *Herod: King of the Jews and friend of the Romans*, 2nd edn (London: Routledge, 2000); Adam K. Marshak, *The Many Faces of Herod the Great* (Grand Rapids, MI: Eerdmans, 2015); Geza Vermes, *The True Herod* (London: Bloomsbury T&T Clark, 2014); Andrea Berlin, 'A Once and Future King', *JRA* 28 (2015): pp. 895–901; and now Martin Goodman, *Herod the Great: Jewish king in a Roman world* (New Haven, CT: Yale University Press, 2024).

59 *Ethnarchos* was a Greek term, combining *ethnos* (people) and *archon* (ruler); it was a lesser title than that of king.

60 Josephus, *War* 1:244; *Ant.* 14:326.

61 See Daniel Schwartz, 'Herodium in History', in Roi Porat, Rachel Chachy and

Yakov Kalman (eds), *Herodium: Final reports of the 1972–2010 excavations directed by Ehud Netzer, vol. 1: Herod's Tomb Precinct* (Jerusalem: Israel Exploration Society, 2015), pp. 1–14.

62 So also Plutarch, *Life of Antony* 36:2.

63 Josephus, *Ant.* 14:359–60; 15:323–5; *War* 1:265, 419–21.

64 Ehud Netzer, *Greater Herodium* (Qedem 13; Jerusalem: Hebrew University, 1981).

65 Jonathan Bourgel and Roi Porat, 'Herodium as a Reflection of Herod's Policy in Judea and Idumea', *ZDPV* 135 (2019): pp. 188–209, at pp. 191–2.

66 See Bourgel and Porat, 'Herodium', pp. 196–8. The list of the new toparchies is given in Josephus, *War* 3:54–5; Schürer, *History*, ed. Vermes, Millar and Black, vol. 1, p. 33. Josephus refers to Bethlehem anachronistically as a toparchy in the days of Solomon: *Ant.* 8:35.

67 Silvia Rozenberg and David Mevorah (eds), *Herod the Great: The king's final journey* (Jerusalem: Israel Museum, 2013); Roi Porat, Rachel Chachy and Yakov Kalman (eds), *Herodium: Final reports of the 1972–2010 excavations directed by Ehud Netzer, vol. I: Herod's Tomb Precinct* (Jerusalem: Israel Exploration Society, 2015), pp. 201–313.

68 Jodi Magness, 'Herod the Great's Self-Representation through His Tomb at Herodium', *JAJ* 10 (2019): pp. 258–87, developing further what she argued previously in Jodi Magness, 'The Mausolea of Augustus, Alexander, and Herod the Great', in Jodi Magness and Seymour Gitin (eds), *Hesed ve-Emet: Studies in honor of Ernest S. Frerichs* (Atlanta, GA: Scholars, 1998), pp. 313–30, that the tomb of Alexander in Egypt was a kind of prototype of other tomb architecture for royal and imperial rulers.

69 Magness, 'Herod the Great's Self-Representation', p. 275, an observation from Abraham Schalit, *King Herod: Portrait of a ruler* (Jerusalem: Mosad Bialik, 1962), p. 228.

70 *Ant.* 14:8; *War* 1:123.

71 See Ben Zion Wacholder, *Nicolaus of Damascus* (University of California Publications in History 5: Berkeley, CA: University of California Press, 1962), pp. 53–8; Kimberley Czajkowski and Benedikt Eckhardt, *Herod in History: Nicolaus of Damascus and the Augustan context* (Oxford: Oxford University Press, 2021).

72 Schalit, *King Herod*, pp. 226–8, 232–9, 234; but see Mordecai Stern, 'A. Schalit's Herod', *JJS* 11 (1960): pp. 49–58, at pp. 55–7.

73 Tal Ilan, 'King David, King Herod, and Nicolaus of Damascus', *JSQ* 5 (1998): pp. 195–240. Ilan notes a number of parallels and considers it likely that Herod himself suggested them to Nicolaus. However, Nicolaus himself could have created these parallels in order to flatter Herod.

74 The unusual term *geiorai* has been traced by Christophe Guignard to an Aramaic word in the Targumic tradition for Exod. 12:38's 'mixed multitude': Christophe Guignard, 'Jesus' Family and Their Genealogy According to the Testimony of Julius Africanus', in Claire Clivaz, Andreas Dettwiler, Luc Devillers and Enrico Norelli (eds), *Infancy Gospels: Stories and identities* (WUNT 281; Tübingen: Mohr Siebeck, 2011), pp. 67–93, at p. 73.

75 Josephus, *Ant.* 13:250, notes that this part is found in Nicolaus of Damascus's history.

76 Freeman-Grenville, Chapman and Taylor, *Onomasticon*, p. 31.

77 Freeman-Grenville, Chapman and Taylor, *Onomasticon*, map 7. Michael Avi-Yonah, *Gazetteer of Roman Palestine* (Jerusalem: Carta/Institute of Archaeology, Hebrew University, 1976), p. 31, thought Jerome was mistaking the Tomb of Rachel for Archelaus's tomb, but this seems unlikely in view of his familiarity with this area.

78 He would not in the end be buried here. See Chapter 7.

4 Born Jesus: the Gospel of Matthew

1 This approach is demonstrated in Annette Merz, 'Matthew's Star, Luke's Census, Bethlehem, and the Quest for the Historical Jesus', in Peter Barthel and George van Kooten (eds), *The Star of Bethlehem and the Magi: Interdisciplinary perspectives from experts on the Ancient Near East, the Greco-Roman world and modern astronomy* (Leiden: Brill, 2015), pp. 463–95.

2 E. P. Sanders, *The Historical Figure of Jesus* (London: Allen Lane/Penguin, 1993), p. 85.

3 Andrew Lincoln, *Born of a Virgin? Reconceiving Jesus in the Bible, tradition and theology* (London: SCM Press, 2013); 'Contested Paternity and Contested Readings: The Conception of Jesus in Matthew 1.18–25', *JSNT* 34 (2012): pp. 211–31, at pp. 211–13; 'How Babies Were Made in Jesus' Time', *BAR* 40/6 (2014): pp. 42–9; 'The Bible, Theology and the Virgin Birth: Continuing a Conversation?', *Journal of Theological Interpretation* 14 (2020): pp. 267–85.

4 Jane Schaberg, *The Illegitimacy of Jesus: A feminist theological interpretation of the infancy narratives* (Sheffield: Sheffield Academic Press, 1995); Gerd Lüdemann, *Virgin Birth? The real story of Mary and her son Jesus* (Harrisburg, PA: Trinity Press International, 1997); Bruce Chilton, *Rabbi Jesus: An intimate biography* (New York, NY: Doubleday, 2002), pp. 3–22; and see also Frank Reilly, 'Jane Schaberg, Raymond E. Brown, and the Problem of the Illegitimacy of Jesus', *JFSR* 21 (2005): pp. 57–80.

5 Antoinette Clark Wire, 'Early Jewish Birth Prophecy Stories and Women's Social

Memory', in Alan K. Kirk and Tom Thatcher (eds), *Memory, Tradition and Text: Uses of the past in early Christianity* (Leiden: Brill, 2005), pp. 173–90, at p. 189. Wire looked at the book of Jubilees and the *Liber antiquitatem biblicarum*, among other works, including the birth stories include the story of Izates (Josephus, *Ant.* 20:17–21) and Rabbi Ishmael, *Midrash on the Ten Martyrs* 2:65; see also Wire, *Holy Lives, Holy Deaths: A close hearing of early Jewish storytellers* (SBL 1; Atlanta, GA: SBL, 2002), pp. 74–101.

6 See James Crossley, *Jesus and the Chaos of History: Redirecting the life of the historical Jesus* (Oxford: Oxford University Press, 2015), p. 1, and see further pp. 13–19, 176–9.

7 For example, James D. Tabor, *The Jesus Dynasty: Stunning new evidence about the hidden history of Jesus* (London: HarperElement, 2006). Richard Bauckham, *Jude and the Relatives of Jesus in the Early Church* (Edinburgh: T&T Clark, 1990), has long been recognised as a significant examination, but it is not much used in historical Jesus studies.

8 John Painter, *Just James: The brother of Jesus in history and tradition*, 2nd edn (Columbia, SC: University of South Carolina Press, 2004).

9 See Chapter 2.

10 Lincoln, *Born of a Virgin?*, pp. 21–39.

11 Eduard Schweizer, 'Matthew's Church', in Graham Stanton (ed.), *The Interpretation of Matthew* (London: SPCK, 1983), pp. 129–55. Schweizer notes the high regard for Peter (e.g. Matt. 16:19) and connects this with Peter's influence in Antioch (Gal. 2:11–14). The focus on maintenance of Jewish law (Matt. 5:17–18) accords with Peter's response to James's instructions, much to the ire of Paul. See Antony Saldarini, *Matthew's Christian-Jewish Community* (Chicago, IL: University of Chicago Press, 1994); David C. Sim, *The Gospel of Matthew and Christian Judaism: The history and social setting of the Matthean community* (Edinburgh: T&T Clark, 1998); see also Craig Keener, *A Commentary on the Gospel of Matthew* (Grand Rapids, MI: Eerdmans, 1999), pp. 38–44; Ulrich Luz, *Matthew 1–7: A commentary* (Minneapolis, MN: Fortress, 2007), pp. 45–59; Hubertus W. M. Van de Sandt (ed.), *Matthew and the Didache: Two documents from the same Jewish-Christian milieu?* (Leiden: Brill, 2005).

12 The category is here used without any assumption of heterodoxy or marginality. The definition of 'Jewish Christian' (without a hyphen) is slippery, and later groups should not all be lumped into one; I have argued that in a praxis-based definition the hyphen is critical: see Joan E. Taylor, 'The Phenomenon of Early Jewish-Christianity: Reality or Scholarly Invention?', *VC* 44 (1990): pp. 313–34, though for clarity it may be better to term them 'Christian Jews'. The issues of

definition are problematic given that Christianity was initially a form of Judaism, and thus one might call all the earliest followers of Jesus 'Jewish-Christians'. The term only has significance relationally, when there were Christians who did *not* identify as Jewish or follow Jewish praxis: a group that became normative. This critique of definition is developed in more detail in Matt Jackson-McCabe, *Jewish Christianity: The making of the Christianity–Judaism divide* (New Haven, CT: Yale University Press, 2020). See also Annette Yoshiko Reed, *Jewish-Christianity and the History of Judaism* (Texts and Studies in Ancient Judaism 171; Tübingen: Mohr Siebeck, 2018).

13 See for the theory that Luke knew Q via Matthew the discussion in: Mark Goodacre, *The Case against Q: Studies in Markan priority and the synoptic problem* (Harrisburg, PA: Trinity Press International, 2002).

14 Maurice Casey, *Jesus of Nazareth: An independent historian's account of his life and teaching* (London: T&T Clark Bloomsbury, 2010), pp. 86–90. That this previous 'Source', Q, was in fact a previous 'Matthew' originally written in Aramaic/Hebrew was the influential argument of Friedrich Schleiermacher in 1832: see Donald A. Hagner, *The Gospel of Matthew* (Word Biblical Commentary; New York, NY: Thomas Nelson, 1993), pp. xliii–xlv. More often today, it is held that Q was composed from the outset in Greek (see Kloppenborg, *Q*, pp. 57–9) and that Q was anonymous, but for memory of authorship regarding the canonical Gospels in general see Simon Gathercole, 'The Alleged Anonymity of the Canonical Gospels', *JTS* 69 (2018): pp. 447–76.

15 See Peter H. Davids, 'Palestinian Traditions in the Epistle of James', in Bruce Chilton and Craig A. Evans (eds), *James the Just and Christian Origins* (Leiden: Brill, 1999), pp. 33–57; Patrick Hartin, *James and the 'Q' Sayings of Jesus* (Sheffield: JSOT Press, 1991).

16 I.e. within Matt. 3:2–6, see Frans Neirynck, 'The Minor Agreements and Q', in Ronald A. Piper (ed.), *The Gospel behind the Gospels: Current studies on Q* (Leiden: Brill, 1995), pp. 49–72, at pp. 65–71; John S. Kloppenborg, 'City and Wasteland: Narrative Word and the Beginning of the Sayings Gospel (Q)', in Dennis E. Smith (ed.), *How the Gospels Began* (Semeia 52; Atlanta: Scholars, 1990), pp. 145–60; John S. Kloppenborg, *Q, the Earliest Gospel: An introduction to the original stories and sayings of Jesus* (London: Westminster John Knox, 2008), pp. 49-50.

17 See Roger Pearse (ed.), *Eusebius of Caesarea, Gospel Problems and Solutions: Quaestiones ad Stephanum et Marinum* (Ipswich: Chieftain, 2010), p. 7.

18 I am grateful to Mina Monier, who has sent me an image of the manuscript in question and pointed out that 'from her' is an addition, written above the line. For

further discussion on the *Diatessaron* and particularly the Arabic version, see Joan E. Taylor and Mina Monier, 'Tatian's *Diatessaron*: The Arabic Version, the Dura Europos Fragment, and the Women Witnesses', *JTS* 72 (2021): pp. 192–230.

19 This is the Old Syriac manuscript tradition evidenced by the Sinaitic and Curetonian Syriac manuscripts of the fourth to fifth century, and by quotations in Aphrahat, Ephrem and other Syrian Christian scholars; see Andreas Juckel, 'Old Syriac Version', in Sebastian P. Brock, Aaron M. Butts, George A. Kiraz and Lucas van Rompay, *Gorgias Encyclopedic Dictionary of the Syriac Heritage*: https://gedsh.bethmardutho.org/Old-Syriac-Version.

20 See William D. Davies and Dale C. Allison, *A Critical and Exegetical Commentary on the Gospel According to Saint Matthew*, vol. 1 (Edinburgh, T&T Clark, 1988), p. 183, n. 7.

21 A part of this text is missing, but it is reconstructed from the *f*13 family as fitting with the surviving letters. For a discussion in favour of the usual reading, see Bruce M. Metzger, *A Textual Commentary on the Greek New Testament* (Grand Rapids, MI: Hendrickson, 2006), pp. 4–6; also John Holland, 'A Text-Critical Discussion of Matthew 1:16', *CBQ* 58 (1996): pp. 665–73. Metzger reads the verb *egennēsen* as referring to Mary rather than Joseph, but this is questionable.

22 Holland, 'Text-Critical Discussion', p. 669, n. 16, disputes this testimony; Metzger, *Textual Commentary*, p. 4, thinks the second part is simply 'a Jewish interpretation of the commonly received text of Mt. 1.16'. However, the Jewish counter-story was that Jesus was the illegitimate son of Pantera (see below).

23 For further discussion see Taylor, 'Phenomenon of Early Jewish-Christianity'.

24 See also Hippolytus, *Ref.* 7:33:1–2; cf. 7:35:1–2; Joan E. Taylor, 'Cerinthus and the Gospel of Mark: The Priority of the Longer Ending', *Comparative Oriental Manuscript Studies Bulletin* 8 (2022): pp. 675–707: http://doi.org/10.25592/uhhfdm.12467.

25 The term meant 'the poor', *ebyonim*, in Mishnaic Hebrew; see Marcus Jastrow, *Dictionary of the Targumim, the Talmud Babli and Yerushalmi and the Midrashic Literature* (New York, NY: Title, 1943), p. 5.

26 See Irenaeus, *Adv. Haer.* 1:26:2; 3:11:7; Eusebius, *Hist. Eccles.* 5:8:10. Origen noted a variant in this gospel in his *Comm. Matt.* 15:14, and see *Comm. Joh.* 2:12.

27 See map in Joan E. Taylor, *Christians and the Holy Places: The myth of Jewish-Christian origins* (Oxford: Clarendon, 1993), p. 37, with discussion on pp. 36–41; also the summary provided by Edwin K. Broadhead, *Jewish Ways of Following Jesus: Redrawing the religious map of antiquity* (Tübingen: Mohr Siebeck, 2010), pp. 346–9.

28 See also Epiphanius, *Pan.* 29:1:1–9:4, and his identification of other villages:

Kochaba (Epiphanius, *Pan.* 29:7:7; cf. 30:2:8–9, 18:1), near Karnaim (map ref. 242250) and Ashtaroth (245246). In Palestine itself, Eusebius mentions 'Jewish-Christian' villages in the area south of Eleutheropolis (Beth Guvrin), the Daromas, for example Anaea (*Onom.* 26:13–14; *Mart. Pal.* 10:1–2) and Iethira (*Onom.* 108:1–4; 110:18; cf. 88:3); see Taylor, *Christians and the Holy Places*, pp. 50, 62.

29 Jerome, *Comm. Matt.* 6:11; 12:13; 23:35; 27:16, 51.

30 'Chaldaico quidem Syroque sermone sed Hebraicis litteris scriptum est', *Adv. Pel.* 3:2.

31 See Andrew Gregory, *The Gospel According to the Hebrews and the Gospel of the Ebionites* (Oxford: Oxford University Press, 2017), who distinguishes only two Jewish-Christian gospels, contra Philipp Vielhauer and Georg Strecker, 'Jewish-Christian Gospels', in Edgar Hennecke (ed.), *New Testament Apocrypha, vol. 1: Gospels and Related Writings*, ed. Wilhelm Schneemelcher, tr. R. McL. Wilson (Philadelphia, PA: Westminster, 1963), pp. 134–78, esp. pp. 139–53; Bart D. Ehrman and Zlatko Pleše, *The Apocryphal Gospels: Texts and translations* (New York, NY: Oxford University Press, 2011), pp. 201–9: the *Gospel of the Hebrews* and the *Gospel of the Ebionites*. The *Gospel of the Ebionites* was based on Matthew but 'not fully whole but falsified and distorted' (Epiphanius, *Pan.* 30:13:2, 6; 14:3), beginning with John's baptism of Jesus, thereby missing the genealogy and nativity accounts. Those who used it asserted that Jesus 'was from the seed of Joseph and from Mary' (*Pan.* 30:14:2; cf. 30:2:2; 30:3:1).

32 Jeremiah Coogan, 'Ways That Parted in the Library: The Gospels According to Matthew and According to the Hebrews in Late Ancient Heresiology', *JEH* 74 (2013): pp. 473–90, at p. 479; Epiphanius, *Pan.* 30:3:7; Jerome, *Comm. Matt.* 4:12:13.

33 Jerome, *Ep.* 20:5; *Tract. Ps.* 135; *Comm. Matt.* 2:5; 12:13; 'as many people maintain, [it is] according to Matthew', *Adv. Pel.* 3:2.

34 Some manuscripts of Matthew note the variants of the 'Jewish gospel' in the margins: MSS 4, 273, 566, 899, 1424; see Ehrman and Pleše, *Apocryphal Gospels*, pp. 208–9. These variants are also noted in Old Latin manuscripts of Matthew, fifth-century Vercellensis and tenth-century diglot Sangermanensis; see Coogan, 'Ways That Parted', pp. 481, 483.

35 See Coogan, 'Ways That Parted'. Scholars should not think of multiple ways of referring to a work as indicating multiple works (contra Ehrman and Pleše, *Apocryphal Gospels*, p. 198, *inter alia*).

36 Bethlehem 'of Judah' rather than Bethlehem 'of Judaea': Jerome, *Comm. Matt.* 2:5, quoting Mic. 5:2, and see *Ep.* 57:8. Gregory, *Gospel According to the Hebrews*, pp. 153–4, suggests 'it seems more likely that it should be attributed to an early

Semitic version of Matthew rather than to the *Gospel according to the Hebrews*,
but he too cautiously avoids equating the Gospel of the Hebrews with an early
'Semitic version' of Matthew.

37 For the claim that they only used Matthew, see Irenaeus, *Adv. Haer.* 1:26:2; 3:11:7.
See also Pseudo-Tertullian, *Adv. Omn. Haer.* 3:1; Origen, *Comm. Matt.* 16:12.
In the fifth-century *Dialogue of Athanasius and Zacchaeus* (43), too, the Jewish
questioner states that Jesus was the son of Joseph.

38 See also Tertullian, *De Virg.* 6:1.

39 Origen, *Letter to Titus*; see Albertus F. J. Klijn and Gerrit J. Reinink, *Patristic
Evidence for Jewish-Christian Sects* (NT Supplement 36; Leiden: Brill, 1973),
pp. 132–3.

40 For Ignatius's knowledge of the Gospel of Matthew see Paul Foster, 'The Epistles
of Ignatius of Antioch and the Writings That Later Formed the New Testament',
in Andrew Gregory and Christopher Tuckett (eds), *The Reception of the New
Testament in the Apostolic Fathers* (Oxford: Oxford University Press, 2005),
pp. 159–86; for Ignatius's different perspective see David C. Sim, 'Matthew and
Ignatius of Antioch', in David C. Sim and Boris Repschinski (eds), *Matthew
and His Christian Contemporaries* (London: Bloomsbury T&T Clark, 2008),
pp. 139–54; see also J. Smit Sibinga, 'Ignatius and Matthew', *NT* 8 (1966): pp.
263–83, who suggests that Ignatius knew a source of Matthew but not the final
Gospel. The recensions of Ignatius are complex, but here I follow Michael W.
Holmes (ed.), *The Apostolic Fathers: Greek texts and English translations*, 3rd edn
(Grand Rapids, MI: Baker Academic, 2007), pp. 166–271.

41 This reading is unstable. The fourth-century Vaticanus manuscript switches these
words around to produce 'Anointed/Christ Jesus'; some ancient manuscripts
simply have 'Jesus' and others only 'Anointed'.

42 BDAG 969–70.

43 For the marriage documents and how they bear on Matthew's story, see Philip F.
Esler, 'The Righteousness of Joseph: Interpreting Matt 1.18–25 in Light of Judean
Legal Papyri', *NTS* 68 (2022): pp. 326–43. Esler reconstructs Mary's *ketubbah* on
the basis of parallel documents.

44 See Esler, 'Righteousness of Joseph', pp. 328–9, who notes there is no mention of
either father.

45 See Michael L. Satlow, *Jewish Marriage in Antiquity* (Princeton, NJ: Princeton
University Press, 2001), pp. 69, 162–81; John J. Collins, 'Marriage, Divorce and
Family in Second Temple Judaism', in Leo G. Perdue, Joseph Blenkinsopp, John
J. Collins and Carol Meyers (eds), *Families in Ancient Israel* (Louisville, KY:
Westminster John Knox, 1997), pp. 104–62.

46 Collins, 'Marriage, Divorce and Family', p. 166, and see p. 298, n. 70, which tells of a rabbi who combined the betrothal and wedding of his daughter in one act, *j.Ket.* 1:1, 24d; Esler, 'Righteousness of Joseph', pp. 332–3, notes also that in P.Mur. 20 the betrothal and wedding/cohabitation appear to have occurred on the same day.

47 Rumours abounded that in Judaea things were a bit loose; see Satlow, *Jewish Marriage*, p. 167.

48 See above, Chapter 1, n. 20. Esler, 'Righteousness of Joseph', p. 335, suggests that Mary's condition would have already been seen when she went out, but actually that would not have happened.

49 For women's clothing of this era, see Joan E. Taylor, 'What Did Mary Magdalene Look Like? Images from the West, the East, Dura and Judaea', in Alicia Batten, Sarah Bloesch and Meredith Minister (eds), *Dress in Mediterranean Antiquity: Greeks, Romans, Jews and Christians* (London: Bloomsbury T&T Clark, 2021), pp. 257–78.

50 Michael Rosenberg, *Signs of Virginity: Testing virgins and making men in late antiquity* (Oxford: Oxford University Press, 2018), pp. 47–54.

51 BDAG 214.

52 See Esler, 'Righteousness of Joseph', pp. 333–5.

53 BDAG 117.

54 The various options are provided in Esler, 'Righteousness of Joseph', pp. 338–41. Esler considers the bill of divorce in P.Mur. 19 in which there is a full return of the dowry, but notes that it could not have spared Mary any shame in a close community.

55 Collins, 'Marriage, Divorce and Family', p. 116.

56 Explored also by Esler, 'Righteousness of Joseph', pp. 342–3.

57 It is associated with marriage or sex, however, in Josephus (*Ant.* 1:302), where it is used for Judah when after seven years he was able to 'take along' Rachel as his wife, and in the Song of Songs (8:2) it is used of a woman bringing along a lover into her mother's house.

58 As James Tabor suggests, 'Perhaps he planned to help her leave town and bear her child in secret': *Jesus Dynasty*, p. 46.

59 Satlow, *Jewish Marriage*, p. 129.

60 See *b.Yev.* 69b–70a. See also Lynn Cohick, *Women in the World of the Earliest Christians: Illuminating ancient ways of life* (Grand Rapids, MI: Baker Academic, 2009), p. 153.

61 Cohick, *Women in the World*, p. 153.

62 Cohick, *Women in the World*, p. 63. Lev. 5:1; Deut. 22:20–1; *m.Sanh.* 11:1.

63 Keener, *Matthew*, p. 87; Geza Vermes, *The Nativity: History and legend* (London: Penguin, 2006), pp. 67–72.

64 Revelatory dreams appear in Gen. 20:3, 6–7; 28:12–15; 31:10–13; 37:5–11; 40:5–8; 41:1–8, 25, 39; Judg. 7:13–14; 1 Kgs 3:5–15; Dan. 1:17; 2:1–11, 19–23; 5:11–12, and sometimes required a skilled dream-interpreter; see David E. Aune, *Prophecy in Early Christianity and the Ancient Mediterranean World* (Grand Rapids, MI: Eerdmans, 1983), p. 82. For an examination of how dreams appear in Matthew's presentation, appealing to audience understandings, see Derek S. Dodson, *Reading Dreams: An audience-critical approach to the dreams in the Gospel of Matthew* (LNTS 397; London: T&T Clark, 2009).

65 See Joan E. Taylor, *The Essenes, the Scrolls and the Dead Sea* (Oxford: Oxford University Press, 2012), pp. 94–5.

66 See below, pp. 165–8; also Aune, *Prophecy*, pp. 139–41.

67 Asher Finkel, 'The Pesher of Dreams and Scriptures', *RQ* 4 (1963): pp. 357–70.

68 After all, it is said by God regarding Moses, uniquely: 'With him I speak mouth to mouth, plainly and not in *riddles* (*behidot*), and he beholds the likeness of God' (Num. 12:8).

69 See also Acts 18:9–10; 23:11; 27:23–4 where revelatory dreams are attributed to Paul; Aune, *Prophecy*, pp. 266–8.

70 Raymond E. Brown, *The Birth of the Messiah: A commentary on the infancy narratives in Matthew and Luke*, rev. edn (New York, NY: Doubleday, 1993), pp. 71–4, in a section titled 'Why the Women?'. This mention of occasional mothers is also found in the genealogies of 1 Chronicles, and Tamar is mentioned at 1 Chr. 2:4.

71 Wayne Manaaki Rihari Te Kaawa, 'Re-visioning Christology through a Maori Lens', thesis submitted in fulfilment of the requirements for the degree of Doctor of Philosophy, University of Otago (Dunedin, 2020), pp. 107–23. Bathsheba is connected to land via Uriah, who is a Hittite, and thus it is his name that is mentioned, rather than hers.

72 Te Kaawa, 'Re-visioning Christology', p. 123.

73 For a summary of explanations, and support of this solution, see Keener, *Matthew*, pp. 78–81; and also see Te Kaawa, 'Re-visioning Christology', pp. 102–6.

74 Sara M. Koenig, *Isn't This Bathsheba? A study in characterization* (Eugene, OR: Pickwick, 2011), pp. 81–2; *b.Sanh.* 101b, 107b.

75 Brown, *Birth*, p. 73.

76 See Lincoln, *Born of a Virgin?*, pp. 78–83.

77 Brown, *Birth*, p. 72.

78 Janice Capel Anderson, 'Mary's Difference: Gender and Patriarchy in the Birth Narratives', *Journal of Religion* 67 (1987): pp. 183–202.

79 So Brown, *Birth*, pp. 73–4.

80 Keener, *Matthew*, p. 79.
81 See also *1 Clem.* 12:1.
82 See *b.Meg.* 14b; Koenig, *Bathsheba*, pp. 154–60.
83 Koenig, *Bathsheba*, pp. 150–4.
84 Ps. 51:7 in Hebrew.
85 Probably dating from the fifth century CE.
86 H. Freedman and M. Simon (eds), *Midrash Rabbah, vol. 4: Leviticus*, tr. Jacob Israelstam and Judah J. Slotki (London: Soncino, 1939), p. 183.
87 Also Ps. 27:10.
88 Lincoln, 'How Babies Were Made', p. 46; *Born of a Virgin?*, p. 85.
89 Philo of Alexandria, ruminating on the commandment 'You shall not commit adultery' (Exod. 20:14) likewise interpreted the law to mean that men should not have sex for pleasure, even with their own wives, comparing those who do with pigs and goats (*Spec.* 3:9, 113; *Jos.* 43); for further discussion see Dale C. Allison, 'Divorce, Celibacy and Joseph', in Dale C. Allsion, *Studies in Matthew: Interpretation past and present* (Grand Rapids, MI: Baker Academic, 2005), pp. 163–75.
90 See Chapter 2.
91 Eyal Ben-Eliyahu, Yehudah Cohn and Fergus Millar, *Handbook of Jewish Literature from Late Antiquity, 135–700 CE* (London: British Academy, 2012), p. 83.
92 There is no reason to see this as a parody of the virgin birth, as does Burton L. Visotsky, *Fathers of the World: Essays in rabbinic and patristic literature* (Tübingen: Mohr Siebeck, 1995), pp. 102–4. For a nuanced and insightful discussion of *Leviticus Rabbah* 14:5 in the light of Davidic characterisation, see Ruth Kara-Ivanov Kaniel, *The Feminine Messiah: King David in the image of the Shekhinah in kabbalistic literature* (Leiden: Brill, 2021), pp. 14–22.
93 LSJ III.1–4, p. 499.
94 LSJ III.6, p. 499.
95 I am grateful to midwife Carol Cooper-McCard who tells me she has encountered three virgin conceptions in her forty-nine years as a midwife; the hymen was unbroken, and no penetrative sex had taken place, but the woman was pregnant as a result of 'heavy petting'. A study of 2013 recorded 45 women out of a group of 7,870 who reported getting pregnant as a virgin without penetrative sex: Amy H. Herring, Samantha M. Attard, Penny Gordon-Larsen, William H. Joyner and Carolyn T. Halpern, 'Like a Virgin (Mother): Analysis of Data from a Longitudinal, US Population Representative Sample Survey', *British Medical Journal* (2013): p. 347: https://doi.org/10.1136/bmj.f7102 (published 17 December 2013): *BMJ* 2013;347:f7102.

96 Lincoln, *Born of a Virgin?*, pp. 83–6.

97 Lincoln, *Born of a Virgin?*, p. 73.

98 Loren T. Stuckenbruck, *The Myth of Rebellious Angels: Studies in Second Temple Judaism and New Testament texts* (Tübingen: Mohr Siebeck, 2014); and see his discussion of the birth narratives, pp. 142–60.

99 In the Dead Sea Scrolls, 'a spirit of holiness' guides the people (1QS 3:18 – 4:26), and therefore actively 'cleanses' them inwardly (1QS 3:6–8; 4:20–2; 1QHab 8:30; 4Q255 2:1) and atones for guilt (1QHab 23:33). The/A spirit provides strength (1QH 7:6–7), truth (1QH 9:32; 1QS 9:3–5), counsel (1QH 12:11–12; 1QH 20:15), knowledge (1QH 13:18–19), understanding (1QH 14:12–13; 1QH 6:24), encouragement (1QH 8:25), delight (1QH 17:32) and comfort (1QH 4:38). The prophets were guided and 'anointed' by this spirit (CD 2:12; 8:16; 4Q270 2:2:14). As a pure spirit that dwells within the community, she/it can be defiled by bad behaviour (CD 5:11–12; 7:3–4): Frederick F. Bruce, 'Holy Spirit in the Qumran Texts', *Annual of Leeds University Oriental Society* 6 (1966/68): pp. 49–55.

100 John R. Levison, *The Spirit in First-Century Judaism* (Arbeiten zur Geschichte des antiken Judentums und des Urchristentums 29; Leiden: Brill, 1997); Eibert Tigchelaar, 'Historical Origins of the Early Christian Concept of the Holy Spirit: Perspectives from the Dead Sea Scrolls', in Jörg Frey, John R. Levison and Andrew Bowden (eds), *The Holy Spirit, Inspiration, and the Cultures of Antiquity: Multidisciplinary perspectives* (Ekstasis: Religious Experience from Antiquity to the Middle Ages 5; Berlin: De Gruyter, 2014), pp. 167–240.

101 Gregory, *Gospel According to the Hebrews*, pp. 32–3, 36–52, 69–74, 94–7.

102 Gregory, *Gospel According to the Hebrews*, pp. 41, 69–74. The motif of the Spirit taking a prophet by the hair is found in Ezek. 8:3.

103 Jerome, *Comm. Isa.* 11:1–3; see Gregory, *Gospel According to the Hebrews*, pp. 110–17; Ehrman and Pleše, *Apocryphal Gospels*, pp. 220–1. This seems to interpret Ezek. 26:25–7, where it is predicted that God will 'sprinkle clean water upon you . . . and I will put my Spirit in you', but also Isa. 42:1–4, which is quoted in full in Matt. 12:18–21.

104 *Comm. Micah* 7:5–7.

105 The term 'gnostic' is used here to refer to a range of different types of early Christianity that focused on esoteric knowledge of the Divine, but for the difficulties of definition see Karen L. King, *What Is Gnosticism?* (Cambridge: Belknap Press, 2003). The *Gospel of Philip* was likely written in Syriac and translated into Greek; see Wesley W. Isenberg, 'Gospel According to Philip, Introduction', in Bentley Layton (ed.), *Nag Hammadi Codex II, 2-7* (Leiden: Brill, 1989), pp. 131–9, at pp. 134–5. The author of *Gos. Phil.* considered their group to

be different from the 'Hebrews'; see Edward Iricinschi, 'If You Got It, Flaunt It: Religious Advertising in the Gospel of Philip', in Edward Iricinschi and Holger M. Zellentin (eds), *Heresy and Identity in Late Antiquity* (Texts and Studies in Ancient Judaism 119; Tübingen: Mohr Siebeck, 2008), pp. 253–72, esp. pp. 256–61.

106 See also Epiphanius, *Pan.* 30:13:7; Theodotius of Byzantium, according to Hippolytus, *Ref.* 7:35:1–2; 10:23:1–2; *Gospel of the Hebrews/Nazarenes*, in Jerome, *Comm. Isa.* 11:1–3.

107 See Carl H. Kraeling, 'The Synagogue', in A. R. Bellinger et al. (eds), *The Excavations at Dura-Europos: Final Report 8, Part 1* (New Haven, CT: Yale University Press, 1956), pp. 161, 183–92, plate 70. Despite the observation that Psyche is used to represent the Spirit (p. 187), Kraeling repeatedly refers to the female figure as 'the Psyche' rather than 'the Spirit'. See also Erwin R. Goodenough, *Jewish Symbols in the Greco-Roman Period*, vol. 10 (New York, NY: Pantheon, 1953), pp. 183–5. The Ezekiel cycle covers the whole of the lower part of the northern wall.

108 Sebastian P. Brock, 'The Holy Spirit as Feminine in Early Syriac Literature', in Sebastian P. Brock, *The Holy Spirit in the Syrian Baptismal Tradition* (Piscataway, NJ: Gorgias, 2013), pp. 175–88.

109 See Gabriele vom Bruck and Barbara Bodenhorn, *The Anthropology of Names and Naming* (Cambridge: Cambridge University Press, 2006).

110 Levi Y. Rahmani, *A Catalogue of Jewish Ossuaries in the Collections of the State of Israel* (Jerusalem: Israel Antiquities Authority/Israel Academy of Sciences and Humanities, 1994). There are even two cases where 'Jesus son of Joseph' is found (no. 9 and no. 704, pp. 77, 203). See also Tal Ilan, *Lexicon of Jewish Names in Late Antiquity, Part I: Palestine 330 BCE–200 CE* (Texts and Studies in Ancient Judaism 91; Tübingen: Mohr Siebeck, 2002), pp. 126–33, 449.

111 See further discussion in John Meier, *A Marginal Jew: Rethinking the historical Jesus, vol. 1: The Roots of the Problem and the Person* (New Haven, CT: Yale University Press, 1991), pp. 205–8; Brown, *Birth*, pp. 130–1.

112 Jastrow, *Dictionary*, p. 600.

113 See e.g. *Test. Mos.* 5–6; Ananda Geyser-Fouche and Young Namgung, 'The Deuteronomic View of History in Second Temple Judaism', *Verbum et Ecclesia* 40 (2019): pp. 1–7: https://dx.doi.org/10.4102/ve.v40i1.1805.

114 Note that ancient 'readers' were often 'hearers', as works were read out to people who were largely illiterate. See the study by William A. Johnson and Holt N. Parker, *Ancient Literacies: The culture of reading in Greece and Rome* (Oxford: Oxford University Press, 2009).

115 For awareness of Herod shown in the text, see Robert Myles, *The Homeless Jesus in the Gospel of Matthew* (Sheffield: Sheffield Phoenix, 2014), pp. 61–3.

116 See above, pp. 64–7.

117 See Helen Jacobus, 'Balaam's "Star Oracle" (Num 24:15–19) in the Dead Sea Scrolls and Bar Kokhba', in Barthel and van Kooten (eds), *Star of Bethlehem*, pp. 399–429.

118 Louis H. Feldman, *Studies in Josephus' Rewritten Bible* (Leiden: Brill, 2021), pp. 110–36. It may have played a part in Josephus's prediction of Vespasian's rule: Craig A. Evans, 'The Star of Balaam and the Prophecy of Josephus Concerning Vespasian', in Craig A. Evans, *Scribal Practice, Text and Canon in the Dead Sea Scrolls* (Leiden: Brill. (2019), pp. 297–333.

119 See George van Kooten, 'Matthew, the Parthians and the Magi: A Contextualization of Matthew's Gospel in Roman–Parthian Relations of the First Centuries BCE and CE', in Barthel and van Kooten (eds), *Star of Bethlehem*, pp. 496–651. Van Kooten suggests that another text, different from Num. 24:17–19, was in view, one proclaiming the advent of a great light (Isa. 8:23 – 9:10).

120 See Joan E. Taylor with David Hay, 'Astrology in Philo of Alexandria's *De Vita Contemplativa*', *ARAM Periodical* 24/2 (2012): pp. 56–74; see also Franz Cumont, 'Lecture 1: The Chaldeans', in *Astrology and Religion among the Greeks and Romans* (New York and London: G. P. Putnam, 1912), pp. 27–46.

121 Brown, *Birth*, pp. 168–70.

122 Judith R. Baskin, 'Origen on Balaam: The Dilemma of the Unworthy Prophet', *VC* 37 (1983): pp. 22–35; Darrell D. Hannah, 'The Star of the Magi and the Prophecy of Balaam in Earliest Christianity, with Special Attention to the Lost Books of Balaam', in Barthel and van Kooten (eds), *Star of Bethlehem*, pp. 433–62, at pp. 438–52. Hannah suggests there was a lost work, the *Books of Balaam*, which had his successors travel to Judaea to honour the Christ-child.

123 Tobias Nicklas, 'Balaam and the Star of the Magi', in Tobias Nicklas, *The Prestige of the Pagan Prophet Balaam in Judaism, Early Christianity and Islam* (Leiden: Brill, 2008), pp. 231–46, at pp. 243–4.

124 He notes that Damascus is now in Syro-Phoenicia: Justin, *Dial.* 78:10.

125 'The evil demon's power' likely refers to the cult of Hadad-Rammon, identified as Zeus-Jupiter.

126 John F. Healey, *The Religion of the Nabataeans: A conspectus* (Leiden: Brill, 2001), esp. pp. 21, 60, 93–5, 160; Peter Alpass, *The Religious Life of Nabataea* (Leiden: Brill, 2013), pp. 209–28.

127 See Taylor with Hay, 'Astrology'.

128 Mathieu Ossendrijver, 'The Story of the Magi in the Light of Alexander the Great's

Encounters with Chaldeans', in Barthel and van Kooten (eds), *Star of Bethlehem*, pp. 217–30.

129 See Josephus, *War* 1:363–77; Ariyeh Kasher, *Jews, Idumaeans and Ancient Arabs: Relations of the Jews in Eretz-Israel with the nations of the frontier and the desert during the Hellenistic and Roman era (332 BCE – 70 CE)* (Tübingen: Mohr Siebeck, 1988), pp. 126–74.

130 Kocku von Stuckrad, 'Stars and Powers: Astrological Thinking in Imperial Politics from the Hasmoneans to Bar Kokhba', in Barthel and van Kooten (eds), *Star of Bethlehem*, pp. 387–98.

131 Rachel Hachlili, 'The Zodiac in Ancient Jewish Art: Representation and Significance', *BASOR* 228 (1977): pp. 61–77; 'The Zodiac in Ancient Jewish Synagogal Art: A Review', *JSQ* 9 (2002): pp. 219–58; Jodi Magness, 'Heaven on Earth: Helios and the Zodiac Cycle in Ancient Palestinian Synagogues', *Dumbarton Oaks Papers* 59 (2005): pp. 1–52.

132 Helen R. Jacobus, *Zodiac Calendars in the Dead Sea Scrolls and Their Reception: Ancient astronomy and astrology in early Judaism* (Brill: Leiden, 2015). For example, there are astrological charts among the scrolls 4Q208 (*4QAstronomical Enocha*) and 4Q209 (*4QAstronomical Enochb*), and 4Q318 (*4QZodiac Calendar and Brontologion*).

133 For discussion see Nicola Denzey, 'A New Star on the Horizon: Astral Christologies and Stellar Debates in Early Christian Discourse', in Scott Noegel and Joel Walker (eds), *Prayer, Magic, and the Stars in the Ancient and Late Antique World* (University Park, PA: Pennsylvania State University Press, 2003), pp. 207–21.

134 David W. Hughes, 'The Star of Bethlehem', *Nature* 264 (1976): pp. 513–17.

135 Stephan Heilan, 'The Star of Bethlehem and Greco-Roman Astrology, Especially Astrological Geography', in Barthel and van Kooten (eds), *Star of Bethlehem*, pp. 297–357.

136 These were coin issues by the legates Quirinius under Augustus in 5/6 CE and Silanus under Augustus in 13/14 CE.

137 Michael R. Molnar, *The Star of Bethlehem: The legacy of the magi* (New Brunswick, NJ: Rutgers, 1999); 'The Historical Basis for the Star of Bethlehem', in Barthel and van Kooten (eds), *Star of Bethlehem*, pp. 17–42. This theory is provided with more detail and support by Bradley E. Schafer, 'An Astronomical and Historical Evaluation of Molnar's Solution', in Barthel and van Kooten (eds), *Star of Bethlehem*, pp. 85–102.

138 Michael R. Molnar, 'The Evidence for Aries the Ram as the Astrological Sign of Judea', *JHA* 34 (2003): pp. 325–7. Molnar also notes that the Roman astronomer

Marcus Manilius (*Astronomica* 4:744–54) includes Syria through to Egypt under the sign of the Ram, as does Vettius Valens (*Anthology* 1:2): Molnar, 'Historical Basis', pp. 24–7. Heilen, in Barthel and van Kooten (eds), *Star of Bethlehem*, pp. 330–3, however, shows how wide the regional associations can be, and also quite various. Nevertheless, Persia and Syria are the countries most frequently associated with Aries.

139 David Pingree, *The Astrological History of Māshāʾallāh* (Cambridge, MA: Harvard University Press, 1971), horoscope 5.

140 Roy F. Baumeister and Stephen Hastings, 'Distortions of Collective Memory: How Groups Flatter and Deceive Themselves', in James W. Pennebaker, Dario Paez and Bernard Rimé (eds), *Collective Memory of Political Events: Social psychological perspectives* (London: Routledge, 1997), pp. 277–93.

141 The image of the fox as a wily and deceitful predator is found in rabbinic 'fox tales'; see the tale of the fox and the fishes (*b.Ber.* 61b; David H. Stern and Mark J. Minsky (eds), *Rabbinic Fantasies: Imaginative narratives from classical Hebrew literature* (New Haven, CT: Yale University Press 1990), pp. 191–4. In the Song of Songs 2:15 there are 'little foxes that spoil and ruin the vineyards'. For the historical echoes of Herod's threat and the displacement theme, see Myles, *Homeless*, pp. 69–73.

142 Roger D. Aus, *Matthew 1–2 and the Virginal Conception in Light of Palestinian and Hellenistic Traditions on the Birth of Israel's First Redeemer, Moses* (Lanham, MD: University Press of America, 2004); Dale C. Allison, *The New Moses: A Matthean typology* (Minneapolis, MN: Augsburg Fortress, 1994).

143 Ben-Eliyahu, Cohn and Millar, *Handbook*, pp. 118–20.

144 See *b.Sot.* 13a; *b.Meg.* 14a.

145 Geza Vermes, *The True Herod* (London: Bloomsbury T&T Clark, 2014), pp. 113–19; Vermes, *Nativity*, pp. 119–26.

146 Vermes, *Herod*, p. 119.

147 Brown, *Birth*, pp. 104–19.

148 Brown, *Birth*, pp. 105–6.

149 Brown, *Birth*, pp. 32–7.

150 Brown, *Birth*, pp. 17–219, with a reconstruction of the main pre-Matthean narrative on p. 109.

151 Brown, *Birth*, pp. 112–14. See a neat summary of the typology in Myles, *Homeless*, pp. 75–7.

152 Brown, *Birth*, pp. 114–16. He notes also *b.Sanh.* 101a; and *Midrash Rabbah* 1:18 on Exod. 1:22, where there are warnings given to Pharaoh by magi-magicians or astrologers. See also Vermes, *Nativity*, pp. 124–5.

153 See above, p. 106.

154 Krister Stendahl, *The School of St. Matthew and Its Use of the Old Testament* (Acta Seminarii Neotestamentici Upsaliensis 20; Uppsala: Almqvist & Wiksell, 1954), p. 14; Robert Gundry, *The Use of the Old Testament in St. Matthew's Gospel* (Leiden: Brill, 1967), p. 174.

155 See Philo of Alexandria, *Abr.* 253; *Cher.* 43; *Congr.* 12; *Spec.* 3:9, 32–4; 4:96–7; *Quaest. Gen.* 2:49; 4:86, 154; William Loader, *Philo, Josephus and the Testaments on Sexuality* (Grand Rapids, MI: Eerdmans, 2011), pp. 61–5. Josephus too commends the Essenes for not having sex with their wives during pregnancy (*War* 2:161) and states overtly that sex is 'only for the procreation of children' (*Apion* 2:199).

156 Mark 6:3 lists the names in this order: James, Joset, Judas and Simon, and Matt. 13:55 lists the names as: James, Joseph, Simon and Judas. In both, sisters are mentioned but not named.

157 The Moses paradigm itself is intriguing, because this is not about a descendant of David. Moses was of the tribe of Levi. However, Deuteronomy ends with Moses' prediction that 'God will raise up for you a prophet like me from among you' (Deut. 18:15, 18). This figure would normally be distinguished from the Messiah, the Anointed (as in John 1:20–1). For Jesus' earliest disciples, the identity of this Prophet was collapsed into the identity of the Messiah, as we see reflected in Acts in the speeches of Peter (Acts 3:22–3) and Stephen (Acts 7:37).

158 Lincoln, *Born of a Virgin?*, p. 163.

159 Origen of Alexandria, *Contra Celsum*, tr. Henry Chadwick (Cambridge: Cambridge University Press, 1980), p. 31.

160 Peter Schäfer, *Jesus in the Talmud* (Princeton, NJ: Princeton University Press, 2007), pp. 16–20, 56. See also Dan Jaffé, 'The Virgin Birth of Jesus in the Talmud: A Philological and Historical Analysis', *Laval théologique et philosophique* 68 (2012): pp. 577–92; Lincoln Blumell, 'A Jew in Celsus' True Doctrine? An Examination of Jewish Anti-Christian Polemic in the Second Century C.E.', *Studies in Religion/Sciences Religieuses* (2007): pp. 297–315, at pp. 301–3; Brown, *Birth*, pp. 535–7.

161 In a third-century story, Rabbi Eliezer Hyrcanus relates how Jacob of Sikhnin came 'in the name of Yeshua son of Panteri' (Tosefta, *Hullin* 2:22–4). There may also be confusions, given that Jesus (Yeshua) was a very common name, so that in one story Yeshua son of Pantera/Pandera has a stepfather who speaks to Rabbi Akiba, a rabbi of the mid-second century (*b.Ber.* 61b). But these stories are told in a world of intense polemic between Christians and Jews.

162 Eusebius, *Eclogae propheticae* 3:10, commenting on Hos. 5:14; Eusebius, *Eclogae*

Propheticae, tr. T. Gaisford (Oxford: Oxford University Press, 1842), p. 11; Schäfer, *Jesus in the Talmud*, p. 151, n. 27.

163 Adolf Deissmann, 'Der Name Panthera', in Carl Bezold (ed.), *Orientalische Studien Theodor Nöldecke gewidmet* (Giessen: Töpelmann, 1906), pp. 871–5.

164 See also Tabor, *Jesus Dynasty*, pp. 70–8. Tabor regards the mentions of Pantera being Jesus' father as accurate and suggests that a tombstone found in 1879 near Bad Kreuznach, Germany, for one Tiberius Julius Abdes Pantera from Sidon, may indeed be his. Certainly, this tombstone does indicate that Pantera was a known name of Roman soldiers.

165 See above, this chapter, n. 4.

166 As well argued by James McGrath, 'Was Jesus Illegitimate? The Evidence of His Social Interactions', *JSHJ* 5 (2007): pp. 81–100; John D. Crossan, 'Virgin Mother or Bastard Child?', in Amy-Jill Levine (ed.), *A Feminist Companion to Mariology* (London: T&T Clark, 2005), pp. 37–55; Lincoln, *Born of a Virgin?*, pp. 81–3.

167 Schäfer, *Jesus in the Talmud*, p. 9. Christians who read Origen and perhaps also knew of these stories independently also reflected the accusation about Jesus' paternity in their own anti-Jewish storytelling. In the fourth century this is found in the portrayal of Jewish accusations indicated in the *Acts of Pilate*, namely that Jesus was born from an act of fornication (2:3). The appellation 'Pantera' relating to Jesus is noted by Epiphanius but attributed to Joseph's father Jacob, named *Panthēr*, and was thus a family name (*Pan.* 78:7:5). Later on, others, such as John of Damascus, suggested instead that Panthera was Mary's great-grandfather (*On the Orthodox Faith* 4:14). See Origen, *Contra Celsum*, ed. Chadwick, p. 31, n. 3. See also the medieval Jewish treatise *Sefer Toledot Yeshu*: Natalie E. Latteri, 'Playing the Whore: Illicit Union and the Biblical Typology of Promiscuity in the Toledot Yeshu Tradition', *Shofar* 33/2 (2015): pp. 87–102, at p. 89.

5 Born Jesus: Luke and beyond

1 But with a missing chunk: Mark 6:45 – 8:26.

2 Usually, the independent source is termed 'L'; see Burnett H. Streeter, *The Four Gospels: A study of origins* (London: Macmillan, 1924).

3 Austin M. Farrer, 'On Dispensing with Q', in Dennis E. Nineham (ed.), *Studies in the Gospels: Essays in memory of R. H. Lightfoot* (Oxford: Blackwell, 1955), pp. 55–88; Michael Goulder, 'Is Q a Juggernaut?', *JBL* 115 (1996): pp. 667–81; Mark Goodacre, *The Case against Q: Studies in Markan priority and the synoptic problem* (Harrisburg, PA: Trinity Press International, 2002); and see Andrew Lincoln, *Born of a Virgin? Reconceiving Jesus in the Bible, tradition and theology* (London: SCM Press, 2013), pp. 99–101.

4 Steve Mason, *Josephus and the New Testament* (Peabody, MA: Hendrickson, 1992).

5 Burton Mack, *Who Wrote the New Testament? The making of the Christian myth* (San Francisco, CA: HarperSanFrancisco, 1995), pp. 161–7.

6 Acts 16:10–17; 20:5–15; 21:1–18; 27:1 – 28:16.

7 For further discussion see Joan E. Taylor, 'Paul's Significant Other in the "We" Passages', in Craig A. Evans and Aaron W. White (eds), *Who Created Christianity? Fresh approaches to the relationship between Paul and Jesus* (Peabody, MA: Hendrickson, 2020), pp. 125–56.

8 On Cerdo, see Irenaeus, *Adv. Haer.* 1:27:1; 3:4:2–3; Hippolytus, *Ref.* 7:37:1; David W. Deakle, 'Harnack and Cerdo: A Reexamination of the Patristic Evidence for Marcion's Mentor', in Gerhard May and Katharina Greschat (eds), *Marcion und seine kirchengeschichtliche Wirkung/Marcion and His Impact on Church History: Vorträge der Internationalen Fachkonferenz zu Marcion, gehalten vom 15.–18. August 2001 in Mainz* (Berlin: De Gruyter, 2002), pp. 177–90. For Marcion see, *inter alia*, Justin, *Dial.* 35:6; Irenaeus, *Adv. Haer.* 1:27; 3:2–15; 4:8, 29–34; Tertullian, *Adv. Marc.*; Eusebius, *Hist. Eccles.* 4:10–12; Sebastian Moll, *The Arch-Heretic Marcion* (WUNT 250; Tübingen: Mohr Siebeck, 2010); Judith Lieu, *Marcion and the Making of a Heretic: God and Scripture in the second century* (Cambridge: Cambridge University Press, 2015).

9 John Knox, *Marcion and the New Testament* (Chicago, IL: University of Chicago Press, 1942), pp. 119–39; Joseph Tyson, *Marcion and Luke-Acts: A defining struggle* (Columbia, SC: University of South Carolina Press, 2006).

10 See the discussion in Jason BeDuhn, *The First New Testament: Marcion's scriptural canon* (Salem, OR: Polebridge, 2013). For the proposal that Marcion's gospel predated both Matthew and Luke, see Matthias Klinghardt, 'The Marcionite Gospel and the Synoptic Problem: A New Suggestion', *NT* 50 (2008): pp. 1–20; *The Oldest Gospel and the Formation of the Canonical Gospels* (Biblical Tools and Studies 41; Leuven: Peeters, 2021); Markus Vinzent, *Marcion and the Dating of the Synoptic Gospels* (Leuven: Peeters, 2013).

11 Tertullian, *Carn.* 1–2.

12 See Vincent Taylor, *Behind the Third Gospel: A study of the Proto-Luke hypothesis* (Oxford: Clarendon, 1926), pp. 164–6.

13 Raymond E. Brown, *The Birth of the Messiah: A commentary on the infancy narratives in Matthew and Luke*, rev. edn (New York, NY: Doubleday, 1993), pp. 239–40.

14 See Brown, *Birth*, pp. 33, 241–5.

15 Joseph B. Tyson, 'The Birth Narratives and the Beginning of Luke's Gospel',

Semeia 52 (1990): pp. 103–20, at p. 109. Tyson considers the narratives fitting for the beginning of canonical Luke, but not original.

16 See Annette Merz, 'Matthew's Star, Luke's Census, Bethlehem, and the Quest for the Historical Jesus', in Peter Barthel and George van Kooten (eds), *The Star of Bethlehem and the Magi: Interdisciplinary perspectives from experts on the Ancient Near East, the Greco-Roman world and modern astronomy* (Leiden: Brill, 2015), pp. 463–95, at pp. 485–6. See also Brown, *Birth*, pp. 415–16; Mina Monier, *Temple and Empire: The context of the temple piety of Luke–Acts* (Lanham, MD: Lexington, 2020), p. 74; Wilhelm Dittenberger, *Orientis Graeci Inscriptiones Selectae: Supplementum Sylloges Inscriptionum Graecarum* 2 (Leipzig: Hirzel, 1905), pp. 48–60.

17 *1 Clem.* 59:3 = Luke 1:52–3; *1 Clem.* 60:3 and Luke 1:71; and *1 Clem.* 61:3 and Luke 1:72. See Donald A. Hagner, *The Use of the Old and New Testaments in Clement of Rome* (Leiden: Brill, 1973), pp. 169–70.

18 Monier, *Temple and Empire*, p. 75.

19 Ultimately, Monier considers both the initial composition and the final redaction of Luke to be placed at this time.

20 Goodacre, *Case against Q*, pp. 56–7.

21 The details of this echoing are identified in Allan J. McNicol, David L. Dungan and David Barrett Peabody, *Beyond the Q Impasse: Luke's use of Matthew* (Valley Forge, PA: Trinity Press International, 1996), pp. 15–21, 47–70. For example, Luke 2:1–23, especially 2:7, 21, echoes Matt. 1:25 and Matt. 2:1–23; Luke 1:31 uses the term *tiktein* (Isa. 7:14 LXX), as does Matt. 1:21–3; the annunciation of Luke 1:39–56 echoes that to Joseph in Matt. 1:18–24.

22 Goodacre, *Case against Q*, p. 57; Lincoln, *Born of a Virgin?*, p. 130.

23 Lincoln, *Born of a Virgin?*, pp. 129–32.

24 Lincoln, *Born of a Virgin?*, p. 136. See also Brown, *Birth*, pp. 32–7.

25 Richard Bauckham (ed.), *The Gospels for All Christians: Rethinking the Gospel audiences* (Grand Rapids, MI: Eerdmans, 1998).

26 The recent work being done on the Gospel of John shows how the Fourth Gospel functions like this in relation to Mark. See the chapters in Eve-Marie Becker, Helen K. Bond and Catrin H. Williams (eds), *John's Transformation of Mark* (London: Bloomsbury, 2021).

27 Agostino Ciasca (ed.), *Tatiani Evangeliorum Harmoniae Arabice* (Rome: Propaganda Fide, 1888), which favours Vatican Arabo 14 (A), dating from the twelfth to thirteenth centuries, and, further, A. Sebastianus Marmardji, *Diatessaron de Tatien* (Beirut: Imprimerie Catholique, 1935).

28 Matthew R. Crawford, 'Reading the Diatessaron with Ephrem: The Word and the Light, the Voice and the Star', *VC* 69 (2015): pp. 70–95, at pp. 79–80.

29 I note now that this proposal has been mooted by Revd Dennis Folds, 'How Luke Re-Wrote Matthew's Nativity Story', on the Bart Ehrman blog: https://ehrmanblog. org/how-luke-rewrote-matthews-nativity-story-platinum-guest-post-by-dennis-j-folds (accessed 12 August 2024).

30 Brown, *Birth*, pp. 256–85, 367–92; Daniel Dapaah, *The Relationship between John the Baptist and Jesus of Nazareth* (Lanham, MD: University Press of America, 2005), pp. 37–64; Joan E. Taylor, *The Immerser: John the Baptist within Second Temple Judaism* (Grand Rapids, MI: Eerdmans, 1997), p. 9.

31 Taylor, *Immerser*, pp. 281–8.

32 Some have suggested that there is use of a nativity story of John the Baptist here; see Paul Winter, 'The Cultural Background for the Narratives in Luke I–II', *JQR* 45 (1954): pp. 159–67, 230–42; 'The Proto-Source of Luke 1', *NT* 1 (1956): pp. 184–99. However, if so, it has been much redacted for Christian use. See Taylor, *Immerser*, p. 9, n. 18.

33 Takamitsu Muraoka, *A Greek-English Lexicon of the Septuagint* (Louvain: Peeters, 2009), p. 206.

34 Muraoka, *A Greek-English Lexicon*, p. 220; BDAG 378–9.

35 Brown, *Birth*, pp. 290–2.

36 See for example J. M. R. Cormack, 'Dedications to Zeus Hypsistos in Beroea', *JRS* 31 (1941): pp. 19–23; Adam Lajtar, 'An Athenian Vow to Zeus Hypsistos', *ZPE* 70 (1980): pp. 165–6; Stephen Mitchell, 'Further Thoughts on the Cult of Theos Hypsistos', in Stephen Mitchell and P. van Nuffelen (eds), *One God: Pagan monotheism in the Roman Empire* (Cambridge: Cambridge University Press, 2010), pp. 167–207.

37 Alexander the Great was conceived after Apollo in the form of a serpent lay with Olympias, the wife of Philip of Macedon (Plutarch, *Alexander* 2, 3). Likewise, Augustus was held to have been conceived after Apollo in the form of a serpent came to his mother Atia (Suetonius, *Augustus* 94:4). Pythagoras was also held to be the son of Apollo (Iamblichus, *Vit. Pyth.* 2). For the Graeco-Roman biographies see Lincoln, *Born of a Virgin?*, pp. 57–67; Robert M. Miller, *Born Divine: The births of Jesus and other sons of God* (Santa Rosa, CA: Polebridge, 2003), pp. 140–50.

38 Robert M. Grant, *Gods and the One God* (Philadelphia, PA: Westminster, 1986), pp. 141–2.

39 It raises issues too about consent: Blake Hereth, 'Mary, Did You Consent?', *Religious Studies* 58 (2021): pp. 1–24.

40 Matthew's use of the term *polis* reflects Aramaic/Hebrew *qiryah*, 'a town', often translated as *polis* in the Septuagint: Muraoka, *A Greek-English Lexicon*, p. 471.

41 E. P. Sanders, *The Historical Figure of Jesus* (London: Allen Lane/Penguin, 1993), pp. 85–6.

42 See Mark D. Smith, 'Of Jesus and Quirinius', *CBQ* 62 (2000): pp. 278–93.

43 Smith, 'Jesus and Quirinius', p. 286.

44 Antipas: Luke 3:1, 19; 8:3; 9:7, 9; 23:7–8, 11–12, 15; Acts 4:27. Herod Agrippa: Acts 12:1, 6, 11, 19–21; 13:1; 23:35.

45 See proposals and the counter-arguments in Merz, 'Matthew's Star', pp. 479–87.

46 Ralph M. Novak, *Christianity and the Roman Empire: Background texts* (London: Continuum, 2001), pp. 293–8.

47 Edward Dąbrowa, 'The Date of the Census of Quirinius and the Chronology of the Governors of the Province of Syria', *ZPE* 178 (2011): pp. 137–42.

48 Merz, 'Matthew's Star', pp. 484–7.

49 Joseph A. Fitzmyer, *The Gospel According to Luke I–IX* (Anchor Bible Commentary; New York, NY: Doubleday, 1981), p. 394; Monier, *Temple and Empire*, p. 74.

50 Taylor, *Immerser*, pp. 255–8.

51 Monier, *Temple and Empire*, p. 74.

52 The story may draw from 1 Sam. 1:22–4, where Hannah, the mother of Samuel, goes to the house of the Lord in Shiloh; see Fitzmyer, *Luke I–IX*, p. 422.

53 See E. P. Sanders, *Judaism: Practice and belief 63 BCE to 66 CE* (London: SCM Press, 1992), p. 151; and Num. 18:15. Matthew Thiessen, 'Luke 2:22, Leviticus 12, and Parturient Impurity', *NT* 54 (2012): pp. 16–29, suggests that this double impurity was known at the time, at least in sectarian circles of *Jubilees* and 4Q265, though he does concede that 4Q266 strongly indicates it is the mother who pays the tax.

54 The initial text was previously defined by Émile de Strycker, *La forme la plus ancienne du Protévangile de Jacques: Recherches sur le Papyrus Bodmer 5 avec une édition critique du texte grec et une traduction annotée* (Brussels: Société des Bollandistes, 1961). The Papyrus Bodmer 5, put together from fragments found in Nag Hammadi in Egypt (see Michel Testuz (ed.), *Papyrus Bodmer V: Nativité de Marie* (Cologny-Genève: Bibliotheca Bodmeriana, 1958)), was thought of as a later adaptation. However, this argument has now been overturned: see George T. Zervos, *The Protevangelium of James: Critical questions of the text and full collations of the Greek manuscripts*, 2 vols (London: Bloomsbury T&T Clark, 2019, 2022), vol. 2, pp. 1–29.

55 Mark Goodacre, 'The *Protevangelium of James* and the Creative Rewriting of *Matthew* and *Luke*', in Francis Watson and Sarah Parkhouse (eds), *Connecting Gospels: Beyond the canonical/non-canonical divide* (Oxford: Oxford University Press, 2018), pp. 57–76, at p. 57.

56 Goodacre, *Protevangelium*, p. 60.

57 For discussion on the titling, attribution and genre of this work see Kimberley A. Fowler, 'The *Protevangelium of James* in Papyrus Bodmer V: Titles, Genres, and Traditions in Transmission', *Religions* 14/636 (2023): https://doi.org/10.3390/rel14050636.

58 John Painter, *Just James: The brother of Jesus in history and tradition*, 2nd edn (Columbia, SC: University of South Carolina Press, 2004), pp. 198–9. The work is likely the one referred to as the 'Book of James' by Origen (*Comm. Matt.* 10:17) in the early third century, when he mentions it as showing that James was the son of Joseph by a previous marriage and as demonstrating the perpetual virginity of Mary. This may nevertheless refer to the *Revelation of James* rather than the *Protevangelium* as we have it.

59 Jan N. Bremmer, 'Author, Date and Provenance of the Protevangelium of James', in Jan N. Bremmer, J. Andrew Doole, Thomas R. Karmann, Tobias Nicklas and Boris Repschinski (eds), *The Protevangelium of James* (Studies on Early Christian Apocrypha 16; Leuven: Peeters, 2020), pp. 49–70.

60 See Bart D. Ehrman and Zlatko Pleše, *The Apocryphal Gospels: Texts and translations* (New York, NY: Oxford University Press, 2011), pp. 33–4.

61 Certain Semitic elements of the *Protevangelium* as a whole have been noted; see Zervos, *Protevangelium*, vol. 2, pp. 6–7, who writes: 'An analysis of the Semitic elements in the *ProtJac* would merit a lengthy commentary of its own which is well beyond the scope of this publication and the expertise of this writer. With this publication I hope to serve future research into the text of the *ProtJac* focusing on the pristine text of *P.Bodm* V and thus preserving the inherent Jewish conceptual and linguistic character of its earliest strata. It is precisely this character that appears to have been diluted by the generations of editors and copyists throughout two millennia who attempted to "correct" what they perceived to have been the deficiencies of the scribe who wrote *P.Bodm* V. Modern editors of the Greek text of the *ProtJac*, most especially de Strycker, amplified this dilution and injected considerable confusion into the already difficult task of reconstituting the original text of the *ProtJac* and of detecting its underlying sources and the evidence of redactional activity that still survives in its text.'

62 See Ehrman and Pleše, *Apocryphal Gospels*, pp. 34–5.

63 Goodacre, *Protevangelium*, pp. 61–2.

64 Goodacre, *Protevangelium*, p. 63. The latter story requires a weaving in of the murder of Zechariah son of Berechiah (Zech. 1:1).

65 Goodacre, *Protevangelium*, p. 63.

66 Goodacre, *Protevangelium*, p. 64.

67 Goodacre, *Protevangelium*, pp. 65–6.

68 This is to follow the Papyrus Bodmer 5. Note that in the majority Greek manuscript tradition the angel asks her *not* to proclaim what she has seen. This proscription in the modified text tallies with the later suppression of women's leadership in churches; see Helen Bond and Joan Taylor, *Women Remembered: Jesus' female disciples* (London: Hodder & Stoughton, 2022), pp. 177–84.

69 Goodacre, *Protevangelium*, notes here (p. 70) that this kind of repetition is also LXX style (e.g. Gen. 22:11; 46:2).

70 Leslie W. Barnard, *Justin Martyr: His life and thought* (Cambridge: Cambridge University Press, pp. 1969), pp. 19–23.

71 The cave for Justin is interpreted using Isa. 33:16, where it was indicated that 'the righteous king' would dwell 'in a cave of mighty rock' (LXX).

72 Gustaf Dalman, *Sacred Sites and Ways: Studies in the topography of the Gospels*, tr. P. P. Levertoff (London: SPCK, 1935), p. 40; Joan E. Taylor, *Christians and the Holy Places: The myth of Jewish-Christian origins* (Oxford: Clarendon, 1993), p. 100.

73 Jacob Neusner, *What Is Midrash?* (Eugene, OR: Wipf & Stock, 2014); Édouard Cothenet, 'Le Protévangile de Jacques: Origine, genre et signification d'un premier midrash chrétien sur la nativité de Marie', *ANRW* 25.6 (1988), pp. 4252–69.

74 Henry Chadwick, *Origen: Contra Celsum* (Cambridge: Cambridge University Press, 1953), pp. 47–8 (italics mine).

75 Origen, *Comm. Matt.* 10:17.

76 See Taylor, *Christians and the Holy Places*, pp. 105–6.

77 Eusebius, *Vita Const.* 3:42–4; Bordeaux Pilgrim, *Itin.* 598; Egeria, *Itin.* 42; Epiphanius, *Pan.* 51:9; 78:15; Socrates, *Hist. Eccles.* 1:17; Sozomen, *Hist. Eccles.* 2:2; Jerome, *Ep.* 108:10.2–3; Eucherius, *Ep. Faust.* 11; Piacenza Pilgrim, *Itin.* 29.

78 See also Andrew Madden, 'A Revised Date for the Mosaic Pavements of the Church of the Nativity, Bethlehem', *Ancient West & East* 11 (2012): pp. 147–90; Bellarmino Bagatti, *Gli antichi edifici sacri di Betlemme* (Jerusalem: Franciscan Printing Press, 1952); Clemens Kopp, *The Holy Places of the Gospels*, tr. Ronald Walls (New York, NY: Herder & Herder, 1963); Robert Weir Schultz (ed.), *The Church of the Nativity at Bethlehem* (London: Byzantine Research Fund / B. T. Batsford, 1910); Edmund Weigand, *Die Geburtskirche von Bethlehem: Eine Untersuchung zur christlichen Antike* (Leipzig: Dieterich, 1911).

79 Jerome refers to the cave also in *Ep.* 147:4.

80 See Chapter 3.

81 For further discussion see Taylor, *Christians and the Holy Places*, pp. 96–112.

82 See Ehrman and Pleše, *Apocryphal Gospels*, pp. 64, 66. For other influences of the

apocryphal gospels on Christian pilgrimage see Tobias Nicklas, 'Beyond "Canon": Christian Apocrypha and Pilgrimage', in Tobias Nicklas, Candida R. Moss, Christopher M. Tuckett and Joseph Verheyden (eds), *The Other Side: Apocryphal perspectives on ancient Christian 'orthodoxies'* (Göttingen: Vandenhoeck & Ruprecht, 2017), pp. 23–38.

83 The story is told in the seventh-to-eighth-century *Gospel of Pseudo-Matthew*, which collects these stories: here the ox and the ass miraculously fall to their knees and worship the infant, along with the biblical shepherds, star, angels and magi (13:6 – 17:2). They already appear in nativity scenes in fourth-to sixth-century Christian art: David R. Cartlidge and J. Keith Elliott, *Art and the Christian Apocrypha* (London: Routledge, 2001), pp. 19, 87, 91.

84 Dalman, *Sacred Sites and Ways*, pp. 4–41.

85 See Brown, *Birth*, pp. 400–1.

86 Dalman, *Sacred Sites and Ways*, p. 42.

87 Hanan Eshel and David Amit, *Refuge Caves of the Bar Kokhba Revolt*, vol. 1 (Jerusalem: Israel Excavation Society, 1998) (Hebrew); Hanan Eshel and Roi Porat, *Refuge Caves of the Bar Kokhba Revolt*, vol. 2 (Jerusalem: Israel Excavation Society, 2009) (Hebrew).

88 The Christmas Cave was identified by John Allegro and Howard Stutchbury on Christmas Day 1960 and excavated by a British team under a Jordanian licence from 1961 to 1963: Kaare Lund Rasmussen, Johannes van der Plicht, Ilaria Degano, Francesca Modugno, Maria Perla Colombini, Guillermo de la Fuente, Thomas Delbey, Amos Frumkin, Uri Davidovich, Roi Porat, Orit Shamir, Naama Sukenik, Greg Doudna, Joan Taylor and Mladen Popović, 'Defining Multiple Inhabitations of a Cave Environment Using Interdisciplinary Archaeometry: The "Christmas Cave" of the Wadi en-Nar/Nahal Qidron, West of the Dead Sea', *Heritage Science* 22/18 (2018): https://doi.org/10.1186/s40494-022-00652-2.

89 Thermoluminescence study of sample KLR 8861 provided a date range of 234 BCE – 50 CE, KLR 8862 yielded 296 BCE – 6 CE, and KLR 8863 yielded 456–92 CE at 1sigma probability (68%); see Rasmussen et al., 'Defining Multiple Inhabitations', p. 8.

90 Joan E. Taylor, 'Babatha's Sisters: Judaean Women Refugees in the Cave of Letters and the Christmas Cave', *Strata: Journal of the Anglo-Israel Archaeological Society* 39 (2021): pp. 35–68.

6 Refugee: into Egypt

1 Robert J. Myles, *The Homeless Jesus in the Gospel of Matthew* (Sheffield: Sheffield Phoenix, 2014), p. 63.

2 See Myles, *Homeless*, pp. 52–5, 62–9.

3 Margaretha M. Wilcke, 'Reconstructing Identity', *Journal of Immigrant & Refugee Studies* 4/2 (2006): pp. 31–47.

4 Max Zettl, Zeynep Akin, Sarah Back, Svenja Taubner, Kirstin Goth, Catharina Zehetmair, Christoph Nikendei, Katja Bertsch, 'Identity Development and Maladaptive Personality Traits in Young Refugees and First- and Second-Generation Migrants', *Frontiers in Psychiatry* 12 (2022), art. 798152: https://doi.org/10.3389/fpsyt.2021.798152.

5 *Ant.* 1:94, 159; 7:101; 12:126–7; 13:250–2; 14:9; 16:183–6. See Ben Zion Wacholder, 'Josephus and Nicolaus of Damascus', in Louis H. Feldman and Gohei Hata (eds), *Josephus, the Bible, and History* (Leiden: Brill, 1989), pp. 147–72; Mark Toher, 'Herod, Augustus and Nicolaus of Damascus', in David M. Jacobson and Nikos Kokkinos, *Herod and Augustus: Papers presented to the IJS Conference, 21st–23rd June, 2005* (Leiden: Brill, 2009), pp. 65–81; Sarah Christine Teets, 'Χαριζομενος Ἡρωδηι: Josephus' Nicolaus of Damascus in the *Judaean Antiquities*', *Histos* 7 (2013): pp. 88–127.

6 For further discussion see Julia Wilker, 'Modelling the Emperor: Representations of Power, Empire, and Dynasty among Eastern Client Kings', in Amy Russell and Monica Hellström (eds), *The Social Dynamics of Imperial Imagery* (Cambridge: Cambridge University Press, 2020), pp. 52–75; David F. Graf, 'The "Client Kings" of Judaea and Nabataea in the 1st Century BCE', *Strata: Journal of the Anglo-Israel Archaeological Society* 40 (2022): pp. 39–100, esp. pp. 41–63; Graf (pp. 40–1) provides a strong defence of the terminology of 'client kings', which is adopted here.

7 See Samuel Rocca, *Herod's Judaea* (Texts and Studies in Ancient Judaism 122; Tübingen: Mohr Siebeck, 2008), pp. 266–7.

8 For the following summary, see discussions in Emil Schürer, *The History of the Jewish People in the Age of Jesus Christ (175 B.C.–A.D. 135)*, vol. 1, rev. and ed. Geza Vermes, Fergus Millar and Matthew Black (Edinburgh: T&T Clark, 1973, pp. 287–32; A. H. M. Jones, *The Herods of Judaea* (Oxford: Clarendon, 1938), pp. 111–55; Peter Richardson and Amy Marie Fisher, *Herod: King of the Jews and friend of the Romans*, 2nd edn (London: Routledge, 2020), pp. 15–36; Ariyeh Kasher with Eliezer Witztum, *King Herod: The persecuted persecutor*, tr. Karen Gold (Berlin: De Gruyter, 2007), pp. 281–404; Martin Goodman, *Herod the Great: Jewish king in a Roman world* (New Haven, CT: Yale University Press, 2024), pp. 116–58; Ernst Baltrusch, *Herodes: König im heiligen Land: Ein Biographie* (Munich: C. H. Beck, 2012). There has been some attempt to rehabilitate Herod, as in the popular work of Geza Vermes, *The True Herod* (London: Bloomsbury

T&T Clark, 2014); or Norman Gelb, *Herod the Great: Statesman, visionary, tyrant* (Lanham, MD: Rowman & Littlefield, 2013); Gelb sees him as effective in Roman terms.

9 For the way Herod involved the Roman imperial authorities in decision-making, see Kimberley Czajkowski, 'Justice in Client Kingdoms: The Many Trials of Herod's Sons', *Historia: Zeitschrift für Alte Geschichte* 65 (2016): pp. 473–96.

10 See above and also Kasher, *Herod*, pp. 281–5.

11 Throughout the narrative, likely taken from Nicolaus, Josephus records the activities and woes of various senior women at court; see Tal Ilan, *Integrating Women into Second Temple History* (Tübingen: Mohr Siebeck, 1999), pp. 97–125. While these instances give us rare glimpses into women's lives, by their inclusion Herod is presented as weak in not managing the women of his house well; see Helen Bond, 'Josephus on Herod's Domestic Intrigue in the "Jewish War"', *JSJ* 43 (2012): pp. 295–314.

12 Ilan, *Integrating Women*, pp. 23–5.

13 Nikos Kokkinos, 'The Royal Court of the Herods', in *The World of the Herods, Vol. 1 of the International Conference 'The World of the Herods and the Nabataeans', British Museum 17–19 April 2002* (Stuttgart: Steiner, 2007), pp. 279–303; Rocca, *Herod's Judaea*, pp. 72–96.

14 Eyal Regev, 'Inside Herod's Courts: Social Relations and Royal Ideology in the Herodian Palaces', *JSJ* 43 (2012): pp. 180–214, at p. 210. There is some question about whether this final development was the work of his son Archelaus, however; see p. 200.

15 He was Roman legate from 6 to 4 BCE.

16 The tomb of Antipater may have been found by a British expedition in 1960. A tomb monument (*nefesh*) was found on the south-west side of Khirbet el-Mird, ancient Hyrcania. It was a square structure with a base 10 m wide and was able to be dated by Herodian sherds. See G. R. H. [Mick] Wright, 'The Archaeological Remains at El Mird in the Wilderness of Judaea', *Biblica* 48 (1961): pp. 1–21, at pp. 14–16.

17 Myles, *Homeless*, p. 63.

18 See above, pp. 68–9.

19 Ariyeh Kasher, *The Jews in Hellenistic and Roman Egypt: The struggle for equal rights* (Texts and Studies in Ancient Judaism 7; Tübingen: Mohr Siebeck, 1985); William Horbury and David Noy, *Jewish Inscriptions of Graeco-Roman Egypt, with an Index of the Jewish Inscriptions of Egypt and Cyrenaica* (Cambridge: Cambridge University Press, 1992); Joseph Mélèze-Modrzejewski, *The Jews of Egypt: From Rameses II to Emperor Hadrian*, tr. Robert Cornman (Princeton, NJ: Princeton

University Press, 1997); Nathalie LaCoste, *Waters of the Exodus: Jewish experiences with water in Ptolemaic and Roman Egypt* (Leiden: Brill, 2018), pp. 25–59.

20 See also Philo, *Flacc.* 8; Josephus, *War* 2:494–8; *Apion* 1:33–5.

21 See also Josephus, *Ant.* 13:353–64; cf. *War* 1:33; 7:421–36; *Ant.* 13:62–73; *Apion* 2:49–56.

22 For example, in 55 BCE the Jewish militia aided Ptolemy XII Auletes and the Roman commander Gabinius (*War* 1:175; *Ant.* 14:98–9). They supported Caesar in 48 BCE (*War* 1:187; *Ant.* 14:127–32) and gained privileges as a result (*Ant.* 14:188–9; *Apion* 2:37). They supported Augustus against Cleopatra VII (*Apion* 2:60) and again gained privileges (Philo, *Flacc.* 50; 74; Josephus, *Ant.* 14:188).

23 Kasher, *Jews in Hellenistic and Roman Egypt*, p. 62.

24 See Philo, *Flacc.*; *Legat.*; Josephus, *War* 2:487–98; *Ant.* 18:257–60. For further discussion on the Jews of Alexandria and Egypt more broadly, see Kasher, *Jews in Hellenistic and Roman Egypt*; John M. G. Barclay, *Jews in the Mediterranean Diaspora: From Alexander to Trajan (323 BCE – 117 CE)* (Edinburgh: T&T Clark, 1996), pp. 19–81; Mary Smallwood, *The Jews under Roman Rule from Pompey to Diocletian: A study in political relations* (Leiden: Brill, 1981), pp. 220–55.

25 Philo's reference to the expected one of Num. 24:7 (*Praem.* 95–7) indicates there would be a future ruler who would put under his hand 'great and populous nations' by means of his forces, which included swarms of wasps (see Exod. 23:28; Deut. 7:20).

26 H. I. Bell, 'Alexandria ad Aegyptum', *JRS* 36 (1946): pp. 130–3.

27 Joan E. Taylor, 'A Second Temple in Egypt: The Evidence for the Zadokite Temple of Onias', *JSJ* 29 (1998): pp. 297–321; Mélèze-Modrzejewski, *Jews of Egypt*, pp. 124–33.

28 See Myles, *Homeless*, p. 66.

29 Naphtali Lewis, 'A Reversal of Tax Policy in Roman Egypt', *Greek, Roman, and Byzantine Studies* 34 (1993): pp. 101–18, at p. 102, n. 2: 'the overwhelming evidence of the Papyri' defines the word *anachōrēsis* as 'essentially resulting from economic ruin or distress'.

30 Robert Myles, 'Echoes of Displacement in Matthew's Genealogy of Jesus', *Colloquium* 45/1 (2013), pp. 31–41, at p. 33; and see Myles, *Homeless*, pp. 66–9.

31 Myles, 'Echoes of Displacement', pp. 36–8; *Homeless*, pp. 58–60.

32 Myles, 'Echoes of Displacement', p. 41.

33 See the Babylonian Talmud, *b.Shabb.* 104b; *b.Sanh.* 107b; Morton Smith, *Jesus the Magician* (New York, NY: Barnes & Noble, 1993), pp. 47–8, 58–9, 67.

34 See Stephen J. Davis, 'Ancient Sources for the Coptic Tradition', in Stephen J. Davis, William Lyster, Cornelis Hulsman and Gawdat Gabra (eds), *Be Thou*

There: The holy family's journey in Egypt (Cairo: Cairo University Press, 2001), pp. 133–62, at p. 137, and see p. 156, n. 4, concerning the textual issues.

35 Davis, Lyster, Hulsman and Gabra (eds), *Be Thou There*; Anne Boud'hors and Ramez Boutros, 'La sainte famille à Gabal al-Tayr et l'homélie du Rocher', in Nathalie Bosson (ed.), *Études coptes VII: Actes de la neuvième journée d'études coptes. Montpelier 3–4 juin 1999* (Cahiers de la Bibliothèque Copte 12; Louvain: Peeters, 2000), pp. 59–76; and also Tony Burke, 'Christian Apocrypha and Pilgrimage, Part 2' (7 November 2017): https://www.apocryphicity.ca/2017/11/07/ christian-apocrypha-and-pilgrimage-part-2 (accessed 13 August 2024); Tony Burke, 'Traveling with Children: Flight Stories and Pilgrimage Routes in the Apocryphal Infancy Gospels', in Sharon Betsworth and Julie Faith Parker (eds), *T&T Clark Handbook of Children in the Bible and the Biblical World* (London: Bloomsbury T&T Clark, 2019), pp. 379–97.

36 Actually to the Apa Apolla monastery of Bawit, near Hermopolis.

37 As in the translation of Rufinus's Latin text by Andrew Cain, *Rufinus of Aquileia, Inquiry about the Monks in Egypt* (The Fathers of the Church 139; Washington, DC: Catholic University of America Press, 2019), p. 103. For the Greek edition, André J. Festugière, *Historia monachorum in Aegypto: Édition critique du texte grec et traduction annotée* (Brussels: Société des Bollandistes, 1961), p. 47.

38 Davis, 'Ancient Sources', pp. 138–40.

39 Davis, 'Ancient Sources', pp. 140–1.

40 Horbury and Noy, *Jewish Inscriptions*, nos 155–6, appendix 3, pp. 247–50.

41 Reading *epi tēs Ioudaikēs lauras*, and see LaCoste, *Waters of the Exodus*, pp. 34, 63.

7 Return: a time of hope

1 1 Kgs 5:2.

2 Raymond E. Brown, *The Birth of the Messiah: A commentary on the infancy narratives in Matthew and Luke* (New York, NY: Doubleday 1993), p. 109.

3 For the biblical concept see Harry M. Orlinsky, 'The Biblical Concept of the Land of Israel: Cornerstone of the Covenant between God and Israel', in Lawrence A. Hoffman (ed.), *The Land of Israel: Jewish perspectives* (Notre Dame, IN: University of Notre Dame Press, 1986), pp. 27–64. It may be that in the second century BCE the Hasmonean dynasty took this concept as a model that justified the expansion of Judaea, including through the area of Samaria held by people who claimed to be Israelites; see Doron Mendels, *The Land of Israel as a Political Concept in Hasmonean Literature: Recourse to history in second century B.C. claims to the Holy Land* (Tübingen: Mohr Siebeck, 1987); however, see Katell Berthelot, *In Search of the Promised Land? The Hasmonean dynasty between biblical models*

and Hellenistic diplomacy, tr. Margaret Rigaud (Journal of Ancient Judaism Supplements 24; Göttingen: Vandenhoeck & Ruprecht, 2018); 'Reclaiming the Land (1 Maccabees 15:28–36): Hasmonean Discourse between Biblical Tradition and Seleucid Rhetoric', *JBL* 133 (2014): pp. 539–59.

4 Simcha Fishbane, '"The Land of Israel Is Holier Than All Lands": Diaspora in Mishnah's Cosmos – the Message', in Simcha Fishbane, Calvin Goldscheider and Jack N. Lightstone (eds), *Exploring Mishnah's World(s): Social scientific approaches* (New York, NY: Palgrave Macmillan, 2020), pp. 63–94, esp. pp. 71–7; Richard S. Sarason, 'The Significance of the Land of Israel in Mishnah', in Hoffman (ed.), *The Land of Israel*, pp. 109–36.

5 Josephus uses instead 'the land of the Israelites': *tēn tōn Israēlitōn gēn* (*Ant.* 8:204; 9:253).

6 Brown, *Birth*, p. 206.

7 *RPC* 1:678, no. 4901. On the Dioscuri symbolism see David M. Jacobson, 'Herod the Great, Augustus Caesar and Herod's "Year 3" Coins', *Strata: Journal of the Anglo-Israel Archaeological Society* 33 (2015): pp. 89–118, at pp. 94–6; David M. Jacobson, 'An Act of Homage to Herod the Great on His Largest Coin', *Strata: Journal of the Anglo-Israel Archaeological Society* 40 (2022): pp. 101–21; Birte Poulsen, 'The Dioscuri and Ruler Ideology', *Symbolae Osloenses* 66 (1991), pp. 119–46; Wolf Wirgin, 'Notes', *IEJ* 11 (1961): pp. 151–4, suggested there may be an idea of Herod being in some way a saviour in choosing this motif.

8 Jodi Magness, 'Herod the Great's Self-Representation through His Tomb at Herodium', *JAJ* 10 (2019): pp. 258–87, at p. 282. Type *RPC* 1, no. 4905, and some types of 4906.

9 *RPC* 1, no. 4907.

10 Ya'akov Meshorer, *A Treasury of Jewish Coins from the Persian Period* (Jerusalem: Yad Ben-Zvi Press, 2001), pp. 65–6. Jacobson thinks the *chi* is just a simplified form of the crossing over of the two palm branches, and that it was Herod's monogram. He rightly notes that palm branches feature on Herod's coinage and there is also the association with a starred *pilos* cap, and thus to the Dioscuri, to connect Herod with heroism. Jacobson also notes that the filleted palm which appears on some of Herod's coins is a symbol of victory: David M. Jacobson, 'Herod the Great's Royal Monogram', *Israel Numismatic Research* 9 (2014): pp. 95–101, at p. 98.

11 Gerhard von Rad, 'The Royal Ritual in Judah', in Gerhard von Rad, *The Problem of the Hexateuch and Other Essays*, tr. E. W. Trueman (London: SCM Press, 1967), pp. 222–31.

12 See discussion also in Joan E. Taylor, *The Essenes, the Scrolls and the Dead Sea*

(Oxford: Oxford University Press, 2012), pp. 192–3, regarding *b.Hag.* 16b. and *j.Hag.* 2:2 (77d).

13 Taylor, *Essenes, Scrolls and Dead Sea*, pp. 92–4.

14 *War* 1:331–2, 340–1; *Ant.* 14:454–5; 462–3; see Kimberley Czajkowski and Benedikt Eckhardt, *Herod in History: Nicolaus of Damascus and the Augustan context* (Oxford: Oxford University Press, 2021), p. 42.

15 Regarding the bath attack, some historians consider that 'the historicity of this encounter is highly doubtful' (Czajkowski and Eckhardt, *Herod in History*, p. 44). However, they do acknowledge this and other aspects of Nicolaus's telling of Herod's story as indicating a narrative of divine support for Herod (pp. 42–7).

16 Once Herod becomes king, he sends for Menahem and asks him about how long he will reign (*Ant.* 13:377–8). After a silence, Menahem states that he might rule for twenty or thirty years, but he would not provide him with an end to the appointed time.

17 Taylor, *Essenes, Scrolls and Dead Sea*, p. 199.

18 See Joan E. Taylor, 'Pharisees, Sadducees and Essenes in Josephus's Writings', in Kenneth Atkinson (ed.), *The Oxford Handbook of Josephus* (Oxford: Oxford University Press, 2024) (forthcoming)..

19 David E. Aune, *Prophecy in Early Christianity and the Ancient Mediterranean World* (Grand Rapids, MI: Eerdmans, 1983), pp. 140–1, lists Gen. 49:10; Dan. 7:13–14; 9:24–7; Num. 24:17.

20 Joseph Blenkinsopp, 'The Oracle of Judah and the Messianic Entry', *JBL* 80 (1961): pp. 55–64, at p. 61.

21 For detailed analysis see Raymond de Hoop, *Genesis 49 in Its Literary and Historical Context* (Leiden: Brill, 1999), pp. 114–48. Gen. 49:10 was probably used by the Hasmoneans to justify their rule as kings, even though they were not Davidic, since the 'Aramaic Levi Document' among the Dead Sea Scrolls states that kingship is not limited to the tribe of Judah (Gen. 49:10; 1Q21 7:2; 4Q213 2 10–18) and that 'the kingdom of priesthood is greater than the kingdom' (1Q21 1); see James Kugel, 'How Old Is the "Aramaic Levi Document"?', *DSD* 14 (2007): pp. 291–312, at p. 295.

22 De Hoop, *Genesis 49*, p. 122, points out that this reading of the LXX presumes a Hebrew text interpreted as '[that] which is for him', possibly validated by Ezek. 21:32.

23 See Moshe J. Bernstein, '4Q252: From Re-written Bible to Biblical Commentary', *JJS* 45 (1994): pp. 1–27; Joseph L. Trafton, 'Commentary on Genesis (4Q252)', in James H. Charlesworth (ed.), *The Dead Sea Scrolls, vol. 6b: Pesharim, Other Commentaries, and Related Documents* (Princeton Theological Seminary Dead

Sea Scrolls Project; Louisville, KY: Westminster John Knox, 2002), pp. 203–19; Daniel K. Falk, *Parabiblical Texts: Strategies for extending the Scriptures among the Dead Sea Scrolls* (London: Bloomsbury T&T Clark, 2007); George Brooke, 'The Thematic Content of 4Q252', *JQR* 85 (1994): pp. 33–59.

24 See also George Brooke, 'The Deuteronomic Character of 4Q252', in John C. Reeves and John Kampen (eds), *Pursuing the Text: Studies in honor of Ben Zion Wacholder on the occasion of his seventieth birthday* (Sheffield: Sheffield Academic Press, 1994), pp. 121–35, at p. 129.

25 The interpretation of 'Shiloh' as indicating the expected eschatological Messiah is found also in the *Targum Onqelos* and *Yerushalmi* translations of Gen. 49:10. For the later interpretations, see de Hoop, *Genesis 49*, pp. 122–4, 129–30.

26 Though Schwartz has read this as referring to the departure from Judah of the monarchic line from the house of David: Daniel Schwartz, 'The Messianic Departure from Judah (4Q Patriarchal Blessings)', *TZ* 37 (1981): pp. 257–66.

27 See Tacitus, *Hist.* 1:10; 5:13; Suetonius, *Vesp.* 4–5; Cassius Dio, *Hist. Rom.* 66:1.

28 Centuries later, Christian scholars thought the 'Herodians' were people who believed that Herod was the Messiah. In the third century, Pseudo-Tertullian (*Adv. Omn. Haer.* 1:1) talks of 'the Herodians who declared Herod to be the Messiah'. Jerome (*Adv. Lucifer.* 23) states that the *Herodiani* were people who assumed King Herod to be Christ (*Herodem regem suscepere pro Christo*). Epiphanius, in his description of the Herodians, has a further messianic supposition (*Pan.* 20:1–2): the Herodians, who believed 'that Herod was Christ, thought that the Christ awaited in all scriptures of the Law and prophets was Herod himself, and were proud of Herod because they were deceived in him'. This misconception likely stems from not quite understanding the nuances of the Essene prediction. For further discussion see Harold H. Rowley, 'Notes and Studies: The Herodians in the Gospels', *JTS* 161 (1940): pp. 14–27, and also Taylor, *Essenes, Scrolls and Dead Sea*, pp. 109–30.

29 Ituraea and Trachonitis was a large non-Jewish area between the Sea of Galilee and northern Nabataea (see Chapter 1, Fig. 1.1).

30 Emil Schürer, *The History of the Jewish People in the Age of Jesus Christ (175 B.C.–A.D. 135)*, vol. 1, rev. and ed. Geza Vermes, Fergus Millar and Matthew Black (Edinburgh: T&T Clark, 1973), pp. 565–7.

31 Jacobson, 'Herod the Great', pp. 105–6, building on Mordechai Narkiss, 'Notes on the Coins of the Herodian Dynasty', *Bulletin of the Jewish Palestine Exploration Society* 1/4 (1934): pp. 8–14 (Hebrew).

32 This presence accounts for how it could be considered a century later to be an area of both Jews and Syrians (*War* 3:57).

33 *Iulius Africanus Chronographiae: The extant fragments*, ed. Martin Wallraff
with Umberto Roberto and Karl Pinggéra, tr. William Adler (Die griechischen
christlichen Schriftsteller der ersten Jahrhunderte, NF 15; Berlin: De Gruyter,
2007), pp. 258–63.

34 For Africanus, of course, this was proven by the arrival of Jesus at this time.

35 See, however, the discussion by Eliezer Paltiel, 'War in Judaea – after Herod's
Death', *Revue belge de philologie et d'histoire* 59 (1981): pp. 107–36; Fausto Parente,
'Flavius Josephus' Account of the Anti-Roman Riots Preceding the 66–70 War,
and Its Relevance for the Reconstruction of Jewish Eschatology during the
First Century A.D.', *JANES* 16–17 (1984–85): pp. 183–205; Nikos Kokkinos, *The
Herodian Dynasty: Origins, role in society and eclipse* (Journal for the Study of the
Pseudepigrapha Supplement 30; Sheffield: Sheffield Academic Press, 1998), pp.
226–9; and Julia Wilker, *Für Rom und Jerusalem: Die herodianische Dynastie im 1.
Jahrhundert n. Chr.* (Frankfurt am Main: Verlag Antike, 2007), pp. 68–76.

36 Schürer, *History*, ed. Vermes, Millar and Black, vol. 1, p. 328.

37 See Steve Mason, *Flavius Josephus: Translation and commentary, vol. 1b: Judean
War 2* (Leiden: Brill, 2009), pp. 7–8.

38 Mason, *Judean War 2*, pp. 8–12. Josephus claims that in 65 CE there were 3
million people present: *War* 2:280.

39 Mason, *Judean War 2*, pp. 12–14.

40 See Kokkinos, *Herodian Dynasty*, pp. 177–92.

41 For further details on Varus, see Hanan Eshel, 'Publius Quinctilius Varus in
Jewish Sources', *JJS* 59 (2008): pp. 112–19.

42 This means he left only one legion behind in Antioch. As legate, he commanded
four legions stationed there: the III Gallica, VI Ferrata, X Fretensis and XII
Fulminata.

43 Mason, *Judean War 2*, pp. 15–28.

44 Mason, *Judean War 2*, pp. 30–4.

45 The Sebasteni appear dedicated to the emperor. In Greek, the term *Sebastē*
corresponds to Latin *Augustus*. Herod had built the city of Sebaste in Samaria as
a special honour for Augustus. The regiment appears in Acts 27:1. For further
details see Michael P. Speidel, 'The Roman Army in Judaea under the Procurators:
The Italian and the Augustan Cohort in the Acts of the Apostles', *Ancient Society*
13/14 (1982): pp. 233–40, esp. pp. 233–5.

46 Mason, *Judean War 2*, pp. 34–7.

47 For these examples see Hanan Eshel and Boaz Zissu, *The Bar Kokhba Revolt: The
archaeological evidence* (Jerusalem: Israel Exploration Society/Yad Izhak Ben-Zvi,
2019), pp. 101–5, 122–38.

48 See Luke 19:14.

49 This was next to the palace of Augustus on the Palatine Hill.

50 Mason, *Judean War 2*, pp. 54–62.

51 Mason, *Judean War 2*, pp. 62–5.

52 See Schürer, *History*, vol. 1, pp. 330–5; Richard Horsley with John S. Hanson, *Bandits, Prophets and Messiahs: Popular movements in the time of Jesus* (Harrisburg, PA: Trinity Press International, 1985), pp. 112–17.

53 See David M. Rhoads, *Israel in Revolution, 6–74 CE: A political history based on the writings of Josephus* (Philadelphia, PA: Fortress, 1976), p. 50; Richard Horsley, *Galilee: History, politics, people* (Harrisburg, PA: Trinity Press International, 1995), pp. 256–75.

54 The arsenal, however, has not been clearly defined, as the building once identified as a fort is no longer assumed to be such; see Eric M. Meyers, Carol L. Meyers and Benjamin D. Gordon (eds), *Sepphoris III Part 1* (Winona Lake, IN: Eisenbrauns: 2018), p. 19. I am grateful to Jonathan Reed for this reference. See also: Mark A. Chancey and Eric M. Meyers, 'How Jewish Was Sepphoris in Jesus' Time?', *Biblical Archaeology Review* 26/4 (2009): pp. 18–33, 61.

55 William R. Farmer, 'Judas, Simon and Athronges', *NTS* 4 (1957–58): pp. 147–55, at pp. 151–2, suggested that these royal claimants were Hasmoneans, and had Hasmonean names; but, as Parente, 'Flavius Josephus' Account', pp. 185–6, argues, the names of the claimants, apart from Athronges, were extremely common. Josephus deemed Judas the son of a bandit chief (*War* 2:204; *Ant.* 14:195), Simon was a slave and Athronges a shepherd, and he seems to scorn their social status.

56 Louis Feldman, 'Josephus' Portrait of David', *HUCA* 60 (1989): pp. 129–74, at pp. 130–1, 173.

57 Mason, *Judean War 2*, p. 3, n. 3, suggests that Archelaus himself stayed in Rome until 3 BCE.

58 See Schürer, *History*, vol. 1, pp. 330–2.

59 Mary Smallwood, *The Jews under Roman Rule from Pompey to Diocletian: A study in political relations* (Leiden: Brill, 1981), pp. 105–8, called those who demonstrated in the Temple 'extremists' and referred to 'riots'; so also Eshel, 'Publius Quinctilius Varus', p. 113, and *passim*.

60 Schürer, *History*, vol. 1, p. 330.

61 Chaim Milikowsky, 'Seder Olam and Jewish Chronography in the Hellenistic and Roman Periods', *Proceedings of the American Academy for Jewish Research* 52 (1985): pp. 115–39; 'Seder Olam', in Shmuel Safrai et al. (eds), *The Literature of the Sages*, Part 2 (Assen: Fortress, 2006), pp. 231–7; *Seder Olam: Critical edition, commentary and introduction*, 2 vols (Jerusalem: Yad Ben-Zvi, 2013).

62 Heinrich W. Guggenheimer, *Seder Olam: The rabbinic view of biblical chronology* (Northvale, NJ: Jason Aronson, 1998), pp. 260–3; Schürer, *History*, vol. 1, p. 534, n. 92.

63 Mason, *Judean War 2*, pp. 45–52.

64 Pseudo-Manetho, *Apotelesmatica* 4:198–9; Petronius, *Satyricon* 111–12; Cicero, *Tusc.* 1:102; Horace, *Ep.* 1:16:48; Juvenal, *Satires* 14:77–8; Artemidorus, *Oneirocritica* 2:53; John Granger Cook, 'Crucifixion and Burial', *NTS* 57 (2011): pp. 193–213; Martin Hengel, *Crucifixion* (Philadelphia, PA: Fortress, 1977), pp. 8–9, 26, 41, 54, 76; Helen Bond, '"You'll Probably Get Away with Crucifixion": Laughing at the Cross in *Brian* and the Ancient World', in Joan E. Taylor (ed.), *Jesus and Brian: Exploring the historical Jesus and his times via Monty Python's Life of Brian* (London: Bloomsbury T&T Clark), pp. 113–26.

65 Schürer, *History*, vol. 1, p. 331, put it down to Sabinus who 'oppressed the people in every sort of way'; Rhoads, *Israel in Revolution*, p. 26, notes there was probably a 'variety of motives' for the outbreaks of rebellion following Herod's death.

66 See Rhoads, *Israel in Revolution*, pp. 50–2, regarding the relationship between Judas son of Hezekiah and Judas the Galilean (*War* 2:56; *Ant.* 17:271–2).

67 This is the translation by John Priest of the single, somewhat confused, Latin text of this important work existing in the Ambrosian library in Milan (C.73 inf), the only text that survives: John Priest, 'The Testament of Moses', in James H. Charlesworth (ed.), *The Old Testament Pseudepigrapha: Apocalyptic literature and testaments* (London: Darton, Longman & Todd, 1983), pp. 927–34, at p. 930. For an alternative translation see Johannes Tromp, *The Assumption of Moses: A critical edition with commentary* (SVTP 10; Leiden: Brill, 1993), pp. 14–17.

68 Eshel, 'Publius Quinctilius Varus', pp. 114–15.

69 Eric M. Meyers, 'Sepphoris on the Eve of the Great Revolt (67–68 C.E.): Archaeology and Josephus', in Eric M. Meyers (ed.), *Galilee through the Centuries: Confluence of cultures* (Winona Lake, IN: Eisenbrauns, 1999), pp. 109–22, at pp. 109–10, 114; Eric M. Meyers and Carol L. Meyers (eds), *Sepphoris, vol. 1: The Pottery from Ancient Sepphoris* (Sepphoris Excavation Reports; Winona Lake, IN: Eisenbrauns, 2013), p. 21; Zeev Weiss, 'Sepphoris', *Oxford Classical Dictionary*, 28 June 2017: https://doi.org/10.1093/acrefore/9780199381135.013.8039 (accessed 13 August 2024).

70 Ehud Netzer and Rachel Bar-Nathan, *Hasmonean and Herodian Palaces at Jericho*, vol. 3 (Jerusalem: Israel Exploration Society, 2022), p. 18, and there has been a suggestion that resettlement at the beginning of Period II at Qumran could relate to events at the beginning of the reign of Archelaus; see Roland de Vaux, *Archaeology and the Dead Sea Scrolls* (Oxford: Oxford University Press, 1973), pp. 34–6; for

material in the caves and the revolts see Joan E. Taylor, 'The Qumran Caves in Their Regional Context: A Chronological Review with a Focus on Bar Kokhba Assemblages', in Marcello Fidanzio (ed.), *The Caves of Qumran: Proceedings of the International Conference, Lugano 2014* (Leiden: Brill, 2016), pp. 7–33.

71 Årstein Justnes and Josephine Munch Rasmussen, 'Hazon Gabriel: A Display of Negligence', *BASOR* 384 (2020): pp. 69–76.

72 See the list in Kenneth Atkinson, 'The Gabriel Revelation (Hazon Gabriel): A Reused Masseba Forgery?', *The Qumran Chronicle* 26 (2018): pp. 113–27, at p. 122. Atkinson himself does not think this artefact is genuine and suggests that modern ink has been applied to an ancient tombstone. However, he notes that inked tombstones have been found in the area of Khirbet Qazone, near where this inscription was recovered. Might the inscription have been written on a tombstone in antiquity?

73 Israel Knohl, 'The Apocalyptic and Messianic Dimensions of the Gabriel Revelation in Their Historical Context', in Matthias Henze (ed.), *Hazon Gabriel: New readings of the Gabriel Revelation* (Atlanta, GA: SBL, 2011), pp. 36–60.

74 Brown, *Birth*, pp. 112–14.

75 Brown, *Birth*, p. 106.

76 Brown, *Birth*, p. 107.

77 This reference to Athronges as a shepherd also makes the angels' appearance to the shepherds (Luke 2:8–18) seem somewhat more significant.

8 Growing up Galilean

1 Matt. 13:54, 57; Mark 6:1, 4; Luke 4:23. BDAG 788: 2: 'a relatively restricted area as locale of one's immediate family and ancestry, home town, one's own part of the country'.

2 John Meier, *A Marginal Jew: Rethinking the historical Jesus, vol. 1: The Roots of the Problem and the Person* (New Haven, CT: Yale University Press, 1991), p. 16.

3 E. P. Sanders, *The Historical Figure of Jesus* (London: Allen Lane/Penguin, 1993), p. 85.

4 Sanders, *Historical Figure*, p. 86.

5 The terminology of 'city' suggests an underlying Aramaic or Hebrew story, because terms such as *qiryat*, meaning a small town, could be translated as 'city' (*polis*) in the Greek Septuagint.

6 Robert J. Myles, *The Homeless Jesus in the Gospel of Matthew* (Sheffield: Sheffield Phoenix, 2014), p. 74.

7 This raises a question, then, as to whether this Gospel quoted Scripture in Hebrew.

8 Hans P. Rüger, 'NAZAREΘ / NAZARA, NAZARHNOS / NAZΩRAIOS', *ZNW*
   72 (1981): pp. 257–63; but see Klaus Berger, 'Jesus als Nasoräer/Nasiräer', *NT*
   38 (1996): pp. 323–35, esp. pp. 330–1, and Maarten J. J. Menken, 'The Sources
   of the Old Testament Quotation in Matthew 2:23', *JBL* 120 (2001): pp. 451–68,
   who argue that the name derives from Judg. 13:5, 7 and is a misquote of 'nazirite'.
   Some have sought to differentiate the meaning of *Nazōraios* from *Nazarenos*
   (found in Mark 1:24; 10:47; 14:67; 16:6); for example, Matthew Black, *An Aramaic
   Approach to the Gospels and Acts*, 3rd edn (Oxford: Blackwell, 1967), pp. 197–200,
   derives the former from the Hebrew root *ntsr* meaning 'guard, observe' and links
   it with Epiphanius's naming of the Jewish Nasaraeans (*Pan.* 18).
9 Krister Stendahl, *The School of St. Matthew and Its Use of the Old Testament* (Acta
   Seminarii Neotestamentici Upsaliensis 20; Uppsala: Almqvist & Wiksell, 1954),
   pp. 103–4, 198–9.
10 In the book of Revelation, dating from a similar time to the Gospel of Matthew,
   Jesus says: 'I . . . have sent my angel' (in a vision) to testify to you [that] I am the
   root (*rhiza*) and the offspring of David, the bright morning star' (Rev. 22:16). In
   another vision, one of the twenty-four crowned elders in heaven speaks of Jesus
   as 'the lion [Gen. 49:9] that is from the tribe of Judah, the root (*rhiza*) of David'
   (Rev. 5:5).
11 See the nuanced discussion in Richard Horsley, *Archaeology, History and Society
   in Galilee: The social context of Jesus and the rabbis* (Valley Forge, PA: Trinity
   Press International, 1996), pp. 162–71: there were likely three languages spoken
   in Galilee: Aramaic, Greek and Mishnaic Hebrew, with Aramaic the most
   widespread, but class and location would have impacted on who spoke what as
   their first language.
12 The noun *nets* or *nats* in Jewish and Christian Palestinian Aramaic means
   'blossom', 'shoot', 'sprout' or 'progeny': Michael Sokoloff, *A Dictionary of Jewish
   Palestinian Aramaic*, rev. edn (Ramat Gan: Bar Ilan University Press, 2017), p. 401.
   However, in the Syriac Peshitta text of Isa. 11:1 the word is *nurba*'.
13 Jessie Payne Smith, *A Compendious Syriac Dictionary* (Oxford: Clarendon, 1903),
   p. 333.
14 Marcus Jastrow, *Dictionary of the Targumim, the Talmud Babli and Yerushalmi
   and the Midrashic Literature* (New York, NY: Title, 1943), p. 930.
15 See also *Jub.* 12:25–7; 4Q464 frag. 3 1 5–9: Steve Weitzman, 'Why Did the
   Qumran Community Write in Hebrew?', *JAOS* 119 (1999): pp. 35–45; John C.
   Poirier, *The Tongues of Angels: The concept of angelic languages in classical Jewish
   and Christian texts* (WUNT 287; Tübingen: Mohr Siebeck, 2010), pp. 9–24.
16 Matt. 4:13; Luke 4:16.

17 Matt. 21:11; Luke 1:26; 2:4, 39, 51; Acts 10:38.

18 Mark 1:9; John 1:45–6.

19 Raymond E. Brown, *The Birth of the Messiah: A commentary on the infancy narratives in Matthew and Luke*, rev. edn (New York, NY: Doubleday, 1993), p. 207; Gustaf Dalman, *Sacred Sites and Ways: Studies in the topography of the Gospels*, tr. P. P. Levertoff (London: SPCK, 1935), p. 58. See Gen. 13:10; 14:2, 8 (and see Jer. 48:34); for Greek references see Michael Avi-Yonah, *Gazetteer of Roman Palestine* (Jerusalem: Carta/Institute of Archaeology, Hebrew University, 1976), p. 104.

20 Joan E. Taylor, 'The *Nazoraeans* as a "Sect" in "Sectarian" Judaism? A Reconsideration of the Current View via the Narrative of Acts and the Meaning of *Hairesis*', in Sacha Stern (ed.), *Sects and Sectarianism in Jewish History* (Leiden: Brill, 2011), pp. 87–118. Mark Lidzbarski, *Mandäische Liturgien* (Berlin: Weidmann, 1920; repr. Hildesheim, Olms, 1971), pp. xvi–xvii, notes that the Mandaeans could call themselves *natsorayya*.

21 See *b.AZ* 6a, 7b; *b.Ta'an.* 27b; *b.Git.* 57a.

22 See Hans H. Schäder, 'Nazoraios/Nazarenos', in Gerhard Kittel (ed.), *Theological Dictionary of the New Testament* (Grand Rapids, MI: Eerdmans, 1964–76), vol. 4, pp. 874–9.

23 James D. Tabor, *The Jesus Dynasty: Stunning new evidence about the hidden history of Jesus* (London: HarperElement, 2006), p. 59, refers to Nazareth as 'Branch Town' with Nazarenes as 'Branchites'.

24 E.g. Matt. 26:71; Luke 18:37; 24:29 (probably); John 18:5, 7; 19:19; Acts 2:22; 3:6; 4:10: 6:14; 22:8; 26:9.

25 Mark 1:24; 10:47; 14:67; 16:6; used also in Luke 4:34; 24:19.

26 Michael Sokoloff, 'Jewish Palestinian Aramaic', in Stefan Weninger et al. (eds), *The Semitic Languages: An international handbook* (Berlin: De Gruyter Mouton, 2012), pp. 610–18, at pp. 612–13; and see Jastrow, *Dictionary*, p. 726. The acknowledged distinctions of Galilean pronunciation are even reflected in what is found in the Gospel of Matthew, where someone says to Peter, in Jerusalem: 'Surely, you're also one of them, for even your speech reveals you' (Matt. 26:73).

27 In the Babylonian Talmud: *b.AZ.* 17a; *b.Ber.* 17b; *b.Sot.* 47a; *b.Sanh.* 43a, 103a, 107a etc.; Tertullian, *Adv. Marc.* 4:8. In *ha-Notsri* the first vowel of *Natsara* is slackened to an 'o' sound and the second has been dropped.

28 William F. Albright, 'The Names Nazareth and Nazorean', *JBL* 65 (1946): pp. 397–401. For references to Nazareth in ancient literature from the second century onwards see Avi-Yonah, *Gazetteer*, pp. 82–3, and see also Jerome's (fourth-century) note that the town was called Nazara (Jerome, *Lib. Loc.* 141).

29 Tabor, *Jesus Dynasty*, p. 59, calls it 'Star Town'. See also Richard Bauckham, *Jude and the Relatives of Jesus in the Early Church* (Edinburgh: T&T Clark, 1990), pp. 63–9.

30 Mentioned in *Pesiqta deRab Kahana* 6:2; Avi-Yonah, *Gazetteer*, p. 50, map ref. 17324; Bellarmino Bagatti, *Ancient Christian Villages of Galilee*, tr. Paul Rotondi (Jerusalem: Franciscan Printing Press, 2001), pp. 101–14; Salomon E. Grootkerk, *Ancient Sites in Galilee: A toponomic gazetteer* (Leiden: Brill, 2000), pp. 180–5. This is likely the birthplace of Rabbi Dosithai (so *Pesiqta Rabbati* 16) and is not to be confused with another town in the Bashan (Gaulanitis) named Kokaba/Chochaba where Jewish-Christians lived in the fourth century (Epiphanius, *Pan.* 29:7:7; 30:2:8–9).

31 Yardenna Alexandre, 'The Settlement History of Nazareth in the Iron Age and Early Roman Period', *'Atiqot* 98 (2020): pp. 25–92.

32 Sean Freyne, *Galilee: From Alexander the Great to Hadrian, 323 B.C.E. to 135 C.E.* (Wilmington, IN: University of Notre Dame Press, 1980); and see also Sean Freyne, 'The Geography, Politics and Economics of Galilee', in Bruce Chilton and Craig A. Evans (eds), *Studying the Historical Jesus: Evaluations of the state of current research* (New York, NY: Brill, 1994), pp. 74–121; *Galilee and Gospel: Collected essays* (Leiden: Brill, 2022).

33 See Mordechai Aviam, *Jews, Pagans and Christians in the Galilee: 25 years of archaeological excavations and surveys: Hellenistic to Byzantine periods* (Rochester, NY: Rochester University Press, 2004); David A. Fiensy and James R. Strange (eds), *Galilee in the Late Second Temple and Mishnaic Periods: The archaeological record from cities, towns and villages*, 2 vols (Minneapolis, MN: Fortress, 2014–15).

34 Danny Syon, *Small Change in Hellenistic-Roman Galilee: The evidence from numismatic site finds as a tool for historical reconstruction* (Numismatic Studies and Researches 11; Jerusalem: The Israel Numismatic Society, 2015), pp. 161–5; Uri Leibner, 'The Origins of the Jewish Settlement in the Galilee in the Second Temple Period: Historical Sources and Archaeological Data', *Zion* 77 (2012): pp. 437–69, at pp. 468–9 (Hebrew; English summary, pp. xxxiii–xxxiv); Zeev Weiss, 'The Transformation from Galil ha-Goyim to Jewish Galilee: The Archaeological Testimony of an Ethnic Change', in Fiensy and Strange (eds), *Galilee*, vol. 2, pp. 9–21; Jonathan Reed, *Archaeology and the Galilean Jesus: A re-examination of the evidence* (Harrisburg, PA: Trinity Press International, 2000), pp. 39–43. However, Richard Horsley is suspicious of a colonising model, noting there were settlements prior to the Hasmoneans that may well have been Jewish: *Archaeology, History and Society*, pp. 109–11.

35 Mark Chancey, *The Myth of a Gentile Galilee* (SNTS Monograph Series 118;

Cambridge: Cambridge University Press, 2002); Mark Chancey and Eric M. Meyers, 'Sepphoris – How Jewish in Jesus' Time?', in Hershel Shanks (ed.), *Where Christianity Was Born* (Washington, DC: Biblical Archaeology Society, 2006), pp. 2–19.

36 Craig A. Evans, 'Context, Family and Formation', in Markus Bockmuehl (ed.), *The Cambridge Companion to Jesus* (Cambridge: Cambridge University Press, 2001), pp. 11–24, at p. 11.

37 See John M. Vonder Bruegge, *Mapping Galilee in Josephus, Luke, and John: Critical geography and the construction of an ancient space* (Ancient Judaism and Early Christianity 93; Leiden: Brill, 2016), pp. 32–90.

38 The following section repeats parts of Joan E. Taylor, 'Jesus as News: Crises of Health and Overpopulation in Galilee', *JSNT* 43 (2021): pp. 8–30.

39 Literally 'over 5,000 added to 10,000'.

40 As Thackeray noted: 'We may suspect exaggeration': Henry St. John Thackeray, *The Jewish War*, books 1–3 (Loeb Classical Library; Cambridge, MA: Harvard University Press, 1926), p. 588, note a). Masterman considered the population figures 'manifestly absurd'; see Ernest W. G. Masterman, 'Galilee in the Time of Christ', *The Biblical World* 32 (1908): pp. 405–16, at p. 407.

41 Chaim Ben David, 'Were There 204 Settlements in Galilee at the Time of Josephus?', *JJS* 62 (2011): pp. 21–36.

42 Magen Broshi, 'The Credibility of Josephus', *JJS* 33 (1982): pp. 379–84.

43 Uri Leibner, *Settlement and History in Hellenistic, Roman, and Byzantine Galilee: An archaeological survey of the eastern Galilee* (Studies and Texts in Antiquity and Christianity 127; Tübingen: Mohr Siebeck, 2009), p. 308.

44 Chester C. McCown, 'The Density of Population in Ancient Palestine', *JBL* 66 (1947): pp. 425–36, thought there were fewer than 1 million inhabitants. Wildly different estimates were noted by Anthony Byatt, 'Josephus and Population Numbers in First Century Palestine', *PEQ* 105 (1973): pp. 51–60, at p. 51, before he suggested a population of 2,265,000 for the whole country, while Seth Schwartz, *Imperialism and Jewish Society, 200 BCE to 640 CE* (Princeton, NJ: Princeton University Press, 2001), assumed there were just 500,000.

45 For example, John Dominic Crossan and Jonathan L. Reed, *Excavating Jesus: Beneath the stones, behind the texts* (San Francisco, CA: HarperSanFrancisco, 2001), pp. 34–5, estimates that Jesus' Nazareth held only 200–400 people. Nathan Schumer, 'The Population of Sepphoris: Rethinking Urbanization in Early and Middle Roman Galilee', *JAJ* 8 (2017): pp. 90–111, suggested that Roman Sepphoris held only 2,000–4,300. Capernaum, with an area of 17 hectares, has been estimated to have had a population of just 1,700 people: Reed, *Archaeology*

and the Galilean Jesus, pp. 82–3; Jonathan Reed, *The Population of Capernaum* (Occasional Papers: Claremont Institute for Antiquity and Christianity 24; Claremont, CA: Institute for Antiquity and Christianity, 1992); and see for further discussion, Jonathan Reed, 'Population Numbers, Urbanization, and Economics: Galilean Archaeology and the Historical Jesus', in Eugene H. Lovering (ed.), *Society of Biblical Literature 1994 Seminar Papers* (Atlanta, GA: Scholars, 1994), pp. 203–19. Even Magen Broshi, who was highly conservative in his estimates, suggested multiplying the coefficient of 400 persons per hectare (40 to 50 people per dunam) by the total combined area of a city, minus public and open spaces: Magen Broshi, 'The Population of Western Palestine in the Roman-Byzantine Period', *BASOR* 236 (1979): pp. 1–10, at p. 5.

46 Rassem Khamaisi et al., *Jerusalem: The Old City: The urban fabric and geopolitical implications* (Jerusalem: International Peace and Cooperation Center: Publication XVII, 2009), p. 22: https://www.ipcc-jerusalem.org/attachment/15/IPCC_Jerusalem_the_Old_City_Urban_Fabric_and_Geopolitical_Implications.pdf.

47 Andrea Arcidiacono et al., 'Environmental Performance and Social Inclusion: A Project for the Rocinha Favela in Rio de Janeiro', *Energy Procedia* 134 (2017): pp. 356–65, at p. 356.

48 Leibner, *Settlement and History*, p. 333 (italics mine); and see also Morten Hørning Jensen, 'Rural Galilee and Rapid Changes: An Investigation of the Socio-Economic Dynamics and Developments in Roman Galilee', *Biblica* 93 (2012): pp. 43–67, at pp. 50–5.

49 For famines see Morten Hørning Jensen, 'Climate, Droughts, Wars and Famines in Galilee as a Background for Understanding the Historical Jesus', *JBL* 131 (2012): pp. 307–24. Jensen notes that Reed has identified in Galilee features that were common in the wider world and these do not necessarily indicate any new social instability (and see his previous work in Jensen, 'Rural Galilee'). However, they would have contributed to long-standing stress.

50 For an important discussion see Camilo Mora, 'Revisiting the Environmental and Socioeconomic Effects of Population Growth: A Fundamental but Fading Issue in Modern Scientific, Public, and Political Circles', *Ecology and Society* 19 (2014), art. 38. While outlining the effects of overpopulation, Mora also notes that in today's world there is a tendency to downplay its effects, not only because population growth is helpful in neoliberal capitalist economics but also because it is assumed that it allows for sustainable care for the retired and elderly. Note that these offset factors were not part of the economics of the ancient world.

51 Giovanni Sarti, Veronica Rossi, Alessandro Amorosi, Stefano De Luca, Anna Lena, Christophe Morhange, Adriano Ribolini, Irene Sammartino, Duccio Bertoni,

Gianni Zanchetta, 'Magdala Harbour Sedimentation (Sea of Galilee): From Natural to Anthropogenic Control', *Quaternary International* 303 (2013): pp. 120–31.

52 Sarti et al., 'Magdala Harbour', p. 129: 'high pollution levels at the base of the HFS [Harbour Foundation Sequence] were induced by harbour activities and a dense human frequentation.'

53 See also John Dominic Crossan, *The Historical Jesus: The life of a Mediterranean Jewish peasant* (San Francisco, CA: HarperSanFrancisco, 1991); Kenneth C. Hanson and Douglas E. Oakman, *Palestine in the Time of Jesus: Social structure and social conflicts*, 2nd edn (Minneapolis, MN: Fortress, 1998); Douglas E. Oakman, *Jesus and the Peasants* (Matrix: The Bible in Mediterranean Context; Eugene, OR: Cascade, 2008).

54 Horsley, *Archaeology, History and Society*, pp. 77–83; Hanson and Oakman, *Palestine*, pp. 105–8; Fabian Udoh, *To Caesar What Is Caesar's: Tribute, taxes and imperial administration in early Roman Palestine (63 BCE–7CE)* (Providence, RI: Brown Judaic Studies, 2005); Bradley W. Root, *First Century Galilee: A fresh examination of the sources* (Tübingen: Mohr Siebeck, 2014), pp. 22–5.

55 Douglas E. Oakman, *Jesus, Debt and the Lord's Prayer: First-century debt and Jesus' intentions* (Cambridge: James Clarke, 2015).

56 As Morten Hørning Jensen has said, this is the answer to the question of 'why Jesus "happened" when he did': 'Rural Galilee and Rapid Changes: An Investigation of the Socio-Economic Dynamics and Developments in Roman Galilee', *Biblica* 93 (2012): pp. 43–67, at p. 43.

57 J. Andrew Overman, 'Jesus of Galilee and the Historical Peasant', in Douglas R. Edwards and C. Thomas McCullough (eds), *Archaeology and the Galilee* (Atlanta, GA: Scholars, 1997), pp. 67–74; Douglas R. Edwards, 'The Socio-Economic and Cultural Ethos of the Lower Galilee in the First Century: Implications for the Nascent Jesus Movement', in Lee I. Levine (ed.), *The Galilee in Late Antiquity* (New York, NY: Jewish Theological Seminary, 1992), pp. 53–74; Mordechai Aviam, 'People, Land, Economy and Belief in First-Century Galilee and Its Origins: A Comprehensive Archaeological Synthesis', in Ralph K. Hawkins and David A. Fiensy (eds), *The Galilean Economy in the Time of Jesus* (Atlanta, GA: SBL, 2013), pp. 5–48, though note that the evidence for a prosperous Galilee is often more related to the second to third century than the first; see C. Thomas McCullough, 'City and Village in Lower Galilee: The Import of the Archeological Excavations at Sepphoris and Khirbet Qana (Cana) for Framing the Economic Context of Jesus', in Hawkins and Fiensy (eds), *Galilean Economy*, pp. 49–74.

58 For further discussion see Joan Taylor, 'Visual Culture', in James Crossley and Chris Keith (eds), *The Next Quest for the Historical Jesus* (forthcoming).

59 Sakari Häkkinen, 'Poverty in the First-Century Galilee', *HTS Teologiese Studies/ HTS Theological Studies* 72/4, a3398: http://dx.doi.org/10.4102/hts.v72i4.3398; James Crossley and Robert Myles, *Jesus: A life in class conflict* (London: John Hunt/Zer0, 2023), pp. 39–47, who critique the idea of 'trickle down' economics leading to prosperity in Galilee. This is not to say there were no village and town elites who could afford imported goods and vessels.

60 Sharon Lee Mattila, 'Revisiting Jesus' Capernaum: A Village of Only Subsistence-Level Fishers and Farmers?', in Hawkins and Fiensy (eds), *Galilean Economy*, pp. 75–138, notes that there is evidence of some imported vessels and luxury items indicative of wealth in the Hellenistic and Roman periods. But this does not counter the general impression presented in the structures of the town from this period, especially on the western (Franciscan) side, even though there are some wealthier structures and public buildings on the eastern (Orthodox) side dating from somewhat later. The town is very different from Tarichaea (later Magdala) where there are well-built structures with hewn stones and even private *miqvaot* in villas. Much of the discussion here seems to boil down to different definitions of 'subsistence level'.

61 Leibner, *Settlement and History*, pp. 210–12; Yinon Shivtiel, 'Artificial Caves Cut into Cliff Tops in the Galilee and Their Historical Significance', *Hypogea 2015 – Proceedings of International Congress of Speleology in Artificial Cavities* (Urbino: AGE Arti Grafiche Editoriali Srl, 2015), pp. 67–76; *Cliff Shelters and Hiding Complexes in the Galilee during the Early Roman Period: The speleological and archaeological evidence* (Göttingen: Vandenhoeck & Ruprecht, 2019).

62 Lincoln Blumell, 'Social Banditry: Galilean Banditry from Herod until the Outbreak of the First Jewish Revolt', *Scripta Classica Israelica* 27 (2008): pp. 35–53, at p. 47.

63 Richard Horsley, 'Josephus and the Bandits', *JSJ* 10 (1979): pp. 37–63; Horsley, *Galilee*, pp. 264–9; Richard Horsley with John S. Hanson, *Bandits, Prophets and Messiahs: Popular movements in the time of Jesus* (Harrisburg, PA: Trinity Press International, 1985), pp. 48–87; Freyne, *Galilee*, pp. 211–16.

64 See Blumell, 'Social Banditry', pp. 41–2. Where 'bandits' are defined as attacking Herodian interests, Roman convoys or strategically significant sites, so might be insurgents.

65 The group of attackers, young men from the village of Dabaritta, took the goods to Josephus, then leader of revolutionary troops in Tarichaea, but were reluctant to agree to the money being sent to Jerusalem to rebuild the walls, as Josephus affirmed he would do; they suspected that he secretly wanted to return them to the owner, which indeed he did (*Life* 128–31).

66 Samuel S. Kottek, *Medicine and Hygiene in the Works of Josephus* (Leiden: Brill, 1994), p. 41. The notion that a change of diet causes disease is found in Hippocrates, *Regimen in Ancient Diseases* 2:63–125.

67 Jonathan Reed, 'Instability in Jesus' Galilee: A Demographic Perspective', *JBL* 129 (2010): pp. 343–65, at p. 345.

68 Reed, 'Instability', p. 355.

69 Reed, 'Instability', p. 357.

70 Samuel S. Kottek and (Manfred) H. F. J. Horstmanshoff (eds), *From Athens to Jerusalem: Medicine in hellenized Jewish lore and in early Christian literature* (Rotterdam: Erasmus, 2000); Stephen T. Newmyer, 'Talmudic Medicine and Graeco-Roman Science: Cross-Currents and Resistance', *ANRW* 2.37.3 (1996): pp. 2895–911.

71 See above, pp. 171–2; Josephus, *War* 2:1–79; *Ant.* 17:200–99.

72 For Sepphoris, see Fiensy and Strange (eds), *Galilee*, vol. 2, pp. 22–87; Rebecca Martin Nagy (ed.), *Sepphoris in Galilee: Crosscurrents of culture* (Raleigh, NC: North Carolina Museum of Art, 1996); Stuart S. Miller, *Studies in the History and Traditions of Sepphoris* (Leiden: Brill, 1984).

73 *Autokrator* is commonly translated as Latin *imperator* in Egyptian inscriptions from the time of Augustus onwards; see Jean-Claude Grenier, 'Le prophète et l'Autokrator', *Revue d'Égyptologie* 37 (1986): pp. 81–9.

74 See James L. Kelso and Dimitri C. Baranki, *Excavations at New Testament Jericho and Khirbet en-Nitla* (New Haven, CT: American Schools of Oriental Research, 1955), pp. 5–8, who noted how Josephus relates that the palace of Archelaus was built in splendid fashion (indeed *ekprepōs* means 'extraordinary', *Ant.* 17:340). The surprisingly weak response by Ehud Netzer, 'The Winter Palace of the Judean Kings at Jericho at the End of the Second Temple Period', *BASOR* 228 (1977): pp. 1–13, at p. 9, was that Herod used a large range of building techniques, and he states that there is no sign of Archelaus's building activity (p. 12).

75 In what is now France, south of Lyon, near the River Rhône.

76 See above, p. 69.

77 Steve Mason, *Flavius Josephus: Translation and commentary, vol. 1b: Judean War 2* (Leiden: Brill, 2009), pp. 78–9. See above, pp. 104, 128–9.

78 See Joan E. Taylor, 'Paul's Caesarea', in Steve Walton, Paul R. Trebilco and David W. J. Gill (eds), *The Urban World and the First Christians* (Grand Rapids, MI: Eerdmans, 2017), pp. 42–67.

79 Mason, *Judean War 2*, p. 81.

80 David M. Rhoads, *Israel in Revolution, 6–74 CE: A political history based on the writings of Josephus* (Philadelphia, PA: Fortress, 1976), p. 48.

81 Rhoads, *Israel in Revolution*, pp. 50–1; Hengel believed that the identification could be made: Martin Hengel, *The Zealots: Investigation into the Jewish freedom movement in the period from Herod I until 70 A.D.* (London: Bloomsbury Academic, 1989), p. 331. For Reza Aslan, the synthesis is essential in terms of the way he defines the 'fourth philosophy': *Zealot: The life and times of Jesus of Nazareth* (New York, NY: Random House, 2013), pp. 40–4.

82 Rhoads, *Israel in Revolution*, p. 51; Fausto Parente, 'Flavius Josephus' Account of the Anti-Roman Riots Preceding the 66–70 War, and Its Relevance for the Reconstruction of Jewish Eschatology during the First Century A.D.', *JANES* 16–17 (1984–85): pp. 183–205, at pp. 189–91; Horsley with Hanson, *Bandits, Prophets and Messiahs*, pp. 191–7.

83 Some have doubted the historicity of the account of Judas, seeing Josephus's treatment as highly rhetorical; see James S. McLaren, *Constructing Judaean History in the Diaspora: Josephus's accounts of Judas*, in John M. G. Barclay (ed.), *Negotiating Diaspora: Jewish strategies in the Roman Empire* (London: T&T Clark, 2004), pp. 90–108; also Gunnar Haaland, 'A Villain and the VIPs: Josephus on Judas the Galilean and the Essenes', in Anders Klostergaard et al. (eds), *Northern Lights on the Dead Sea Scrolls: Proceedings of the Nordic Qumran Network 2003–2006* (STDJ 80; Leiden: Brill, 2009), pp. 241–4; Gunnar Haaland, 'What Difference Does Philosophy Make?', in Zuleika Rodgers (ed.), *Making History: Josephus and historical method* (Leiden: Brill, 2007), pp. 262–88, esp. pp. 271–2. The trouble with such arguments is that rhetoricity does not at all invalidate historicity.

84 See above, pp. 151–2.

85 For these schools see Joan E. Taylor, 'Pharisees, Sadducees and Essenes in Josephus's Writings', in Kenneth Atkinson (ed.), *The Oxford Handbook of Josephus* (Oxford: Oxford University Press, 2024) (forthcoming).

86 See Joan E. Taylor, *The Essenes, the Scrolls and the Dead Sea* (Oxford: Oxford University Press, 2012), pp. 55, 62–4. Two sons of Judas, James and Simon, were crucified under the procurator Tiberius Julius Alexander, *c.*47 CE (*Ant.* 10:102). The revolutionary leader Menahem was allegedly also the son of this Judas (*War* 2:433); this is not impossible if he was born *c.*5–6 CE. Another revolutionary leader, Eleazar son of Jairus, was a grandson (*War* 7:253). Various revolutionary groups, called by Josephus 'zealots' or 'sicarii', appear under the designation of the 'fourth philosophy'; for further discussion, see Rhoads, *Israel in Revolution*, p. 57.

87 *War* 4:151–8. See also Luke 1:9.

88 One should not think of it as a 'sect' of 'Zealots' and something coherent from the outset: see Richard A. Horsley, 'The Sicarii: Ancient Jewish "Terrorists"', *Journal of Religion* 59 (1979): pp. 435–58.

89 Rhoads thinks therefore that the revolt was actually quite small and insignificant: *Israel in Revolution*, pp. 47–60.

90 Ralph M. Novak, *Christianity and the Roman Empire: Background texts* (London: Continuum, 2001), pp. 293–8.

91 Annette Merz, 'Matthew's Star, Luke's Census, Bethlehem, and the Quest for the Historical Jesus', in Peter Barthel and George van Kooten (eds), *The Star of Bethlehem and the Magi: Interdisciplinary perspectives from experts on the Ancient Near East, the Greco-Roman world and modern astronomy* (Leiden: Brill, 2015), pp. 463–95, at pp. 484–7.

92 See Hannah Cotton and Jonas Greenfield, 'Babatha's Property and the Law of Succession in the Babatha Archive', *ZPE* 104 (1994): pp. 211–24. For a full investigation of Babatha and her legal issues, see Philip F. Esler, *Babatha's Orchard: The Yadin Papyri and an ancient Jewish family tale retold* (Oxford: Oxford University Press, 2017).

93 Scott Leckie, 'Housing and Property Issues for Refugees and Internally Displaced Persons in the Context of Return: Key Considerations for UNHCR Policy and Practice', *Refugee Survey Quarterly* 19 (2000): pp. 5–63.

94 *War* 2:433–4.

95 *War* 7:26–32.

9 Growing up Jesus

1 John Meier, *A Marginal Jew: Rethinking the historical Jesus, vol. 1: The Roots of the Problem and the Person* (New Haven, CT: Yale University Press, 1991), p. 352. Meier bases this assessment on his analysis of Jesus' early years as told in the canonical Gospels (pp. 202–351), though Matt. 1 – 2 are not considered historically relevant, except for a few points of agreement with Luke (pp. 208–14).

2 See among many studies Cindy C. Sangalang and Cindy Vang, 'Intergenerational Trauma in Refugee Families: A Systematic Review', *Journal of Immigrant and Minority Health* 19/3 (2017): pp. 745–54.

3 Bellarmino Bagatti, *Ancient Christian Villages of Galilee*, tr. Paul Rotondi (Jerusalem: Franciscan Printing Press, 2001), p. 93.

4 See for overviews James F. Strange, 'Nazareth', in David A. Fiensy and James R. Strange (eds), *Galilee in the Late Second Temple and Mishnaic Periods: The archaeological record from cities, towns and villages*, 2 vols (Minneapolis, MN: Fortress, 2014–15), vol. 2, pp. 167–80.

5 Yardenna Alexandre, *Mary's Well, Nazareth: The late Hellenistic to the Ottoman periods* (Jerusalem: Israel Antiquities Authority, 2012). A bath-house complex was found in excavations behind the 'Cactus' shop close to Mary's Well, which

indicates that water was channelled here, and while there was discussion about more ancient remains, this seems likely to date to the Crusader period: Tzvi Shacham, 'Bathhouse from the Crusader Period in Nazareth', in *Spa: Sanitas per Aquam, Aachen 18–22 March, 2009: Proceedings of the International Frontinus Symposium* (Leuven: Peeters, 2012), pp. 319–26.

6 Asad Mansur, '"The Virgin's Fountain," Nazareth', *PEFQSt* (1913): pp. 149–53; Bagatti, *Ancient Christian Villages*, pp. 30–2; Alexandre, *Mary's Well*.

7 See Ken R. Dark, *The Archaeology of Jesus' Nazareth* (Oxford: Oxford University Press, 2023), pp. 31–2.

8 The agricultural life of Nazareth has been preserved in the Nazareth Village Farm project, lying some 400 m from remains found underneath the Sisters of Nazareth Convent: Stephen Pfann, Ross Voss and Yehudah Rapuano, 'Surveys and Excavations at the Nazareth Village Farm (1997–2002): Final Report', *Bulletin of the Anglo-Israel Archaeological Society* 25 (2007): pp. 19–79.

9 Walid Atrash, 'Nazareth (West), Preliminary Report', *Hadashot Arkheologiyot* 121 (2009): http://hadashot-esi.org.il/report_detail_eng.aspx?id=1073&mag_id=115 (accessed 14 August 2024).

10 Clemens Kopp, 'Beiträge zur Geschichte Nazareths', *JPOS* 18 (1938): pp. 191–228; Joan E. Taylor, *Christians and the Holy Places: The myth of Jewish-Christian origins* (Oxford: Clarendon, 1993), p. 233; Alexandre, *Mary's Well*, 9; Ken R. Dark, 'The Byzantine Church of the Nutrition in Nazareth Rediscovered', *PEQ* 144 (2012): pp. 164–84, at p. 165.

11 Dark, *Archaeology*, pp. 37–8. Dark notes that the objects indicate 'high status burials' and 'far more of these burials than might be expected if it was simply a small agricultural hamlet'.

12 E.g. see Nurit Feig, 'Nazareth Illit', *IEJ* 33 (1983): pp. 116–17. This tomb is probably second to third century.

13 Michael Avi-Yonah, 'A List of Priestly Courses from Caesarea', *IEJ* 12 (1962): pp. 137–9.

14 Dark, *Archaeology*, pp. 116–18. See also Ken R. Dark, 'Early Roman-Period Nazareth and the Sisters of Nazareth Convent', *Antiquaries Journal* 92 (2012): pp. 37–64; Dark, 'Byzantine Church'.

15 Dark, 'Byzantine Church', p. 165; Dark, *Archaeology*, pp. 69–71.

16 See illustrations in Jean-Bernard Livio, 'Nazareth: Les fouilles chez les religieuses de Nazareth', *Le Monde de la Bible* 16 (1967): pp. 26–34, at p. 29; Dark, *Archaeology*, fig. 1.8.

17 Dark, *Archaeology*, p. 37.

18 For a summary of evidence, see Yardenna Alexandre, 'The Settlement History of

Nazareth in the Iron Age and Early Roman Period', *'Atiqot* 98 (2020): pp. 25–92, at p. 86.

19 These took place initially in 1892; see Benedict Vlaminck, *A Report of the Recent Excavations and Explorations Conducted at the Sanctuary of Nazareth* (Washington, DC: Commissariat of the Holy Land, 1900), and work continued at the site in subsequent years: Prosper Viaud, *Nazareth et ses deux Églises de l'Annonciation et de Saint-Joseph d'après les fouilles récentes* (Paris: A. Picard, 1910). More extensive excavations took place in the 1950s and 1960s; see Bellarmino Bagatti, *Excavations in Nazareth*, tr. E. Hoade (Jerusalem: Franciscan Printing Press, 1969), pp. 259–63; Bagatti, *Ancient Christian Villages*, pp. 23–36. Viaud uncovered rock-hewn silos and cisterns in the area of the Terra Santa convent, but the records were destroyed in the Second World War. For further analysis see Taylor, *Christians and the Holy Places*, pp. 230–67; Alexandre, *Mary's Well*, pp. 5–9; Alexandre, 'Settlement History', pp. 28–9.

20 See Gustaf Dalman, *Sacred Sites and Ways: Studies in the topography of the Gospels*, tr. P. P. Levertoff (London: SPCK, 1935), pp. 57–80.

21 Livio, 'Nazareth', p. 30.

22 Though see Livio, 'Nazareth'.

23 Dark, 'Early Roman-Period Nazareth'; Ken R. Dark, *The Sisters of Nazareth Convent: A Roman-period, Byzantine and Crusader site in central Nazareth* (Routledge: London, 2021); Dark, *Archaeology*, pp. 106–25.

24 These were quite likely manufactured nearby at a quarry and stone-vessel facility, such as the one at Einot Amitai; see Yonatan Adler and Dennis Mizzi, 'A Roman-Era Chalk Quarry and Chalk-Vessel Workshop at 'Einot Amitai in Lower Galilee: A Preliminary Report', *IEJ* 72 (2022): pp. 113–32.

25 This is in locus 153, which contains what is called an 'underground pit complex': Alexandre, 'Settlement History', pp. 43–4.

26 Alexandre, 'Settlement History', p. 46.

27 Alexandre, 'Settlement History', p. 81.

28 Viaud, *Nazareth*, pp. 134–5, 142–4; Bagatti, *Excavations in Nazareth*, pp. 223–7, no. 62. At Japha (Yafi'a), just 2 miles (3 km) south-west of Nazareth, there was a similar three-level complex: Claude R. Conder and Horatio H. Kitchener, *The Survey of Western Palestine, vol. 1: Galilee* (London: Palestine Exploration Fund, 1881), pp. 353–4.

29 Clemens Kopp, *The Holy Places of the Gospels*, tr. Ronald Walls (New York, NY: Herder & Herder, 1963), pp. 82–6.

30 See Taylor, *Christians and the Holy Places*, pp. 246–50; Bagatti, *Excavations in Nazareth*, pp. 28–9; Viaud, *Nazareth*, pp. 142–4.

31 Bagatti, *Excavations in Nazareth*, pp. 27–59; Taylor, *Christians and the Holy Places*, pp. 230–3, 250–2.

32 Dark, *Archaeology*, pp. 43–5.

33 This was not the 'Large Cave' as identified by Dark, *Archaeology*, pp. 15–17, 111, since this was cut later on, but rather a smaller cave on the edge; see pp. 111–12.

34 Bagatti, *Ancient Christian Villages*, p. 26.

35 On road 6089, opposite the Old Muslim Cemetery.

36 Nazareth Cultural & Tourism Association, 'A World Hidden Underground', *Nazareth Today* (Dec. 2011), pp. 4–5.

37 Human habitation in the Palaeolithic and Neolithic eras has been evidenced in several places. Flints from the late Neolithic and late Chalcolithic were noted at Mary's Well; see Alexandre, *Mary's Well*, pp. 13–56. Middle Palaeolithic flints were found in excavations at the Rashidiya School: Yotam Tepper, 'Nazareth, Final Report', *Hadashot Arkheologiyot* 121 (2009): http://hadashot-esi.org.il/report_detail_eng.aspx?id=1132&mag_id=115 (accessed 14 August 2024). Palaeolithic burials and artefacts were found in the Qafzeh Cave under Mount Precipice: Bernard Vandermeersch and Ofer Bar-Yosef, 'The Paleolithic Burials at Qafzeh Cave, Israel', *Paleo* 30–31 (2019): pp. 256–75; Erella Hovers, *The Lithic Assemblages of Qafzeh Cave* (Oxford: Oxford University Press, 2009).

38 Matthew K. Robinson, '"Is This Not the Τέκτων?" Revisiting Jesus's Vocation in Mark 6:3', *Neotestamentica* 55 (2021): pp. 431–45; see also James D. Tabor, *The Jesus Dynasty: Stunning new evidence about the hidden history of Jesus* (London: HarperElement, 2006), pp. 100–2.

39 Geza Vermes, *Jesus the Jew* (London: SCM Press, 1973), pp. 21–2, notes that this term corresponds to Aramaic *naggar*, 'craftsman', found in *b.AZ* 50b metaphorically in terms of skill in interpretation.

40 This is a translation of the Syriac text of *Acts. Thom.* 3 in Albertus F. J. Klijn, *The Acts of Thomas* (Leiden: Brill, 1962), p. 66. See also Harold Attridge and Julian Hills (eds), *The Acts of Thomas* (London: Polebridge, 2010).

41 Origen in fact rejects the suggestion that Jesus was a carpenter (*Against Celsus* 6:36), indicating that he himself only knew manuscripts of Mark with the reading corresponding to Matthew's phrase 'son of a carpenter' (Matt. 13:55). This is indeed found in some early Greek manuscripts of Mark, e.g. the third-century papyrus P45, and Greek manuscript families *f*13 and 33. See Chris Keith, *Jesus against the Scribal Elite: The origins of the conflict* (Grand Rapids, MI: Baker Academic, 2014), pp. 53–6.

42 Jodi Magness, Shua Kisilevitz, Matthew Grey, Dennis Mizzi and Karen Britt, 'Huqoq – 2017 Preliminary Report', *Hadashot Arkheologiyot* 130 (2018): https://

www.hadashot-esi.org.il/Report_Detail_Eng.aspx?id=25419. I am grateful to Jodi Magness and Jim Haberman for the photograph of the woodworker.

43 See Rüdiger Schwarz, 'Adze-plane, Skeparnon, Multipurpose Adze or Two-handled Adze? Practical Work with an Alleged Predecessor of the Woodworking Plane', *EXARC Journal* 2018/1: https://exarc.net/ark:/88735/10329.

44 This was first mooted by Shirley Jackson Case, 'Jesus and Sepphoris', *JBL* 45 (1926): pp. 14–22, and more extensively proposed by Richard A. Batey, 'Is Not This the Carpenter?' *NTS* 30 (1984): pp. 249–58; *Jesus and the Forgotten City: New light on Sepphoris and the urban world of Jesus* (Grand Rapids, MI: Baker Book House, 1991); see also Douglas R. Edwards, 'The Socio-economic and Cultural Ethos of the Lower Galilee in the First Century: Implications for the Nascent Jesus Movement', in Lee I. Levine (ed.), *The Galilee in Late Antiquity* (New York, NY: Jewish Theological Seminary, 1992), pp. 53–74, at pp. 62–3; Tabor, *Jesus Dynasty*, pp. 104–6; Jean-Pierre Isbouts, *Young Jesus: Restoring the 'lost years' of a social activist and religious dissident* (New York, NY: Sterling, 2008), pp. 119–23.

45 Mark Chancey, *Greco-Roman Culture and the Galilee of Jesus* (Cambridge: Cambridge University Press, 2005), p. 83.

46 Richard Horsley, *Archaeology, History and Society in Galilee: The social context of Jesus and the rabbis* (Valley Forge, PA: Trinity Press International, 1996), pp. 118–30.

47 Ken R. Dark, 'The Roman-Period and Byzantine Landscape between Sepphoris and Nazareth', *PEQ* 140 (2008): pp. 87–102; Dark, *Archaeology*, pp. 3–7; Dark, 'Roman-Period and Byzantine Landscape'; Ken R. Dark, *Nazareth Archaeological Project: A preliminary report on the fourth season in 2007* (London: Late Antiquity Research Group, 2008); *Nazareth Archaeological Project: A preliminary report on the fifth season in 2008* (London: Late Antiquity Research Group, 2009); *Roman-Period and Byzantine Nazareth and Its Hinterland* (London: Routledge, 2020).

48 See Eric M. Meyers, Carol L. Meyers and Benjamin D. Gordon, 'Sepphoris B: Residential Area of Western Summit', in Fiensy and Strange (eds), *Galilee*, vol. 2, pp. 39–53, at p. 45; James F. Strange, 'Some Implications of Archaeology for New Testament Studies', in James H. Charlesworth and Walter P. Weaver (eds), *What Has Archaeology to Do with Faith?* (Philadelphia, PA: Trinity Press International, 1992), pp. 32–5.

49 See Jonathan Reed, *Archaeology and the Galilean Jesus: A re-examination of the evidence* (Harrisburg, PA: Trinity Press International, 2000), pp. 132–3.

50 Keith, *Jesus against the Scribal Elite*, pp. 27–49.

51 James Crossley and Robert Myles, *Jesus: A life in class conflict* (London: John Hunt/Zer0, 2023), p. 37.

52 In the story as told in Luke 4:16–30 the town is named as Nazareth, but it is not named in Matthew's retelling (Matt. 13:54–8). See also John 4:44.

53 Keith, *Jesus against the Scribal Elite*, pp. 44–50.

54 Philo, *Legat.* 312–13; *Mos.* 21:6; *Praem.* 66; *Spec.* 2:62; see also *Spec.* 2:60–2.

55 Hagith Sivan, *Jewish Childhood in the Roman World* (Cambridge: Cambridge University Press, 2018), pp. 105–7; see *m.'Abot* 5:21; *j.Qidd.* 1:7, and for further on teaching Torah, pp. 108–13.

56 See also Maurice Casey, *Jesus of Nazareth: An independent historian's account of his life and teaching* (London: T&T Clark Bloomsbury, 2010), pp. 158–62.

57 As was common; see Libanius, *Oration* 1:8, 11, 88.

58 Jerusalem Talmud, *j.Meg.* 3:1 [73d]; *j.Ket.* 13:1 [35d].

59 See *m.Ber.* 4:2; *m.Dem.* 2:3, 7:5; *m.Ter.* 11:10; *m.Shabb.* 16:1; 18:1; *m.Pes.* 4:4; *m.Betz.* 3:5; *m.'Abot* 5:14; *m.Men.* 10:9; *m.Yad.* 4:3–4; *Gen. Rab.* 63:10. Also called a Beth Talmud; see *j.Meg.* 3:1 [73d].

60 For further discussion see Joan E. Taylor, 'Gender and Space in Early Synagogue Complexes: Reflections on the *Andrōn* and the *Gunaikōnitis* in Texts and Archaeology', in Dennis Mizzi, M. Grey and Tina Rassalle (eds), *Pushing Sacred Boundaries in Early Judaism and Roman Palestine: Essays in honor of Jodi Magness* (Supplements to the Journal for the Study of Judaism 208; Leiden: Brill, 2023), pp. 490–528.

61 See Michael Hilton, *Bar Mitzvah: A history* (Lincoln, NE: University of Nebraska Press, 2014), pp. 1–34.

62 Reidar Aasgaard, *The Childhood of Jesus: Decoding the apocryphal Infancy Gospel of Thomas* (Cambridge: James Clarke, 2011); Stephen J. Davis, *Christ Child: Cultural memories of a young Jesus* (New Haven, CT: Yale University Press, 2014); J. Robert C. Cousland, *Holy Terror: Jesus in the Infancy Gospel of Thomas* (Library of New Testament Studies 560; London: Bloomsbury T&T Clark, 2018).

63 Tony Burke has defined the earliest form of Greek manuscript tradition with help from readings of early translations: Tony Burke, *De infantia Iesu euangelium Thomae graece* (CCSA 17; Turnhout: Brepols, 2011); Tony Chartrand-Burke, 'Completing the Gospel: The Infancy Gospel of Thomas as a Supplement to the Gospel of Luke', in Lorenzo DiTommaso and Lucian Turcescu (eds), *The Reception and Interpretation of the Bible in Late Antiquity* (Leiden: Brill, 2008), pp. 101–19, at pp. 118–19. The oldest full Greek text is the eleventh-century Greek manuscript Saba 259 (fols 66r–72r), known as 'S', now in the Greek Orthodox patriarchate library, Jerusalem. It is itself not the initial Greek text but rather the closest surviving Greek form of the text that survives better in early translations, as identified by Sever J. Voicu, 'Notes sur l'histoire du texte de L'Histoire de

l'enfance de Jésus', *Apocrypha* 2 (1991): pp. 119–32. Recently, a fragment of this older text (2:3 – 3:1) has been found in Greek in the collection of the Staats- und Universitätsbibliothek in Hamburg and dated to the fourth to fifth century; see Lajos Berkes and Gabriel Nocchi Macedo, 'The Earliest Manuscript of the So-Called Infancy Gospel of Thomas: Editio Princeps of P.Hamb.Graec. 1011', *ZPE* 229 (2024): pp. 68–74.

64 See Bart D. Ehrman and Zlatko Pleše, *The Apocryphal Gospels: Texts and translations* (New York, NY: Oxford University Press, 2011), pp. 3–156.

65 As Hagith Sivan notes, with particular focus on rabbinic examples, physical violence towards boys in school 'was proverbial in ancient writings': *Jewish Childhood*, p. 77.

66 Davis, *Christ Child*, p. 108.

67 Davis, *Christ Child*, pp. 92–108.

68 A. Carlotta Dionisotti, 'From Ausonius' Schooldays?' *JRS* 72 (1982): pp. 83–125; Rafaella Cribiore, *Gymnastics of the Mind: Greek education in Hellenistic and Roman Egypt* (Princeton, NJ: Princeton University Press, 2001), pp. 15–17 and, for the following, see Joan E. Taylor, '4Q341: A Writing Exercise Remembered', in Ariel Feldman, Maria Cioată and Charlotte Hempel (eds), *Is There a Text in This Cave? Studies in the textuality of the Dead Sea Scrolls in honour of George J. Brooke* (STDJ 119; Leiden: Brill, 2017), pp. 133–51, at pp. 146–8.

69 *Hermeneumata Einsidlensia*, in Georg Goetz (ed.), *Corpus Glossariorum Latinorum*, 7 vols (Leipzig: Teubner, 1888–1923), vol. 3, p. 225 (56); Cribiore, *Gymnastics*, p. 15.

70 Davis, *Christ Child*, p. 109.

71 Here Quintilian notes types of syllabaries in elementary education: 'As regards syllables, no short cut is possible: they must all be learnt, and there is no good in putting off learning the most difficult; this is the general practice, but the sole result is bad spelling' (*Institutiones* 1:1.30): Quintilian, *Institutio Oratoria* (Loeb Classical Library; Cambridge, MA: Harvard University Press, 1920).

72 *'Abot R. Nat.* 6, 15; *t.Yad.* 2:11; Catherine Hezser, *Jewish Literacy in Roman Palestine* (Tübingen: Mohr Siebeck, 2001), p. 76.

73 This leads Hezser to wonder whether there was any significant elementary education involving writing in Judaea in the Second Temple period. However, Michael Wise has argued for skills in writing on the basis of surviving papyrological material: Michael Wise, *Language and Literacy in Roman Judaea: A study of the Bar Kokhba documents* (New Haven, CT: Yale University Press, 2015).

74 For further discussion see Shemuel Safrai and Menahem Stern, with David Flusser and Willem Cornelis van Unnik (eds), *The Jewish People in the First*

Century: Historical geography, political history, social, cultural and religious life and institutions, vol. 2 (Assen: Van Gorcum, 1976), p. 947; Burke, *De infantia*, pp. 236–7.

75 Educated women within rabbinic tradition appear to have learnt Torah at home, though a woman is reported as attending the school of Rabbi Meir in order to hear him, much to the irritation of her husband, who considered her to have neglected her primary household duties (*j.Sot.* 1:4, 16d).

76 Taylor, *Christians and the Holy Places*, pp. 228–9; Davis, *Christ Child*, pp. 139–43.

77 Greville S. P. Freeman-Grenville, *The Basilica of the Annunciation at Nazareth and Adjacent Shrines* (Jerusalem: Carta, 1994), pp. 43–54, though see Ken Dark and Eliya Ribak, 'An Unpublished Excavation by Roland de Vaux at the "Synagogue Church" in Nazareth, Israel', *Reading Medieval Studies* 35 (2009): pp. 93–100.

78 Bagatti, *Excavations in Nazareth*, pp. 233–4; Dalman, *Sacred Sites and Ways*, p. 68.

79 For further discussion see James McGrath, *What Jesus Learned from Women* (Eugene, OR: Cascade, 2021).

80 See Helen Bond and Joan Taylor, *Women Remembered: Jesus' female disciples* (London: Hodder & Stoughton, 2002), pp. 126–8.

81 Andries van Aarde, *Fatherless in Galilee: Jesus as a child of God* (Harrisburg, PA: Trinity Press International, 2001), esp. pp. 132–4, developing his previous work in van Aarde, 'Social Identity, Status Envy and Jesus' Abba', *Pastoral Psychology* 45 (1997): pp. 451–72.

82 See pp. 112–14.

83 Van Aarde sweeps away the nativity accounts of the Gospels, and paints a picture of Galilee that is out of step with contemporary research in being quite non-Jewish, labouring under the weight of an oppressive Temple system.

84 Donald Capps, *Jesus: A psychological biography* (Eugene, OR: Wipf & Stock, 2000), pp. 129–64.

85 Tabor, *Jesus Dynasty*, pp. 88–92, 102, thinks that Mary actually married Clopas. The time when a boy came of age might be around 13 years, but surviving legal documents from the first and second centuries are not precise; see Carolien Oudshoorn, *The Relationship between Roman and Local Law in the Babatha and Salome Komaise Archives: General analysis and three case studies on law of succession, guardianship and marriage* (Leiden: Brill, 2007), pp. 299–377.

86 John W. Miller, *Jesus at Thirty: A psychological and historical portrait* (Minneapolis, MN: Fortress, 1997), 35.

87 See Jeroen K. Van Ginneken, 'Prolonged Breastfeeding as a Birth Spacing Method', *Studies in Family Planning* 5 (1974): pp. 201–6; Siobhan Mattison, Katharine Wander and Katie Hinde, 'Breastfeeding over Two Years Is Associated with

Longer Birth Intervals, but Not Measures of Growth or Health, among Children in Kilimanjaro, TZ', *American Journal of Human Biology* 27 (2015): pp. 807–15: https://doi.org/10.1002/ajhb.22729.

88 Sivan, *Jewish Childhood*, p. 85; and see Patricia Smith and Joe Zias, 'Skeletal Remains from the Late Hellenistic French Hill Tomb', *IEJ* 30 (1980): pp. 109–15, at p. 111 (comparative table).

89 See Miller, *Jesus at Thirty*, p. 39.

90 See Deut. 21:15–17; Philo, *Spec.* 2:133–4; see also Kyu Seop Kim, *The Firstborn Son in Ancient Judaism and Early Christianity: A study of primogeniture and Christology* (Biblical Interpretation Series, 171; Leiden: Brill, 2019), pp. 40–7.

91 Miller, *Jesus at Thirty*, 36; see also Sivan, *Jewish Childhood*, pp. 92–105, 127–8.

92 Bruce Malina, *The Social Gospel of Jesus: The kingdom of God in Mediterranean perspective* (Minneapolis, MN: Fortress, 2001), pp. 133–9, 152–3. In Q the community of sibling disciples are asked to break family ties if necessary (see Matt. 10:34–7; Luke 12:51–3; 14:26). This teaching may have influenced how the family of Jesus is presented. See Bond and Taylor, *Women Remembered*, pp. 129–31.

93 As John Painter well argues, Mark 3:20–1 should not be understood as referring to Jesus' immediate family: *Just James: The brother of Jesus in history and tradition*, 2nd edn (Columbia, SC: University of South Carolina Press, 2004), pp. 21–8.

94 For a view of the mother and siblings as being faithfully alongside Jesus in John see Painter, *Just James*, pp. 12–18.

95 This 'mountain' was on the other side of the lake, the Sea of Galilee, where he had been with his disciples; see John 6:3.

96 This image of Jesus taking himself off away to the hills or wilderness to be alone to pray is already found in Mark (1:35–7; 6:46–7), and repeated in other Gospels (e.g. Luke 6:12), and given this we may well wonder if it was a distinctive practice of his.

97 See the translation of the New International Version, for example, and the interpretation of John R. Donahue and Daniel J. Harrington, *The Gospel of Mark* (Sacra Pagina Series 2; Collegeville, MN: Liturgical Press, 2002), pp. 128–9; Richard T. France, *The Gospel of Mark* (NIGTC; Grand Rapids, MI: Eerdmans, 2002), pp. 164–7.

98 It is positioned in the narrative to lead on to a description of scribes from Jerusalem stating that Jesus is possessed by Beelzebub (Mark 3:22). In some manuscripts of the Western textual tradition, 3:21, then, there are changes to the text to indicate Jesus' opposition, thus: 'after hearing about him, the scribes and the others went off to grab him . . .'

99 See Andrew Gregory, *The Gospel According to the Hebrews and the Gospel of the Ebionites* (Oxford: Oxford University Press, 2017), pp. 120–5, who also notes the similarity with *Gos. Thom.* 104.

100 See above, pp. 93–4.

101 Gregory, *Gospel According to the Hebrews*, pp. 98–102.

102 See Hanan Eshel, 'The Bar Kochba Revolt, 132–135 CE', in Steven T. Katz (ed.), *The Cambridge History of Judaism* (Cambridge: Cambridge University Press, 2006), vol. 4, pp. 105–27.

103 See p. 77 and Taylor, *Christians and the Holy Places*, pp. 36–41.

104 Painter, *Just James*, pp. 11–82.

105 Painter, *Just James*, p. 312.

10 Boy Jesus in the Temple

1 See for example the painting by Millais discussed in George P. Landow, *Victorian Types, Victorian Shadows: Biblical typology in Victorian literature, art, and thought* (London: Routledge & Kegan Paul 1980), pp. 49, 123–5. The subject of Jesus in Joseph's carpentry workshop was in the Middle Ages associated with an apocryphal story of Jesus helping Joseph in his workshop (see below): David R. Cartlidge and J. Keith Elliot, *Art and the Christian Apocrypha* (London: Routledge, 2001), pp. 111–13; Adey Horton, *The Child Jesus* (London: Geoffrey Chapman, 1975), pp. 178–9, and plate 96, p. 186.

2 Likewise, this subject picks up on apocryphal stories; see Cartlidge and Elliot, *Art and the Christian Apocrypha*, pp. 106–16; Horton, *Child Jesus*, pp. 175–86.

3 In Holman Hunt's *The Finding of the Saviour in the Temple* (1854–60), the teachers in the Temple are presented negatively; they sit together in a group on the left side of the painting, while the holy family are on the right, and behind them is a poor blind beggar, recalling Christ's miraculous healings as an adult: Landow, *Victorian Types*, pp. 125–7.

4 Teresa Morgan, *Literate Education in the Hellenistic and Roman Worlds* (Cambridge: Cambridge University Press, 1998), pp. 132, 194–5. For Philo, the aim of education is the acquisition of wisdom (*sophia, Congr.* 79–81); this included for Philo music, geometry, astronomy, dialectic and grammar (*Congr.* 11–18).

5 Raymond E. Brown, *The Birth of the Messiah: A commentary on the infancy narratives in Matthew and Luke*, rev. edn (New York, NY: Doubleday, 1993), p. 479.

6 Christopher Pelling, 'Childhood and Personality in Greek Biography', in Christopher Pelling (ed.), *Characterization and Individuality in Greek*

Literature (Oxford: Oxford University Press, 2009): https://doi.org/10.1093/oso/9780198140580.003.0010; M. David Litwa, *How the Gospels Became History: Jesus and Mediterranean myths* (New Haven, CT: Yale University Press, 2019), pp. 122–5.

7 See Suetonius, *Div. Aug.* 89; Libanius, *Oration* 1:4–13.

8 Also known as the Infancy Gospel of Thomas.

9 See Robert C. Cousland, 'Soundings in the Christology of the Infancy Gospel of Thomas: The Rewriting of Luke 2:41–52 in Paidika 17', *CBQ* 81 (2019): pp. 657–78; Brown, *Birth*, pp. 485–95.

10 Tony Chartrand-Burke, 'Completing the Gospel: The Infancy Gospel of Thomas as a Supplement to the Gospel of Luke', in Lorenzo DiTommaso and Lucian Turcescu (eds), *The Reception and Interpretation of the Bible in Late Antiquity* (Leiden: Brill, 2008), pp. 101–19, at p. 115.

11 See above, p. 85.

12 The attribution of the work to Judas Thomas, Jesus' supposed twin brother, is late and not found in early manuscripts; see Tony Burke, *De infantia Iesu euangelium Thomae graece* (CCSA 17; Turnhout: Brepols, 2011), pp. 205–6; Stephen J. Davis, *Christ Child: Cultural memories of a young Jesus* (New Haven, CT: Yale University Press, 2014), pp. 22–4.

13 For these Johannine echoes and more, see Robert C. Cousland, *Holy Terror: Jesus in the Infancy Gospel of Thomas* (Library of New Testament Studies 560; London: Bloomsbury T&T Clark, 2018), pp. 78–87; Cousland, 'Soundings in the Christology of the Infancy Gospel'.

14 Burke, *De infantia*, pp. 104, 182–4. Burke sees the Johannine echoes as apparent only in later forms of the text. See also Henk J. de Jonge, 'Sonship, Wisdom, Infancy: Luke ii. 41–51a', *NTS* 24 (1978): pp. 317–54, at pp. 346–7.

15 See Burke, 'Completing the Gospel', p. 109: it aims 'to supplement Luke with new childhood tales and additions to the Temple story'.

16 Brown, *Birth*, p. 483.

17 See Tony Burke, *The Syriac Tradition of the Infancy Gospel of Thomas: A critical edition* (Piscataway, NJ: Gorgias Press, 2017), p. 5, and his rejection of this: Burke, *De infantia*, pp. 209–11.

18 Diane G. Chen, *God as Father in Luke-Acts* (New York, NY: Peter Lang, 2006).

19 In the book of *Jubilees*, from the second century BCE, the people of Israel are collectively 'the children of the living God' (*Jub.* 1:24–8): Jacques van Ruiten, 'Divine Sonship in the Book of Jubilees', in Felix Albrecht and Reinhard Feldmeier (eds), *The Divine Father: Religious and philosophical concepts of divine parenthood in antiquity* (Leiden: Brill, 2014), pp. 85–105.

Further reading

Aasgaard, Reidar, *The Childhood of Jesus: Decoding the apocryphal Infancy Gospel of Thomas* (Cambridge: James Clarke, 2011).

Alexandre, Yardenna, *Mary's Well, Nazareth: The late Hellenistic to the Ottoman periods* (Jerusalem: Israel Antiquities Authority, 2012).

Barthel, Peter, and George van Kooten (eds), *The Star of Bethlehem and the Magi: Interdisciplinary perspectives from experts on the Ancient Near East, the Greco-Roman world and modern astronomy* (Leiden: Brill, 2015).

Bauckham, Richard, *Jude and the Relatives of Jesus in the Early Church* (Edinburgh: T&T Clark, 1990).

Becker, Eve-Marie, Helen K. Bond and Catrin H. Williams (eds), *John's Transformation of Mark* (London: Bloomsbury, 2021).

Bond, Helen K., *Jesus: A guide for the perplexed* (London: Bloomsbury T&T Clark, 2012).

Bond, Helen K., *Jesus: A very brief history* (London: SPCK, 2017).

Brown, Raymond E., *The Birth of the Messiah: A commentary on the infancy narratives in Matthew and Luke*, rev. edn (New York, NY: Doubleday, 1993).

Casey, Maurice, *Jesus of Nazareth: An independent historian's account of his life and teaching* (London: T&T Clark Bloomsbury, 2010).

Collins, John J., *The Sceptre and the Star: Messianism in light of the Dead Sea Scrolls*, 2nd edn (Grand Rapids, MI: Eerdmans, 2010).

Crossan, John Dominic, and Jonathan L. Reed, *Excavating Jesus: Beneath the stones, behind the texts* (San Francisco, CA: HarperSanFrancisco, 2001).

Crossley, James, and Robert Myles, *Jesus: A life in class conflict* (London: John Hunt/Zer0, 2023).

Dark, Ken R., *The Archaeology of Jesus' Nazareth* (Oxford: Oxford University Press, 2023).

Dark, Ken R., *Roman-Period and Byzantine Nazareth and Its Hinterland* (London: Routledge, 2020).

Davis, Stephen J., *Christ Child: Cultural memories of a young Jesus* (New Haven, CT: Yale University Press, 2014).

Elliott, James K., *The Apocryphal New Testament: A collection of apocryphal Christian literature in an English translation* (Oxford: Oxford University Press, 1993).

Fiensy, David A., and James R. Strange (eds), *Galilee in the Late Second Temple and Mishnaic Periods: The archaeological record from cities, towns and villages*, 2 vols (Minneapolis, MN: Fortress, 2014–15).

Fredriksen, Paula, *Jesus of Nazareth, King of the Jews: A Jewish life and the emergence of Christianity* (New York, NY: Vintage, 2000).

Freyne, Sean, *Galilee and Gospel: Collected essays* (Leiden: Brill, 2022).

Goodman, Martin, *Herod the Great: Jewish king in a Roman world* (New Haven, CT: Yale University Press, 2024).

Gregory, Andrew, *The Gospel According to the Hebrews and the Gospel of the Ebionites* (Oxford: Oxford University Press, 2017).

Hanson, Kenneth C., and Douglas E. Oakman, *Palestine in the Time of Jesus: Social structure and social conflicts*, 2nd edn (Minneapolis, MN: Fortress, 1998).

Horsley, Richard, *Archaeology, History and Society in Galilee: The social context of Jesus and the rabbis* (Valley Forge, PA: Trinity Press International, 1996).

Horsley, Richard, *Galilee: History, politics, people* (Harrisburg, PA: Trinity Press International, 1995).

Horsley, Richard, with John S. Hanson, *Bandits, Prophets and Messiahs: Popular movements in the time of Jesus* (Harrisburg, PA: Trinity Press International, 1985).

Isbouts, Jean-Pierre, *Young Jesus: Restoring the 'lost years' of a social activist and religious dissident* (New York, NY: Sterling, 2008).

Kasher, Ariyeh, with Eliezer Witztum, *King Herod: The persecuted persecutor*, tr. Karen Gold (Berlin: De Gruyter, 2007).

Keith, Chris, *Jesus against the Scribal Elite: The origins of the conflict* (Grand Rapids, MI: Baker Academic, 2014).

Levine, Amy-Jill, *The Misunderstood Jew: The Church and the scandal of the Jewish Jesus* (New York, NY: HarperOne, 2006).

Lincoln, Andrew, *Born of a Virgin? Reconceiving Jesus in the Bible, tradition and theology* (London: SCM Press, 2013).

Mason, Steve, *Josephus and the New Testament* (Peabody, MA: Hendrickson, 1992).

Meier, John P., *A Marginal Jew: Rethinking the historical Jesus, vol. 1: The Roots of the Problem and the Person* (New Haven, CT: Yale University Press, 1991).

Miller, Robert M., *Born Divine: The births of Jesus and other sons of God* (Santa Rosa, CA: Polebridge, 2003).

Myles, Robert J., *The Homeless Jesus in the Gospel of Matthew* (Sheffield: Sheffield Phoenix, 2014).

Novenson, Matthew V., *The Grammar of Messianism: An ancient Jewish political idiom and its users* (Oxford: Oxford University Press, 2017).

Painter, John, *Just James: The brother of Jesus in history and tradition*, 2nd edn (Columbia, SC: University of South Carolina Press, 2004).

Reed, Jonathan, *Archaeology and the Galilean Jesus: A re-examination of the evidence* (Harrisburg, PA: Trinity Press International, 2000).

Richardson, Peter, and Amy Marie Fisher, *Herod: King of the Jews and friend of the Romans*, 2nd edn (London: Routledge, 2020).

Root, Bradley W., *First Century Galilee: A fresh examination of the sources* (Tübingen: Mohr Siebeck, 2014).

Schürer, Emil, *The History of the Jewish People in the Age of Jesus Christ (175 B.C.–A.D. 135)*, vol. 1, rev. and ed. Geza Vermes, Fergus Millar and Matthew Black (Edinburgh: T&T Clark, 1973).

Tabor, James D., *The Jesus Dynasty: Stunning new evidence about the hidden history of Jesus* (London: HarperElement, 2006).

Taylor, Joan E., *Christians and the Holy Places: The myth of Jewish-Christian origins* (Oxford: Clarendon, 1993).

Taylor, Joan E., *What Did Jesus Look Like?* (London: Bloomsbury T&T Clark, 2018).

Vermes, Geza, *The Nativity: History and legend* (London: Penguin, 2006).

Vermes, Geza, *The True Herod* (London: Bloomsbury: T&T Clark, 2014).

Watson, Francis, and Sarah Parkhouse (eds), *Connecting Gospels: Beyond the canonical/non-canonical divide* (Oxford: Oxford University Press, 2018).

Zervos, George T., *The Protevangelium of James: Critical questions of the text and full collations of the Greek manuscripts*, vols 1 and 2 (London: Bloomsbury T&T Clark, 2019, 2022).

Index

Note: Page numbers in italics refer to illustrations.

Abraham 16, 17, 21, 39, 42, 91, 100
Adomnan 57, 59, 60–1, 62
Africanus, Julius 38, 45, 46, 47, 68, 215; and Nazareth 190; prediction of Herod as king 168–9, 179
Alexander the Great 13, 19, 102, 155, 296 n37
Alexandre, Yardena *211*, 212, 321 n5
Alexandria 8, 19, 154–6; Jewish refugees in 155–6
ancestry/heritage 15, 17–18, 20, 25, 30, 42, 54; and grave sites 63; *see also* Davidic dynasty
angels 82, 83, 93, 95, 131, 135; and Hebrew as heavenly language 187–8; messages/ revelations of 85, 105, 108, 109, 111, 118, 120, *122–3*, 161, 171, 180–5; *see also* Egypt, flight to; Gabriel (angel); Land of Israel, return; prediction
Antigonus Mattathias 64–6, 69, 97, 99, 101, 103, 107, 114, 144, 164, 174, 196
Antipas (Herod) xvi, 107, 151, 152, 172, 173, 177, 183, 196, 199, 200, 201, 205, 217, 245
Antipater xv, 21, 67, 147–52, 170; Herod's execution of xv, 152, 170, 181
apostles 6, 100, 230; Last Supper 6; *see also* disciples; Paul; Peter
Archelaus xv–xvi, 69, 128, 152, 170–5, 181, 182–3, 184, 198–9, 200, 204; removal/banishment of 200–1, 205; suppression and massacre in the Temple 171–2, 177, 181, 198, 242

Aslan, Reza 14, 27
astrology 99, 100, 101, 102, 104–5, 137; and date of Jesus' birth 105–6
Athronges 175, 178, 183

Babylon 29, 30, 39
baptism 36, 94, 231, 232; *see also* John the Baptist
Bar Kokhba 56, 99, 180, 233
Bartimaeus 33–5, 37
Basilica of the Nativity, Bethlehem 54–5, *55, 57*, 58, 61, 69, 138, 139
Bathsheba 29, 85, 86, 89, 90
Bauckham, Richard 41
Bethlehem 18, 23, 28, 32, 38, 45, 49–70, 115, 136–7, 204, 209; aqueduct in 50, *51, 52*; Herod's massacre of male children in 106–8, 109, 127, 134; as Jesus' birthplace 49, 53, 63, 96–7, 120, *122*, 126–8, 134, 136–7, 185, 186; Mary's property in 204; *see also* censuses, Roman; City of David; nativity stories
birth stories 71–3; *see also* nativity stories
Bond, Helen 38
Bordeaux Pilgrim 58–9, 60, 63
Botner, Max 36, 37
Brown, Raymond 86, 108–9, 182, 236, 240–1
Burke, Tony 240, 326 n63

Cassius Dio 56, 65, 200–1
Capps, Donald 227

carpenter (*tektōn*) 216–20; Jesus defined as 216, 218; as Joseph's profession 213, 216, 217ff.; social class of 218–19

Cave of the Annunciation 214

cave of the nativity 134–5, 136, 137–40; Basilica on 55, 138

caves, use as hiding places 213–15; Joseph's workshop 213

Caesar Augustus 129, 147, 148, 149, 151, 156

Celsus 49, 112–13, 138, 157–8, 216, 227

censuses, Roman 128–9, 185, 203–4; in Bethlehem 53, 121, *122*, 126–8, 134, 140, 141, 185, 203–4; Judas' rebellion against 6 CE 210–5, 244; memory in stories of 203

childhood of Jesus 71, 74, 157, 179, 184, 185–6, 201, 203–35, 244–5; class, social conditions and stigma 219–20, 227, 245; education and teaching of 219–24, 240, 245; and effect on identity 186, 205, 207, 234, 235, 244, 245; and family duties of 223–4, 228; father absence of 226–7, 228; historical and archaeological scholarship of 185, 207, 210–15, 244; in Nazareth 199, 205–15, 219, 225; revolt/rebellion experience of 203, 205–6, 244, 245; skills and training 216, 218, 235, 245, 330 n1; in the Temple 239–43; see *also* Galilee; Nazareth; siblings and family of Jesus; teachings of Jesus

Christian pilgrims and pilgrimage 58, 61–2

Church of the Annunciation 211, 212, 214

Church of the Nativity see Basilica of the Nativity

circumcision 8, 11, 12, 20, 95, *123*, 124, 127, 133, 140, 143, 228

City of David 52, 53, 58, 60, 67, *122*, 127, 131, 274 n45; and Bethlehem 135

Clark Wire, Antoinette 72, 278 n5

clothing 2, 24, 80, 223

coins 163, 173; political use of 163–4, 168, 173, 305 n10

Collins, John J. 11–12

Crossley, James 72, 219

crucifixion 6, 35

Dark, Ken *209*, 212, 218

David, King 15, 27–9, 33, 36, 39, 40–3, 52, 115; conception of 90–2; Tomb of xi, 58–60, 62–3, 68–9, 97, 153, 154, 159

Davidic dynasty 15, 24–49, 52–4, 59, 68–70, 79, 85, 90–2, 175–6, 191, 245; Gospel genealogies of 38–43, 46, 79, 85–6, 91; Jesus as seed/son of 25–6, 33–5, 37–8, 43, 47–8, 52, 73–4, 75, 78, 84, 91–2, 94, 95, 96, 114, 159, 207, 232, 234, 244; and Mary 134; persecution of 46–8, 70, 115, 146, 159, 215, 245; women in 85–6; see *also* Bethlehem; Herod; Messiah; siblings and family of Jesus

Davis, Stephen J. 221–2

Dead Sea Scrolls 12, 23, 33, 81, 85, 102, 162, 167

Diodorus Siculus 102, 155, 198

disciples 6, 7, 33–5, 45, 125–6, 188, 221, 228ff., 245; as spiritual brothers of Jesus 232; see *also* apostles

dreams 58, 84–5, 94, 95, 105, 165, 221; as divine messages 110; in Moses story 108; as revelation 58, 84, 98, 110; see *also* Egypt, flight to; interpretation; prediction

education 220–2; and basic literacy 222–3, 327 n71; in Hellenic context 221–2, 326 n63; Mosaic law in 220, 222; synagogues as 'schools' 220–1; training in Scripture in 220, 221, 241

Egeria 59, 62

Egypt: as place of refuge 146, 154–5, 160; treatment of Judaeans in 154–6; *see also* Egypt, flight to; refugee

Egypt, flight to: from Herod's threat 144, 146, 154, 156, 159–60, 204; and Joseph's dream 105–6, 108–9, 111, 115, 144, 154, 161, 232; return to Israel *see* Land of Israel, return; stories of life in 158–61; *see also* Egypt; refugee

Elizabeth, mother of John the Baptist 118, 121, *122, 123,* 124, 125, 126, 134, 237; and conception of John 124

Essenes 203; dreams/predictions of 84, 163–70, 180; Josephus and Vespasian 165–6; Menahem and Herod 163–4, 165, 168–70; and use of Scripture 164, 165–70; *see also* Africanus, Julius; Josephus

Eusebius 44, 55, 56, 68, 77, 79–80, 81, 83, 138–9, 215

exorcism 4, 14, 36

France, Richard 37
funerals and mourning rituals 63

Gabriel (angel) *122,* 124, 125, 127, 180; and Gabriel Revelation tablet 180

Galilee 1, 6, 183, *189,* 190–201, 207; bandits and crime in 196–7; disease and plague in 197–8; and Joseph's return 183; in Josephus 192–3, 195ff.; as Judaean settlement 192, 195; population density impact in 193–6, 198; and social inequality/poverty 196–7; *see also* Nazareth

genealogy and genealogical records 42–3, 68, 75, 87; in Matthew/Luke 38–43, 46; *see also* ancestry/heritage, Davidic dynasty

gnostic sources 44, 45
Goodacre, Mark 119, 133, 135
Greek Hellenic influence 19–20, 22, 23

Hasmonean dynasty 20, 21, 22, 67, 68, 177–8, 191, 203

healing 4, 33, 34, 36, 135, 159, 225
Hegesippus 44, 45, 46, 47
Hermopolis 158, 159, 160
Herod 3, 21, 22, 60, 64–7, 96–7, 102, 105–8, 120–1, 128, 144, 163, 179; claim of divine rule of 163–4, 169–70; death of 103–4, 111, 148, 170–1, 177; as enemy of Davidic line 67–8, 97, 99, 107, 114, 148, 154, 159; massacre of boys 106–8, 114, 140, 146, 152; as threat to Jesus 97–8, 103–6, 144, 150, 154, 159; tomb of 64, 66–7, 69, 97, 171; tyranny of 144, 146–153, 173; *see also* prediction

Herodion 54, 64, 65–6, 69, 97, 114, 149, 150, 159, 170–1, 172

Holy Spirit 75, 78, 93, 232; as divine Mother 93–4, 232; and Mary's divine impregnation 83, 92–5, *122,* 124, 125–6; as Wisdom 93

identity 4–5, 15, 24, 25, 27, 31, 42, 49, 53, 186; Jesus as Jewish 2–3, 4, 5–15, 24, *123,* 130–1, 244; and place identity 49, 53, 63, 146; *see also* Ioudaios; Judahites; refugee

interpretation 78, 84–5, 109–12, 114–15, 165–70, 179, 245; of dreams 84–5, 107, 109–10; role of Joseph in 109–12, 115, 221, 245; used for hope 162, 184, 245; *see also* nativity stories

Ioudaios 1, 2, 5, 7–8, 9, 19; concept of 5, 8, 49; Jesus as 2, 5, 7–8, 15, 17, 18, 24, 49; and Judaism 5–8

Israel 1, 2, 4, 31, 96, 161–2; messianic saviour of 31–3, 46, 245; twelve tribes of 15, 16, 18, 20, 28; *see also* Davidic dynasty; Land of Israel, return

Jacob/Israel 1, 5, 15, 16, 161, 162; twelve sons of *16;* Spring of 1–2

James, brother of Jesus 6, 7, 43–4,
45, 47, 72–3, 74, 227; execution of
44, 226; significance of 232–4; as
successor to Jesus 43–4, 234; *see also*
Protevangelium of James; siblings and
family of Jesus
Japha 193, 208, 214, 217, 226
Jerusalem 5–6, 14, 19, 21, 23, 28, 30,
55, 56, 97, 115, 194; as City of David
58; Jesus' entry into 33–5, 37; Roman
conquest of 47; Temple 5, 11, 13, 20,
30, 37, 53, 69, 130; *see also* Judaism
John the Baptist 36, 118, *122*, 123–5, 129,
134, 183, 231, 232, 236, 245; and link
with Jesus 124–5
Joseph, father of Jesus 26, 38–9, 41, 44, 45,
47, 53, 72, 74, 78–85, 105–6, 108–12,
226–8, 235, 268 n71; as a carpenter 213,
216–20; and Mary's pregnancy 80–4,
86, 89, 90–1, 94–5, 111, 113–14, 232; as
real father of Jesus 75–8, 86, 89, 92, 94,
112–15, 226–7; as son of Jacob 1, *16*,
38; *see also* Egypt, flight to; interpretation; Land of Israel, return; prediction
Josephus 12, 19, 25, 42, 44, 50, 56, 58ff.,
84, 85, 97, 99, 102, 107, 108, 109, 115,
128, 134, 146ff., 156, 161–79, 220, 241,
244, 318 n65; prediction of Vespasian
as emperor 165ff., 169, 175; scriptural
interpretation of 166–8; War of Varus
depiction 170–9
Joset, or Joseph, brother of Jesus 44, 73,
219, 227, 233
Judaeans (Judaea) 1–2, *3*, 5, 12, 18–24,
49, 56, 95, 192, 194, 201–2, 207; census
rebellion 6 CE 210–6, 244; insurrection
and revolt 4 BCE 170–9; Jesus as
Judaean 18–24, 207, 244, 245; law/
ruling class in 23
Judahites 15–18, 19, 20–1, 23, 28, 29–30,
32, 39, 43, 49; Jesus as 15–18, 24, 244
Judaism 5–6, 7–8, 10–13, 14–15; and

Jewish identity 7–15; law/tradition in
10–13, 19
Judas the Galilean (of Gamala) 202–5;
and census rebellion 6 CE 201–6, 217
Jude, or Judas, brother of Jesus 44–6, 73,
216, 219, 227, 233
Justin Martyr 100–1, 126, 136–7

'Land of Israel, the', concept and use of
161–2, 181, 304 n3
Land of Israel, return 161–2, 170–1, 199,
204, 232: Galilee as Joseph's choice 183;
and hope after Herod 162, 170, 171,
179, 181–3, 198; and Joseph's revelations
161, 171, 181–5, 186; insurrection and
War of Varus 4 BCE 170–80, 181ff., 199
Lincoln, Andrew 83, 92, 112, 120

magi (*magoi*) 96, 99–101, 114; use of
term 100; as 'wise men' 100, 102
magi/star story 96, 97–105, 110, 114,
123, 130, 134–5, 139, 232; and flight
to Egypt 105–6; significance of star in
98–9, 100, 102–5, 232
Magness, Jodi 66–7
manger in the nativity 128, 134–41, 143;
reason for use of 134; *see also* cave of
the nativity
Marcion 117, 118, 121, 130
marriage and betrothal 80–2, 86, 91; and
Jesus 228; of Mary and Joseph 79–84,
86, 89; men as 'righteous' in 79, 83–92;
and virginity 81–3
Mary, mother of Jesus 44, 45, 72, 75, 76,
78, 124–6; in nativity narratives 79–80,
122–3; pregnancy of 80–4, 86, 91–2,
113, 124–6; virginity of 77–8, 79, 81–3,
84, 92–5, 113, 114, 124, 125, 133, 135,
227, 241; *see also* Joseph, father of
Jesus; siblings and family of Jesus
Mary, sister of Jesus 45, 73, 227
Mary Magdalene 45

Mary of Nazareth International Centre 211, 212, *213*

memory/memories 27, 58, 64, 98, 105, 112, 114, 115, 129, 139, 203, 240–2, 244; of Joseph in Matthew 105–7, 115, 116; of Mary in Luke *123*, 131–2, 240, 243; and presumed knowledge 78

Menahem 163–4, 165, 168–70, 179, 204, 306 n16, 320 n86

Merz, Annette 129

Messiah 32, 33, 36, 46, 167, 175, 184, 186; Jesus as 'son of God'/Messiah 29, 31–2, 36, 37–8, 47, 53, 98, 234, 266 n43; and messianic prophecy 34, 84, 191; *see also* Davidic dynasty; magi/star story

Milk Grotto 69

miracles 33, 94, 229; in conception 92–5

Monier, Mina 118, 119, 130

Moses 7, 13, 37, 107–8, 109, 111, 115, 178, 182, 220, 242

Myles, Robert 144, 153, 157, 186, 219

naming 95; of Jesus 75, 95–6, 98, 119, 121

nativity stories 26, 43, 71–3, 78, 112–14, 131–2, 244; counter-narratives to 112–14; historical actuality in 114–15, 129–30, 137; in Gospel of Luke 116–30, 131–2, 182, 236, 237; in Gospel of Matthew 74–8, 80–5, 89, 91, 95, 96, 98–9, 108, 113–17, 119–21, *122–3*, 131, 244; interpretation/retelling in 78, 84–5, 114–15, 143, 236; *see also* censuses, Roman; magi/star story; manger in the nativity

Nazarene (*Nazōraios*), Jesus as 126–30, 160, 185, 186–7; and scriptural interpretation 187–8

Nazareth 38, 44, 49, 53, *122*, 125, 126–30, 181, 185, *189*, *190*, 191, 198, 205–14, 217, 226, 236; archaeological remains in 208–9, 211–14; and association with prophecy 191; fear of Roman army in

199, 205; hiding places and caverns in 212–15; Joseph's choice of 183–4, 185, 186, 191, 198, 205, 225; *see also* childhood of Jesus

Nicolaus of Damascus 67–8, 146, 150, 151, 162, 174, 244

Nigro, Lorenzo 63

nobility/nobleness 25, 42, 43, 46, 68

Origen 78, 93, 100, 112, 138–9, 324 n41

Paidika 216, 221–3, 226; Jesus in the Temple story in 237, *238–9*, 240

Palestine *see* Syria Palestina

Parthians 13, 19, 99–100

Passover 5, 104, 126, 171, 172, 237, *238*, 241–3

Paul, apostle 6–9, 13, 15, 23, 44, 73, 233; letters of 6, 7, 9, 15, 25–6, 43, 44; mission and travel of 116

Persia 13, 19

Peter, apostle 8, 44

Philistines 28, 29

Philo 12, 13, 25, 93, 95–6, 99, 100, 109, 154, 155, 194, 220

Phoenicia *see* Syria Phoenicia

physical appearance of Jesus 17

Piacenza Pilgrim 59, 60, 223

Pontius Pilate 2, 129

prediction 32, 72, 84, 95, 99, 102, 106, 109–12, 163–5, 184; of Herod as divine king 163–4, 165, 168–9; Joseph's method of 106, 109–12, 115, 181; *see also* dreams; Essenes; interpretation

Protevangelium of James 132–3, 134–5, 139–40, 141, 158, 170, 172, 185, 216, 227, 237, 298 n61

purification 130–1

Rahab (of Jericho) 85, 87–8, 91

Reed, Jonathan 198

refugee 146, 154, 204; displacement effect of 146, 156–7; Jesus' life as 146, 156–8, 186, 207, 245
resurrection 6, 9, 216, 233
Romans, revolt against: 6 BCE census rebellion 201–6; 4 BCE insurrection 170–9; First Revolt 66 CE xvi, 142, 154, 170, 173, 176, 180, 203, 204–5, 213, 218; second Bar Kochba Revolt 132–6 CE xvi, 56, 142, 173, 176, 180, 233; *see also* Land of Israel, return
Ruth (Moabite) 52, 68, 85, 86, 88–9

Sabbath 10, 14, 65
Salome (midwife) 81, 135
Salome, sister of Herod 148, 152, 172–3
Salome, sister of Jesus 45, 73, 227
Samaria (Samaritans) 1, 4, 16–17, 21
Sanders, E. P. 11, 71, 127, 185
Schäfer, Peter 113
Schröter, Jens 26–7
Sepphoris (Autokratoris) 21, 174 ff., 180, 183, *190*, 191, 193, 196, 199, 202, 205, 208, 209, 217–18
shepherds, motif of 131
siblings and family of Jesus 43–8, 73, 111–12, 133, 134, 184, 216, 223–4, 226, 227–35, 244–5; as not Mary's children 134, 227; protection of Jesus by 231; support and understanding of 228–31, 234; *see also* James, brother of Jesus
Simeon, cousin of Jesus 44, 47
Simon, brother of Jesus 44, 73, 219, 227, 233
Simon bar Kosiba, *see* Bar Kokhba
Simon the Slave 175, 180, 183, 200
sisters of Jesus 44, 219, 233; *see also* Mary, sister of Jesus; Salome, sister of Jesus
Sisters of Nazareth Convent 210, 214, 223
storytelling 71–2, 137; and scriptural retelling 4, 16, 107–9, 115, 121, 132, 134, 137, 140, 143, 184, 236, 241
Syria Palestina/Syro-Palestinians 1, 19, 22, 56, 139, 154, 173, 191, 192, 194, 201, 233, 244
Syria Phoenicia/Syro-Phoenicians 3, 4, 7, 14, 19, 22, 23, 85, 174, 191, 192, 194, 224, 244

Tamar (Canaanite) 85, 86, 87
teachers: in the Jerusalem Temple 241–2; Jesus as student 221–2, 239–40; and physical punishment 222; synagogues used for 220–1, 222; *see also* education
teachings of Jesus: claim to prophecy in 219, 224–5, 234; danger of 225; in the Jerusalem Temple 37, 236–43; Joseph's absence in 226; message as offensive and upsetting 219–20, 224–6; in the synagogue 219, 220, 224–5

Van Aarde, Andries 226–7, 328 n83
Varus, P. Quinctilius 128, 151, 173, 175, 205; War of 4 BCE xvi, 175–9, 180ff., 199, 214, 217, 242, 244
Vermes, Geza 10–11, 14, 26, 41–2, 108, 324 n39
Vespasian's rule 47, 142, 165–6, 175, 176, 193, 214, 215; and First Revolt 176; Josephus' prediction of 84, 165ff., 169, 175

wisdom (*sophia*), of Jesus 14, 219, 222, 225, 236; use of term 93, 236; *see also* Holy Spirit
women; characterisation/focus of 86–92, 125; in Davidic genealogies 85–6, 91–2; *see also* marriage and betrothal

Zechariah, father of John the Baptist 121, *122*, 123, 129, 130, 134
Zechariah (prophet) 34, 35, 124
Zerubbabel 30, 39, *40*, 41
Zoroastrians 13–14